To Ri

MW00946086

RACE

MY STORY AND HUMANITY'S BOTTOM LINE

Enjoy The read and remember to....

Believe in Humanity!

Lauren

RACE

MY STORY AND HUMANITY'S BOTTOM LINE

More than a Book . . . . It's an Experience

LAUREN JOICHIN NILE

iUniverse LLC
Bloomington

RACE: My Story & Humanity's Bottom Line
More than a Book . . . . It's an Experience

iUniverse books may be ordered through booksellers or by contacting:

iUniverse LLC
1663 Liberty Drive
Bloomington, IN 47403
www.iuniverse.com
1-800-Authors (1-800-288-4677)

ISBN: 978-1-4917-0307-6 (sc)
ISBN: 978-1-4917-0308-3 (hc)
ISBN: 978-1-4917-0309-0 (e)

Library of Congress Control Number: 2013918762

Printed in the United States of America

iUniverse rev. date: 03/03/2014

Reach Lauren Joichin Nile on the worldwide web at www.LaurenNile.com

Dedication

RACE: My Story & Humanity's Bottom Line is one of five segments of the first book of a trilogy on which I'm currently working, *The Grand Trilogy to Save and Mature Humanity.* Each book of the trilogy is both focused on and titled for one of Three Great Truths—We Are One, We Are Brilliant and We Are Divine.

I have felt The Trilogy deep within me since I was a very young child. It almost feels as if The Creator reached down into my mother's womb when I was inside it, and with an index finger, gently but quite decidedly etched the three books onto my tiny little heart, gave it a few, good, slow pats, then smiled.

I dedicate the first truth of The Trilogy, "We Are One", to my mother, Mrs. Selina Gray Joichin, whose indescribable love and powerful life lessons of compassion, poise, maturity, dignity, citizenship, deep concern for the less fortunate and hope for a just and compassionate world, have been my foundation throughout my life. Her example continues to inspire me to this day.

I dedicate *The Grand Trilogy of Truth* to The Divine Source which wholly inspired it, the Source of all truth, all love, and all of us.

CONTENTS

Dedication v

Acknowledgements xiii

Notes xv

Introduction in Three Parts xvii

About the Author xvii
The Grand Trilogy of Truth xxvii
The View from One Hundred Thousand xxxvi

I. My Racial Memoir: The Making of a Compassionate Activist 1

II. The Conventional View of Race: Our Very Simple Story 114

III. The Fundamental Truth About Race: Africans Are The Parents of Humanity We *All* Began as African 117

IV. Our Racial Past: A Profoundly Tragic Tale 134

A. How It All Began 135

B. The Effect of Racism on the Entire Human Race 140

C. The Psychology of Racism: Its Effect on Americans of Color 140

1. Physical Unattractiveness 141
2. Intellectual Inferiority 150
3. Historical Irrelevance 151
4. Social Deviance 154

D. The Practice of Racism Against People and Americans of Color 156

1. Slavery 157
2. Colonization 158
3. Discrimination—Harassment—Violence 164

a. All People of Color 166
b. Indigenous People of the Western Hemisphere 167
c. Asian People and Asian Americans 179
d. Latin People and Latin Americans 188
e. African People and African Americans 194
f. Muslim People and Muslim Americans 241

Note on the Question: "Why haven't black Americans achieved as much as white Americans after being here all this time?"

4. Lack of Adult Role Models in Positions of National Power and in the Entertainment Industry 242

A. Positions of National Power 242
B. The Entertainment Industry 243

5. Eurocentrism 249

E. The Psychology of Racism: Its Effect on European Americans 255

F. The Practice of Prejudice Against European Americans 257

1. All European Americans 257
2. Jewish Americans 258

G. A Final Comment on Our Racial History 260

V. The Impact of Our Racial Past on Our Universal Racial Present 267

A. Two Worlds Within a World 267

B. Two Worlds Within Nations 267

C. An Incalculable Tragic Waste of Human Potential 271

D. A Social Structure of Unearned Privilege for Some and Daily Indignities for Others 274

1. Unearned Privilege 274
2. The Daily Indignities 278

VI. Our Racial Present: Mixed but Encouraging 295

The United States 295

The Planet 304

VII. Inverse Realities: Walking in Another's Moccasins 309

VIII. Our Racial Future: A Way Forward 344

A. Structural Racial Inequality 344

1. The United States 344
2. The Planet 346

B. Racial Prejudice 347

1. The United States 348

a. Education—What We Must Know 348
b. Action—What We Must Do 356

2. Prejudice—The Planet....364

IX. Race: Humanity's Bottom Line....366

X. We Are One: A Trilogy of Great Unity....370

Notes....371

Note One....371
The Most Cruel Form of Psychological Racism Practiced Against People of Color—Particularly African Americans

Note Two....379
History and Accomplishments of People of Color
A Representative Sample

Note Three....404
Unearned Privilege

Note Four....408
Common Responses to Conversations about Racially-Based Daily Indignities

Note Five....427
Societal Attempts to Address the Present Day Effects of Past Discrimination

Note Six....453
How As Children, We Acquire Racial Stereotypes and Their Accompanying Feelings

Study Group Questions....455

Short Video Clips....460

Documentaries....467

Movies & Television Miniseries 470

Training Videos 473

Websites 474

Book I We Are One (A Five Part Series) 482

Coming Next in Book I The We Are One Series: 483
Religion: Different Paths—Same Journey:
The Fundamental Truth about Faith and Spirituality

Book II Truth II—We Are Brilliant 484

Book III Truth III—We Are Divine 485

Postscript 486

Acknowledgements

I thank my loving partner Barbara, for her extraordinary patience throughout my writing process. For your understanding on all of the evenings and weekends during which I did nothing but work on this project, and for your faith both in me and in this work, I am exceptionally grateful. I love you, honey.

My sincere gratitude goes to my brother Lambert who helped me to fact check my memories of people, places and things from my childhood. You were a tremendous help during all of those long phone calls. Thanks Lambert.

Genuine thank you to my Aunt Johnnie for keeping and sending me the only picture of Grandpa Jim that survived Hurricane Katrina. For all of our long, delightful conversations about our family history, thank you as well, Johnnie. They mean a lot to me.

My heartfelt appreciation goes to my dear friends, Theresa Sayles and Jack Straton, for agreeing to be my readers on this project. Theresa and Jack's editorial suggestions have been utterly invaluable. Jack, (Jack C. Straton, Ph.D., Associate Professor of Physics at Portland State University), was also very helpful with some of the genetic science discussed in this work. Theresa and Jack, sincere thanks.

In addition, I extend my genuine gratitude to my wonderful friend, Tom Finn, for also reading my manuscript. Thank you as well Tom, for your magnificent enthusiasm about its content. Your feedback was extremely helpful.

Finally, a sincere thank you goes to my neighbor, Lael Littke, for reading the first draft of the book's introduction and conclusion and for providing my initial editorial assistance.

Notes

My goal is that as you read this book, you have as close an experience as possible, of actually hearing my voice. Words that appear in bold are those which in a **reading** of this work, I would speak with emphasis. For that reason, I have used bolding quite liberally throughout.

My use of capitalization is both unorthodox and intentional. I have capitalized the names of groups of people in a manner that is unconventional, but have done so to show the utmost respect to those groups. I have also capitalized the names of items which I consider to be important.

In an effort to make its electronic format as much of a fully interactive experience as possible, I have included in *RACE: My Story and Humanity's Bottom Line*, many websites of short video clips. A list of the sites referenced throughout is provided for those who prefer to read the book in its entirety before viewing them. All of the links included herein were active at the time of publication. For any links that become inactive, an internet search by either subject-matter or title, when available, will most likely result in an active url for the desired information. A few urls may not work when clicked on. Those may need to be copied and pasted into your browser. I am hopeful, however, that whether you are reading the hard copy or the electronic version, this book will be an adventure on which you will travel with me page by page.

While the content of this work covers racial issues which impact the entire planet, its **primary** focus is on **the United States**, its racial history and present racial reality.

Finally, I wrote *RACE: My Story and Humanity's Bottom Line*, not for scholars. I wrote it, rather, for the average person. My intention was to make its message accessible to the largest number of those who are deeply interested in matters of race and the oneness of humanity.

Introduction in Three Parts

Part One

About the Author

I was born black and to non-college educated parents in the Deep South, New Orleans, specifically, in a time during which the southern states were still enforcing the last legally sanctioned vestige of slavery—segregation. The year was 1953.

I **loved** my childhood!

I was enormously blessed that four **extremely** fortunate circumstances severely limited what was the potentially **enormously** negative impact that the larger society into which I was born, **could** have had on my development as a healthy human being. They were, indeed, my emotional sanctuaries.

First, I was born to a mother and grandmother who showered pure, total and **complete** love upon me from the moment I was born. Second, in addition to her deep love, my **mother** also provided me with a **powerful** example of how to live a conscious life of integrity, poise, dignity, compassion, generosity of spirit and civic engagement. Third, I grew up in a beautiful, middle class African-American community in which I had **many** role models of adults who, even while living with the daily indignities of segregation, led lives in which they modeled self-respect, maturity and community involvement. Fourth, I was born with a **fierce** intellectual curiosity, the result of which as a child, I both **loved** science and had an **incredible** inner life of fantasy, imagination and wonder.

Gramzie, my mother's mother, (**Miss** Gramzie to all the kids in her neighborhood), told me that, beginning as an adolescent, my mother "always" wanted a daughter. My mother, an avid reader, wanted a daughter **so** badly, in fact, that **in high school**, she began saving her favorite books for the daughter she dreamt of having some day. After having two sons, Lemar Jr. and Lambert, born respectively nearly ten and six years before me, and then **losing** a baby girl at birth, my mother **really** wanted me. She wanted me **so** desperately, that even though she was a practicing Methodist, (and Methodists decidedly do **not** pray to statutes), she made a novena, a special prayer, for a little girl, to a statute of the Virgin Mary **every day** after discovering that she was expecting me. The story, as Gramzie told me, was that my parents' Catholic neighbor told my mother that if an expectant mother wanted to have a little girl, upon learning of her future bundle, she had to make a novena to the Blessed Virgin **every single day without fail** until the baby's birth, asking the Virgin to bless her with a baby daughter. My mother wanted a little girl so badly that this, Gramzie said, is **exactly** what she **faithfully** did to a little statuette of the Virgin Mary **every single day** for eight months prior to my birth. Then, two weeks premature, I was born on August 15th, **the Feast Day of the Blessed Virgin**! [1] It was a sure sign, as my mother saw it, that I was indeed the **literal** answer to all of her many prayers. And oh my goodness—how my mother loved me. **Oh my goodness**.

Gramzie, for her part, had five grandsons before me, Lemar Jr. and Lambert, and my cousins Joseph, Gerard and Drexel, the step son and two younger boys of Mama's older brother, my Uncle Isaac. Need I say it? Right. I had from Gramzie, a **second** dose of extreme love, extreme in the sense that extreme sports are extreme—intense, powerful and concentrated. I **know** though, that Gramzie didn't love me any **more** than she loved my brothers and cousins. In watching her with the boys, it was **absolutely** clear to me how **very** much she also loved them.

---

1 The day of the year within Roman Catholicism on which The Virgin Mary's believed assumption into heaven is to have taken place and is celebrated.

Now, I suspect that in addition to my being her first granddaughter, Gramzie's deep love for me was as much the result of the happiness that my long-awaited birth brought to her Selina, the eldest of her three girls, whom, like her two younger daughters, my aunts Verlie and Johnnie, she adored beyond description. Because my birth so delighted and thrilled my mother, I was to Gramzie, **also** heaven's blessing.

So . . . . it was late on that Saturday afternoon of August 15, 1953 at precisely 4:58 P.M., that I entered the world with my very own little personal double halo.

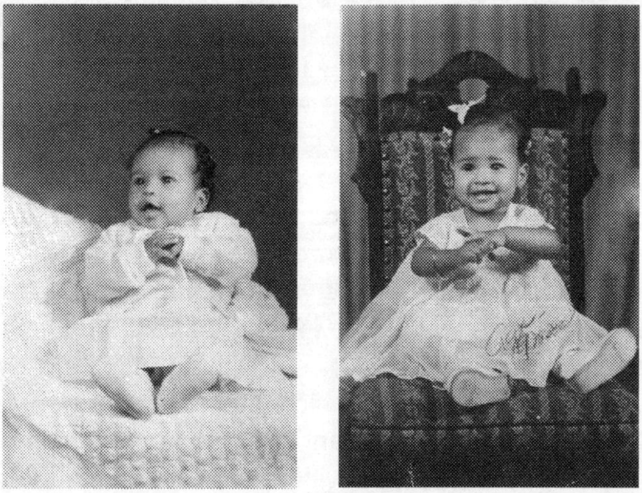

Me at Three and Nine Months

Despite the fact that I was the little girl that my mother wanted desperately, however, it was completely clear to me that like Gramzie who loved all of her grandchildren the same, Mama loved Lemar Jr. and Lambert **every single bit** as much as she loved me. I heard her say more than once, "I don't believe in making a difference between children. I love all my children the same." I **knew** that that was categorically true.

My mother and I were **always** together. While Lemar Jr. and Lambert were either at home or with their friends, Mama and I would be together, running her many errands—grocery shopping, buying our school clothes, buying our school **supplies**, getting something or other for the house, doing Gramzie's food shopping and picking up her medications, or buying some item for the church, among numerous other possible tasks that **always** seemed to need doing. Mama and I were together so much, in fact, that she told me numerous times, "Laurie, you're my little shadow."

My mother took surprising pride in my smallest accomplishments. The first time I combed my hair without her help when I was about nine, she called Gramzie and said with such love and happiness in her voice, "Mother, my little girl just combed her hair and put it in the cutest little pony tail, all by herself!" Overhearing that conversation from my bedroom, I smiled from ear to ear, happy that I had made Mama proud.

Shortly after my fifteenth birthday, my mother began having "the talks" with me. At one point during one of those conversations, she asked me what I would do if I liked a boy, was alone with him and he asked me to become intimate with him. I told her that I wouldn't do it. "Even if no one would know?", she asked. "**I'd** know Mama", I responded. "I have a conscience." Within a minute, I overheard yet another conversation in which Mama had called Gramzie, and with her voice trembling from the emotion she was obviously feeling, said, "Mother, I was having another talk with Laurie today and I asked her what she would do if . . . . and do you know what that child said to me? She said, 'Well **I'd** know, Mama. I have a conscience.' I was **so** proud of her, Mother". I'm sure Mama didn't know that I had overheard **that** conversation as well, but as I did, hearing how deeply **she** had been touched, I also became full, my eyes welling up with tears.

During my high school years, I'd sometimes take the bus uptown to my mother's job at the New Orleans Urban League after school and then ride home in the car with her. On one such afternoon, I walked into her office when Gloria Bartley, her much younger colleague and friend who happened to be sitting in Mama's office when I arrived, looked at me, and with a big warm smile, said, "Oh, there she is Laurie Joichin.[2] That's all we hear about—Laurie, Laurie, Laurie. Laurie did this. Laurie did that. Young lady, you're all your mother talks about!" Whether it was the progress I was making in my piano lessons, my ninth grade science project having been chosen for a regional science competition, getting my driver's license, or any of my other quite ordinary adolescent landmarks, my mother's pride in me was endless. [3]

The love that I felt so intensely from both my mother and my grandmother when I was a child was powerful. It was tender. It was adoring. That double dose of indescribable love from the two women who directly preceded me in my birth line was unquestionably the source of both the happiness which was ninety percent of the emotional template of my childhood and also of whatever amount of strength, dignity and compassion with which I have lived my adult life.

My mother's example, the second reality that helped emotionally shelter me from the effects of segregated New Orleans of the 1950's and '60's, came in the form of a two-tiered lesson. On one level was her message, very lovingly taught, that a lady has good posture, good manners, good grammar, a beautiful smile,

---

2 I changed my last name to "Nile" when I was in my late 30's. Even though I hadn't actually done the research to unequivocally establish it, I assumed, quite safely I believe, that "Joichin" was the name of one of my father's ancestors' French captors. I decided at that point, that while I could do nothing to **change** that tragic history, I did not have to carry it's vestige in my very identity. I chose "Nile" as a name that connects me with both the African continent and with the great Nile Valley Civilization. I chose to **publish** using the "Joichin" name in order to potentially connect with the many people from my early life who know me as Lauren Joichin.

3 Lemar Jr. and Lambert were out of the house by then so it wasn't that my mother wasn't also proud of them. They just were just no longer in our everyday family life at that point.

and most importantly, beautiful "ways", (poise, charm and a lovely, genuinely warm personality), all of which she personally and exquisitely modeled. They were lessons about how to hold a fork, (which I received when I was so young, that I don't remember ever holding my fork any other way **but** in the manner she taught me), of covering my mouth before yawning, answering questions in complete sentences, saying, "Yes please", "No thank you" and "You're welcome" and her **many** other lessons in proper decorum. On a far deeper level, however, were Mama's lessons of character. She taught me that no matter how attractive a person may be on the outside, if they have "ugly ways", i.e., if they're ugly on the **inside**, their looks don't matter one bit. Mama taught me how to be compassionate and empathetic to others—**all** others, especially those less fortunate. They were **profound** lessons—lessons of true character. [4]

Later, I'll share much more about my third childhood sanctuary—my neighborhood.

Now as for my fourth emotional shelter, that imagination of mine. Consider: On a hot summer day when I was about nine, while waiting my turn at bat during a day camp softball game, I picked a blade of grass from the ground, looked at it for several seconds, and then asked Mrs. Green, the camp director sitting nearby, "Hey Mrs. Green, you think maybe there's a whole **nother** universe on this blade of grass, or maybe a whole **lot** of universes on it? And you think maybe **our** universe might be on a blade of grass in some other, **really big** universe?" Mrs. Green turned, and as she looked at me **in utter astonishment,** responded, "Little girl, there's that imagination of yours again! I've never **seen** a child with such an imagination!" I was a genuine little science geek.

---

[4] My mother's character as exemplified by her unmistakable sincerity—her total non-pretentiousness, her genuine warmth and politeness, her sincere concern **for** and kindness **to** others and her strong social activism, **in addition to** her poise, grammar and posture, all seemed so natural to her. I wanted, more than anything, to be just like her when I grew up.

Curiosity and imagination truly **were** my two best childhood friends.

Because of the love that Mama and Gramzie showered on me, Mama's example, my childhood neighborhood and my rich inner life of fantasy and wonderment, I was for the most part, amazingly happy as a kid. The small part of me that **wasn't** happy, was the result of my father's parenting style. Four things about Daddy made me uncomfortable when I was young and caused me, during my childhood, to never really emotionally bond with or even get in touch with any feelings of love toward with him.

First, and characteristic of many men of his era, my father, Lemar Louis Joichin, Sr.,[5] was somewhat detached and rather emotionally unavailable. Shortly after my eighteenth birthday, after several years of wanting to but never having the nerve, I finally asked him, "Daddy, can't you show any emotion?" "No. My daddy didn't do it and I'm not going to do it. Men don't do that." His response deeply hurt. After that conversation, I lowered my expectations of my father and never again expected him to be emotionally available. I was sad, but it also felt tremendously liberating.

Second, despite the fact that he was a quiet, reserved man, my father expressed his anger in bouts of yelling. When something upset him, if, for example, one of my brothers or I had the volume on the stereo too high, he'd stew in bed quietly for as long as he could take it, then suddenly storm into the living room and yell, "Turn that G_____D_____music down!" We would, then he'd go right back to the bedroom. The whole thing lasted about five seconds. It didn't happen often, thankfully, but I didn't like it when it did, and it frightened me.[6]

---

5 "Joichin" is pronounced, "Joysin". The "h" is silent.

6 I'm **painfully** aware that there is a bit of that temperament in me. While I'm not a yeller, I **can** be exasperated by a situation. I feel exasperation almost exclusively when either I personally receive,

Third, Daddy drank excessively on weekends. He was as straight as an arrow and went to work **every** day during the week. (In fact, in nearly thirty-five years on his job, while I'm sure he must have, I don't ever **remember** him missing a **single** day of work.) Then, every Friday and Saturday night, he gorged on beer at the neighborhood Clubhouse, which, I imagine, may have qualified him for the term, "weekend alcoholic". Fortunately though, Daddy wasn't **abusive** toward us when he drank. Indeed, it was after he'd been drinking that he'd sometimes come home and actually talk quite pleasantly with me in a way that he otherwise never did. The end of those conversations was always the same, "Li'l girl, you know your Daddy loves you." Then pointing to his right cheek, "C'mon, give your Daddy a kiss." I would, then he'd smile and give me a five dollar bill. Those conversations happened perhaps every tenth time he'd come home sloshed. Usually though, he'd just go straight to the refrigerator, and after staring into it for a good five minutes, grab a left over pork chop, or piece of hot sausage, make and eat a sandwich, then go to bed.

Fourth and finally, and more than his emotional unavailability, his stints of expressed anger **or** his weekend beer binges, the thing that **by far** saddened me most during my childhood, was my father's emotional distance toward my mother. She bought him Christmas presents every Christmas, made him a big Easter basket with his favorite candy every Easter, reminded him of their anniversary every July and gave him a birthday present every September. I saw my mother trying **so** hard to make her marriage what she wanted it to be, but **never** saw my father respond to her in kind. I wanted him to be as loving and as kind toward her as she was toward him. Tragically, he was utterly incapable. His lack of emotional warmth, his temper, (expressed toward her in arguments, usually about the fact that he thought she spent too

---

or witness directed toward others, behavior that I experience as absent of concern, understanding and compassion. When that **does h**appen, I try my absolute best to handle the challenge with my mother's poise. I am not always successful, but fortunately, it is seldom that I'm in that position.

much money on us and on the house), and his weekend drinking, hurt my mother deeply. It was a very difficult marriage for my mother. I **knew** that, and because I loved **her** so deeply, it also hurt **me** tremendously.

Many years later, sometime in my mid-thirties, I realized that my father was an absolute product of his time, that he was an extremely responsible man and an excellent provider, that he did his unqualified best toward me and that he loved me. I also realized—that I loved him.

> [My father was indeed a very responsible man. The January 18, 1949 official transcript of his military record reads as follows:
>
> - **Civilian Occupation and Number**: Student X-02
> - **Summary of Military Occupations**: Cargo Checker—Checked cargo from ship to shore. Kept records and tally sheets of all materials. Turned records in to be filed. Supervised four men working as checkers. Checked all records and tally sheets of men under him to check correctness.
> - **Battles & Campaigns**: Normandy, Northern France
> - **Decoration & Citations**: EAME Campaign Medal w/2 Bronze Service Stars, Good Conduct Medal and Victory Medal WWII
>
> My father was a young man of 21-24 years old during the years of his military service. He was there, on D-Day, not fighting, but supporting those who did, at the Battle of Normandy.]

I am fortunate that even though during my childhood I didn't have a very close emotional bond with my father, because of **Mama and Gramzie's** powerful love, I nonetheless grew up feeling cherished and adored. It was that tremendous love that I received so early in my life that has in large measure inspired me to write this book, for I have written it out of my great love for humanity, a love which I am able to deeply feel only because of the great love that I experienced upon entering this world and throughout my formative years.

The seeds of *The Grand Trilogy* originated very early in my childhood, about which you now know a little. I cannot, however, represent that I am its **source**. It feels far more honest to say that I was merely its **recipient**. My fervent hope is that The Trilogy will help **to heal** humanity and to guide us into a future of wisdom, maturity and compassion.

Part Two

The Grand Trilogy of Truth

For thousands of years, we human beings have constructed told and believed many stories about every aspect of reality as we know it to be. We are taught that our stories provide us with all of the information we need about both the most fascinating questions and the most profound mysteries with which we live each and every day of our lives. We have developed stories to name just three, about why people look different from each other, (and the significance of those differences), about the essential potential of human beings, and about Ultimate Reality—The Great Mysteries, i.e., The Divine. Our stories in those three areas give us all of the "answers" to many of the most difficult questions that we may **raise** about **our differences**, that **exist** about our **potential**, and that we may **posit** about **The Divine**. They have for centuries, been a source of support, of emotional security for us. It is **those** stories, I believe, that more than **all** others, have most greatly affected us as a species, profoundly influencing our psyche, and therefore our emotional maturity and spiritual evolution. In essence, our stories in those three areas have allowed us to wrap a very easy, very tight, and often a very **simple** bow around what are **exceedingly** complex questions.

The vast majority of us around the world accept without doubt in **some form**, the stories about our differences, about our human potential and about The Divine, with which we were raised. Our widespread, unquestioned acceptance of our stories about our differences has in some instances, had a somewhat stabilizing effect **within** cultures.[7] It has also, however, resulted, time and again, in extreme conflict and human suffering **between** cultures. Such conflict has occurred when, for example, human beings of

7 In those same cultures, however, that acceptance has also often resulted in the oppression of those within the culture who **according to the culture's story**, were inferior.

one race use the story of **their** racial superiority, as justification for the oppression of human beings of **other** races; when human beings of one **sex** use the story of their **sex-**based superiority, to oppress human beings of the **other** sex;[8] when **able-**bodied human beings use the story of their **physical** superiority, to oppress human beings who live with physical and mental impairments[9]; when human beings who are **heterosexual** use the story of the moral superiority of **their** sexual orientation, to oppress human beings who are **not** heterosexual, and when human beings of **one** religion, use the story of the correctness of only **their** view of The Divine, to oppress human beings of **other** religions who have a **different one**.

In three books, *The Grand Trilogy of Truth to Save and Mature Humanity*, I shall examine both those **stories**, and the three ultimate **truths** to which they often blind us, the truths that "*We Are One", "We Are Brilliant*", and "*We Are Divine*".

The first book of the trilogy, *We Are One*, concentrates on our stories about our **differences**. In it, we will look at how our "difference stories" have affected our past societal behaviors and our present collective consciousness. Our difference stories will

---

8 While I seem to be implying here that there are only two sexes, presumably female and male, human beings are actually born into **three** sexes, female, male and inter-sexed. Additionally, I refer here specifically to sex, not gender. We'll consider the difference between the two in Fact Two of *We Are One*, "In the Beginning, In Utero, We All Begin as Female: The Fundamental Truth About Our Sexes."

9 None of the words and phrases used to describe people who are not considered able-bodied are acceptable to all. Many people who live with what may commonly be thought of as a physical, mental, emotional or learning disability or impairment, do not **consider** themselves to be disabled or impaired. Unfortunately, there is no term of which all will approve. In this work, I shall use the term which is currently considered the most appropriate, "people with disabilities."

lead us, finally, to a consideration of **who, as human beings, we truly are to each other**.

The **specific** focus of *We Are One*, is five particular differences among our human family that we have historically used to divide us, and to oppress billions of our sister and brother human beings across the planet. Those five differences are race, sex, disability, gender identity/gender expression/sexual orientation and religion.

With respect to those five human differences, are Five Great Facts of which, on a global level, we must be aware. Those facts are summarized in the following acronym "WISER" in the truth that humanity must be wiser.:

Who Are the Parents of Humanity? Africans We All Began as African
The Fundamental Truth about Race

In the Beginning, In Utero, We All Begin as Female
The Fundamental Truth about Our Sexes

Sometimes the Same is a Little Different
The Fundamental Truth about People with Disabilities

Either Be Straight or Be Wrong—Why That's Just Not Right
The Fundamental Truth about Gender Identity, Gender Expression and Sexual Orientation

Religion: Different Paths—Same Journey
The Fundamental Truth about Faith and Spirituality

With **respect** to our differences in those five areas, we have constructed many **extremely** simple stories. They are stories of superiority and inferiority, of right and of wrong. Specifically, our stories tell us that based upon our **differences** some of us are either superior or inferior to others of us, and that based upon what some identify as our **behaviors**, (specifically the lives that we live consistent with our gender identity, gender expression and sexual orientation), some of us are morally **right** and others of us, morally **wrong**.

Our stories about our differences share two essential characteristics:

1. They make **our** group and **our** beliefs superior and correct, and **other** groups and **their** beliefs **in**ferior and **in**correct; and,

2. They have a kind of simplicity that is utterly inconsistent with reality. The "bottom line" of the belief system of our stories, is that there are good people and there are bad people. There is right behavior and there is wrong behavior and it truly is as simple as that.

Our ignorance and misinformation **about** and fear **of** our five specific differences of race, gender, disability, the category of gender identity, gender expression and sexual orientation and finally, our religious differences, have resulted both historically and internationally, in perhaps more needless human pain and suffering than has been caused by any other of our human shortcomings. It is for that reason that of all of the many possible human differences on which I **could** have focused, in We Are One, I have chosen to focus on our stories about those **specific** differences.[10] I am writing *We Are One*, as a five-part series with each part focused on one of them. This, the first installment of the series, is about the first of the five differences—race.

In the United States, we have had national dialogues and town hall meetings about race. We have racial dialogue groups with well-meaning participants occurring all across the country.

---

[10] In many societies around the world, class has also historically been used as a deep dividing line among human beings. It is, therefore, **another** important divider worthy of serious analysis, deep understanding and social activism to correct injustices based upon it. In the United States, political orientation is also rapidly becoming a serious social division, thus, we must engage in a concerted attempt to move beyond **it** as well.

Conversations about race, **when skillfully facilitated**, can, of course, be quite helpful. Deep sharing and listening with an open heart to each other's thoughts and feelings **about** and experiences **with** race, under the right circumstances, **can** indeed, be cathartic. In truth, I believe that such conversations are an absolute **necessity** in our national racial healing process. But while such dialogues and town hall meetings are necessary, they are **not** sufficient. We can have all of the dialogues and all of the town hall meetings about race that we can possibly want, but in order for them to have any chance of **success**, for them to have any possibility of leading to great **understanding** and thus, deep compassion among human beings, **before** we talk, we must **first** share a body of knowledge about three essential things:

1. The fundamental facts about the biology of race;
2. The facts about our racial past; and,
3. The facts about how our racial past has influenced and continues to influence our racial present.

The many thousands of people who voluntarily engage in racial dialogues in cities and towns across the U.S., arrive "at the table" with a certain desire to explore, learn about and become more "conscious" with respect to matters of race and racism. I suspect that the vast majority of dialogues attended by such participants are respectful, **regardless** of the attendees' level of knowledge. Racial dialogues that are attended by participants whose attendance is required, however, (as is often the case in employer-sponsored diversity training, for example), and who do not have a basic, shared understanding of the facts about race and racism, are on occasion unhelpful and may actually do harm. Such dialogues may result in the following kinds of proverbial thoughts and sometimes even verbal exchanges:

> "Well you all weren't the only ones who had it hard, you know. Other people, the Irish, the Poles, we were discriminated against too." "Well at least you weren't slaves. The agricultural South which **fueled** the industrial North, i.e., the success of **this entire country**, was built

on our backs, and what did we get for it? Nothing" "Well why should **I** feel guilty? I never owned any slaves." "Well look at **my** grandparents. They didn't do **anything**. They were innocent, **and they were American citizens** and **yet** they were locked up in a camp in California for years during World War II, and they lost **everything**, their home, **and t**heir business. They had absolutely **nothing** when the government finally let them out. They had to start all over again. Do you have **any** idea how that affected my parents' lives and now mine?" "Yeah, well at least they weren't putting you into crematoriums and trying to kill off your entire race in the camps **you** went to. At least you didn't have whole families, whole towns killed off in **your** camps. You went to **internment** camps. We went to **extermination** camps." "Yeah, well what about us? You know how wrong it is for us to be treated like "illegals"? This was Mexico **before** the United States government took it and made it part of the U.S. Now **we're** the illegals? You guys weren't 'settlers. You were invaders then occupiers, then land thieves, then oppressors." "Well, we say to **all** of you that this is **our** land. We were here **15,000 years** before **everybod**y else who's now living on this land, and yes, for a time, many of **us** were slaves here too, **and on our own land.** You're **all** squatters." "You guys are always playing the race card. All of you. Everything that happens to you happens because of your race. You never want to take any responsibility for anything that happens to you. I'm sick of the whining."

Obviously, such conversations accomplish nothing. While today, (with the exception of some politicians and radio talk show pundits), far fewer people seem to be publicly **expressing** such thoughts, my very strong suspicion is that with respect to the issue of race, many of the thoughts themselves **and** the often strong feelings that accompany them, are still prevalent in many of us.

As discouraging as that thought may be, however, I am heartened by my **equally** strong belief that with a clear cognitive understanding of the basic truths about race, about our racial history, and about how that history has impacted and continues to impact our racial present, our dialogues, our sincere, heartfelt sharing with each other of our thoughts and feelings **about** and experiences **with** race, will lead to a depth of understanding and clarity of insight that have the potential to result in both profound personal growth and **in time, over the long haul**, utter societal transformation. I have attempted, in this work, to provide what I consider to be some of the most significant of those truths.

We will concentrate in Book Two, *We Are Brilliant*, on **our essential human potential**. In **it**, we will reflect upon our story **about** that potential, and **compare** that narrative to what current scientific evidence is telling us is the true potential of our brains. We will reflect upon some of the many wonders of which we may be individually capable if only we were able to utilize even an additional **tiny fraction** more than we currently do, of our brains and thus our human intelligence. Then, based upon that unimaginably enriched potential of each of us, together we will dream about the wonders of which our human family may be **collectively** capable. Our central focus in *We Are Brilliant*, is **<u>what, as human beings, we actually can be</u>**.

Ultimate Reality—The Great Mysteries—The Divine**,** is the subject of Book Three, *We Are Divine*. In **it**, we will examine our many stories about the **existence** of a Creator, about the **nature** of that Creator, and about what that Creator teaches us are our highest calling and reason for being. We'll examine what some believe to be evidence both that in addition to our **physical** universe, a **non**-physical, a **spiritual** universe exists and that we live independently of our bodies, **in** that spiritual universe. Most importantly, we will embark upon an enthralling journey of exploration of whether it is possible for us, in our human finiteness, to experience the infinite. We will muse about whether we can touch The Divine that I believe exists, whether, in essence . . . . we can know God. At the end of our look into the Great Mysteries, I will posit my belief about **<u>what, as human beings, we essentially are</u>**.

RACE: My Story & Humanity's Bottom Line

In this, the first installment of *We Are One,* we will consider, among others, the following specific questions:

- How did growing up in New Orleans under segregation in the 1950's and '60's affect me as a child? How did it impact my early and later adult life?
- What is humanity's universal, racial story?
- Why do human beings of different races often look so dramatically different from each other?
- What is the fundamental truth about race? Does biological race, as we commonly think of it, really even exist? If so, are there **truly** superior and inferior races?
- What are some of the most important events of our racial past that continue to impact us today, including the earliest first contacts between the races?
- What are some of the most important realities of our racial present that are either largely unknown or greatly misunderstood?
- What is humanity's racial bottom line?
- Is it realistic to think that humanity will **ever** mature beyond our wretched racist past into a mature compassionate racial future?
- If so, what are the specific steps that we must take in order to do so?

In order for humanity to finally and permanently leave our adolescence behind and ultimately mature, we must:

1. Recognize fully, our conventional **beliefs about** our differences, (i.e., understand our stories about them);

2. Understand thoroughly and acknowledge completely, the history of what we have **done in response to** our differences;

3. Comprehend deeply the fundamental **truth about** our differences; &

4. Embrace unreservedly, a more compassionate, evolved **view of** our differences.

Finally, before beginning our examination of the five differences that comprise, *We Are One,* I shall share with you my memoir, my personal experiences with each.

Part Three

The View from One Hundred Thousand

The view from one hundred thousand—from one hundred thousand feet above the Earth. Wow. It's **so** quiet up here. It's peaceful beyond measure, beyond anything that I can describe in words. It's absolutely **serene** here. And the **beauty**—you have to **see** the beauty to understand it. You have to see the remarkable brilliance of the light and of the soft, gentle colors. The calm, the tranquility, and on some extraordinarily deep level, the **familiarity**, the utter but inexplicable familiarity of this place, are comforting beyond words. Equally incredible, is the feeling here of goodness, of **pure** heavenliness. But most powerful of **all**, is the realization, the **absolute** and absolutely mystifying **knowing** that this good and beautiful, **perfectly tranquil** place, reflects our true human nature—our true being—our true selves.

As I gently descend, I begin to get my first glimpse of our small, beautiful planet, of the magnificent blue water that fills it and the stunning green continents that rest upon it. I can hear the hypnotizing sound of the oceans' waves. I can see the Earth's grand mountains, Everest, Kilimanjaro, the Alps, and the Pyrenees, as well as its gigantic rain forests and mammoth deserts. I am mesmerized by its majestic waterfalls, Angel, Victoria and Yosemite.

As I descend farther still, I begin to see the graceful and regal soaring of Eagles, Condors, Falcons and thousands of other species of birds. I start to see the Earth's majestic animals—the noble lions and great apes of Africa, the gigantic elephants of India, and the armies of Emperor and King Penguins of Antarctica, among thousands of others.

I can see our cities and hear the sound of our technology, our trains, our planes, and automobiles.

As I descend still closer to the Earth, I begin to see us, humanity, seven billion cousins, sharing our world, Australians and South Americans, Africans and Europeans, Central and North Americans, Asians and the millions of our world's island inhabitants. I see the vast, **utterly inter-connected** collage of the family of humanity in pursuit of our ordinary, daily affairs. In observing us carrying **out** those affairs, **I see human kindness everywhere**. I see generosity. I see self-awareness and maturity. I see compassion. **Everywhere I look**, I see love. I see mothers caring for their children with unconditional adoration, and fathers kissing those children goodbye as they leave them at school. I witness grandparents affectionately passing on to their **grand**children, the wisdom that they lacked as **parents**, to impart to their **children**. I observe friends happily sharing meals together. I see nurses, doctors, teachers, social workers, and lawyers, **heroically** serving those in need. I am a witness to people who live in poverty, unselfishly helping each other in their shared circumstances. I see many with wealth donating large sums of their money, and infinitely more importantly, their **time**, in aid to those who live in poverty. I perceive firefighters saving lives, police officers protecting the innocent, and politicians legislating for the common good. I see researchers in pursuit of cures to our illnesses and solutions to the harm that we have done to the Earth and its atmosphere. I see artists—writers, painters, playwrights and screenwriters producing works of art that deeply touch our hearts and help us to profoundly feel our humanity. I see musicians making music that stirs our souls. I see those who love peace, and those who seek justice, speaking and working tirelessly on behalf of each. Perhaps most importantly, I see visionaries helping us to glimpse what is possible for ourselves and thus for our world, inspiring us through their words and at times their example, to live the true greatness of our Divine potential, to **become**, in essence, the Beloved Community.[11] All of

11 The Beloved Community is the vision of Philosopher-Theologian Josiah Royce, popularized by Dr. Martin Luther King, Jr., of a human society without poverty, hunger, violence and bigotry of all kinds. It is the family of humanity living in a just and peaceful world.

these things, all of this human love, I see on every continent and in every nation, in every city and every town, in every village and in every hamlet. **Everywhere I look**, I see human beings living lives of wisdom, lives of compassion. **All over the Earth**, I see what is possible for us. I see The Divine in action **through** us.

But my descent toward the Earth also allows me to see the other, the **distorted** side of our nature. As I continue to descend, I see extreme human apathy in every place—**in every single site**—severe hunger existing **simultaneously** with massive, multi-billion dollar sports and entertainment industries. I observe the glamorization of violence in all forms of entertainment. On **six** continents, I witness the abject sexualization of women in both live and still imagery, and an international sex slave industry that targets primarily women and children. As I continue to descend, I am a first-hand witness to constant war on Earth, occurring right now, in **numerous** places all **over** the Earth. I see physical suffering—genocide and torture. I witness mental suffering—the mental suffering that accompanies mental illness. I see emotional suffering—people being emotionally violent toward their fellow human beings, responding with apathy, resentment, jealousy, and hostility to strangers, co-workers, friends and yes, even those they love most dearly. I see the resulting fear, depression, anger, greed, selfishness, xenophobia and hatred, all expressed, as among other things, racism, anti-Semitism and other forms of religious intolerance, homophobia and heterosexism, ableism, sexism, ageism, classism, and nationalism. What I see is **us**, the human species, existing in a horrifyingly dense cloud of miserable ignorance and wretched immaturity.

Tragically, (but perhaps inevitably), we have lived in that ignorance and that immaturity for the majority of our human existence. The reason, very simply, is that we had been, for the **majority** of that existence, in our childhood stage of development. Throughout the vast majority of this stage, we lived on savannahs, in forests, and in caves. Our personal survival and that of our family and/or clan was our total focus. We lived in the fight or flight, kill or be killed mode. It was the stage of our development during which we had no rules, no social sanctions against cruelty. Indeed, for **most** of this time, we had no **concept** of cruelty, of right and wrong, good and bad, moral and immoral, humane and inhumane. For all intents and purposes, during this stage of our development, we were truly psychological and emotional juveniles.

The long epoch of our human childhood ended, however, long ago. It ended when and wherever the first social prohibition emerged forbidding an oppressive or inhumane act toward another. We know neither when nor in which civilization that prohibition initially appeared, or whether it perhaps appeared in many civilizations somewhat simultaneously, but with those first notions of right and wrong, with that consciousness, that burgeoning sense of morality, and the rules which we created based **upon** it, where and **when**ever they first appeared, we took a great leap in our human development **out** of our childhood, and **into** our adolescence . . . . and what a gigantic leap it was.

Throughout much of our adolescence, we lived in nomadic hunter-gatherer communities, later in agricultural societies, then finally and presently, in nation-states.[12] In all of those various human living arrangements, we had thoughts about what was right and what was wrong. Based **upon** those thoughts, we developed both rules that governed our behavior, and consequences for violating them.

Still, throughout our adolescence, **century after century**, we engaged in countless, spiritually bankrupt, immoral and indeed **evil** acts of inhumanity toward our fellow human beings, causing **immeasurable** pain and **devastating** suffering. Perhaps our most extreme method of doing so was our numerous historical attempts at genocide, a malevolence **which plagues us to this day**. The most recent genocidal campaign occurring already within this new 21st century, resulted in the death of thousands

---

12 After agricultural societies and before nation states, the feudal state also existed, specifically in Europe, between the 9th and 15th centuries.

and by some estimates, **hundreds** of thousands of innocent people who were massacred in a brutal civil war in the Darfur region of Sudan. In the twentieth century we witnessed the murder of between five hundred thousand and **one and one-half million** Armenian human beings by the Turkish government; of **six million** Jewish human beings by the German Third Reich; of millions of other human beings by the Third Reich for their disability, sexual orientation and/or political activity; **of one and one-half million** human beings by Cambodia's Khmer Rouge; of thousands of Muslim men and boys during the Bosnian war; and of between **eight hundred thousand and one million** Rwandan human beings by their fellow Rwandans based upon their tribal membership. Additionally, genocide was a tactic that was historically used by European conquerors against the Indigenous People of the West. Although clearly **bondage** rather than **genocide** was the goal of the enslavement of **African** human beings in the Americas, in any accounting of genocides, **the sheer number** of African People who either died or were murdered during the Trans-Atlantic Slave Trade, (estimates vary from 4.5 million-10 million, 10-15 million and 15-20 million), requires that we acknowledge them as well. As is true of the Trans-Atlantic slave trade, genocide was not the intention of the World War II bombings of Hiroshima and Nagasaki. Nonetheless, **the sheer number** of those who perished in them, the one hundred fifty thousand Japanese human beings killed in Hiroshima and the seventy five thousand human beings killed in Nagasaki, also requires full acknowledgement.

Estimates of the number of female human beings that we burned alive at the stake in Europe for over **two-hundred years**, based upon the belief, (and often only the **purported** belief), that they were witches, range from thirty thousand to nine million. We inflicted massive human suffering in fighting the Crusades, in carrying out the Inquisition, and in oppressing, torturing and killing scientists during Europe's Middle ages, including Giordano Bruno, burned at the stake for advancing the theory that the Sun, not the Earth was the center of the Solar System, and Galilei Galileo, imprisoned and under house arrest for many years until his death, for championing it. Over the last six hundred years alone, we human beings have engaged in mass rape and slaughter in the colonization, (the taking and pillaging) of society after society, ... after society, the world over.

For **thousands of years** now, our mental, emotional and spiritual evolution has progressed **exceedingly** slowly, resulting in **tremendous** human pain and indescribable suffering. The period of our human adolescence has been long. It has been painful. It has been abominable.

As a species, we are **still** in our adolescence, our technological, emotional and spiritual adolescence, specifically.

In our **technological** adolescence, we have very seriously endangered **our actual physical existence on the planet** by allowing our technology to poison the air, water and soil of the Earth, our only home, by exterminating thousands of its non-human species, endangering the existence of thousands of others, and by delivering ourselves to the very brink of nuclear annihilation.[13] We are producing disease and chemical-filled food that causes frequent outbreaks of sometimes fatal illness. We must be plugged in at all times to an electronic matrix which makes us constantly accessible to anyone, at any time, for any reason. We persist in creating forms of entertainment that take our minds and spirits farther and farther away from stillness which in turn, takes **us** farther away from internal peace, and thus from

13 We have been hanging on the precipice of nuclear annihilation since the invention of the atomic bomb over sixty-five years ago. The 1962 Cuban Missile Crisis was our closest call. While the nuclear tension that existed for a generation between the U.S. and the USSR is now nothing more than an historical relic of a time gone by, nuclear weapons around the planet still number in the thousands and are capable of destroying the Earth many times over. Additionally, for the first time in our history, we now face the threat of such weapons being used by not only nations, but by rogue terrorists, putting our existence at **perhaps** even greater peril.

our true selves. We have allowed our technology to dominate our consciousness and in some sense, to actually **rule** our very lives.

Because we are **emotional** adolescents, we continue to construct artificial divisions among us based upon false demarcations of among other things, race, sex, disability, gender identity/gender expression/sexual orientation and religion, and attempt to use violence on a **massive** scale, to resolve the conflicts that are the inevitable and quite predictable **result** of those and other false divisions.

Our state of **spiritual** adolescence is characterized by the continuing predominance of religions that rob us of our innate curiosity about the complete mystery of the universe, give us **extraordinarily** simple answers to **extremely** complex questions about the nature of reality, and in **some** instances, even teach us that **our** religious beliefs are the **only** ones that are **true**.

Yet, in all of our foolish beliefs **about** and cruel ventures **toward** our fellow human beings, we had within us, the full potential to know that both what we **believed about** and what we were **doing to** each other, were wrong. We had the **complete** capability to know that some of our most basic **beliefs** about each other were foolhardy and that the **actions** that we took based **upon** them, were ominous.

That potential, (which we possessed **in abundance** as we engaged in **every** one of our tragic human follies), was being **aware of**, **listening to** and behaving **in accordance with** the Divinely-inspired higher consciousness that I believe resides within each of us.[14] It is the consciousness of The Three Ultimate Truths of our existence—The Three Truths which comprise The Grand Trilogy—We Are One, We Are Brilliant and We Are Divine.

---

14 Our "higher consciousness" is our awareness of our oneness, our brilliance and our Divinity as a human species.

Had we, throughout our adolescence, accessed and acted in accordance with our higher consciousness, we **could**, over the past millennium, have avoided **enormous** human suffering. What would our contemporary world **be** like, for instance, if in 1948, the Palestinians and the then new Israelis had been able to begin and to **continue** to live respectfully and in peace with each other? That state of affairs is so unlike our **actual** reality of the very bloody and seemingly intractable, decades-long war between those two peoples, that we can simply not **imagine** what our world would be like today without that devastating sixty-five year old conflict.

Can we even **begin** to envision the Western Hemisphere had its Indigenous People not been subjugated **in**, and in many cases, forcibly removed **from** their lands? What if the Europeans who began arriving on their shores in massive numbers over five-hundred years ago, attempted to live in peace and in harmony with the first inhabitants of the Americas? I dare say that we cannot in any meaningful way, **truly** picture what our world would now be had **that** been our history instead of the massive oppression of Indigenous People and the forceful taking of their land that is our **actual** past. [15]

How might contemporary human civilization now be different, had the first **and all subsequent** meetings of Africans and Europeans been on the basis of friendship, mutual esteem and shared learning? That scenario is so **far** removed from the reality of our history of the enslavement of tens of millions of African People for over two centuries throughout all of the Americas, that **we simply cannot visualize it**.

What if women, over the last five-thousand years of human history, had been **full** contributors in every society around the world? We can imagine neither the human pain and suffering that

---

15 A number of different terms are used to identify people who fall within the group commonly referred to as, "Native American." I shall use the term, "Indigenous People" in referring to people who are indigenous or native to the Western Hemisphere.

may have been avoided, nor the present level of maturity in which our species may now exist, had women and men contributed their thoughts, their talents and their abilities **in equal measure**, in building our contemporary human civilization.[16]

While I **do** wonder about all of those alternate histories that **could** have been ours, I am **enormously relieved** that as a species, we are **not** in the position of having to wonder what the world would be today if during the Cuban Missile Crisis, the United States and Cuba had not engaged in a nuclear exchange. I am **extremely thankful** that we are as human beings, not now in the position of having to wonder what the world would today be like if Hitler hadn't won World War II. I am **eternally gratified** that as a nation, the United States does not have to try to imagine what American society would now be like had the North won the Civil War, or had the Civil Rights Movement not failed. I can imagine such a world only in my worst nightmares.

I sincerely **mourn** the fact that we **are** in the position of having to only **try** to imagine our present world without our tragic past of genocide, of the Holocaust, of African slavery, of the total oppression of the Indigenous Peoples of the Americas, Australia and the Earth's other islands, and without so many of our other intentionally engaged in, historical human tragedies.

Yet, while our past has surely been no less than **devastating** to our present world in **so** many ways, evidence **abounds** that we **shall** do better in the future. We shall do better because our adolescence of the present is distinguished from our childhood of the past by one **extremely** important factor, **the** factor which, over time, will **utterly** transform our human condition. That factor, is awareness. Throughout our adolescence, we have been, and are now, more fully **aware** of what is right, even if we do not

16 Going back to **ancient** history, I also wonder how our contemporary world may be different if over the last millennium, we could have benefitted from all of the wisdom that tragically burned in the Libraries of Alexandria and Persepolis.

always, or even often **do** that which is right. Although, genocide, for example, continues to exist in our present, and even though the world is still often far too slow to **respond** to it, we at least **know** that it is evil, and **in that knowing**, will eventually abolish it from the face of the Earth. We have for all intents and purposes, banished slavery based upon skin color, the world over. Although both rings of human sexual slavery and the trafficking of humans for lifelong servitude exist worldwide, we know that **they** are evil, and in **that** knowing, will eventually abolish **them** from the planet. Although women **still** do not participate as full members in **any** society, whether developing or industrialized, in **most** cultures, the importance of achieving the **goal** of women's full equality and participation, is fully taken for granted. Thus, in time, **it** will also, ultimately be achieved.

Our awareness of what is right, moral and just, has resulted in the major movements toward consciousness over at least the last century and a half—the American abolitionist, suffrage, labor, civil rights, peace, women's, and LGBTQ movements; the movement to end communism in the Soviet Union and Eastern Europe; the movement to end apartheid in South Africa; the burgeoning movement for women's equality in India and other parts of Asia and the Middle East, and the worldwide environmental movement, to name but a few. Those movements have resulted in strict legal prohibitions against inhumane treatment toward other human beings—in the U.S. alone, the Equal Pay Act, the Civil Rights Act, the Voting Rights Act, the Age Discrimination in Employment Act, the Americans with Disabilities Act, and Hate Crime Laws among others—and those American laws have counterparts in countries the world over.

While all of those movements, however, and in some respects, their highly successful results, unquestionably indicate that we are now **significantly** more aware, significantly more **conscious** than we were in the era of our **childhood**, we are still largely not **acting** upon our awareness. We are not yet **behaving** consistently with it. Yet, it is **that**, it is our **behavior,** squarely rooted in our burgeoning higher **consciousness that** will **finally and forever**, mark the end of our protracted human adolescence. Just as surely as the darkest moment of the night gives rise to the dawn, it is **our conscious behavior** that will **finally** birth our maturity.

Tragically, over the course of human history, at the same times during which we were advancing in scientific knowledge and technology, in the **same** times during which we were experiencing remarkable **intellectual** growth, we were **dreadfully** paralyzed in our **emotional** growth. Thus, ultimately, **at the same time that we were beginning to explore space**, we, in the United States were also attempting to integrate public restrooms and water fountains.[17] I literally cannot imagine where humanity would be in our development, what kind of progress we would have made over the past six hundred years, had racism not been present on the Earth. What genius and **geniuses** might we have spawned!

The time has now come for us to mature. The time has come for us to mature beyond the Saddam Husseins, the Francois Duvaliers, the Josef Stalins, the Kim Il Sungs, and the Adolf Hitlers of our past. We must mature both in our thoughts **and** in our behavior, and we must do so **now**. We must do so now because never before has humankind stood on a double precipice of possible self-annihilation—environmental destruction through the poisoning and/or over-population of the Earth, and nuclear obliteration, the likelihood of which may be greater now than ever in our past.

Although the possibility of human self-destruction based on **both** threats looms large before us, I believe very strongly that as a species, we are **not** going to destroy ourselves. I believe that we **are** going to make it. I can neither see nor can I predict the future, but my belief that humanity will survive is **so** strong, it is **so** deep, that indeed, it doesn't feel like a **belief** at all. It feels, rather, like a profound and yet utterly inexplicable "**knowing**".

---

17 Acknowledgement goes to MSNBC's Melissa Harris Perry show for that analogy.

I "know" that we are going to make it because as a species, **over the long march of history**, we have consistently marched in the right direction. We have evolved beyond gladiator sports, beyond burning women as witches, beyond crucifying people on crosses, and beyond race-based slavery. Just as we have matured in those and countless other ways, I "know" that ultimately, we will mature beyond sexual slavery, beyond terrorism, beyond war. I "know" that from our **present** level of understanding and development, we are simply **incapable** of imagining the emotionally and spiritually advanced human culture that in the future, we **will**, as a species, develop.[18]

I "know" these things, **intuitively**, of course, and not in fact. Time will **tell** whether I am either triumphantly correct, or tragically mistaken.

I do **in reality**, however, know this: If we **do** indeed survive our immaturity, our emotional, technological and spiritual adolescence, as I adamantly believe we shall, two **very** different, very **divergent** paths are available to us in the process. One is The Path of Wisdom. The other, the Path of Foolhardiness.

On The Path of Wisdom, we become aware of our higher consciousness and **sincerely** attempt to both understand, and live consistently with it. Specifically, on that path, we will do the following three things: make every attempt to come together in love as one human family, deeply understand the presently unfathomable potential of our minds, and spiritually mature.

On the Path of Foolhardiness, we remain utterly unaware of our higher consciousness and thus neither seek nor heed it. As a

[18] My use of the term, "we", in this book is contextual. Sometimes it references my membership in the Human Race. At other times, it references, more specifically, my membership in the groups, "People of Color" and "Americans of Color." At still other times, it references, even more specifically, my membership in the group, "African Americans."

consequence, we will both continue to put the health of the Earth at risk and learn our **every** lesson about how we should live together on the Earth, **slowly**, and with continued **tremendous** future human suffering in the forms, among others, of continual war, constant terrorism, perpetual genocide, the chronic subjugation of women, continued racial and other oppression, unrelenting religious conflict, unremitting hunger, and unyielding disease. In other words, with both a kind **and amount** of needless human suffering that tragically, is our present existence.

What I **don't** know, is which path we will take on our journey toward maturity, i.e., whether we will continue down The Path of Foolhardiness on which as a species, we have traveled since our birth, and on which we remain to this day, or whether we will take the proverbial "fork in the road" to The Path of Wisdom. Thus, I know neither to what extent the human condition may deteriorate, nor **how long** that deterioration will last **before** our maturation begins. I believe, however, that when we **do** mature, humanity will experience a giant leap of consciousness in which we will become **exceedingly** more mentally stable, emotionally healthy and spiritually mature. On the other side of our transition into maturity, we will live in a state of civility and peace unlike any we have **ever** experienced. I suspect that we may now be nearing the beginning of that transition. It is possible that within the not too distant future, we will begin the process of escaping the catastrophic limitations of our human childhood and adolescence **bursting**, finally, into the brilliant light of the freedom of what will be the ever expanding awareness of our maturity. Whether we do so either soon or in the distant future, however, I am confident that **as a species,** we **will** ultimately live in a state of higher consciousness. My great hope is that in reaching it, we will follow The Path of Wisdom.

My mission in writing *The Grand Trilogy* is to share with you:

- What I believe are the three profound truths that . . . .

  We Are One—We Are Brilliant—and—We Are Divine;

- The transformative collective actions that we must take with respect to those three truths; and,

- A vision of our personal Divine being.

I believe that those truths, those actions and that vision, provide a doorway, a roadmap, a kind of guide, to The Path of Wisdom.

The one hundred thousand foot view of Earth reveals our true human spirit, what we were **meant** to be—compassionate, self-aware, peaceful and mature. *The Grand Trilogy of Truth*, if we allow it, can serve as a beacon along our journey to that evolved existence. We can choose to either learn *The Grand Trilogy of Truth* quickly and relatively easily, to our enormous benefit, or we can choose to ignore it, to our great peril. About that, we have **total** choice, and that choice, is ours.

I. My Racial Memoir: The Making of a Compassionate Activist[19]

Picture: A little girl about ten, sitting on Santa's lap, wearing Harry Potter glasses, a pencil behind her right ear, reading quite deliberately from a spiral notepad.

The words on the pad: "Let's see now, did I mention world peace? And of course, cures for all the horrible diseases in the world, places for everyone to live, an end to all hatred, a spiritual awakening for everyone, a solution to pollution, and for me—maybe just a few little trinkets. You know what I—You choose."

The Inscription: "Lauren—Is this the perfect card for you or what?! Hope you have a great 1993. Looking forward to spending more of it with you. Love, Tom & Kathleen"

I received that card from my dear friend Tom Finn twenty years ago.

That little girl on the card was really an amazing reflection of me as an adolescent beginning at age thirteen. I did absolutely **love** science throughout my childhood, and the little insatiably curious scientist was still very much present, but beginning at age thirteen, Lauren, the little outraged activist began to emerge. I was beginning to develop a very strong intellectual and emotional orientation toward integrity, peace, economic equality and social justice.

You see, the little girl who was so greatly loved by her mother and grandmother, that extremely curious little kid with the amazing inner life, the kid who had enough intellectual curiosity and imagination to wonder during a summer camp softball game about whether a

---

19 I want to thank my dear friend Theresa for encouraging me to tell my personal racial story as part of this work.

whole other universe existed on a blade of grass, that kid who was a wonder-filled little ball of energy, when outside of the safe cocoon of her family, community and school, lived within a larger society as a second class citizen. Throughout my elementary school years, until I was nearly eleven years old, I both saw the **symbols** and lived in the **reality** of segregation every day. The "White Only" signs were **everywhere**.

Images of segregation:
https://www.youtube.com/watch?v=c-7eNRB2_0Q

I couldn't drink from the same water fountains white kids drank from. I couldn't use the same restrooms they used. In some places, there were three restrooms, "Men, Women and Colored". I couldn't eat with my parents at the same restaurants at which they ate with their parents.[20]

I couldn't go to Pontchartrain Beach, (the city's formerly "White Only" amusement park, right on Lake Pontchartrain and Lakeshore Drive that was a five minute drive from our home in Pontchartrain Park), which I **really** wanted to do, to ride what seemed to me to be the most amazing roller coaster in the world.[21]

When we went to "the Lakefront"[22] for Fourth of July, Memorial Day or Labor Day family picnics, we, along with all of the city's

---

[20] The two African American restaurants that my family went to, Dooky Chase and Levata's Oyster House, like all of the city's other black eating establishments, had **incredible** food, so fortunately, we were not at a "food disadvantage" by eating at segregated restaurants. It may have been the only way in which segregation did not result in a social and economic hardship to us.

[21] Our separate, much smaller and utterly unequal amusement park was Lincoln Beach, located down a two lane street on which there was no public transportation, a full twelve miles from downtown New Orleans.

[22] New Orleanians refer to Lakeshore Drive, a long, very pleasant avenue which runs along Lake Pontchartrain, the city's northern

other African-American residents,[23] had to try to find a spot between Seabrook and Franklin Avenue, which I would guess is perhaps a fifth to a quarter of the entire Lakefront Drive area. **The entire remainder of the lakefront**, from Franklin Avenue all the way out to its end at the Southern Yacht Club, was "White Only".

Early one summer afternoon in the early 60's, my extended family, after arriving at Mandeville Louisiana's Fontainebleu State Park for a family picnic, nearly left after about 45 minutes of riding around looking for the park's Colored section. Fortunately, we eventually did find it, and had our picnic. But if looks could kill, those we received from the European American patrons in the white section would surely have made that our last day.

I couldn't go into the Howard Johnson's ice cream parlor on the corner of Congress Drive and Chef Menteur Highway that we passed **every single day** on the way home from school to have any of the twenty-eight flavors of ice cream that were so prominently and colorfully displayed on its front window. When we went to the train station to get my great uncle Marshall who lived in New York City and came down by train to visit us every summer, we had to sit in the "Colored" section, which was perhaps one-third of the station. The entire rest of Union Station was the "White Only" seating area.

My mother and I went grocery shopping at the Gentilly Schwegmann's supermarket every other Saturday, which was billed, at the time, as "The Largest Supermarket in the World". On the inside, it literally went on for as far as my eyes could see. It was in terms of size, the 1960's precursor to Costco. When Mama and I stopped at its long, L-shaped lunch counter at the front of the store for a sandwich and soda, we weren't allowed to sit and

---

border, as, "the Lakefront". For its entire length, the lake is on one side of Lakeshore Drive, and a very nice picnic area is on the other.

23 I shall use the terms "African American" and "black", and "European American" and "white" interchangeably.

eat our meal at the large front section with the nice counter stools. We had to go around to the shorter side of the "L", the much smaller side counter where there were no stools. African American customers had to order lunch on that side and then either stand while eating or sit on the adjacent staircase. My mother and I never did. In retrospect, I believe that the indignity of doing so was probably simply far too much for my mother. We bought our sandwich and soda and then left. I'll never forget the visual of White People sitting comfortably at the front counter eating their lunch, and Black People at the small side counter eating while either standing or sitting on the nearby tile staircase—essentially, the floor. There was sometimes so many people sitting on those steps that they'd be half-way up the entire staircase, always with a passageway on the right side as you looked up. Walking along the passageway were White People who were going either upstairs to, or downstairs from the second floor business offices.

In the front section of the store were two water fountains, each on either side of a large, white round, floor-to-ceiling support column. Down one side, in big, black, capital letters, the word, "W-H-I-T-E" was painted. Down the other, "C-O-L-O-R-E-D". The "white fountain" was tall, silver, metal, and cold. Ours was low, white, porcelain and hot. Judging from the frost that accumulated so quickly on the mouthpiece, the "white fountain" had a strong steady stream of icy cold water. Ours, a trickle of warm.

When we went to the Shrine Circus at the Municipal Auditorium, we had to sit so high up in the auditorium's Colored section, the "nosebleed" seats, that it was virtually impossible to see the action taking place on the stage floor below. It was the same segregated Municipal Auditorium in which Lemar Jr. and his friends attended concerts of their favorite groups. The Coasters, the Platters, and the Drifters were his three favorites. He and his friends sat up in the segregated balcony high above all the white teens in the orchestra seats below them, as they **all** watched the African American performers on the stage.

My parents couldn't go to listen to jazz in any of the French Quarter clubs, the same clubs in which black musicians were performing.

We watched the Mardi Gras parades on either Claiborne Avenue or Canal Street. While Jim Crow laws didn't **prohibit** us from being there, it was known that St. Charles Avenue, the "uptown" section of New Orleans, was the area where the city's white residents watched the parades. It was a kind of **de facto** segregation.

My mother absolutely **loved** musicals. I grew up with the 33rpm soundtracks of the Broadway productions of among others, The Sound of Music, The King and I, My Fair Lady, and South Pacific. I don't know whether any of them were performed in New Orleans at that time, but **had** they been, we wouldn't have been able to see them since they would most certainly have been performed at the Saenger Theatre or some other "White Only" venue.

In addition to Lemar Jr.'s Ray Charles, Temptations, Marvin Gaye and Tammy Terrell and Sam Cooke albums, Lambert's Earth Wind and Fire, Miles Davis, Eddie Harris, Wes Montgomery, Dave Brubeck, Astraud Gilberto, and Chicago albums and the music I liked, the Supremes, Simon and Garfunkel, Stevie Wonder, the Mamas and the Papas, The Fifth Dimension, Dionne Warwick, the Beatles, the Shirelles and John Denver, I also grew up listening to the classical music which my mother loved. I have in my garage to this day, in vinyl, her favorites—Dvorak's New World Symphony performed by the Vienna Tonkuenstler Symphony Orchestra; Handel's Water Music and Royal Fireworks Suites performed by the Philadelphia Orchestra, Eugene Ormandy conducting; Beethoven's "Pastoral" Symphony No 6 performed by the Vienna Philharmonic, Pierre Monteux conducting; Rimsky Korsakov's Scheherazade performed by the Philadelphia Orchestra, Eugene Ormandy conducting; and her two absolute favorites, Finlandia and Swedish Rhapsody performed by the Philadelphia Orchestra, Eugene Ormandy conducting, and Handel's Messiah, performed by the New York Philharmonic with the Mormon Tabernacle Choir, Leonard Bernstein conducting.

Mama loved classical music so much, that she wanted to instill a love for it in me. Her plan—Go to Werleins Music Store on Canal Street to buy me a piano, (the only place of any reputation to buy a piano in the city), and send me to piano lessons. After my lessons began, every time she went shopping, it seemed, she bought my yet another album of piano music. My favorites are The Exciting Pianos of Ferrante and Teicher, performed, of course, by them; My Favorite Chopin, performed by Van Cliburn; and my all time favorite, Rachmaninoff's Piano Concerto No. 2 in C Minor, performed by Taylor Edwards with the Royal Festival Orchestra. I don't know whether any of those orchestras ever performed in New Orleans at that time, but if they **had**, they **too** would have been performed at "White Only" theaters.

My mother took me to see the Disney movies—Mary Poppins, 101 Dalmations, Lady and the Tramp, Chitty Bang Bang are the ones I remember. To every Sidney Poitier movie that came to the theater—Lilies of the Field, To Sir With Love, A Patch of Blue, Guess Who's Coming to Dinner, and In the Heat of the Night. To the biblical movies she loved—The Greatest Story Ever Told, The Ten Commandments and King of Kings. And to the James Bond films she enjoyed—From Russia with Love, Goldfinger and Dr. No. When she did, went to either one of the city's five "Colored" movie theaters, the Claiborne, the Carver, the Gallo, the Famous and the Caffin, or to one of its segregated theaters, the Circle and the RKO Orpheum, where we sat upstairs in the "Colored" section. There were even separate **concessions stands** in the segregated theaters, one for white and one for colored.

In addition to the city's colored and segregated movie theaters, there were also some that were "White Only", of course, the Saenger Orleans and the Joy, on Canal Street, the Fox, on Elysian Fields, the Tiger on Franklin Avenue and the one closest to our house, the Gentilly Art, on Gentilly Boulevard.

I saw no black salespeople or cashiers in department stores, drug stores, grocery stores, furniture stores—**no** stores. I saw African Americans only sweeping and mopping their floors. I saw only white men as news reporters, news anchors, meteorologists, sports casters, and politicians.

Even the city's **cemeteries** were segregated, as they were all over the South. The descendants of the **same** people, some of whom lived with European Americans in their plantation homes, waiting on them "hand and foot" from the moment they woke up in the morning until the moment they went to bed at night, the descendants of the **same** people who during slavery, cleaned their homes, cooked their food and cared for their children, the descendants of the **same** African American women who, during slavery, **breastfed their children**, the descendants of **those same people** were not good enough to have their remains buried in the same cemeteries as the descendants of their European American captors. [24]

During those, my childhood years, I was struck by the absolute **unfairness** of segregation. The reality that was by far the hardest for me to comprehend is that we—my brothers, my parents and grandparents, cousins, aunts and uncles, all of whom I loved so much, all my friends and their parents to whom I looked up so much—**because of how we looked, because of physical characteristics with which we were born**, were being treated, every day of our lives, as second class citizens. My thought was, "But White People were born white just like we were born brown. (Children think in colors, not in categories.) They didn't choose being born white and we didn't choose being born brown. It's not fair."

Years later, as an adult, I realized that in addition to being **morally** bankrupt, segregation was also tremendously **financially** unjust. Throughout the entire time that we were forced to live as second class citizens in a segregated society, we paid not a single **penny** less for our goods and services, and not a **cent** less in taxes. No "discrimination adjustment" was made for us. Apparently, lawmakers didn't opine, "Well, since they're getting lesser treatment, we really **should** charge them less. It may hurt us a bit financially, but it's well

24 I use the word, "captor" and not "owner" because I do not believe that one human being can ever own another.

worth it to not have our children go to school with them, to not sit next to them at the movies or see them in our amusement parks, to not have to eat with them, use the bathroom with them, share water fountains with them, and sit next to them on the buses." If any such discussions based on a fairness argument **did** occur among lawmakers, those who advocated for such a two-tiered economic structure, lost. The reality was that while being required by law to sit in only the back of the bus, we paid **the exact same fare** as white riders who rode in the front. While standing and sitting on the stairs adjacent to the side section of Schwegmann's lunch counter, we paid **the exact same price** for our sandwiches and sodas as the white patrons who sat at the nice counter stools in the front. While being consigned to the smaller section of Fontainebleau State Park with its inferior picnic area and inadequate restroom facilities, our parents paid **the exact same state income taxes** for the park's maintenance as did white citizens. In all the stores in which we weren't allowed to try on clothes, hats and shoes, or to return them if they didn't fit, we paid **the exact same price for and sales tax on** that clothing. My parents and all of the city's other African American residents who were fortunate enough to be able to buy a home, paid **the exact same** real estate taxes on **their** homes as white home owners paid on theirs. Math has never been my strong suit, but one needn't be a math wiz to realize that it would have been a **tremendous** economic benefit to African American families and communities if, as an acknowledgement of the **crippling** discrimination under which we were forced to live, **by law**, (when we shopped, when we ate in restaurants, when we used public transportation, public restrooms, public parks and **every other kind** of public facility), we had been charged 33, 25, 20, 15 or even 10 percent less for goods and services and paid even 10 percent less in income and sales taxes. It was a benefit that tragically, we were denied. We paid the same **for everything**. We paid . . . . to be humiliated—publicly.[25]

---

25 Among the most memorable conversations that I have ever had about the discrimination that I experienced during my earliest years of life, was that which I had with a white European man who was my friend for a few years, about five years ago. He was from Romania and had

In retrospect, I realize that the **utter** injustice of segregation, **could** very well have scarred me as a child. **But** because my mother told me that segregation was **wrong**, that the people who **believed** in it were wrong in that belief, and that **we** were on the right side, the just side, the moral side of the issue, not only did segregation **not** affect my self-esteem, it actually provided me an emotional template on which I and everyone I knew and loved, were fighting a valiant battle of right against wrong, of justice against injustice. I felt good being on the "right" side, the side, I thought, of the people who were intelligent and mature, the side that was ultimately destined to win.

---

grown up in his country, under communism. I will **never** forget my friend's reaction to my story, to my telling him that if he and his parents had been able to visit the United States during that time, and had they come to New Orleans during their visit, they would have been able to go to amusement parks, restaurants, theaters, movie houses and many other places that my parents and I would have been prohibited from entering; that my parents and I would not have been able to drink from the same water fountains as he and his parents; that we wouldn't have been able to use the same restrooms that he and his parents used; that we would have had to sit behind them on public service busses; that he and I would not have been able to attend the same school; that our families would likely not have been able to live in the same neighborhood, and that **all** of those things, the water fountains, restrooms, lunch counters, **everything** that **we** had, would have been **vastly** inferior to everything that **they** had. As he looked at me in pure amazement, my friend responded, "Lauren, in Romania, we didn't know **anything** about this. All we knew was that the United States was the land of freedom, and we all wanted to come here. I can't believe that **your own country** would treat you and your parents and other black Americans like that. I can't believe that me, a foreigner, could have come here and been treated better than you and your parents, **you, who are Americans.** It was different, but **kind** of like me growing up in communism. You had no freedom. Lauren, you and me, we're human beings. We're human beings. There's no difference. I'm sorry Lauren." And as through his thick Romanian accent, he uttered that last sentence, my friend, a large, fit, muscular blonde haired, blue eyed man of over six feet, wiped tears from his eyes.

As a child, I was totally unaware that that very struggle of what I thought of as good against evil, was providing me with a very early backdrop against which I was already beginning to develop as a value, the goal of living a conscious, examined life of principle. [26]

What I have described in **much** abbreviated fashion, is that both the time **at** and place **in which** I was born, resulted in my experiencing the ugliness of segregation as a part of my introduction to life. It is ironic that in a different way, I was born during America's golden age. It was our golden **economic** age, a time during which millions of us whose parents had been raised in poverty during the depression, as were mine, became our families' first generation to grow up middle class. There **had** been middle class African American families during the decades after emancipation and preceding the 1950's, primarily those of attorneys, physicians, ministers and business owners, but they were by far the exception. Primarily as a result of the legacy of slavery, every generation of African-Americans during that period, was significantly poorer than European Americans. We were, in the 50's, the first generation of black kids to grow up middle class **in any appreciable numbers** and whose parents were not primarily lawyers, doctors, ministers and entrepreneurs.

We were Baby Boomers who grew up in the post-World War II economy. Many of our fathers were veterans of the war, making a college education through the G.I Bill, possible for many of

[26] I have been struck, in many conversations with Barbara, by how different her childhood was in New Jersey during the 1950's and 60's. She and her family are also African American and as a child, her parents took her and her siblings to see the Rockettes at Radio City Music Hall. They had Sunday outings to Baskin Robbins. They visited the Philadelphia Museum of Art and rode on all the rides in Atlantic City. Barbara listens to the stories of my childhood under segregation with nothing but pure amazement. She was aware of the **existence** of segregation, of course, but had never before heard actual **stories** of what it was like to actually **live** in it every day and of what happened, initially when it ended. My stories have been a real eye opener for Barbara.

them. Our parents, members of The Greatest Generation, were able to purchase their homes with either FHA, (Federal Housing Administration) or VA (Veterans Administration) loans. Certain kinds of government jobs were, becoming available on a limited basis to People of Color for the first time at the Federal, state and municipal levels. While it was a time of **crippling** discrimination against People of Color, **still**, the African American community in which I grew up was a **total** product of America's economic golden age.[27]

The wonderful African American community of my childhood was Pontchartrain Park, named for Lake Pontchartrain which was walking distance away. Pontchartrain Park is recognized as one of the first, (if not **the** first), middle class African American sub-divisions in the country and is a National Register Historic District. It was built in the Gentilly section of New Orleans, widely known as a pleasant, middle class, residential segment of the upper part of the city's Ninth Ward.[28]
http://www.nola.com/175years/index.ssf/2011/11/1955_pontchartrain_park_opens.html
(Paste this url into your browser to get to the correct website.)

---

27 Knowing that my **parents** had both more education, (high school diplomas) and more employment opportunities than my **grand**parents, and that **my** generation lived much more comfortably than my **parents** did when **they** were children, I thought, as a child and young adult, that I was simply witnessing the progressive march of history, society merely becoming smarter and better. I never **dreamed** that in reality, those of us who are Baby Boomers had actually won the birth lottery. I **never** thought that for the generation after us, it would be **harder** to afford a college education, **harder** to find meaningful employment in one's chosen field, **harder** to purchase a home, **harder** to be in the middle class. We had no way of knowing that we may actually have been born during a brief window in time during which we had **tremendous** opportunities that a generation later, may not exist for our children.

28 The city's large Ninth Ward also encompasses the "Lower Ninth", which was "below", i.e., on the other side of the Industrial Canal, that received so much national media coverage in the aftermath of Hurricane Katrina.

http://nutrias.org/photos/parkways/ppark/pparkphotos1.htm

History of Pontchartrain Park

Ariel View of Pontchartrain Park Before Construction of Homes and Golf Course Louisiana Division/City Archives, New Orleans Public Library

Breaking Ground Louisiana Division/City Archives, New Orleans Public Library

Dedication of Pontchartrain Park Louisiana Division/City Archives, New Orleans Public Library

New Subdivision Sign[29] Louisiana Division/City Archives, New Orleans Public Library

29 The sign was later changed to read simply, "Pontchartrain Park."

http://nutrias.org/~nopl/photos/ragas/015/015_01.jpg

Dedication of Pontchartrain Park, January 31, 1955

The Club House
Louisiana Division/City Archives,
New Orleans Public Library

The Golf Course
Louisiana Division/City Archives,
New Orleans Public Library

Kids at the 1 of 2 Playgrounds
Louisiana Division/City Archives,
New Orleans Public Library

Kids at the Playground
Louisiana Division/City Archives,
New Orleans Public Library

Pontchartrain Park was a brand new, beautiful, middle and upper middle class African-American community of single-family homes with meticulously manicured lawns. It was officially dedicated in January of 1955 and was truly one of the most beautiful neighborhoods in the city, black or white.

African American couples began touring the subdivision's model homes immediately upon their availability.[30]

http://photos.nola.com/tpphotos/2011/11/175pontchartrain_6.html
Prospective buyers tour newly built homes in the Pontchartrain Park neighborhood of New Orleans in the mid-1950's

The community was oval-shaped, and in the middle was an 18 hole golf course with two large, lagoons[31] and a clubhouse for golfers. It was a neighborhood of back yards filled with various colors, kinds and sizes of gym sets and round, plastic, two and three ring inflatable kids' pools. At the back of the community was Lake Pontchartrain, tennis courts, basketball courts, picnic grounds, a baseball field for the kids in the community and right beside the baseball **field**, a baseball **stadium** for the city's schools. There were two playgrounds with swings, merry-go-rounds, see-saws and monkey bars. Saturday mornings were filled with the sound of lawnmowers from every direction, the overpowering smell of freshly cut St. Augustine grass, and dozens

---

[30] Pontchartrain Park was also built just behind the all-white Gentilly Woods subdivision. The two communities were by either accident or design, separated by a trench. It was a very clean trench, with thick, very neatly cut grass that grew on both sides and the bottom, but it was a trench, a divider, nonetheless.

[31] The larger island, "Nanny Goat Island", was wooded and actually had goats living on it that were clearly visible from the golf course. The popular story among us kids that there was a rickety old shack in the middle of the woods with a little old man living in it, intrigued my imagination to no end.

of men walking along the golf course, including my father, who after a couple of years of the following comment about the golfers, “Look at those fools, out there doing all that walking, chasing a little white ball around”, became an **avid** golfer himself. Judging from the three trophies he was awarded by the Pontchartrain Park Golf Club, Daddy was pretty decent on the course. [32]

Golfers pose at the opening of the Pontchartrain Park Golf Course
http://photos.nola.com/tpphotos/2011/11/175pontchartrain_4.html

My Father After Receiving One of His Golf Trophies

My Father, (Right) with His Golf Buddies

We moved to “The Park”, as it was widely known throughout New Orleans' “colored” community, on Thanksgiving Day, 1955. My understanding is that we were the second family to move in.

---

[32] In the dining room of the house, my father taught me how to swing a golf club. I **loved** playing with his little green, plastic electric putting machine that spat the ball back to the putter, but I never did catch the golf “bug”. He was much more successful, though, with Lemar Jr. and Lambert, who are to this day, absolute golf fanatics. As for me, I play a pretty mean game of putt putt.

Indeed, after looking at the plans for the entire community, my parents bought our home from the architectural plans before it was actually built. Every Saturday morning while the house was being built, my mother would pick up her younger sister, my Aunt Verlie, drive out to our lot, and very excitedly look at the progress that had been made in the construction the prior week. On Thanksgiving Day of 1955 when we moved in, Lemar Jr. was twelve. Lambert was eight and I was two.

My Mother, Lemar Jr., Lambert and I at home in the Living Room.

It was from my perspective as a child, a world of the Etch-A-Sketch, of Give-A-Show Projectors, Pogo Sticks, Snow Cone Machines, of Slinkies, Silly Putty, finger painting, Pick-Up Stix, Jumping Beans, Play-Doh, and the wonders of the View Master's astounding 3-D pictures. It was a time, years before Sesame Street's cultural diversity, of Captain Kangaroo and Mr. Green Jeans, Shari Lewis and Lamb Chop, Howdy Doody and Bozo the Clown. My favorite cartoons were Mighty Mouse, Gumby and Pokey, Popeye, and Rocky & Bullwinkle with their cast of characters, Sherman, Mr. Peabody, Nell, Dudley Do-Right, Oil Can Harry and the Fractured Fairy Tales. Dick Tracy, Annie, Beetle Bailey and Blondie were "required" reading **every** Sunday morning.

These were the pre-FM days. Radio was only AM, and in New Orleans, the four most popular stations for our generation were

WBOK and WYLD which played “black kids’ music”, and WNOE and WTIX which played “white kids’ music”.

For television, we had the three major networks and PBS. In New Orleans, they were Channel 4, WWL, (CBS), Channel 6, WDSU, (NBC) Channel 8, WVUE, (ABC), and Channel 12, (then later Channel 13), WYES, (PBS). Channel 26, WGNO, came along much later. Remote controls and channel surfing were the stuff of sci-fi.

My two favorite TV shows, both science fiction, The Twilight Zone and The Outer Limits, were scaring the life out of me and every other kid I knew. Leonard Bernstein’s Sunday afternoon Young People’s Concerts, the holiday season television airing of The Sound of Music and the Wizard of Oz and the Easter season television airing of Peter Pan with Mary Martin were **never** missed.[33] Mama and I always watched them together. If you grew up in New Orleans, Morgas and Chopsley were compulsory Saturday night viewing, and Mr. Bingle was a daily visitor during the Christmas season.

The three month summer vacation from school felt like three years, and summer was a time of hand suckers, pink, blue and white coconut pralines, and nickel huck-a-bucks, (sweet frozen cups). It was a time of S & H Green Stamps and of the milk man who delivered right to your front door, fresh milk in glass bottles with cardboard tops. We ate Sugar Daddy suckers after school, and had Sugar Smacks, Sugar Frosted Flakes and the “Snap, Crackle and Pop” of Sugar **Pops**, (that sometimes even came in a really cool three-way fold-out cardboard box) for breakfast. Tony the Tiger was telling us to put corn flakes in our stomach, and Esso was telling us to put a tiger in our tank. This was the time of mimeograph machines with their amazing smelling ink and frost

---

33 When I think about that Peter Pan production now, I find the portrayal of its Indigenous characters enormously disconcerting. Both its stereotypes and the use of the term, “Red Skin”, while shocking by **current** standards of cultural appropriateness, were, unfortunately, quite commonplace when the production was performed in the early 1960’s.

covered silver metal ice trays with handles so cold they stuck to your fingers. Both Bosco and Brylcreem were "boss", and people who brushed with Pepsodent wondered where the yellow went. I dreamed of seeing the USA in a (convertible) Chevrolet. When adults talked about "the war", everybody knew without question, that it was World War II. Music was on 45's, and 33's and a few of your parents' heavy old 78's were still around.

The Park was like "Black Leave It to Beaver Land". We were all two-parent families. I don't remember a **single** family going through a divorce the entire time I was growing up there, from the time I was two, until I left after graduating from college, when I was twenty. With the exception of one family that moved to California in the mid '60's, I don't even remember any families **moving out** of the Park. We were an **extremely** stable community of black families, the Woods', the Gougises, the Glapions, the Allens, the Vickmans, Aguillards, Nelsons, Bushes, Kennedys, LeBlancs, Washingtons, Gardners, Merrimans, Durrels, Villavasos, the Coulliets, the Permillions, Uncle Ikee and his family, who lived four blocks from us, and so many others.[34]

> [Despite how amazing a place Pontchartrain Park was in which to grow up, it was built for a disturbing, nefarious reason—to keep the city's new and growing middle and upper middle class African American population from moving into white subdivisions during the post-World War II, Jim Crow era. Fortunately, as children, we were totally unaware of the Park's raison d'etre.]

---

34 I was an older teenager when I learned that one of my friends was from a blended family. I'll refer to them as the Smiths. I learned that Mrs. Smith had been married prior to being married to Mr. Smith, and that my friend's two older brothers had a different last name and a different father from herself and her younger brother - Mrs. Smith's first husband. I was totally surprised by that information and realized that the Smiths were the most atypical of any family I knew in my entire neighborhood.

In its earliest days, Pontchartrain Park had a governing board, on which my mother served. The Board was followed in time, by the Pontchartrain Park Improvement Association, of which she was the secretary. She was also the editor of the early editions of the community newspaper, the Pontchartrain Park Patriot, and an organizer of the House of the Month Club. [35]

http://photos.nola.com/tpphotos/2011/11/175pontchartrain.html
Pontchartrain Park Improvement Association Directors' Meeting Nov. 3, 1957: From left: F.T. Bechet; C.W. Acox; Mrs. J.B. Vickman; H.S. Dorsey, chairman; Permillion, president; Mrs. Selina Joichin; Rev. A.A. Jones, Chaplain.

I remember that on one occasion, members of the Improvement Association met with the manager of the Gentilly Arts Movie Theater, requesting that they set aside one day per week on which we could see movies there, a kind of "Negro Night." I don't know whether the Association was successful, but because I have no memory of ever having gone to the Gentilly Arts, I doubt that it was.

I have in my possession to this day, the inch-and-a-half thick binder of notes that my mother took at all of those Pontchartrain Park Improvement Association meetings, and as such, am **acutely** aware that I am sitting on an absolute **gold mine** of history.

I have memories of growing up in Pontchartrain Park that will remain with me forever. There was the jingle of the ice cream truck, (that I still remember and can hum to this day), that passed through the neighborhood **every** summer evening without fail, the sound of bicycle bells, metal skates, (with keys), on cement, boys playing football, and the sound of kids practicing drums, flutes, clarinets and trumpets.

---

[35] Homes were judged each month for the beauty of their front lawn and landscaping. The house judged **most** beautiful, was awarded the "Pontchartrain Park House of the Month" front lawn sign.

Every year on Halloween night, it seemed that there were at least ten thousand kids out Trick-or-Treating, all in costumes. At Christmas, I don't remember a single house not being beautifully decorated. On Christmas morning, the neighborhood **lawns and sidewalks** were filled with kids playing with wooden croquet sets, tin kaleidoscopes, a myriad of board games, plastic bowling pins and balls, kid-sized golf sets, dolls, and matchbox cars, while the **streets** were overrun with traffic jams of kids on skaters and shiny new bicycles. They are memories that are as clear for me today as if it all happened yesterday.

Pontchartrain Park was a community of African-American adults who were remarkable role models of grace, maturity and exquisite dignity in the face of the incredible daily indignities of segregation. Many of our parents were active members of the New Orleans NAACP and Urban League. As Lambert and I have said in our numerous conversations about the adults who were in our lives during our childhood, they were extremely "civic-minded."

Our parents had inspiring dignity. I **never** heard either my mother or Gramzie, utter a single curse word—never, **not once**. Our mothers even used the word, "expecting". I **never** heard the word, "pregnant", and we kids weren't supposed to use it. "Pregnant", as it turns out, was a bad word. Even though they were all on a friendly, first name basis with each other, in talking to us kids about another adult, our parents referred to their peers by their title and last name—"I spoke to Mrs. Saunders this morning and she said she'd be happy to give you a ride to school in the mornings with Terry and Kenneth", or, "Mr. Williams said that he'll be taking the Cub Scouts on a field trip next month."

We were referred to as young ladies and young men. It may have been the little boy standing up in the front row of the kids' movies Mama showed at our church on Saturday nights to raise money for the building of the new sanctuary, whom she addressed as follows, "Young man! Young man! Sit down in front please." It may have been the teenager who, when my mother stopped at a stop sign on her way home from work one evening, opened the front passenger door of her car, grabbed her purse from the seat and ran. The kid made the mistake of running into a dead end alley and unbelievably, my mother ran after him. When his back was against the alley's back wall, and he was clutching my mother's purse and looking right at her, she said to him, "**Young man**, I'm sure your mother doesn't know that you're out here doing these kinds of things. Now you can have the money that's in my bag, but I need my purse back." The kid then dropped her purse and dashed past her, out of the alley. It may have been any of the girls at church who'd done something particularly nice on a given Sunday, about whom she'd say, "She's such a nice young lady."

On New York Circle, the little cul-du-sac in which my family lived, there were our next door neighbors on the corner, Mr. and Mrs. Morial and their kids Julie and Marc, [36] then my family at 5019 New York Circle, then on the other side were Mr. and Mrs. Acox and their son, Clarence Junior. Next to the Acoxes were Mr. and Mrs. Wharton and their six kids, Larry, their two sets of twins Sandra and Sandrine, Ronald and Donald, another boy whose name I can't remember, and their youngest, Leah. Next door to the Whartons were Dr. and Mrs. Burgeron, then next to them, Mr.

---

[36] Mr. Morial later served two terms as the first black mayor of New Orleans. In the Fall of 1977 when he was elected to his first term, he spoke at the University of Pennsylvania where his son, Marc and I were both students and quite coincidentally, next door neighbors again in the W.E.B. DuBois residential living facility, "the black dorm". The first thing Mr. Morial said to me when I went up to greet him after his remarks, was, "Laurie Joichin. Look at you, all grown up, and working on your doctorate. Young lady, your mother would be **so** proud of you. If Selina could see you now." I called my father the next day and told him about that exchange. Although after his initial susrprise, "You saw Dutch?" (Mr. Morial's nickname which he was called by many of his peers), he responded with his customary "Uh huh", it was uttered this time with a chuckle. I knew that he delighted in hearing Mr. Morial's comment. Years later, Marc, (currently the Executive Director of the National Urban League), also served two terms as mayor of the city.

and Mrs. Carr and their daughters Shelly and much later, Stacy. Next to the Carrs were Mr. and Mrs. Hayes and their daughter[37] and then on the other corner of the circle were Mr. and Mrs. Doucette and their five kids, Gaynelle, Lloyd Junior, Terri, Michelle and their youngest, their little boy Dion.

On DeBore Drive, just outside of the circle, were Mr. and Mrs. Rubion and their kids Barbara and Lemar Jr.'s best friend, Lil Pat, (Mr. Rubion was Patrick Sr., i.e., "Big Pat"), and Mr. and Mrs. Sneed and their four daughters Gwen, Roz, Deb and Karen. Around the corner on Congress Drive in the gorgeous big, white, sprawling house on the hill, were Dr. and Mrs. Adams and their daughter Carolyn.

Lemar Jr. Lambert and I in Front of Our Parents' New 1959 Ford Fairlane 500

There were two churches in Pontchartrain Park. In "the new section", as we called it, built in the 60's on the other side of the golf course, was Holy Cross Lutheran Church. On our side was the church my family attended, Bethany Methodist Church. Bethany was chartered

37 Mr. and Mrs. Hayes were extremely protective of their daughter and with the exception of going to school, didn't allow her to be outside very much. For that reason, and also because she was in Lemar Jr.'s group - about ten years older than me - I don't remember her name.

in 1957, two years after Pontchartrain Park opened. Before Bethany was built, ours was one of the homes in which church service was held on a rotating basis. My mother was one of Bethany's founding members, the lead soprano of its Sanctuary Choir, Chair of its Pastoral Relations Committee, and a member of it Bi-Racial Dialogue Group. As a member of Bethany's Building committee, Mama worked tirelessly on getting the new sanctuary built. To say that my mother truly **loved** Bethany would be an understatement of **mammoth** proportions. My mother was **totally** committed to Bethany. It was exceptionally close to her heart. She had a profound and abiding religious faith. My mother's deep-seated faith in God was one of the pivotal foundations of her life. I'm sure that Gramzie, also woman of deep faith, was her model. [38]

My Mother with Methodist Women's Guild (Third from Right)

We were a **real** community. The way in which our parents in the circle came together to beautify their homes typifies the munificent neighborhood spirit they all shared. They decided, at some point, that in addition to **cutting** their lawns, they also wanted to **edge** them. Consequently, they held a meeting and decided that they'd all pitch in toward the cost of an electric edger. I can still see that

[38] After the 1968 merger of the Methodist Church with the Evangelical United Brethren Church, the name was changed to the United Methodist Church, after which Bethany became Bethany United Methodist Church.

edger in my mind's eye. It was red and three-wheeled and at **our** house most of the time. I was probably about eight when I finally stopped being afraid of the sparks that flew when its steel blade nipped the sidewalk. We shared that edger for years.

Although we lived in the midst of a racist, segregated society, racism manifested in New Orleans in such a way that we were spared the emotional pain of seeing our parents be **personally deferential** to European Americans. We never saw them drop their eyes in the presence of, step off a sidewalk for, or say "Yes Sir" and "Yes Ma'am" to them. Perhaps it was a function of being in a large city as opposed to a rural area where, for African Americans, not engaging in such personal indignities was often a matter of life and death. Instead, as children, we watched our parents work responsibly at their jobs as secretaries, teachers and school principals, as mailmen, high school coaches and guidance counselors, as elementary school nurses, and for a few of us, doctors and lawyers.

> [My mother had a career as an administrative assistant which she very much enjoyed, but had her life circumstances been different, she would have gone to college as she planned and wanted so badly to do. Her father, my Grandpa Jim, told her very late in her process of preparing to attend Southern University in Baton Rouge, that he didn't have the money to send her. My Aunt Johnnie believes that if she had graduated from college, my mother would most likely have majored in Business Education with the intention of going into elementary and secondary educational administration and classroom teaching as a back-up because that is exactly what she advised Johnnie to do when she entered college.[39] When

---

[39] My Aunt Johnnie didn't want to go to college. She admired my mother tremendously, and wanted to be a "secretary" just like her big sister, Nina. Mama, however, was very clear that Johnnie should go to college and coordinated all of the details that made it happen. I was too young to remember, but I can imagine the pride Mama must have felt at her baby sister's college graduation. And Gramzie,

Grandpa Jim told Mama that he didn't have the money to send her to college, she was devastated, but immediately enrolled in Straight Business School in New Orleans, as an alternative, from which she graduated.

As for my father's career, he told me several years after he retired, that he'd always hated his job in the Post Office, a fact which I had never before known. He loved science, medicine particularly, and wanted to be a doctor. Daddy was actually a freshman at Southern when he was drafted for "The War."]

It was a time at which a couple such as my parents, a public school secretary and a mailman, could **afford** to buy a suburban home **and** a nice car **and** live comfortably.[40] I watched my mother go to work every day in a professional dress, matching earrings and necklace and coordinating pumps and purse. We watched our parents during the Civil Rights Movement as, despite any resulting **personal** inconvenience, they courageously took a stand against discrimination by among things, participating in boycotts of stores

who worked as a hotel maid for years? She must have been simply **overflowing** with pride to see her youngest earn a college degree in Business Education with a minor in English. My Aunt Johnnie retired from the New Orleans Public School System after thirty-five years as a teacher of Business Education.

40 City jobs as police officers, fire fighters and employees in Federal, state and city agencies were still largely not available to African Americans. The segregated public school system and the U.S. Post Office, in which my parents both worked when we moved to the Park, were perhaps the two employers that beginning in the 50's, most contributed to the existence of an African American middle class.

My grandparents' generation supported their families principally as janitors, domestics in private homes, laborers, hotel maids, (as was Gramzie when she was young), truck drivers, (as was Gramps, my father's father), and river front workers, (as did Gramzie's brothers, my great uncles William and Paul, and her sister, my great aunt Celie).

that engaged in discriminatory employment practices.[41] We watched them coordinate community and civic meetings that were organized around issues of discrimination. We watched them as active members of church committees fighting segregation and other forms of discrimination. We observed them battle evil **outside** of our community, while **internally**, we watched them **simultaneously** coach our little league teams, direct our summer camps, lead our scout troops and attend **with so much pride**, our recitals and ballet concerts. We watched our parents be amazing examples of both strength **and** tenderness, compassion **and** wisdom.

While the adults in our community were role models for all of the neighborhood kids, my **mother** was without question, **my** most powerful role model. She was a community activist who gave from her heart, always attempting to meaningfully contribute to Bethany, her church, Pontchartrain Park, her community, and the United States, her country. Mama was on Pontchartrain Park's Governing Board. She later served as a member of the Pontchartrain Park Improvement Association. She was the Editor of the early editions of our neighborhood newspaper, *The Pontchartrain Park Patriot*. She was Chairperson of Bethany's Pastor-Parish Relations Committee and a member of its Bi-Racial Dialog Group. She was an active member of the Methodist Women's Guild, lead soprano of Bethany's Sanctuary Choir, and an active member of its Building (fundraising) Campaign. My mother was both a member and an employee of the New Orleans Urban League and was deeply committed to its goals of economic opportunity for African Americans. It was my mother's deep compassion for others that compelled her activism. Gramzie was

---

41 In order to shop during the long Civil Right Era boycotts of Gentilly stores, our parents drove all the way to the sections of the city in which they had grown up. Every Saturday for well over a year, my mother drove up to the Circle Food Store in the city's Seventh Ward where she grew up, to do our grocery shopping, passing up the Gentilly Schwegmann's, which was on Chef Menteur Highway, five minutes outside of the Park.

an **astonishingly** compassionate person and she **clearly** instilled that same level of compassion in my mother.

My mother was also the Organizer-In-Chief of our entire extended family. She took care of all of Gramzie's needs. She informed Uncle Ikee about Pontchartrain Park and encouraged him to consider purchasing a home there, which he did, in 1956 and owned until Hurricane Katrina destroyed it fifty-one years later. She got my Aunt Johnnie into and through college and helped both my aunts Verlie and Johnnie find homes and jobs. When Uncle Ikee lost his wife, my Aunt Gerlie, leaving him with two very young boys, my cousins Gerard and Drexel, she stepped in, cooking for them and helping with the boys every day until Uncle Ikee remarried. She organized our family gatherings and in every other sense, "was there" for **all** of us—Gramzie, her, (Mama's) siblings **and** their children—and of course, us, her own family.

Family was **extremely** important to my mother. She went from her job to either Gramzie's or my Aunt Verlie's for lunch almost every day. My Aunt Verlie and my mother were very close and Verlie shared with me once that she always enjoyed having lunch with my mother on those days, just the two of them. Mama's surprise wedding gift to my Aunt Johnnie epitomizes the many ways in which she demonstrated her love to all of us. Several days before my Aunt Johnnie's wedding, she and her fiancé, with the help of several family members and friends, brought all of their new furniture and other belongings to the home in which they were going to live. When Johnnie and her new husband arrived at the house very late on their wedding night, they expected to find it just as they'd left it a couple of days earlier, filled with boxes and with a made-up bed as the only semblance of order. When the newlyweds opened the front door of their home on that night, to their utter amazement, all the curtains had been hung, pictures were on the wall, rugs were on the floors, all their clothes were unpacked, neatly folded and in their drawers, their shoes and hanging clothes were in the closets, and the refrigerator and freezer were full. Johnnie knew **in an instant** that what she was seeing was Mama's handiwork in action. The instant she opened the door of her new home, she saw her big sister Nina's loving fingerprint. It was my mother's very same loving fingerprint that touched us all.

My mother was the pillar of our family, a leader in our community and the center of my world.

In the midst of the tremendously racist society which was 1950's and 60's New Orleans, our parents taught us that violence was not only immoral, it was also unproductive, (and thus a **tremendous** waste of precious time), because it was **always and ultimately** doomed to fail. They taught us that it was **non**-violence that would change the world. They taught us that **all** people are created equal, and that we must **never** hate White People. They taught us that there were many thousands of White Americans of conscience and integrity who, often putting their own personal safety at **grave** risk, both supported and actively **participated** in the Civil Rights Movement. They taught us that we should not hate those who hated us, for they were simply unaware. Our parents told us that in being blind to the image of God in which **we** were created, they were also blind to their own. They taught us that love is **infinitely** more powerful than hate and that it is **love** which in the **final** analysis, without fail, always wins.

But perhaps more than any others, there were two **immeasurably** valuable lessons that our parents gave us. The first, and unquestionably the most important, was that we were **immensely** loved, that we were wonderful, smart, good, talented kids, and that **no one** was better than us, no matter **what** societal messages we received about the inferiority of blackness. The second message, which they **dutifully** drilled into us, was that if we "**applied**" ourselves, ("You have to **'apply'** yourself," was one of my mother's most used admonitions to us whenever we didn't perform at our best at something), did well in school and worked hard, we could both **do** anything and **be** anything we wanted and thus that there was **nothing** that we couldn't accomplish, crippling discrimination notwithstanding.[42]

---

[42] In retrospect, I suspect that our parents may not have **actually** believed that. They were very **well** aware that if as adults, we faced

We, their children, are the **infinitely** blessed beneficiaries of **all** of those indescribably inspiring messages. We are the beneficiaries of watching our parents in the 50's and 60's not just **teach** us all of those lessons, but indeed **live** them all. I cannot describe in words the tremendous wisdom, strength and dignity with which our parents responded to racism and segregation. One would had to have **experienced** them at that time to truly understand their poise, their self-respect and in turn, the compelling impact which their example had on us, their kids.

Our parents' lesson of self-respect and their message that we weren't inferior to **anybody,** were never more clearly illustrated as the day a handful of white golfers showed up at the golf clubhouse attempting to pay their fee and play nine holes on the course. Mr. Lassiter, the Clubhouse proprietor, reminded the men that segregation was the law, that the law went **both** ways, and that theirs was the City Park Golf Course, uptown. He then very politely turned them away. The white golfers protested, but Mr. Lassiter stood his ground until the men left.[43]

But there was also **another** lesson that my mother taught Lemar Jr., Lambert and I. It was the lesson that just as no one was better

---

the same kind and the same level of racism with which they were living **their** adult lives, there were many opportunities that would be **totally** unavailable to us. But in their love for us, their **intention** was to encourage us, to build our developing self-esteem. My guess is that as our parents **encouraged** us, they deeply **hoped** and fervently **prayed** that their promise to us would not be, as it was for them, a dream deferred, but would, instead, be our adult reality.

I learned as an adult, that some black parents told their children that they had to be twice as good as a white person to get half as far. The intention, I imagine, was to both prepare their children for the reality of American society as it was, and to motivate them to work very hard.

[43] I am aware of that story only because my father came home that day and beaming with pride, told my mother and I of the incident.

than **us**, **we** were no better than anyone else. My mother **always** taught us that we should **never** either believe **or behave** as if we were better than other people because we lived in Pontchartrain Park, and that "having a little more than other children" didn't mean that we were any **better** than them. She taught us that **all** people had equal worth, equal value. and that we were **all** children of God. Mama believed that with all her heart and wanted to be sure that we did as well. I have clear memories of my mother expressing deep and sincere concern about people who are poor not only in the United States, but indeed around the world. Perhaps it was herself having grown up very poor during the depression that caused her to feel so deeply for those in need.

I was reminded of that message every day at school. From kindergarten through sixth grade where elementary school ended, I attended Robert R. Moton Elementary. Moton was in the heart of the Desire Project, one of the city's largest public housing developments. For several years after it opened in 1949, and throughout the time I attended school there, 1957-'64, the Desire was for working class African Americans, a pretty nice place to live. Compared to the housing in which many of the city's African American residents lived years earlier during the depression, it may indeed have been considered a **very** nice place to live. All the buildings, sidewalks and streets were relatively new, less than ten years old, and they looked it. The apartments were large and sunny. There was no stigma to living in the projects then. They were just the places where people who were low wage earners lived. Its residents were the maids and bellmen of the French Quarter hotels. They were the custodians of downtown office buildings. They were the "lunch ladies" and janitors in the African American public schools. In the projects, in those days, there were no teenagers hanging out all night, no sound of police sirens, no gun shots. There were no gangs. There was simply the sound of hundreds of kids playing outside whenever school was out—hopscotch, football jump rope, and with dolls, marbles, hula hoops, jacks, wooden yoyo's, tops and kites.

I knew what the Desire sounded like after school because Gramzie lived there at that time and my mother dropped me off with her every day both before and after school. Mama moved Gramzie to the Desire not long after it opened. A year or two prior, a number of Gramzie's relatives had moved into and thoroughly taken over her house in the Seventh Ward. Not liking that situation one bit, my mother told Gramzie about a nice new housing development where she thought Gramzie and her two younger sisters Verlie and Johnnie, would be comfortable. Gramzie looked at the apartment and at the development itself and after some initial reluctance and subsequent persuasion, finally agreed. She lived in the Desire until I was in eighth grade when again, Mama moved her because the project was just beginning to "get rough" at that time. Gramzie's Desire Project address, 3351 Desire Parkway, Apartment A, and her phone number, Whitehall, (WH) 3-5804, will remain with me for the rest of my life. After Gramzie moved out, over time, the Desire Project became widely known as the worst, i.e., the most crime-ridden project in the city.

I'm quite amused, thinking back now, about the reason I attended Moton . . . . By the time I was three, I cried **every day**, wanting, so badly, to attend school. I mean I **really** wanted to go to school . . . . and I **really** cried about it. I wanted to go to school so badly, in fact, that for Christmas when I was three, I got a miniature school desk, (we called it a peg table at that time), so that I could **pretend** that I was in school. My mother was the secretary for Moton's principal, Mrs. Anna B. Henry, so, when I turned four, in order to stop my daily, "I wanna go to school!" protests, my mother asked Mrs. Henry if I could just **sit in** with the kindergarten class at Moton. The plan was for me to then **officially** enroll in kindergarten the following year at Valena C. Jones Elementary, my parents' my Uncle Ikee, my aunts Verlie and Johnnie and Lemar Jr. and Lambert's elementary school. Mrs. Henry agreed and my mother got a permit from the School Board for me to attend Moton since it was not the school which based upon my zip code, I was supposed to attend. Because I was born in August, I was in kindergarten the entire school year. Well, as it turned out, my kindergarten teacher, Mrs. Bertrand, told my mother at the end of the year that I had done very well in the classroom, both socially and academically, and that it would therefore be a real shame for me to have to spend an entire year **repeating** kindergarten. She suggested, although I'd just be turning five, that I be put into first grade there at Moton as a test, just to see if I was academically ready for it and was able to keep up. If it turned out that I couldn't, I'd then go back to kindergarten. Apparently, I did just fine in Ms. Napoleon's first grade class because I never saw kindergarten again. [44]

By the end of first grade, I had all my friends and knew most of the teachers at Moton—it was my third home, (Gramzie's house was my second), and I loved it. Moton was a beautiful new school in which all of the classrooms had an entire wall of glass which we decorated for every holiday. There were lots of maps and world globes, books, puzzles and games in the classrooms.[45] The teachers, all my mom's friends, were dedicated to making sure that we received a good education, despite and perhaps **because**

---

[44] My mother dropped me off at Gramzie's house every morning before going to work at Moton. When I was very young, my Aunt Verlie, who then lived with Gramzie, combed my hair, dressed me and walked me to school when it was time. After school, I went to my mother's office and played in the space under her desk where her feet were, until it was time for us to go home. When I was a little older, I'd go to Gramzie's after school in order to play with my friends, the children of Gramzie's neighbors, until Mama picked me up. Because I attended the same school at which my mother worked **and** because that school was in my grandmother's neighborhood, I was **never** physically very far away from either of them, whether I was at home or at school. The result was that I felt my mother and grandmother's love and protection at **all** times, **wherever** I was.

[45] I suspect that as is true of dedicated teachers today, Moton's teachers may have used some of their personal funds to supplement whatever the school district provided for our classrooms, to buy many of the teaching aids we used in the class.

of the fact that our school was in the project. Indeed, Mrs. Henry was **so** dedicated to the kids, that for our kindergarten graduation, we wore satin caps and gowns in Moton's orange and white school colors, and marched to "Pomp and Circumstance." Having discovered through conversations with junior high schoolmates who'd attended other elementary schools that none of **them** graduated from kindergarten in caps and gowns, I asked my mother sometime during my early teen years, why **we** had caps and gown at Moton. She explained to me that Mrs. Henry knew that many of my classmates, simply because of the circumstances of their birth, may well not finish high school and that she, (Mrs. Henry), wanted the kids to be able to remember that they **did** wear a cap and gown, at least **once** in their lives.

Moton was, of course, all black, all the kids, all the teachers, the cafeteria workers, the custodians, the principal, Mrs. Henry, and the two secretaries, my mother and Mrs. Height. I **loved** Moton. I was fascinated by everything I was learning in geography, in history, and of course, in science. In retrospect, in view of my later experiences with colorism in junior high and racism in senior high school, I understand how very fortunate I was to have to have experienced all of **elementary** school, to have lived the first ten years of my life—without experiencing either. Nobody asked to feel my hair. I didn't get asked how chitterlings are cooked. The tan that I returned to school with after a summer vacation of playing outside all day didn't surprise anybody. I didn't come back to school to, "You're so brown! I didn't know **you** could tan!" In all of my classrooms, and in my Brownie and Girl Scout troops, I was just another kid in the class and in the troop. I was, and was able to **be** just a kid.

We worked hard in class every day, and had lots of homework every night. I got a **terrific** education at Moton.

Me at Four
in Annie Oakley Outfit

Me in Third Grade Play
as Cinderella's Fairy Godmother

One of the best things to have ever happened in what was my entire life at that point, occurred the summer after I finished fourth grade. My parents, in their late thirties by then, learned that they were going to have a mid-life surprise—and it was indeed a surprise. Of course, "expecting" was the only word I heard when the adults discussed it. "Your mother's 'expecting' again!" I was almost nine when seven months later, my little sister, Lorna, came into the world. Mama and Mrs. Henry were such good friends, irrespective of their roles at work, that she, my mother, asked Mrs. Henry to be Lorna's godmother, to which she very happily agreed. Our family of five, was now a family of six.

Mama, Daddy & the Four of Us

Mama now had a second little girl to adore . . . . and adore her she did. Shortly after Lorna was born, my mother once said to me, "Well, Laurie, after you've left home and gone away to college, I'll still have my little Lorna with me." Even though we were nearly nine years apart in age, I was **elated** to have a baby sister and I loved her **dearly**. "Mama and Her Shadow" were now "The Three Musketeers".

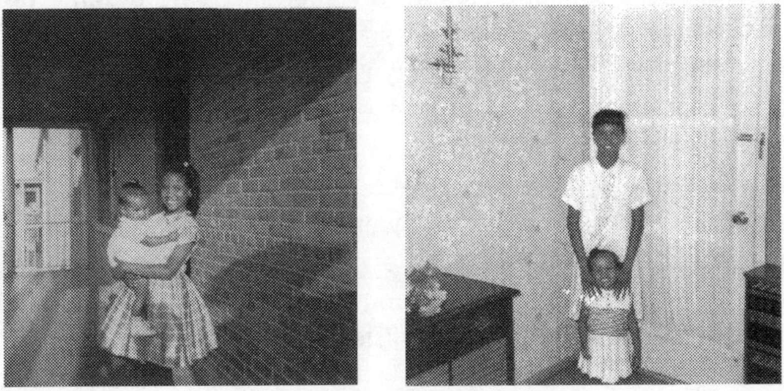

Lorna and I in 1963 and 1964

I played a lot and learned well during my seven years at Moton. One of my most valuable experiences there, however, was that of having fully enforced, my mother's lesson that all human beings are equal. I saw and learned **through my own lived experience**, that the children that I went to school with at Moton, the kids who lived in the project, those kids whose lives were so different from mine, were **just like** me. I saw that they were no different from me and from my friends in Pontchartrain Park. I saw that it didn't' matter if you were poor. You were **still** a human being with the same feelings and the same dreams as other people. I saw it every day in my school friends who wanted to grow up to be nurses and teachers, police officers and fire fighters. I saw that while they had far fewer **material** comforts than we did, many of the apartments in which my friends from school lived were just as clean and just as neat as was my home and that of many of my friends who lived in the Park.

The harsh reality for Moton's kids, however, was that **simply because of an accident of their birth**, i.e., because of the economic circumstances into which they just **happened** to have been born, the likelihood that they would be able to pursue their dreams, was much smaller than it was for the kids who lived in the Park, racism notwithstanding.[46] That being so, I'm **sure** that **some** of Moton's kids **did** go on to complete high school and college and that **some** may even have graduated from graduate, medical and law school. I'm confident of that because there were some **really** smart kids at Moton—really smart. I had very good grades, but one of my classmates, Gwendolyn Hamilton, in addition to having grades that were equivalent to mine in every **other** subject, **also** did well in arithmetic, my academic nemesis. That advantage made Gwendolyn, overall, a better student than me. Because of that, at the end of fifth grade, Gwendolyn got the gold Citizenship Award for Girls and I got the silver . . . . and Gwendolyn was a kid from the project. Gwendolyn, along with my friend Glenda, brother and sister Gentry and Kimberly Stevens, my friend Joseph Rose and **so** many others, were only a few of **many really** smart kids that lived in the Desire. They needed opportunity. Those kids just needed a chance.[47]

---

46 Even as a child, I was able to understand that the financial disadvantage that my school friends faced because of an "**economic** accident of their birth", was as happenstance and in my mind, as **unfair**, as was the discrimination that we **all** faced, (**regardless** of our economic differences), because of a "**racial** accident of birth".

47 I recently heard it said on a radio show that many European Americans do not see African American children as children, that they do not attribute to them the innocence of childhood. Rather, they see black **children** as just small black **people**, with the same mental and emotional attributes that in their stereotypes, they attribute to black adults. Even as we learned about the utter unfairness of society, I and all my friends, (both in Pontchartrain Park and the Desire Project), had every bit as much of childhood's wonderful innocence and naivety as all other children. The knowledge that many people do not see black children as children, is therefore **heart-rending** for me. I believe that European Americans who adopt African American children, as well as those who have bi-racial

My mother never told me to not talk about our home and our neighborhood with my friends at school, but I knew, **intuitively**, that I shouldn't. I knew not to talk about my room with its white French provincial furniture and canopy top bed. I knew not to mention all my stuffed animals that **lived** on my bed, or going to see Disney movies with my mother. I knew not to mention that one of my favorite things was to watch old Fred Astaire and Ginger Rogers movies at home with my mother. [Mama **loved** watching them dance. "Just look at that. They're **so** graceful", she'd always say.] I knew not to talk about my marionette puppet show and all the other toys I made a bee line from my bed to the Christmas tree to see, that were waiting for me every Christmas morning. I knew not to mention the fact that every year, the night before Easter, Mama and I dyed and tattooed all of the Easter eggs for our Easter baskets, or to talk about the big pink, green and yellow basket full of candy I woke up to every Easter Sunday. I knew not to mention the two sets of encyclopedias, Colliers and World Book, and the accompanying set of children's books in the living room, that I enjoyed reading. At school, I didn't talk about our complete 1959 six record set of The Golden Record Library's recordings, "A Musical Heritage for Young America", which included "The Treasury of Great Classic Fairy Tales" that I listened to incessantly, and my **absolute** favorite, "The Instruments of the Orchestra". I didn't talk about my family's traditions of seafood, potato salad and green peas almost every Friday night, donuts and chocolate milk every Saturday morning, and a big breakfast of grits, eggs, bacon, biscuits and pineapple juice every Sunday

---

biological children who are African American in appearance, are fully aware of the innocence of **all** children. The oneness of humanity, and specifically racial unity, is one of the most fundamental tenets of the Baha'i faith. Members of the faith inter-racially marry perhaps more than any other group. For that reason, Bahai's are conceivably more conscious of the universal innocence of all children than the majority of human beings. I describe the Baha'i faith and my experience with it along my spiritual journey, in "My Spiritual Memoir", the first section of *Religion: Different Paths—Same Journey,* to be published next in the *We Are One: Book One* series.

morning. I knew that my friends at school, in all likelihood, neither did, nor **had** many of those things, and **instinctively**, I knew not to mention that I did. I didn't want to make my friends feel badly.

I feel incredibly fortunate that I learned so early in life, that not only are there no superior and inferior people based upon **race**, there are **also** none based upon **class**. Living in Pontchartrain Park and attending school in the Desire Project taught me that lesson in a very **deep** and profound way, early in my life. It taught me both respect and compassion for those who are financially less fortunate than I.

Segregation ended with President Johnson's signing of the Civil Rights Act on July 2, 1964, one month after I graduated from Moton. My grandparents were in their 60's, my parents, their early 40's. Lemar Jr. was 20, Lambert, 16, I was ten and Lorna hadn't quite turned two.[48] We watched the news report of the signing of the Act on the nightly news. I remember that night as if it were **last** night. I had seen adults share a profound collective **grief** when President Kennedy was assassinated. I had seen them share what as a child I experienced as very real collective **fear** during the Cuban Missile Crisis, but I had **never** seen them share a collective **elation**. That is **exactly** what happened the day the Civil Rights Act of 1964 was passed.

Following the news that night, the phone in my house rang "off the hook." Gramzie, Uncle Ikee, my aunts Verlie and Johnnie, the neighbors and my other parents' friends, were **all** calling. I wanted to know what was going on, why all of the adults were so happy. I asked my mother what the law said and why the grown-ups were so excited. "Well Laurie", she said to me, "You know the twenty-eight flavors of ice cream you've been wanting to try at Howard Johnson's?" "Yeah" I said in great anticipation of what might be coming. "Well", my mother continued, "This new law says that we can go there now. We can go to the Howard Johnson's ice cream parlor now." "And we can eat the twenty-eight flavors

[48] The Act prohibited segregation in all public accommodations.

of ice cream?" I asked with even more anticipation. "Well", she said smiling, "We'll take them one at a time, but yes, we can go to Howard Johnson's, **sit at the counter** and have ice cream now." I responded with one word, "Wow." My mother continued, "And now we can go to Pontchartrain Beach, and ride that big roller coaster you see all the time." She went on to explain that the law said that we could get a hamburger at Royal Castle if we wanted to, and eat at Morrison's Cafeteria if we wanted to, that my Girl Scout troop could go to City Park and ride the kids' train around the park. I'll never forget thinking in that moment, "This one law is doing all of that?! That's a powerful law". It was an evening I'll never forget.

Within days, I also saw that at Schwegmann's supermarket, Mama and I no longer had to drink from the "colored" fountain. We could now drink from the tall, cold, silver, metal fountain, the one on the side of the column on which the soon-to-be-gone letters, "W-H-I-T-E" were painted, from which icy cold water was dispensed. Within those same few days I also learned that my mother and I could now use the "Ladies Room", and that the third or "Colored" lavatory of the familiar three restroom lineup, "Men", "Women" and "Colored", would soon be gone. The adults in my life could now go to a French Quarter club to listen to jazz. African American families could now go to the Gentilly Maison Blanche restaurant for dinner. It seemed to my ten year old consciousness that the entire **world** was changing.

But the process of integrating what had since the end of slavery, been a **completely** racially segregated society, was hard. It was painful and for me as a child, often frightening. From birth until the end of my tenth year, which was also the end of elementary school for me, my sole experience of racism had not been personal. It had been comprised solely of my exposure to segregation, a phenomenon which, while very much a **part** of my world, was also, in a very real sense, **outside** of it, outside, that is, of the immediate world of my family, neighbors, teachers and friends, the world which mattered most to me.

Ironically, the **end** of segregation occasioned my first **personal** experience with racism. I had graduated from Moton and entered seventh grade at Rivers Frederick Junior High School and for the first time, had to ride city busses to school. It was September, 1964, just two months after President Johnson signed the Civil Rights Act into law. Among the many public accommodations that, upon passage of the bill, were required to be integrated immediately, were city busses. Prior to the passage of the law, African Americans were required to sit in the back of the bus behind a tin sign that attached to the top of the seat located adjacent to the back door of the bus. It read, "These Seats Are Reserved For Our Colored Patrons Only." After riding **all their lives** on the front of the bus with us seated in the smaller back section, (and often standing back there even when seats were available in the front), it must have been visually quite shocking to white New Orleanians, to see us suddenly and for the very first time, sitting in the **front** of the bus, **especially** in those instances when it required **them** to stand.

I was one of about thirty kids from Pontchartrain Park who rode three city busses every day to and from Rivers Frederick Junior High School, which I attended for seventh and eighth grades, the Congress to the Broad to the Elysian Fields bus. The morning commute was fine because our neighbor, Mr. Sanders, gave me and his own two kids, Terri and Kenneth, a ride to the Elysian Fields bus stop, resulting in our having to ride only the Elysian Fields bus, which wasn't a problem. In the afternoon, the Congress bus, the last of the three on our trip, was also fine. But that afternoon cross town ride on the Broad Street bus was **horrendous**. When the 3:15 bell rang, ending the school day, the thirty or so of us walked to the Elysian Fields bus stop. As we did, all I could do was think with sheer dread, about what was soon coming—the **unmerciful** harassment and abuse we received on the Broad bus, every day, from the older and much larger white boys from Cor Jesu Senior High. After the Elysian Fields bus ride, we'd get on the Broad bus at the corner of Elysian Fields and Gentilly and because of the new law, sit anywhere there was a seat. The Cor Jesu boys got on at the next stop, and seeing us sitting in the front, would lean over and yell any number of hate-filled epithets and messages in our ears. The one I remember most clearly, was, "Lil nigga, you think you good as a white man now just 'cause you can sit on the front of the bus?! Is that what you think? Huh? You'll **never** be good as a white man no matter **what** the damn president says! You **still** nothin' but a monkey!" We sat there stoically, as twelve, thirteen and fourteen years olds, looking straight ahead, terrified on the inside but blank-faced and as still as posts on the outside. Some of the white boys while yelling in our ears, would also thump our boys on their heads with either their hands or their books. That would lead, inevitably**, every day**, to fights, right there on the bus, between the white and the black boys. When it started, the girls would run to the back of the bus. The consistent and inevitable result was that our junior high school boys, who were younger and therefore considerably smaller than the Cor Jesu senior high school boys, would exit the bus with bloody noses and black eyes, **everyday**. It was **terrifying** to both watch and to be so physically close to. The white bus driver, (there were **only** white bus drivers in those days), **never** intervened, not once.

I believe the white Cor Jesu boys thought that if they intimidated us enough, we'd just give up and go back to sitting in the back of the bus. But those white kids didn't know our parents. They didn't know us. The lenses through which they saw us were so clouded that they could not see who we were. The dignity that our parents had instilled in us wouldn't allow us to sit in the back. We sat our ground. I realized as an adult looking back on that time, that the act of sitting on the front of the bus **every day**, **knowing full well** what was coming, was my and my schoolmates' small bit of activism during the Civil Rights Movement. While I wasn't consciously aware of it at the time, I now think of it as my personal connection with Mrs. Rosa Parks.

By the end of the school year, some nine months later, the white boys had finally stopped harassing us. Most white passengers on city busses had gotten used to integrated seating by then. Only a few were still either jumping up and standing the second one of us sat next to them, or scooting all the way over to be sure nothing was touching. It was a **tremendous** relief when the daily harassment and abuse by the Cor Jesu boys finally ended. That horrible afternoon Broad Street bus ride made seventh grade **treacherous**. I was eleven.

Tragically, at the same time that I had on city busses, my first personal experience with **racism**, I also had my first personal experience with **colorism**, the discrimination that People of Color engage in against each other. Colorism is very clearly described by the old adage that I and I suspect millions of other African Americans of my generation learned in childhood, "If you're light, you're alright. If you're brown, stick around. If you're black, get back."[49] Historically, that message has created a human hierarchy **within** groups of color, (based upon and reflecting the same racial hierarchy of the entire human race), with light-skinned people at the top, medium brown-skinned people in the middle, and dark brown-skinned people at the bottom. Colorism has wreaked indescribable emotional and psychological pain and suffering **within** groups of color and within those **groups**, in families.

Frederick was in the Seventh Ward of New Orleans. The residents of the Seventh Ward at that time, and indeed until Hurricane Katrina hit, were not exclusively, but certainly **overwhelmingly** Creole—very light-skinned African Americans who often had green or blue eyes and very straight, sometimes light colored hair. The Seventh Ward was almost a kind of mini "color city" within the city. Frederick was in the **heart** of the Seventh Ward. During my two years there, I observed that some of the teachers, (not the

[49] As a child growing up in New Orleans, I knew many light-skinned, straight-haired African Americans, some of whom thought of and referred to themselves as, "Creole." The majority of Creoles married and taught their children to marry only **other** Creoles in order to "keep the light skin and straight hair in the family." Many thought of themselves as being superior to the city's other African American residents. Still others considered themselves to be a different race entirely - the Creole race.

majority, fortunately), all of whom were African American, were more comfortable with and therefore, were warmer toward the light-skinned Creole kids. As for the students, some of the dark brown-skinned and light brown-skinned kids disliked each other **automatically,** on the basis of skin color.[50]
I was, of course, **aware** of colorism before I started junior high school. It would have been **impossible** to have lived in New Orleans for eleven years without at least **knowing** about colorism, but prior to going to school every day in the Seventh Ward, it hadn't actually **affected** me. It was during my seventh and eighth grade years at Frederick that I saw colorism "up close" for the first time.

I was neither light nor dark-skinned. With skin that was medium brown, I was in the middle. Even my **hair** was in the middle. It was neither straight nor napped. [51] It was fuzzy, but it was long. The

---

50 I had thought for years that colorism was unique to New Orleans' African American community. I learned as an adult, however, that colorism **is** and has historically **been** present in African American communities across the United States. In conducting several months of training at Howard University in the mid-1990's, the first time I walked down the hall to the President's office, I noticed immediately, that the pictures of most of the past presidents that lined the wall leading to his office, were not only male, which was no surprise, but also unmistakably light-skinned. Colorism among African Americans is the subject of Spike Lee's 1988 film, "School Daze", set at an African American university. At the end of the film, one of the characters, utterly frustrated by the colorism that plagued the school, stood in the middle of one of the campus quads, both hands in the air, and yelled at the very top of his lungs to all within shouting distance, "Wake Up!"

51 The term, "nappy" in reference to African hair has become a pejorative, connoting "bad" hair. For that reason, I have used the term, "napped" to describe African hair. Our hair is not curly in the largely traditional understanding of that word. Rather, it is napped in

former was bad. The latter, good. I felt as if I was in a really weird kind of color/hair limbo.

The whole "color thing" was very painful to me because like **most** African American families, mine has members who are at both ends and also in the middle of the range of human skin color. Gramzie had thirteen grandchildren, four from Uncle Ikee, four from my mother, three from Aunt Verlie and two from Aunt Johnnie. Our skin colors run the gamut of the complexion spectrum, and Gramzie loved all of us, all thirteen of us, the same. With all of our complexion diversity, we **never** played the color card in my family. Never.[52]

But colorism ran deep in New Orleans. For decades, it was the strict practice of certain African American sororities and fraternities to admit as members, only those whose skin was of a "certain" hue. In some, membership was open to those whose skin was a bit darker, but only **if** they had "good", i.e., straight hair. For many years, a New Orleans social club for African American men informally excluded black men who were not light-skinned.

I was at Rivers Frederick from September 1964 until June 1966. I found the colorism that I experienced there particularly painful because of the reality of my mother and grandmother's lives.

---

the same sense that Berber rugs are napped. Thus, I use the term, "napped" as just a factual, neutral descriptor of African hair.

52 My Aunt Johnnie shared with me when I became an adult, that my mother bought her a beautiful red coat to take with her to college, but because she, (Aunt Johnnie, who was considerably darker in complexion than my mother), had heard over her entire life that dark brown skinned people were not supposed to wear certain colors, red among them, because they accentuated their "darkness", she was too embarrassed to wear it. My mother talked to her younger sister and told her that she did **not** want her to feel that way, that she should absolutely **not** be ashamed of her color and that the coat looked beautiful on her. Aunt Johnnie wore that red coat with pride throughout her college years. Colorism touched us all.

Gramzie had dark brown skin, African hair, African facial features and apparently, (judging strictly from appearance, which is absolutely **not** an indicator), none of the European American genes that millions of African Americans possess as the result of the rape of thousands upon thousands of African American women by their European American captors during the long legacy of American slavery. Gramzie didn't appear to be "mixed" with anything. She had the appearance of a beautiful African woman. Mama looked very different. Indeed, one might look at the two of them and not even believe that they **were** mother and daughter. Mama was very light-skinned and had European facial features and very straight black hair.

Gramzie had always told us that my mother looked like one of her great aunts, a very old picture of whom she had shown me since I was little. The woman in the picture, however, while very light-skinned with straight hair, didn't look anything like my mother. As a child though, I accepted without question, what Gramzie told me. I didn't know until I was eighteen, the real reason why there was no resemblance between my mother and the woman in the picture.

In February of 1924, Gramzie was a very young woman who worked as a maid cleaning rooms in the New Orleans Jung Hotel. Although she was only eighteen, she was already married to Jim Gray. "Grandpa Jim" had the same complexion, hair texture and type of facial features as Gramzie.

One of Gramzie's work days in early February of 1924, began, I'm sure, like any other. She had no way of knowing that **after** that day, her life would be changed forever. At some point during what was otherwise probably quite a routine work day, one of the white patrons "had his way with her", and nine months later, my mother was the result. That is literally all the detail I know. It was the kind of thing that adults just didn't talk about.

My father was the one who told me the story. It happened during a conversation one night during which he was quite sloshed. In response to a question I had just asked about Grandpa Jim, my father looked at me and said, "Laurie, now . . . . you know your Grandpa

Jim isn't your real grandpa, right?" "Huh? Grandpa Jim not my real grandpa?" I replied in utter surprise. "Think about it, Laurie. How could a woman like your Gramzie and a man like your Grandpa Jim get together and make a baby that looks like your Mama? What happened is that your Gramzie was a young girl working at the Jung Hotel and one day, one of the white patrons had his way with her, and that's how your Mama came to be." To say that I was shocked in that moment would be a **total** understatement. I was at a complete loss for words. After several seconds, I managed to ask two questions—whether Gramzie told Grandpa Jim what happened before Mama was born, and if so, how he reacted. In response, my father told me that he didn't know whether Gramzie had told Grandpa Jim what happened before my mother was born, but went on to say that whether or not she told him at the time, my mother's appearance at birth **must've** made it obvious to him that he wasn't her biological father. The last thing he said about the matter was that Grandpa Jim loved my mother **dearly** nonetheless, and raised her as his own. He explained that Grandpa Jim trusted Gramzie **completely**, and understood that what had happened to her, happened to **a lot** of young African American women at that time, especially those who worked in hotels and private homes.

My father didn't decide to tell me that story because he thought that at eighteen, I was old enough to know. The conversation happened quite accidentally. If it hadn't happened during one of our "enhanced" talks, (that happened only after he'd been drinking), I may never have known the truth about my mother's conception. That was the only conversation my father and I ever had about the matter. I don't even know whether he remembered, the next day, that it happened. I never once asked Gramzie about it.

Gramzie

Mama

Grandpa Jim

Although at the time I didn't know the actual story of my mother's conception, I understood even as a child, (I was about ten), why she cried so much when she and I watched at home in the living room, the original 1934 version of the movie, "Imitation of Life". The film centered on the relationship of an African American mother and daughter. In the plot, the very light-skinned daughter passed for white and in so doing, totally denied her dark brown-skinned mother. Even though Mama never did and never **would** have done such a thing to Gramzie, I knew **exactly** why the movie's plot moved her so deeply. I knew that on some fundamental level, the characters reminded her of she and Gramzie. Sitting there in the living room with her, I just put my arms around her, patted her back, and tried, in my child-like way, to comfort her.

In addition to Mama and Gramzie, my parents were **also** dark and light-skinned. My father had dark brown skin and African hair. Unlike many African American New Orleaneans who shared her physical appearance, my mother didn't marry a man who looked like her in order to have children who had light skin and straight hair.

My Parents' Wedding Pictures[53]

[53] The little girl in the front on the left is my mother's younger sister, my Aunt Verlie. She was four. Aunt Johnnie was two - too young to be in the wedding.

Witnessing and deeply feeling, as I did, the **immense** love between Gramzie and Mama, and loving them both as **much** as I did, (my love for them was as deep and as intense as their love for me), **combined** with the fact that my father was dark brown-skinned, I found the colorism at Frederick **immensely** disturbing. Just as with racism, I had the insight, even at that young age, to clearly see both the **insanity** and the **inhumanity** of colorism. I knew that as African Americans, we were doing to each **other**, the very same thing that European Americans had historically done and were **continuing** to do, to all of us.

After spending seventh and eighth grades at Frederick, in early September of 1966, just days after my thirteenth birthday, I began my freshman year of senior high school at The Academy of the Holy Angels, "AHA", or "Holy Angels" as we usually called it. One morning early in my freshman year, I rode the Louisa to the Galvez bus and walked the four or five blocks down St. Claude Avenue from the Galvez bus stop to school. On that walk, I had to pass in front of Nicholls Public High School, which had been all white before integration, and which may still have been at that time, or at least predominantly so. That was one of **the** most harrowing walks of my young life. As I walked in front of the school, a group of twenty or thirty students, while yelling, "Niggah!", and "Niggah girl", broke soda bottles on the sidewalk and threw the glass fragments at my legs. I had **never** been as frightened in my entire life, but **did** not and knew that I **could** not show it. With my heart thumping in my chest at what felt like ten times its normal rate, I just kept walking and showed no fear. I somehow escaped that nightmare essentially unharmed, with just a few small bloody nicks to my calves. Luckily, I had tissues with me and before arriving at school, was able to clean up the little bits of blood that were streaming down my legs. Later that evening when I told my mother what appened to me, she was appalled, frightened and **very** worried. She told me to **never** walk in front of that school again and instead, to start taking the St. Claude Avenue bus the few blocks from Galvez Street to school. I did.

There were roughly five-hundred-fifty girls at Holy Angels. When I arrived, all were white except for one senior, four or five sophomores and roughly ten of us freshmen who were African-American. At the beginning of the school year, all freshmen were assigned, by lottery, to a senior who was to be her "Big Sister" for the first two weeks of school. The "Big Sister, Little Sister" program was AHA's freshman orientation with a bit of very light "hazing" thrown in. The hazing was simply having to take orders from your big sister—to bring her lunch to her, or carry her books to her next class, for example. Suffice it to say that **my** big sister, who was **not** the one African-American in the senior class, was far less than happy to have wound up paired with me. Her very first order was for me to come to school the next day with my hair in braids all over my head, with a big ribbon at the end of each, every one in a different color. I refused. I was thirteen and quite little and she was seventeen or eighteen and quite large, but the dignity that my mother had instilled in me, even at that tender age, made such an instruction utterly unthinkable for me. I never told Mama about that "assignment" because I knew how deeply it would hurt her. I also have absolutely no doubt that she would not have allowed me to comply with it. That was the **only** order my big sister ever managed to give me because I literally hid from her for the remainder of the two weeks of freshman orientation. In comparing notes with the nine or so other black kids in my class, I discovered that they had somewhat normal experiences with their big sisters. Mine was the worst. It was horrible.

My four years at Holy Angels were, to say the least, not the best. Among the nuns, a few of the older ones, two or three at most, while not in any way hostile, seemed noticeably **uncomfortable** with black students. **All** of the other sisters, however, were fine, and several were really very nice. Two in particular, Sister Mary Dominic Savio, my tenth grade biology teacher, and Sister Mary Rose Elizabeth, my senior homeroom and English teacher, were actually **very** sweet to me. As for the students, the ratio was just the reverse. A few were sincerely nice. I remember their names and can see their faces to this day. One in particular, my friend Janis who sat behind me in Sister Mary Margaret's freshman homeroom class because her last name came just after mine alphabetically, was

very kind. **Many** more of the students, however, while not externally antagonistic, were visibly unwelcoming and distant. I was only thirteen when I began high school at Holy Angels, but I understood the racism I was experiencing there every day.

One specific explanation of racism that my mother gave me when I was very young, was that White People who treat us badly were simply behaving consistently with the way they had been taught their entire lives to behave, and that one day, they would realize that they were wrong, and then would change. Those words were front-and-center in my mind as I experienced the coldness of some of my white schoolmates every day. I was aware of the stereotypes of African Americans that my European-American classmates probably held and knew that for many of them, we were in all likelihood, the very first African-Americans they had ever experienced in any significant way. That understanding, however, while useful to me on an **intellectual** level, didn't make the daily **emotional** experience of being in what felt like a generally frosty atmosphere, one bit more comfortable.

Suffice it to say, I didn't become involved in any extra-curricular activities at Holy Angels. The one activity I **did** try, was outside of school. It was Junior Achievement, a national program with a focus on entrepreneurship and preparing young people for the business world. Its goal was to teach kids the skills necessary to become financially literate and empowered.

I had absolutely no interest in either business or entrepreneurship, **none**; but, the Junior Achievement representative who pitched the program to the AHA student body was so charismatic, and his presentation so exciting, that I decided to try it. In the program, students were organized into units which were called "companies". Each company had approximately eight-to-ten or so kids. The companies made a product of some kind, developed a marketing strategy for it and then sold it. The more a company sold, the more valuable was its stock. I was **so** excited about starting with my company. I looked forward to brainstorming what product we'd make, to the imagination required in designing and figuring out how to make it, and to the ingenuity of developing a sales approach and marketing strategy for it. It all seemed as if it would be so much **creative** fun.

The very first thing I noticed at my company's initial meeting, was that I was the only African-American kid **in** the company. I tried my best to offer my suggestions. I wanted to be a good team member, and I **knew** I had great ideas. I quit two months later. None, **not one** of the other kids in my company would talk to me. I got the silent treatment the entire two months. I remember that there **were** two kids who **wanted** to be nice to me—a girl and a boy. I could tell because they'd smile kindly at me when no one else was looking. I understood, though, that they were under tremendous unspoken peer pressure to **not** acknowledge me and I felt badly for them. At the end of those two months, I was hurt and extremely disappointed that I was not going to have the Junior Achievement experience.

The abuse and harassment that my Rivers Frederick classmates and I experienced from the Cor Jesu boys on the city bus, the verbal and physical abuse I experienced from the Nicholls High students, albeit on only one morning, the alienation that I felt **throughout** my four years of high school, the experience of being ignored in my Junior Achievement company, and my many other experiences with racism that I've chosen to not even write about here, made my junior and senior high school years, the six years between 1964 and 1970, the first six years after integration, **very** difficult, as they were for **many** African American children of that era, not only in New Orleans, but across the South, and indeed the country.

The story of Ruby Bridges is perhaps the best known account of an African American student's life during that time. It describes Ms. Bridges' experience as a first grader at New Orleans' historically all white William Frantz Elementary School. The parents of many of Frantz's European American students withdrew their children from the school because **one** African American student, Ruby, had enrolled. For the rest of that entire academic year, Ruby was the **only** child who was taught by her courageous first grade teacher, Mrs. Barbara Henry. This was happening while I was in school at Moton just a couple of miles away.[54] Ms. Bridges tells her story in her book, *Through My Eyes.*

Ruby Bridges' Book, *Through My Eyes*
http://www.barnesandnoble.com/s/through-my-eyes-ruby-bridges?store=allproducts&keyword=through+my+eyes+ruby+bridges

The Narrated Story of Ruby Bridges (for children)
http://www.youtube.com/watch?v=dYM-72AftEo

It wasn't only the integration of the **schools** that was tough, however. Integration didn't come easily to New Orleans in **any** context. For some time after the passage of the Civil Rights Act, there were small outbreaks of violence across the city. One of the results of that violence I remember most vividly was that rather than **integrate** its three largest pools at Pontchartrain Beach, Audubon Park and City Park, the city **closed** them in order to prevent the likely violence that would have occurred in the water.

Our parents also experienced the discomfort of the early days of integration. I remember seeing the utterly icy and often downright hostile looks on the majority of the white patrons' faces the first time we went into any formerly "White Only" establishment. Our parents saw them as well. As adults, they experienced the discomfort of going into formally "White Only" restaurants, restrooms, and clothing store fitting rooms, of sitting in the formally "White Only" section of the train station, bus station and airport, and being in a myriad of other early integration situations. I heard adult conversations, for example, about being refused service in restaurants, sitting there sometimes for more than an hour, being totally ignored.

---

[54] My Aunt Johnnie lived walking distance from Frantz School until Hurricane Katrina destroyed her home, Two of her grandchildren, my second cousins, Dominic and Darius, attended Frantz before Hurricane Katrina destroyed her home of forty years.

That very thing happened to my father one night in what had always been a "White Only" steakhouse on Chef Menteur Highway that he'd passed every day for years on his way to and from work. He decided to eat at the restaurant one night, just because now, after integration, he could. After the waiter ignored my father for close to a half hour, he left, but only long enough to go outside, use a pay phone and call a few of his buddies. Fifteen minutes later, when there were **ten** black men sitting in that little steakhouse, the wait staff "jumped to it", bringing my father and his friends their steaks and drinks without missing a beat. That was only **one** example, (probably among many others, of which I remain unaware to this day), of our parents' courage and quiet grace during that difficult time.

It was just six weeks shy of my 11th birthday when segregation ended. I cannot imagine living as an **adult**, in its debilitating indignity. My parents, however, did just that. They were in their early forties when it ended. My grandparents, in their sixties, lived in it for the majority of their entire lives. I **so** wish I could give back to my parents and grandparents, all of those years of their lives to live in dignity and freedom. Tragically, I cannot. No one can. For them, justice delayed truly **was** justice denied.

Still, it felt to me that we, the kids who were integrating the schools, were on our own "front lines" during the early days of integration because we dealt with the often extreme reaction from so many of our European American peers **every day**. Most of our parents by contrast, because they worked primarily in environments that were either all or predominantly African American, didn't spend a lot of time around White People during the week. They also drove cars and thus, didn't ride city busses as we did. Our grandparents were retired by then. Since, however, our parents lived with the indignities of segregation well into adulthood, and our grandparents **almost their entire lives**, they had paid their dues and **then** some, dues they never owed; dues which over the course of my parents' lives, deprived each of them on at least one occasion, of well-earned promotions on their jobs.

> [Shortly after the passage of the Civil Rights Act, my mother left the public school system and took a job with the Veterans Administration, becoming the agency's first African American secretary in the city. She ultimately left that job because a young European American woman half her age who had been promoted over her and to whom she began reporting, spoke to her in a manner that was both mean and patronizing, a situation which was intolerable. Thankfully, after my mother left the Federal government, she took a job which she truly loved, with the New Orleans Urban League.]

Those "dues" made it only fair for my parents and their peers to have been spared what turned out to be the utterly **insane** daily indignities of ending segregation that we, their children endured every day,

That said, I am **very** well aware that **many** of the city's African American adults **indeed** experienced those indignities every day both on their jobs and while riding city busses. They were the African American adults who likely worked in jobs as maids, porters and bell hops in city hotels and janitors in downtown office buildings. They were the adults who worked, **every day** in the presence of European Americans, many of whom may have been very angry about the passage of the Civil Rights Act and who, through their personal demeanor, may have, on a daily basis, taken **out** that anger on them.

The racial discrimination and harassment that during my early life I both **personally** experienced and witnessed **all** African Americans experience, imprinted upon me **a keen, finely-tuned, razor sharp** awareness of what as human beings, we are capable of doing to each other when we are unaware that we are one human family. The experience of **acquiring** that awareness was bitter, with a sharp, painful, cutting edge; one that **no** child deserves. That said, I wouldn't exchange my experiences for the world, for I'd be a **very** different person today without the understanding and wisdom that they afforded me.

Most significant, I believe that my experiences gave me both an intellectual awareness and an emotional sensitivity that left me with a **dogged** determination to do something **profoundly** important to bring understanding and compassion to the world, to help humanity evolve and mature. Also, in addition to being moved by my personal **experiences**, I was a child during the heyday of the Civil Rights Movement and was **very** deeply inspired by it.

Predictably, then, another side of me, (which was quite different from little Lauren the junior scientist), began developing in my early teens—the young activist with an intense passion for fairness and social justice.

I was also personally inspired by my Aunt Johnnie who was a student at Southern University in Baton Rouge, Louisiana, an historically black university, in the early 60's. Johnnie marched in student demonstrations at the downtown Baton Rouge Woolworth's Department Store which Southern's students organized in response to the store's segregated lunch counter. The Sothern University students named their movement, "5,000 Strong". My aunt told us that they marched **every** day, and that nearly **all** of the university's students participated in it. Johnnie told us that because when they left campus, she and her fellow students never knew whether they were going to survive another day, they began their daily marches by walking from the campus to a local church to pray. She said that she and her fellow students fully understood the danger of their activities, but that they were totally willing to die for their convictions, After prayer, the students continued by walking from the church all the way to the downtown Woolworth's. Upon arrival, carrying signs, and either silently or while singing freedom songs, they walked around the store for hours. On one of her visits home during that time, my Aunt Johnnie told us that she and her fellow students had been tear gassed during a recent demonstration, and that they regularly faced big angry, frothy, barking police dogs, and water streams from city fire hoses that could knock a horse over. Her experiences seemed to perfectly mirror all of the images of civil rights sit-ins and demonstrations that were being televised nearly every night on the national news.

Mama and Gramzie were at the same time, both **extremely** proud of Johnnie, and **dreadfully** frightened for her safety—but I remember their **fear** far more than their pride.

> [My aunt Johnnie reported feeling that her life and the lives of all of her fellow student demonstrators were potentially at risk every day they demonstrated. Fortunately, however, she had only one brush with actual physical danger. It was an experience during which she and other students ran and jumped over a fence to escape police dogs. In the end, Woolworth's did indeed integrate its lunch counters.]

But it was Dr. King's speeches that were exceptionally moving for me. I was old enough and **aware** enough, for both Dr. King's **words** and the **remarkably** compelling, poetic eloquence with which he **delivered** them, to often quite literally move me to tears. I **knew** that Dr. King was engaged in a just movement because I and all those I knew and loved were living the **injustice** that the movement was designed to address. His speeches about the power of love and non-violence went straight to my heart, **deeply** touching me. His "Drum Major Instinct" sermon is my favorite, by far, of **all** of his sermons and speeches.

Dr. Martin Luther King Jr.'s Sermon—"The Drum Major Instinct"
https://www.youtube.com/watch?v=BcuifZJdyaY

I was fourteen on April 4, 1968, the day Dr. King was assassinated. My mother, Lorna and I were in the car and almost home at the end of the day when the radio announcer read the statement. Reverend Martin Luther King, Jr. had been shot and killed in Memphis. In that instant, my mother cried out in sheer anguish, "Oh my God, Dr. King is dead!"

When we got home, what followed was yet another evening during which our phone rang incessantly with family members and many of my parents' friends calling well into the night. This time though, it wasn't elation that they were sharing. It was disbelief and **painful, intense sorrow**. I hadn't seen the adults in my life so terribly shaken and anguished since the day, nearly five years before, when President Kennedy was assassinated. On the night of Dr. King's death, **my** heart and that of every person I knew, was **heavy** with grief. It was one month before the end of my sophomore year of high school, and was, up to that point, the saddest day of my entire fourteen years.

On the day of Dr. King's funeral, I sat on the floor, inches from our den television, with my little portable reel-to-reel tape recorder, taping as much of the service as I had blank tape to accommodate. I knew that I was witnessing history and I wanted to save it. I still have that little reel-to-reel, as well as the tapes on which I recorded the ceremony. The tape recorder, unfortunately, hasn't worked in decades.

Exactly two months and two days later, on June 6,1968, Bobby Kennedy, whom I admired profoundly, was assassinated. It felt to me that Bobby Kennedy exuded true compassion for the poor from every fiber of his being. My fourteen year old heart was once again devastated.[55]

I became a young activist the following summer, the summer of 1969. Mama was at that time, the Administrative Assistant to Mr. Clarence Barney, the Executive Director of the New Orleans Urban League. As such, she assisted in the coordination of the League's summer voter registration drives, the objective of which, of course, was to get African-Americans registered to vote. The program's "boots on the ground' were high school students under the direction of an Urban League staff member. That summer, it was Mrs. Oretha Haley. The students were essentially volunteers, receiving only a very small stipend for bus fair and lunch. From the moment my mother told me about the program, I wanted in. It was the summer before my senior year at Holy Angels. I was fifteen.

55 It was for that reason that I was **extremely** disappointed when I learned as an adult years later, that as Attorney General, Bobby Kennedy, even though he may have done so reluctantly, ordered the FBI to wiretap Dr. King's telephones.

The Urban League's voter registration drive that summer, was my very first experience doing grass roots "activist" work, and I enjoyed it **immensely**. I **knew** how important it was to vote. My parents were always interested in both what was going on politically and in current events. The three local newspapers, the Times Picayune, (the morning paper), the States Item, (the evening paper), and the Louisiana Weekly, (the local African American paper), were all delivered to the house. I saw my parents both vote, **without fail,** in **every** election, national, state and local, and I knew that they took both voting and their Democratic politics very seriously. Additionally, although it hadn't been a part of any history class curriculum in school, I had read on my own that African-American men had gained the right to vote in 1870 with the passage of the fifteenth amendment, but that women, **no** women, including **white** women, were allowed vote until 1920, a full **fifty years** after black men received the right. I learned that women's vote came about **only** in response to the suffrage movement, without which, women may not have gained the right to vote for another several decades. I remember Dr. King speaking about how African-Americans' constitutional right to vote was being trampled on in many places in the South through the use of bogus and totally illegal poll taxes, literacy tests and Ku Klux Klan intimidation tactics.

When I began working on the Urban League's voter registration drive that summer of 1969, **all** of that history, as well my knowledge of what civil rights voter registration activists had gone through only a few years earlier, came vividly alive for me. I thought about the fact that James Chaney, Andrew Goodman and Michael Schwerner, all three in their early twenties, had actually been **killed** by the Klan for doing **exactly** what we were doing that summer—helping African Americans register to vote. I found **completely** gratifying, the process of knocking on doors, talking to people about the importance of registering to vote, and on the spot, arranging a ride for them to the registration location, knowing that another volunteer was waiting for them there, ready to walk them through the process, at the end of which there would be another African-American who was registered to vote.[56]

The experience of working on the New Orleans Urban League's voter registration drive as a high school student that summer, was the beginning of what became my lifelong attempt to make the world a fairer, more just place that reflected what I **deeply** believed was a higher, Divinely-inspired human consciousness. I desperately wanted two things. First, I wanted fairness. I wanted justice for people who had been discriminated against for so long. I wanted us to be genuinely **regarded** and in every way **treated**, as the full human beings that we are with all of the accompanying dignity and equality thereby required. I wanted **all** people to understand on a deep level, that we are **all** equal. Secondly, I wanted European-Americans to experience their lives from a place of far greater emotional maturity. I wanted them to at least **glimpse** the unimaginable possibilities that existed for their lives, how they would behave and far more importantly, **how they would feel in their hearts**, were they capable of truly experiencing African Americans and all other People of Color as their sisters and brothers in the family of humanity. Essentially, I wanted for all

56 As a teenager in 1969, I could have never **imagined** that in 2013, nearly fifty years after the passage of the Voting Rights Act, African and now also Latin Americans, would again face horrible and quite obvious attempts to both suppress our vote and intimidate us into not voting. I could not have imagined that our nation's highest court would have gutted the strongest section of the 1965 Voting Rights Act. It is almost **unbelievable** to me that our nation is **once again** fighting that tired, old, weary battle. It is a common saying within the community of civil rights activists, that every generation has to win its freedom anew. It seems to be just accepted. That apparent acceptance of having to fight similar battles all over again in every generation makes me extremely uncomfortable, and yet, I know that it is indeed the reality. With each successive battle, however, I tell myself, "Just as a pendulum swings back and forth several times before the swinging stops and it finally settles into a strong, stable mid-point, this too, **in time**, shall end."

of humanity, both the intellectual **and** the emotional freedom that I knew was possible for us if we truly understood and deeply felt that we are all equal. I knew that I wanted to do **something** significant in my life to make that emotional freedom our reality.

So there I was in the summer of 1969, the summer before my senior year of high school, a happy, very seriously committed little fifteen year old voter registration volunteer. Wednesday, July 2nd of that summer, was my parents' 26th wedding anniversary. The next day, Thursday, July 3rd, my entire world was turned upside down, inside out and knocked completely out of its orbit when suddenly and completely unexpectedly, Mama died after a routine and very minor female surgery. She was forty-four and in the prime of her enormously vibrant and active life. On Sunday morning, June 29th, my mother was, as always, at church, in front, singing lead soprano in the choir. One week later, on Sunday, July 6th, she was in front of Bethany again, but this time, in a casket.

Two weeks later, Lambert, who was twenty-one and in the Air Force, was shipped off to Clark Air Force Base in Manila, Philippines. Several **months** later, Lemar Jr., who was twenty-five and in the Army, was shipped off to a Vietnamese jungle. It was three weeks before Lorna's seventh birthday and six weeks before my sixteenth. Lorna was going into second grade at Coghill Elementary. I was headed into my last year at Holy Angels and suddenly and without warning, Mama was gone from all of our lives.

My parents had known each other their entire lives. They grew up together on the same block of the 7th ward, on La Harpe Street as next door neighbors, attended Valena C. Jones Elementary and McDonough 35 High School together and married as teenagers. In the blink of an eye, their relationship of over forty years and their marriage of over twenty five years had ended, and my father was a forty-five year old widower.

There are no words to describe the anguish I experienced when my mother died. Mama was the center of my entire universe and neither my love for her nor my pain at her death, can ever be expressed in words. As I headed into my senior year of high school, I was a depressed, devastated, emotional wreck.

Because Lemar Jr. and Lambert left so soon after my mother died and were then so far away from home for so long, I wasn't able to really witness their immediate grief. And Lorna? She was **so** young. For a week or so after Mama died, she'd ask every time the doorbell rang, "Is that Mama?" Her question **devastated** my father. He **had** explained to her that Mama had died. She was far too young, however, to really understand the concept of death. Shortly thereafter, she just stopped asking.

My mother's siblings, Uncle Ikee and my aunts Verlie and Johnnie were **crushed**. Uncle Ikee deeply loved his younger sister, Selina, and Aunt Verlie and Aunt Johnnie loved and admired their big sister, "Nina" to no end. Uncle Ikee spent the entire night Mama died walking around his back yard until the sun came up the following morning. Sometime in the late1990's, more than twenty-five years after my mother died, I interviewed my Aunt Verlie about our family history, recording more than two hours of conversation with her. Talking about Mama, Verlie said, "Nina was my sister, and I love her and I still miss her."

My Mother on Uncle Ikee's Patio at a Family Gathering

But it was **Gramzie** for whom, by far, my heart ached most. Her grief seemed to be an infinite, bottomless pit of **profound** anguish. She had lost her eldest daughter, her beloved Selina. It absolutely **tortured** me that Gramzie was hurting so severely and that there was absolutely **nothing** I could do to help her. I **did** step into my mother's shoes after she was gone, and took care of all of her needs—cashed her sixty-five dollar Social Security check, paid her seven dollar monthly rent, did her grocery shopping and picked up her medications from the pharmacy. Doing all those things for Gramzie, however, did absolutely nothing for my feeling of absolute helplessness, because I couldn't take away her indescribable pain. My hurt over Mama's loss was **compounded** by the pain that I saw Gramzie experience.

My cap and gown pictures arrived in the mail from the photography studio on Saturday afternoon, just two days after my mother's death. Upon opening them, I cried inconsolably, saying over and over again, "Mama would have been so proud of me. She would have been so proud."

The following week, my father sat me down on the living room couch one night to talk to me about his plan. He would go to work, of course, do the food shopping, (or "make groceries" as we say in New Orleans), cook—which he did **very** well, and do the laundry. I'd go to school, naturally, keep the house clean and take care of Lorna. With our hearts ailing with severe pain, the two of us followed Daddy's plan and it worked. We went on, as we had to, and on a practical level, did ok.[57]

---

[57] It never occurred to me that going from a two to a one income family may have had a dramatic impact on our standard of living. The reality, however, is that it did not. My father, on his U.S. Letter Carrier annual salary of $18,000, was able to pay our $75.00 monthly mortgage, all of our other household expenses, my senior year tuition at Holy Angels, and later, my college tuition and books. He was even able to buy me a little used Toyota Corolla during my senior year of college.

My mother's death sent shock waves through the entire Pontchartrain Park community. She was without question, from the beginning, one of its pillars, and was truly beloved by the **entire** community. The notice of her death published the next month in the Pontchartrain Park Patriot read in part:

> August, 1969
>
> Residents of Pontchartrain Park were saddened last month in the announcement of the sudden death of Mrs. Selina Joichin. Mrs. Joichin was a tireless community worker. She had served on numerous boards in both civic organizations and Bethany Church. She leaves to mourn . . . . a host of relatives and friends and the entire community of Pontchartrain Park.

Mama was adored as well by our minister, Reverend Kennedy, and our entire Bethany church family. Upon her death, the members of Bethany's Bi-Racial Dialogue Group, of which she was a member, wrote the following letter to Reverend Kennedy:

> July 21, 1969
>
> The Rev. Edward A. Kennedy Jr.:
>
> When we first came together as a Bi-Racial Dialogue Group almost a year ago, none of us knew just what to expect. We shared a common hope, however, that through an open and honest sharing of ideas and feelings, we would each gain a better understanding of ourselves and a deeper appreciation of one another as persons. We believed then, as we do now, that this kind of understanding is desperately needed in the face of the racial distrust and tension which burdens our land.
>
> One member of our group who contributed immeasurably to its success was Mrs. Lemar L. Joichin. Selina brought so many things—she brought a warm and cheerful

> personality; she brought ideas and insights which grew out of her work with the Urban League; she brought a religious conviction which few experience in concern for other people as individuals and for her community. In all of these ways she enriched the lives of those of us who were privileged to know her.
>
> In token of our gratitude for that privilege, we desire to have some small share in the future of Bethany Methodist Church which meant so much to her. It is our understanding that the music room in the new (church) building will be dedicated to Mrs. Joichin. If possible, we hope that the enclosed check can be applied to the purchase of some item for that room. We hope that this gift will in some small way express our appreciation for what Selina meant to us.

After her death, Bethany's choir room was indeed dedicated to my mother's memory. A bronze plaque with an engraved dedication was placed above its entrance. Beside the door, a picture of her with her choir robe folded over her left arm was hung.[58]

The week after Mama died, we received a letter, addressed to "Joichin Family":

> We thought that you would like to know the persons who have made contributions to Bethany United Methodist Church as of this date, in memory of your wife and mother, Mrs. Selina G. Joichin.
>
> [List of all the contributors' names and the amount of their contributions.]

---

[58] Many years later, Uncle Ikee told me that it was he who hung Mama's picture beside the entrance of Bethany's choir room. Uncle Ikee was not a member of Bethany, or of any church, but he knew how very much Bethany meant to my mother, and was proud of the plaque that hung over the choir room door in her memory.

Clarence W. Acox,
Financial Secretary

On July 3, 1994, the **twenty-fifth** anniversary of my mother's death, I was in New Orleans visiting family. I hadn't planned to be there on that specific date; it just happened that it was a convenient time for me to make the trip. July 3rd, that year, was a Sunday. I attended church at Bethany that morning. To my utter surprise, the printed program for the service had a full page dedication to my mother which included two pictures of her, the dates of her birth and death, and the following words:

> Remembering Mrs. Selina G. Joichin on the anniversary of her death. Selina Joichin was a devoted member of Bethany. She became a member of Bethany during its infancy. During her time at Bethany, Selina served as a member of the Sanctuary Choir. Selina had a beautiful voice and used it to praise God.
>
> While serving as Chairperson of the Pastor-Parish Relations Committee in 1966, she was among the persons who were instrumental in having our then pastor, Rev. Edward A. Kennedy, Jr. continue in service at Bethany.
>
> Mrs. Joichin was an Executive Secretary of the Urban League. She used her skills to serve as secretary to . . . . serve Bethany without remuneration until the time of her passing.
>
> The choir room was named the Selina Joichin Choir Room, in her memory. Many persons, members and friends gave donations to the church in her memory to help defray the cost of furnishing the choir room.
>
> There is a photograph of Mrs. Joichin on the wall outside the choir room. We who knew Selina Joichin thank God for having her pass this way on her Christian journey. We shall always remember her with love.

Unfortunately, Hurricane Katrina damaged Bethany severely, destroying my mother's dedication plaque and photo that had hung for years outside the choir room. The church was rebuilt, but without those two things which meant so much to me.

My Mother (Center) with the Choir of Laharpe Street Methodist Church[57]

My Mother with Her Choir Robe Outside of Bethany.

My mother was also **genuinely** loved on her job at the New Orleans Urban League. At the behest of the League's Acting Executive Director at the time of her death, Mr. Larry Cager, the 1970 Convention of the National Urban League in Washington, D.C., was dedicated to her memory.

Program of the 1969 National Urban League Conference Dedicated to My Mother

The 1969-'70 Annual Report of the **New Orleans** Urban League was dedicated to her memory as well. Her dedication on the report's inside front cover read:

THE 1970 ANNUAL REPORT IS DEDICATED TO MRS. SELINA G. JOICHIN. PRIOR TO HER UNTIMELY DEATH LAST YEAR, SHE EXEMPLIFIED THE BEST IN URBAN LEAGUE COMMITMENT AND COMPETENCY DURING HER THREE YEARS OF SERVICE AS ADMINISTRATIVE ASSISTANT. HER HOPE FOR THE TRUE AMERICA, CONCERN FOR THE DISADVANTAGED, DEDICATION TO EXCELLENCE, AND PRIDE IN BLACKNESS EMBODIED THE ESSENCE OF URBAN LEAGUE PURPOSE AND HER MEMORY CONTINUES TO INSPIRE US ALL.

THE NEW ORLEANS URBAN LEAGUE

Selina

Brightly, life engulfed her heart
and danced her to the joy of living,
hoping, dreaming,
laughing, giving . . .

Deeply, suffering grieved her soul
and stirred her to a sense of doing,
prodding, working,
pushing, moving . . .

Gently, dusk enshrined her eyes
and cloaked her in its sable grace,
Black and lovely - -
God's gift to every race.

Eugene P. McManus, S.S.J.

1969-1970 New Orleans Urban League Annual Report Dedicated to My Mother

Within days of Mama's death, the New Orleans Urban League forwarded the following letter to the house:

To: The Family of the Late Selina Joichin
c/o Urban League of Greater New Orleans
1821 Orleans Avenue
New Orleans, Louisiana 70116

Dear Friends:

The shocking news of the loss of your beloved Selina reached our office this morning.

All of the Members of the Administrative and Clerical Council of the National Urban League are deeply grieved over her death.

We remember her as the vivacious, efficient Administrative Assistant of the New Orleans Urban League who did so much last year to make our stay during the (national) conference memorable.

We share your sorrow and mourn your loss.

Sincerely,
Theresa M. Moss
Theresa M. Moss, President
Administrative & Clerical Council
National Urban League

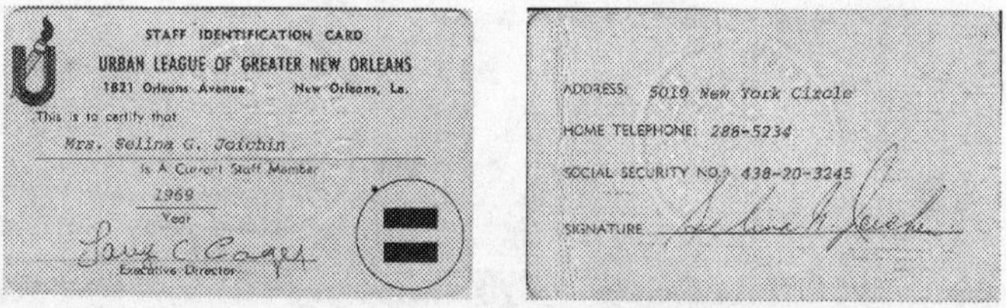

My Mother's Urban League Membership Card

Anyone who knew my mother, knew that she was not only highly **respected** for her activism, she was also sincerely **loved** for her sincerity, warmth and deep compassion for others. Mr. John Pecoul, New Orleans Urban League Housing Director, was one of **many** who were well aware of that. Mr. Pecoul wrote on the inside cover of a sympathy card which he sent to my father:

> Dear Mr. Joichin:
>
> We were shocked and saddened to hear about Selina. Being with her was like being in the sunshine. We extend our deepest sympathies to you.

Ms. Gloria Bartley, one of the young women with whom my mother worked at the Urban League, had feelings of such endearment toward Mama, that on Mother's Day of 1969, Gloria sent her the biggest, most beautiful bouquet of flowers I had ever seen. I imagine that Gloria may have experienced my mother as a mother figure to herself. Two weeks after my mother's funeral, Gloria called me at home saying that she wanted to take me to dinner. Over the meal, she shared her profound grief with me. She told me that the week after Mama died, she went to see Mama's doctor and said the following to him, "Doctor, this was supposed to be a routine, very minor surgery. Now Mrs. Joichin is gone. How could this have happened?" Gloria said that the doctor responded, "It's just one of those things that happens sometimes that we don't understand." I was deeply moved that Gloria had done that. A few years later, after she married and had a son, Gloria gave birth to a baby girl. She named her Selina.

My mother was very deeply committed to the goals of the Urban League—improving the lives of African Americans through economic equality and opportunity. She died only five years after the passage of the Civil Rights Act and thus, had only five years of freedom. I'd give both my arms to have been able to change that for her.

At sixteen, I was a high school senior and a teenage mother with a seven year old. Despite my youth and my depression, Mama's example of a powerfully loving mother left me strong enough to be aware of how crucial it was for Lorna to have a happy childhood. I was **painfully** aware that I couldn't bring my mother back to her, but I wanted her, in every **other** way, to have everything I had as a child.

For all of Lorna's birthdays, including her seventh birthday three weeks after Mama died, I gave her the exact same kind of big birthday party that my mother had given both of us, every year.

I bought her costume and took her trick-or-treating every Halloween.

I made sure that she woke up to a big Easter basket every Easter morning.

Just as my mother had watched the kids TV specials of my time with me, I watched the ones of Lorna's time with her—Rogers and Hammerstein's 1965 production of Cinderella and Fred Wolf and Harry Nilsson's absolutely wonderful 1971 animation, "The Point" are the ones I remember.

Just as my mother had also watched the kids' **holiday** TV shows of my time with me, I also watched the kids' **holiday** shows of **Lorna's** time with **her**—The 1964 animated TV Christmas special, "Rudolph the Red-nosed Reindeer"; the 1965 "Charlie Brown Christmas Special", the 1966 "Grinch that Stole Christmas", and the 1969 "Frosty the Snowman" animated TV Christmas special.

Every Christmas, I played Christmas Carols in the house and put up a Christmas tree for Lorna. My father gave me the money for her toys, and just as my mother had done for us, I went from store to store, getting every single item on her Santa list, and then brought them all to Gramzie's where I very carefully hid them until Christmas Eve. Then, on Christmas Eve night, I set out Santa's cookies and milk on the dining room table with her, gave her a bath, told her that Santa would be coming later in the night, and then tucked her into bed. She always went to bed **very** excited. Then, after she was soundly asleep, I'd drive up to Gramzie's, pick up her toys, go home and lay them all out under the tree, looking forward to seeing her utter delight the next morning.

I taught Lorna all the things about proper decorum that my mother, in her most gentle loving way, had taught me, among them, to speak in "correct" English, to not be "loud and common" in public, to be polite and say, "yes please" and "no thank you", to chew with her mouth closed, to cover her mouth when she yawned, to not sit on public toilets and to let her lips touch only the water when drinking from public water fountains.

But **far** more importantly, I attempted to give Lorna the same emotional template in her formative years that I had received in mine—the same simultaneous warmth **and** strength of character that my mother had so exquisitely modeled for me. I also wanted to give her a spiritual base for her life, so I took her to church with me for as long as I attended.[59] I remember telling her once before my seventeenth birthday, to always remember that God loved her much, much more than **any** human being did. I tried to teach Lorna all the lessons that my mother had taught me about respecting **all** people, regardless of their class, their race, their complexion, their religion, their disability, or any other characteristic that we human beings use to divide ourselves. I tried to teach her the compassion that I learned from nearly sixteen years of watching Mama and Gramzie in the world.

I loved Lorna **tremendously**, and because tragically, she doesn't remember my mother and knew only me as her **surrogate** mother, she also loved **me**—very much. For that reason, Lorna and I bonded in a way that I believe resulted in our being closer than most sisters. I was her caregiver—her mother and she was my little girl. Today, Lorna remembers well, attending the ballet lessons in which my mother enrolled her,[60] and all of the **material** vestiges of Mama's love for her, her backyard gym set, sand box,

---

59 I stopped attending Bethany when I was eighteen and a sophomore in college. The reasons and my spiritual journey thereafter are described in "My Spiritual Memoir" of Fact Five of *We Are One*—"Religion: *Different Faiths Same Journey*".

60 Seeing all of those beautiful, little tiny African American girls in their tutus, ballet shoes, braids and curls every time Mama and I took Lorna to dance class touched me, even as a teenager.

merry-go-round, see saw and picnic table, as well as her little girl's room with her white, French provincial furniture, canopy bed, kitchen set, mini table and chairs, blackboard, and Show N' Tell video/record player. But it hurts me **deeply** that she remembers **only** those physical remnants of my mother's love for her, and has only bits and pieces, mere flashes, really, of minor memories of Mama as a person. She was just too young.

My senior year at Holy Angels was the worst year of my life. I was **severely** grieving my mother's death and therefore in a **deep** depression. During that year, a few of my African American classmates and I exchanged books written by black authors, *The Autobiography of Malcolm X*, Claude Brown's, *Manchild in the Promised Land*, James Baldwin's *The Fire Next Time* and Ralph Ellison's *The Invisible Man* among them. Even in the midst of my personal profound depression during which, overall, I felt emotionally numb, I was able to feel distress in being introduced for the first time, (especially in Malcolm X's autobiography), to a world about which I knew next to nothing, the world of northern black urban poverty. The descriptions of the abject economic deprivation, drug dealing, prostitution and violent crime that typified it shocked me. I remember my reaction well—"Why do our people have to suffer so much, even in a place like **Massachusetts**, (where Malcolm lived.) As much as we've suffered down here . . . . I thought the North was better." I felt outrage. Although that was some forty-three years ago, I remember it clearly.

I graduated in May of 1970, ten months after my Mama died. The ceremony was held in the French Quarter's St. Louis Basilica in Jackson Square. At the end of the graduation, as I marched with my classmates down the center aisle of the cathedral to the front door, my eyes overflowing with tears, searched the ceiling from left to right for a glimpse of my mother's smiling face.

I entered Louisiana State University in New Orleans, LSUNO, in the fall of 1970. I was still **severely** grieving Mama's death and therefore **still** in a deep depression during my freshman year. I did nothing but attend class and go home.

It was in my sophomore year that I found what was for me, a figurative lifesaver—the LSUNO NAACP College Chapter.

Finding the College Chapter at the beginning of my second year was **the** thing that helped me finally begin to emerge from my depression. After two years of having a **very** heavy heart and doing nothing but going to school and returning home, I was both making friends and working with them on issues that were especially meaningful to me. We were a small group of a little more than ten, Claude, Bobby, John, Margie, Hannah, Gilda, Simonette, David, Henry, Larry, Anthony and I, but we were an **active** little College Chapter. On Friday evenings, we met at a different member's home, planned our civil rights activities and then played Jeopardy. We met **every** Friday night. I had found my undergraduate home.

Our faculty advisor was Dr. Joseph Logsdon, a professor in the History Department. Originally from Boston, Dr. Logsdon was European American, probably in his mid-forties at that time, married with two pre-teenage daughters, and just a down-to-Earth, salt-of-the-Earth, trustworthy, compassionate, sincere, decent, and **good** human being.

Our NAACP College Chapter met with LSUNO's Chancellor, Dr. Homer Hitt, about the university's small number of faculty and staff of color; we held demonstrations at the foot of Canal Street on the site of a statue which commemorated white supremacy; we sponsored "Easter Kiddie Day" every year during which we brought kids from the city's public housing projects to campus for an Easter Egg Hunt;[61] we organized "Thanksgiving in the Ghetto"

[61] New Orleans, at the time, had a **lot** of projects - the Desire Project, the Florida Avenue Project, (which had historically been "All White" and was walking distance from both the Desire Project and William Frantz Elementary School, attended by Ruby Bridges), the St. Bernard Project, the Lafitte Project, the Iberville Project, (which was

programs, in which we collected and delivered a Thanksgiving dinner to residents of the city's projects; we raised funds for our various programs through can shakes during which we'd stand in front of various grocery stores throughout the city with a can labeled, "NAACP" in our hands, shaking them, and saying over and over again to store patrons as they entered and exited, "Give to the NAACP. Give to the NAACP". We always did pretty well with our can shakes. We were just teenage college students, but we **worked** our little NAACP College Chapter.

Of **all** the activities in which we engaged, **most** memorable for me was our picketing of perhaps a half dozen or so Canal Street stores during the summer of 1972. The targeted stores, as policy, or a matter of practice, hired either no or very few African-Americans. Those that did, subjected them to biased disciplinary practices and fired them unjustly. I don't know whether the New Orleans NAACP Branch, (the adult division of the NAACP), asked us to do the picketing, but as a **College Chapter**, upon receiving permission from the NAACP national office in New York, **we took it on**. For close to eight weeks, **every afternoon**, in that burning hot New Orleans summer sun and sweltering humidity, we'd meet at an appointed time in front of a particular store, form a circle, hold hands and open with a prayer. We'd then split up to go to our respective stores, in front of which we'd walk in silence, in a circle, for a couple of hours carrying our heavy signs, with inscriptions such as, "Discriminatory Hiring and Firing Practices. The NAACP Asks You to Please Boycott This Merchant." Afterwards, we'd all meet where we started, put our signs down, and once again in a circle holding hands, sing a few freedom songs, end with a closing prayer, then go home. Some people crossed the picket lines, but many more did not.

I **loved** those old freedom songs. They moved me. They did so both in the same way, yet also differently from the way the Methodist hymns with which I'd grown up, moved me. Both

---

also historically "All White), the Fisher Homes Project, the Calliope Project, the St. Thomas Project and the Melphomene Project.

touched my internal chord of being in love with goodness, with justice, with charity and with compassion. My favorites included:

Aint Gonna Let Nobody Turn Me 'Roun

Aint gonna let nobody turn me 'roun, turn me 'roun, turn me roun,
Aint gonna let nobody turn me 'roun,
We're gonna keep on a walkin', keep on a talkin'
March'n up to freedom land.

http://www.gospelsonglyrics.org/songs/aint_gonna_let_nobody_turn_me_around.html

We Shall Not Be Moved

We shall not, we shall not be moved.
We shall not, we shall not be moved,
Just like a tree that's planted by the water,
We shall not be moved.

http://www.youtube.com/watch?v=4WXSI6PcjkE

Oh Freedom

Ooooh freedom, Ooooh freedom
Oh freedom over me, over me
And before I be a slave, I'll be buried in my grave
And go home to my Lord and be free.

http://www.youtube.com/watch?v=yHmUPql6w9g

At times, we'd sing the anthem of the Civil Rights Movement itself.

We Shall Overcome:

We shall overcome, we shall overcome,

We shall overcome someday.
Ooooh deep in my heart, I do believe
We shall overcome someday.

http://www.youtube.com/watch?v=qRWR6lZ3pF8
http://www.youtube.com/watch?v=130J-FdZDtY
http://www.youtube.com/watch?v=bKDVNSpsBZE

We marched in front of those stores, in those circles, in the hot New Orleans sun, until their management agreed to meet and talk. Members of the city's adult NAACP Branch attended those meetings and were successful in reaching a fair compromise on every issue with every store. Before long, the number of black cashiers and sales people in the stores was noticeable.

Our LSUNO College Chapter received the National NAACP award for being the most active Chapter in the country at least once, and I believe twice, during the three years during which I was active in it. We deserved it.

Lorna graduated from Coghill Elementary and I graduated from college with a bachelor's degree in Philosophy, in 1974. That fall, Lorna moved to Washington, D.C. to live with Lemar Jr. and his family and I started a Master's Degree Program in Philosophy at UCONN, The University of Connecticut.

> [Although that was 1974, and I never lived in my childhood home again, it still hurts that today, in the aftermath of Hurricane Katrina, Pontchartrain Park looks as if an atomic bomb had been dropped on it. In pictures taken shortly after the storm, only the very tops of roves could be seen. My home, 5019 New York Circle, is now gone. Only an address marker remains on the lot. Uncle Ikee's home that was just a couple of blocks away, was also destroyed by Katrina.]

http://photos.nola.com/tpphotos/2011/11/175pontchartrain_2.html
Pontchartrain Park in the Aftermath of Hurricane Katrina

As a result of my childhood experiences with racism, (both segregation and personal harassment), followed by my civil rights activism at LSUNO, when I left home for graduate school, I was determined to do **whatever** I was able, to help young African Americans reach their greatest human potential. That determination lead me as a graduate student, to found and charter the UCONN Black Graduate Student Organization, (BGSO), the purpose of which was to provide a forum within which black **graduate** students could academically tutor, counsel and support black **undergraduate** students. Mine was only a one year Master's program, after which I left UCONN so I don't know whether the BGSO continued after my graduation from the university, but I do hope that it did and that if so, the life of at least **one** African American student, undergraduate **or** graduate, was positively influenced through it; that at least **one** student was encouraged; that through the organization, at least **one** student was profoundly inspired. I hope that the Black Graduate Student Organization made **some** difference. I shall never know.

I enjoyed my year of grad school at The University of Connecticut and graduated from UCONN with my Master's Degree in Philosophy in May, 1975.

Lorna and I at my Master's Degree Graduation
May 1975

Following my year at UCONN, I was fortunate to be hired as Assistant Dean of Admissions at Wesleyan University in

Middletown, Connecticut. I started at Wesleyan on August 1, 1975, two weeks before my twenty second birthday. It wasn't until after I had been at Wesleyan for a few months that I began to understand the affluence of the world I had entered. New England old wealth, from which many of Wesleyan's students came, was unlike anything that I had experienced in my life to that point. In the midst of that influence, I was fully aware of the irony that as a twenty-two year old Assistant Dean of Admissions at one of the country's most prestigious universities, just eleven years earlier, I could by law neither drink from the same water fountains nor use the same restrooms as European American children.

During my first year at Wesleyan, I along with two colleagues, Donna Ireland, an Admissions Officer at Trinity College and Ron Ancrum, an Admissions Officer at Connecticut College, were invited to an ABAFAOILSSS, (pronounced "Abafoils") Association of Black Admissions and Financial Aid Officers of the Ivy League and Seven Sisters Schools meeting at Harvard. Ron, Donna and I were highly impressed by the meeting and as a result, requested admission to the organization. Our three universities, while among the nation's most highly prestigious and competitive liberal arts institutions of higher education, in the country, were not, however, part of the Ivy League and its Seven Sister Schools. We were a tier below. As a result, our request to join was rejected, leaving the three of us wondering why we were invited to the meeting in the first place. But Donna, Ron and I were **determined** to provide the same benefits to the student applicants of color of **our** and similarly ranked universities, as ABAFAOILSS allowed its members to provide to **their** student applicants of color. Within months, we founded NECBAC, the New England Consortium of Black Admissions Counselors.

I was one of six admissions officers at Wesleyan. We each had two student populations for which we were responsible in the admissions process. Not surprisingly, one of mine was applicants of color. Over the course of my two years at Wesleyan, I recruited dozens of primarily African American and Latin American high school seniors in Westchester County, New York, Brooklyn,

Philadelphia, Atlanta, Miami, Chicago, New Orleans, San Juan, Puerto Rico and a host of other cities.

The student whom I recruited from the farthest location, was Kofi A. Kofi was a kid from Accra, Ghana, whose path I crossed while traveling in West Africa during the summer of 1976. We met by chance on his neighbor's patio during a ping pong game on a rainy July afternoon. Actually, I no longer believe that **anything** happens by chance. We are **all**, I believe, in the lives of every other one of us for a reason. I was obviously destined to be there on that patio, in that ping pong game, on that rainy July afternoon, at the exact time Kofi arrived.

Some of the Latin and African American students I recruited to Wesleyan were from privileged, upper class backgrounds, the children of attorneys and physicians. Some were from middle class families. Most, however, were from pretty tough circumstances, the projects of Brooklyn, the Bronx, Chicago, Atlanta and Miami. I feel privileged to have been fortunate enough to have played just a small part in the process of those kids' both getting into college and attending an institution of Wesleyan's caliber.

NECBAC celebrated its 35th anniversary last year, but under a new name, "The New England Consortium of Counselors of Color Bridging Access to College". Over the last thirty-five years, the organization has helped thousands of kids of color to attend college. I am humbly grateful for having played a small role in its inception.

When I began working at Wesleyan, I planned to work for two years and then return to graduate school. Eastern Philosophy, (Hinduism, and Buddhism, primarily) was my passion and I desperately wanted to pursue an academic career specializing in it. Thus, in the fall of 1977, two months after leaving Wesleyan, I entered a Ph.D. program in Comparative Religion at the University of Pennsylvania. I was anxious to begin serious preparation for my career in academia. For reasons explained in, *Fact Five: "Religion: Different Faiths Same Journey",* however, I spent only a year in the program, after which I decided to pursue a very different profession.

Following my year in my Ph.D. program, I worked as an Equal Opportunity Specialist in the Higher Education Division of The U.S. Department of Education's Office for Civil Rights (OCR).[62]

My job at OCR was, as a member of a team, to investigate complaints of discrimination and harassment filed by employees of colleges and universities, and subsequently write a Report of Findings in which the university was found either guilty or not guilty of having engaged in alleged discriminatory employment practices. The Report of Findings was then submitted to the agency's Regional Attorney's Office where, if the university **had** been found to have engaged in discrimination, a decision was made concerning the method to be used to bring the institution into compliance with Title VI of the Civil Rights Act of 1964. In such cases, complainants were awarded some combination of back pay, damages and reinstatement of their job. Not only was that work extremely **intellectually** exciting to me, it was also an **emotional** high. During my time at the Office for Civil Rights, I saw OCR help people who were innocent targets of discrimination, to receive fairness. I saw them receive justice. I had seen close up, the **tremendous** difference that attorneys were able to make in the lives of people who had been hurt by discrimination. I decided at the end of my time at OCR, to apply to law school.[63]

---

62 At the time, the Department of Education was a part of The Department of Health Education and Welfare, or "HEW", as it was commonly called.

63 My life during the years 1970 to 1981, my college, graduate school and early professional years, were, fortunately, largely race neutral. I experienced racism during those years only through the daily racial indignities that occurred in society-at-large. One such indignity that I experienced during that time, in the summer of 1980 that stands out in my memory, is that of being followed around a small, open-front New York City produce store. As I walked from one aisle to another,

Two years later, I entered Cornell Law School in Ithaca New York. The year was 1981. I was twenty-eight.

Cornell Law School was overwhelmingly white, with only eight to ten or so African American students in my class, a handful in the two classes above me, and an even smaller number of Latin, Asian and Indigenous students.

Entering Cornell law school in September of 1981 took me right back to my high school years more than a decade earlier. Just as was the case at Holy Angels, the majority of European American students at the law school, while not visibly **hostile**, were visibly **uncomfortable** with people who did not look like them. And, not unlike the majority of my white high school classmates, many exhibited the resulting chilly, aloof behavior toward us.

First year law students shared their locker with one other student. The classmate with whom I was assigned to share **my** locker, was European American. **For the entire year** that we shared our locker, my locker mate did not speak to me. The experience was always the same. If I happened to get to the locker first either at the beginning or end of the day or between classes, she stood behind me and waited until I left. If **she** reached the locker first, she'd hurriedly get her things and then scurry off. If I said "hi", she **would** respond, but with only a serious-faced, low, muted, "hi", That was the full extent of my locker mate's interaction with me the entire year. I was deeply saddened that my feelings of frustration and level of fatigue with the racist behavior that I was receiving

---

the store owner walked to and stood at the front of whichever aisle I was on. When I noticed the owner's behavior, I was so outraged, that I slammed down the package of raspberries that was in my hand, on the table in front of me and as I stormed out of the store, yelled at him, "I'm not a thief!." I was **particularly** infuriated because two European American customers who had come in after me, were shopping without being monitored in any way. As it turns out, I needed that "break" in preparation for the very challenging three-year experience that I was about to have.

felt so hauntingly familiar even after more than a decade had passed since I'd last felt them in that context. I just felt emotionally exhausted by the situation. My feeling was, "Enough! I've had enough! I'm just a human being, just like you! Why can't you see that?!"

The most serious consequence to my life that racism has ever had, was that of potentially getting kicked out of law school on a trumped-up honor code violation. My mistake was that of very honestly sharing, during a meeting of the Women's Law Caucus, (WLC), in my first semester, how I was experiencing the law school, or more precisely, how my European American classmates were responding to me as "other". Two months later, I found myself in a class taught by the WLC's Faculty Advisor who was present at the meeting. She both gave me an "F" in the class and alleged that I had intentionally plagiarized the paper that I wrote for it. Several weeks later, during my hearing before the law school's Honor Board, with the help of my student attorneys, my friends Gretchen and Ellen, not only was I able to prove that the allegation was false, I was **also** able to prove that at the time my professor **filed** the charge against me, she had to have **known** that it was false. The administration directed her to change my grade. She gave me a "C". Had I been found guilty of the charge, I would have been expelled from law school. I am not aware that the professor faced any consequence for her actions.

Late in my first semester at Cornell, in December of 1981, as was my practice, I called my father early on a Sunday morning to touch base with and check up on him. [64] There was no answer. I found it strange that he **didn't** answer the phone because Daddy was **always** at home on Sunday mornings, cooking his breakfast and

[64] Although Lorna returned home after two years in Washington, she was away at college by then, so my father was living alone at the time. He was also not working by then. After thirty-three years of service in the U.S. Post Office, and two years of service during World War II, he had retired several years earlier with thirty-five years of Federal service.

dinner before heading out for the golf course in the afternoon. It was his Sunday ritual which he carried out **every** Sunday. I called Lambert, who lived ten minutes away in New Orleans East, to ask if he'd heard from him. "Daddy's in the hospital but he didn't want me to tell you, Lem Jr. and Lorna. He didn't want to worry you", he said with a deep sadness. Four months later, in April of 1982, my father died, one month before the end of my first year of law school. Thirty years of smoking had taken their final toll on his lungs. He was fifty seven and I was twenty eight. My father knew me, so before he died, he **knew** that I was innocent of the honor code violation allegation. The hearing hadn't yet occurred at the time of his death. He died worrying about it.

It wasn't until after Daddy died that I got fully in touch with how much he loved us. He took good care of Lorna and I after Mama died. He cooked almost **every** day, and when he didn't, he'd give me a twenty dollar bill and the car keys and sent me to "the highway", (nearby Chef Menteur highway on which there were shopping centers and fast food restaurants), to get burgers, fries and malts for us. He washed and folded the laundry every week, leaving our clean, folded mound of clothes on the foot of my and Lorna's beds. He paid our high school tuitions and my college tuition. From his regular question to me, "Have you heard from your brothers?" during Lemar Jr.'s thirteen months in Vietnam, and Lambert's year in the Philippines, it was obvious to me that he was very much concerned about and loved them too.

In retrospect, I realize that during the first seven years after I left home, the years before my father died, I lived with the unconscious awareness that if, for **whatever** reason, I ever needed to return home, my bedroom at the end of the hall of 5019 New York Circle would be there. It was my security blanket. I never thought about it after I finished college and moved away, but Daddy's death suddenly made me hyper-aware of the level of safety and security I had felt in the world because on an unconscious level, I knew I **had** that security blanket—my father and my childhood home.[65] We still owned the house, but with Mama and Daddy **both** gone now, the house alone, **despite** my love for it as the repository of my childhood memories, wasn't enough to maintain my emotional safety blanket. With my father's death, it was gone.

My grief at losing my father, coupled with my feeling of being a true orphan at that point, quite abruptly made **whatever** racial insanity I was experiencing at school, (including my locker mate's inability to treat me like a human being), no more than a minor annoyance. I was both grieving Daddy's loss and crushed by my deep regret that he would never see me graduate from law school. Those two very personal hurts consumed **all** the space in my heart and wedged out, for a time, the cruel sting of racism at school.

The physical landscape of Ithaca itself was also of tremendous help after my father's death. I have **always** absolutely **loved** nature. Stunning landscapes and beautiful soft, ambient, meditation music are among the things in life that more than **all** others, provide me with an **unparalleled** inner peace. The two together, (with one exception that I describe in, "My Spiritual Memoir, A Lifelong Journey—A Pilgrim's Path", the first section of Book Five of *We Are* One, *Religion: Different Paths—Same Journey—The Fundamental Truth about Theology and Spirituality),* give me a feeling which is as close to heaven on Earth as I believe I can **ever** have.

I was extremely fortunate that the racism that I withstood at Cornell Law School was often abated by that very experience. Cornell, located in the Finger Lakes Region of Upstate New York, is in the middle of a kind of natural beauty that is no less than magnificent—the Spring season filled with young, light green

[65] I used my security blanket in March of 1979 when, while living in New York City, I very quickly made a plane reservation and went home for a week because of my fear of the partial nuclear meltdown that occurred at Pennsylvania's Three Mile Island nuclear facility.

leaves, and azaleas of utterly saturated pink, red, yellow, fuchsia, purple and white; radiant Fall colors of amber, orange, red and brown; winters of brilliantly white first snows; summers of deep blue skies filled with mesmerizing white, puffy, cirrus clouds, rolling green hills speckled with farms, red barns and old rusty wagons from at least the 1930's, and of course, stunning views of Lake Cayuga, over which the campus sits. But most of all, **Ithaca has waterfalls!** The then popular bumper sticker, "Ithaca is Gorges", is **literally** true. Ithaca's gorges were my life savers throughout law school. Within a few minutes ride from campus were three **stunning** falls, Taughannock, Buttermilk, and my unqualified favorite, Treman. **All three** were for me, a safe harbor. Being able to get into my car, no matter how cold it was, (indeed, the snow white winter landscape had its own unique beauty), play one of my Gregorian Chant cassette tapes,[66] and take a peaceful ride out to either the country or to one of the waterfalls, was my personal retreat. It was my way of regaining my center and then returning home in peace and serenity, no matter **what** degree of frustration I was feeling after the latest racial incident at school. Being in Ithaca softened, significantly, the emotional blow of my experiences at Cornell. I took more "nature rides" than usual upon my return to school after we buried my father.

Two years later, in 1984, just before graduation, I wrote an article that was published in the May 20th edition of the Dicta, the law school's student newspaper, describing my experiences and those of some of the other black law students at Cornell. In it, I described what it felt like to be racially objectified by the majority of our peers **throughout** our entire law school experience. I was thirty when I wrote it in May of 1984. The article follows below in its entirety:

I wish that for a day, for just one day, I could make half of America's white population experience American society as black Americans experience it. Twenty-four short hours would suffice.

---

[66] Ambient music, my absolute favorite musical genre, didn't yet exist, making Gregorian chant, at the time, my soft, relaxing music default.

What would they experience during those twenty-four hours? They would experience the American culture from a perspective which for most, would be shattering, shattering myths, stereotypes, pre-conceived ideas, lies. Within those brief twenty-four hours they would gain an awareness of the subtleties of racism of which they otherwise may have remained totally ignorant. They would experience being the fourth person in a supermarket checkout line, seeing all three people ahead of them receive a friendly, "hello", from the cashier and they not a word; they would experience white people's assumption that they are interested in only "black things", which manifests itself, for example, in white peoples' questions to them regarding what they think about Jesse Jackson's campaign or Martin King's birthday becoming a national holiday, or some other such "black concern". They would experience what it feels like to have white people tell them all about the black people whom they have known in the past. They would experience what it feels to be in a society in which the vast majority of its members harbor an entire set of often unconscious but nonetheless firmly entrenched beliefs and attitudes about them, all of which are based almost exclusively upon the color of their skin, i.e., that they are less intelligent than white people, that they lack the full range of human emotion, sensitivity and sensibilities which white people, by their very birthright, naturally possess—the ability to appreciate nature's beauty, to be touched by a poem, to look up at the stars with awe. In essence, they would experience what it is like to be thought of and responded to as inferior, to lose their individuality, to be responded to as "a black person", to lose their personhood, to be dehumanized. They would no doubt see quite clearly that many white people are totally and utterly unconscious of their preconceived notions about black people. They would see the specific ways in which many white people relate to black people differently from the way in which they relate to white people, and they would understand, no doubt with far more depth than "real" black Americans, that the ways in which white people relate to them is the result solely of their social conditioning. They would see clearly that most white people are not deliberately or maliciously racist, but they would truly and experientially understand that that lack of deliberateness and malice does not alleviate the pain of losing their individuality, their personhood, a big piece of their humanity. They would see clearly that it does not alleviate the pain of being objectified, the pain of dehumanization.

On still another level, in addition to experiencing the feelings of being a member of a group which is consciously and unconsciously thought of and treated as inferior by the majority of society, they would also experience the reality of being a member of a group which is a ***numerical*** *minority in this society—to walk into a movie theatre, restaurant, bookstore, classroom, one's work environment . . . and be one of only a handful of brown faces, and possible the only one . . . .*

I am convinced that it can be fairly safely assumed that most white people, after only half of that day, would probably be driven to cry out, "I am white! I am white! This is going to wear off in only twelve hours! I am white!" Most could simply not take being classified, being responded to by automatic impulse on the basis of the color of their skin, walking through city streets and just being in society in general with the knowledge that when white people look at them, they, (white people), see a black person first, their sex second, and not much else. With their exclamations, they would in essence be proclaiming and reclaiming their full personhood, their humanity. They would be shouting to the world that they really are a "regular person".

After those twenty-four hours had elapsed and the "black/white" people had returned to their ordinary state, I would like to sit in on a discussion in which the "black/white" people try to explain to the inexperienced half of the white persons present, what it was like to be black for a day. I would love to listen to them attempt to explain how differently they, the inexperienced half, responded to them, (when they responded to them at all), as black people, what it felt like to be denied the common courtesy of a "hello" from a supermarket cashier, to have white people talk to them about "black things", obviously with the assumption not only that they are interested in nothing else, but also that they probably do not know much about anything else. I'd like to listen to them try to explain what it felt like to walk into a movie theatre, bookstore, restaurant, classroom, one's work environment . . . and be one of a very few or the only black face present. I would like to hear them describe what it was like to experience the American media and advertising industries as a black person. I would **love** *to listen to that conversation.*

My thirty years of experience as a black American unequivocally inform me that the inexperienced white people would respond to their comments and perceptions with total skepticism and even disbelief. They would be utterly unable to hear, to really hear, to listen to the descriptions of the patronizing, rote manner in which the inexperienced white people related to the "black/ whites". Without actually having lived as a black person for a period of time, albeit a very short one, there is simply no way for the inexperienced whites to understand the experience of being black in America. Finally, they would for the very first time truly understand that most white people simply do not see the racism in their interactions with black people.

My three years at Cornell Law School have, not surprisingly, proven that the law school reflects the racism in society-at-large, the kind or racism described above. I wish that for just one day, I could make the entire white Cornell Law School student body truly understand what it is like to walk through Myron Taylor Hall as a black law student—to sit in those classrooms knowing that the majority of your white colleagues view you as . . . . less intelligent and less articulate than they, solely because of your race, that you are incapable of thinking very well in the logical, coherent, comprehensive manner which is required of attorneys. . . . They would learn much from experiencing what it feels like to have your intelligence, you ability to think critically and analytically, your articulateness, your ability to be an excellent attorney, discounted, ignored, indeed, not even seen.

Obviously, one cannot magically transform white people into black people. One cannot through mental telepathy make them suddenly aware of their unconscious racism. How then does one make them understand the invidiousness of unconscious racism? How can they be made aware of the all-pervasive extent and effects of that unconsciousness on those of whom they are unconscious? How can they be made aware that their unconscious racism also adversely affects their own lives? How does one expose myths for what they are? How does one open eyes? Minds? How does one force white people to grow, to identify, and subsequently eradicate their world view in which to be a white person is to be a person and to be a black person is to be a black person? How does one give them the simple ability to see and respond to people who are racially different from themselves as intelligent, sensitive human beings? How is that awesome feat accomplished? Do I go around the law school proclaiming that my favorite composers are Sibelius and Rachmaninoff, that I write poetry, that I keep a journal, that I love orange sunsets and rocky beaches? Do I go around explaining that I don't spend every waking moment of my day wallowing in my oppression, that I enjoy skating, exercising, and writing letters to friends? Do I yell out that my mother loved poetry and opera, that my father, a postman of thirty-five years was a science enthusiast and part-time mystic and Egyptologist?

I do not have the answers to those questions. Freeing minds and changing solidly established behavior patterns is extremely difficult work. That task requires generations. I am greatly encouraged, however, by the good, serious anti-racism work which so many black and white feminists have recently done and are presently doing. After six long years of working arduously in feminist organizations in Philadelphia and New York City with Indigenous American women, black women, Asian American women, WASP women and Jewish women on issues of racism, anti-Semitism, sexism, classism, homophobia, ageism and able-bodied people's discrimination against the physically challenged, the past three years at Cornell Law School have been excruciatingly painful for me. The following are but a few of the numerous racist incidents which have occurred during my three-year tenure at Cornell Law School: A Law Practice Dynamics lecturer very clearly implied that all black people are thieves and hustlers; a guest speaker judge addressing a group of students in the West lounge, referred to his Nigerian law clerk's countrymen and women as running around in the woods throwing spears, (for which he later apologized); a professor informed two black students whom he planned to call on the next day what their question was going to be; placement office personnel continually informed a black student about opportunities in a District Attorney's office despite her constant and adamant indications that she was not interested in prosecutorial work . . . .

. . . . Consciousness raising can indeed be done, but not without both a sincere desire and serious commitment on the part of white people to work on their racism. It requires reading, consciousness-raising groups, an awareness in the moment of one's reaction to a person of color, as well as the reasons which underlie them. It requires a vision, a vision of what their life could be like if they were emotionally free to respond to every single person as an individual and a desire to have that life to the extent that it is possible. It requires a vision of what the world should and can be.

I have a list of several very good sources of information (primarily books and pamphlets) on how to "unlearn" racism and will be more than happy to provide it to anyone who drops a note in my pendaflex.

Among the stories that I **didn't** share in the article, was a conversation that I had with one of my African American classmates at the beginning of our third year. During the conversation, she described her sheer shock and horror in response to an incident that she had experienced while working as a summer associate at a major New York City law firm. At one point during the summer, she attended a social function of some kind at which several of the firm's partners, associates and law student summer associates were present, along with a few New York City judges. Two of the judges, one of whom was African American and the other, European American, had an apparently well-known history with each other as what may be described as at least professional competitors and perhaps even rivals. At some point during the evening, my friend saw the European American judge, after he'd had, "a few too many", walk over to the African American judge and overheard him say to his rival, "You know, if slavery ever came back, I'd love to own you."

Upon hearing of my friend's experience, I shared her horror. **Then,** I felt immediate and absolute empathy for the African American judge. And **then,** I thought, "Nothing, not being an intelligent person, not being a good person, not a college degree, not an Ivy League legal education, **not even being a judge, nothing**, can insulate you from this insanity."

The day the article was published, I ran into my first year locker mate as she was entering and I was leaving the women's room at school. After neither speaking to nor even acknowledging me for three years, she looked at me and said with what sounded and appeared on her face to be utter shame and guilt, "I really like that article you wrote." I responded with a very cool, austere, "Thank you", then walked out. After sharing a locker with me **for an entire year**, after sitting in a number of classrooms with me **for three full years**, after **seeing** me five out of seven days a week over the **course** of those three years, I believe that as a result of reading my article, that young woman, (whose name I don't even remember because we never interacted), **finally** saw my humanity. Perhaps my stoicism in that moment gave her quite a lot to think about. I wish, however, that I had been **able**, in that moment, to have both felt more compassion **for**, and shown more compassion **to** to her. I wish I had possessed the maturity in that brief exchange, to have actually smiled at her and said warmly, "Thank you. I appreciate your saying that." It is what my mother would have done.[67]

---

[67] I remain both professional and personally respectful, but I can become "cool" toward people whom I feel have treated me or others insensitively. We are all works of personal growth in progress. In addition to being professional and respectful, continuing to be **warm**

Upon graduating from law school the following month, in May 1984, I moved to Washington and worked there for several years, in the public sector, as an attorney. I wanted to do whatever I could, to contribute to making the world and especially American society, more ethical, more just, more fair, and I wanted to use my law degree in that endeavor. After several years of legal practice, however, I grew restless. I wanted to write, to teach, to do public speaking, to facilitate adult learning about oppression/liberation issues. I was absolutely **driven** by a desire to open minds and soften hearts.

My Life Today

In 1990, six years after graduating from law school, I stopped practicing.[68] I was fortunate enough to be able to begin a career in the field of consulting and training, the decision which, to date, was **the** best of my professional life. I **love** being a trainer.

It was actually my passion for the issue of diversity that **afforded** me the opportunity to transition from the legal to the training field. I was a labor lawyer at the time, a staff attorney with NTEU, the National Treasury Employees Union. I don't know exactly how, but **somehow**, someone brought to the attention of management, that while there **was** a considerable amount of racial diversity among the union's **staff** attorneys, there was **none** among either its **Chief** Attorneys **or** its officers. Indeed, there was only one **woman** among the ranks of the union's officers. **All** of the other members of the union's top administration were European

to another when I have experienced them as being insensitive is an individual personal growth objective on which I continue to work.

68 In pursuing a legal career in Washington, my desire was to work on Capitol Hill as a Legislative Assistant to a member of either the House or the Senate. While that opportunity never materialized, I felt good about the work that I did at the Maryland Legal Aid Bureau, the Women's Equity Action League and the National Treasury Employees Union during those years.

American men. The conversation about NTEU's lack of racial diversity in its leadership team, led to diversity training for staff members. Whether the session was voluntary or mandatory, I do not remember. What was **significant**, is that it became the springboard which launched my career as a trainer.

The workshop was my first experience participating in facilitated dialogue about race, and interactive exercises, the objective of which was for all of us to leave with heightened awareness of the ways in which we can all be more culturally competent. It was the very first time that I had participated in a learning endeavor designed to raise awareness of issues of racial privilege and disadvantage, racial sensitivity and insensitivity, racial justice and injustice. **I was utterly enthralled**.

At the end of the two-day session, I immediately walked up to the trainer, Lucia E., and said to her with resolute determination, "Lucia, I want to do what you do.' Lucia looked at me, and with sheer astonishment, uttered, "But Lauren, you're a lawyer." "Yeah, and a very unhappy one, too", I responded without missing a beat." The conversation ended with an invitation to attend a party at Lucia's three weeks later, which would allow me to meet other trainers and thus, begin making connections with other professionals in the field.

As one who has **never** been very comfortable at informal social gatherings, when the day of Lucia's party arrived, I hesitated. Deciding, as I ultimately did, to **go** to the party, changed my life, for it was at that party that I met Dr. Bill E., a Director of a group of internal trainers of a Maryland-based consulting firm. Upon meeting Bill, we spoke for about twenty minutes. We talked about Lucia's gorgeous, ultra-modern home for the first two or three, then for the remainder of the time, discussed his work, about which I had **many** questions. After that part of the conversation, Bill and I had the following exchange:

Bill: So what do **you** do?

Lauren: I'm a lawyer but I don't like it,

Bill: Well . . . . What do you **want** to do?

Lauren: What **you** do.

Bill: (After a few seconds of obvious contemplation and while looking at me with a noticeable degree of surprise), I'm looking to hire someone.

Lauren: I'm looking to be hired.

From that moment, my days as a lawyer were numbered. Bill hired me, I joined his training team and began a new career.

Over the past twenty three years of my career as a trainer, I trained in a myriad of organizations from small non-profits to large corporations and at all levels of government. I've trained in venues from a small, Virginia furniture store, to the White House. My workshops have been in the areas, among others, of leadership, team building, communication, workplace etiquette, working with temperament differences, and conflict resolution. I've facilitated hundreds of sessions in the areas of working effectively with cultural diversity and minimizing and effectively responding to all forms of harassment in the workplace. **I love my work!** Over the course of my career as a trainer, I've felt no less than **called** to do training, and especially in the area of helping us all to see and experience our humanity across **all** of our differences.

In my diversity workshops, specifically, I develop agendas that I hope will raise both the participants' awareness **and empathy** in relating to their colleagues who they perceive to be different from themselves. I want us as human beings, to understand the universality of our humanity.

As serious as such sessions by their very nature **can** be, in **most**, there are also periods of lightness and laughter. But then—**when it is safe enough**, people begin to share their personal stories.

I have found, over the years, that when we can listen to each other's experiences with neither judgment nor blame, (similar to the way in which members of twelve step programs share and listen to each other's stories), minds can change and hearts can be touched. Among my most important jobs as a trainer is that of making the room safe enough for people to both share and listen to each other with an open heart. Workshops often **truly** start, when the story telling begins. There is **tremendous** power in our stories.

I have listened to the stories of second and third generation Asian Americans share the frustration of not having their specific and very distinct Vietnamese, Japanese, Laotian, Cambodian, Thai and other cultures acknowledged. It is the pain and frustration of being seen as one large Asian monolith, specifically Chinese, and thus, being perceived as being all alike.[69] I have listened as some Asian Americans have described the pain and anger of having people speak to them v-e-r-y s-l-o-w-l-y a-n-d l-o-u-d-l-y and with exaggerated expression. I've heard Asian Americans, born and raised in the United States describe their experiences of being asked in that same tone, "Where—are—you—from?" I've heard many of the different ways in which some Asian Americans respond to the "model minority" label. I've listened to what have often been compelling personal stories of Asian Americans who, in violation of the stereotype, grew up poor. I've heard the accounts of others, of how it felt throughout twelve years of elementary, middle and high school, to be "misfits" because they loved literature, for example and had absolutely no math, engineering or computer science ability.

I have listened to Latin Americans in many diversity workshops **also** talk about how frustrating and distressing it is to have others assume that **they** are not American. I have heard Latin Americans

---

[69] In that instance, two important points are missed - that there is much rich diversity among Asian Americans of many nationalities, **and** that that same abundance of diversity exists **within** the population of Chinese and Chinese American people.

from Nicaragua, Ecuador, El Salvador, Costa Rica and other Latin American countries describe their many instances of being assumed to be Mexican, i.e., of having the uniqueness of **their** cultures as well, **also** erased by others' mental tapes both that all Latin people are Mexican. and that all Mexican People are alike.[70] I have listened as young Latin American men describe their experiences of being stopped by police for no apparent reason. I've heard numerous Latin Americans describe the pain and embarrassment of having many of their elementary school teachers assume that because at that time they had not yet learned English, they were of low intelligence. I have listened to the accounts of Latin Americans who were born and raised in the United States, of how it feels when they are assumed to be not only "**foreign**", but **illegal** as well.

Over the past twenty three years, there have, unfortunately, been very few people in my workshops whom I have been aware were Indigenous.[71] As a result, both I and the thousands of workshop participants whom I have trained over that time, are much less aware of the reality of the lives of Indigenous People than we otherwise **would** have been had we been privileged to hear some of their stories. I **did** learn a lot, however, from being on a training team with two Indigenous American colleagues some years ago, both Blackfeet, one female, the other male, one of whom grew up on a reservation and the other of whom did not. I learned a **great** deal from hearing their extremely different growing up stories which resulted in part from the differences between their two

---

[70] The same two points are missed in **this** instance, as in the stereotyping of all Asian Americans as Chinese, i.e., the richness of the diversity of the many nationalities of Latin Americans as well as **within** Mexican and Mexican American populations.

[71] There may have been many instances in which an Indigenous Person was present in the session, but I was unable to physically identify him/her as such, and nothing s/he said informed me that s/he was indeed Indigenous.

families, but also from the **completely** different cultures in which they were raised.

In the **absence** of the voices of Indigenous People in the room, I **try**, to the best of my ability, to at least **include** the historical and present-day experiences of Indigenous People in all discussions of our different experiences with diversity in the United States. In so doing, I am **never** confident that I have done an adequate job, and indeed, in **most** instances, despite both my sincere desire **and** valiant attempt to do so, probably have not. Indeed, the very fact that I lack the lived experience of an Indigenous Person, makes it **impossible** for me to. I do my best, however, and genuinely hope that as a result, the participants leave the workshop with at least a **slightly** deeper understanding of the history and experiences of our Indigenous sisters and brothers.

Over the course of my career as a trainer, I have listened to African American men try to help others in the workshop understand the feeling of being stopped by the police numerous times, a phenomenon which for many, began in their early adolescent years. I have listened to the heartbreak of African American parents as they described their resentment of having to have "the talk" with their young sons, the talk in which they tell their boys that they **must** be deferential to the police if they are stopped, specifically **how** to be, and that their life may depend upon just how **successfully** deferential they are. I have listened with much empathy, to the painful stories of African American women who worked **very** hard on their jobs in corporate America, in academia and a myriad of other employment settings, earned a promotion on the **basis** of that work, and were then subsequently told by a colleague, often "in jest", that the only reason they **received** the promotion is that they were a "twofer", black **and** female. I have listened as African American women **and** men have described their frustration and anger when they experience the phenomenon sometimes referred to as "shopping while black", i.e., of being watched carefully and often **followed** by sales people in retail establishments. In many sessions, African American parents have shared, and **tearfully** so on more than one occasion, **painful** stories of their child having been put into the "slow" reading group in school **without ever having been tested**. I have listened to African American women share their outrage, sorrow and disappointment when an African American man harasses them in the workplace. The sentiment that I've heard them express most often in this regard, is, "How **dare** he! How dare **he**! **He** should know better. Given his experiences with **racism**? He should know better!" I have listened, in many workshops, to an African American man share what it feels like when the simple physical manifestation of the combination of his race and gender, i.e., the very fact that he **is** a black man, instills obvious fear in strangers on the street; that the same thing often happens with a person with whom he is interacting, and that depending upon the situation, he may attempt to put the person at ease. I have deeply listened as African American men share how psychologically and emotionally exhausting it is to continuously both **experience** people being afraid of them, **and** to go through the "It's ok, I'm really a good guy" exercise on the numerous occasions on which they have in their lives. I have watched as **every other African American man in the room** nods in understanding, each time the fear experience was shared.

Two stories, both of which were shared in diversity sessions that I facilitated more than ten years ago, are particularly powerful for me. One was told by a young African American man; the other, by a young European American woman.[72] The young man worked in management for a large Florida-based supermarket chain. During the afternoon of the first day of the workshop, he described a personal experience that had occurred at a gas station convenience store earlier that morning:

> On my way to the training this morning, I stopped at a gas station convenience store to get a cup of coffee. After pouring my coffee, I got in line to pay for it. The guy in front of me was also black. All of a sudden, for no reason that

72 Although the two narratives are told in first person, and do accurately represent the message, they are not verbatim accounts.

I could see, this guy started going off on the cashier, who was white. I mean he was screaming at her, calling her names, everything. I think maybe the guy was mentally ill. He left, then **I** was next in line. When I walked up to the counter, that lady looked like she saw a ghost. I know what she was probably thinking. She was probably thinking, "Oh God. Here comes another one!" I didn't even **know** that guy. I didn't know him from Adam. Now, if I had been a **white** guy in line behind another **white** guy that had just gone off on her, she probably would've looked at me and said something like, "What was **his** problem?!" But as a **black** man, I have no individuality. That hurts like hell.

In my brief interaction with that young man, I experienced him as polite and soft spoken. Absolutely **nothing** about him was threatening.[73]

---

73 That young man's story reminded me of an experience that my cousin Joe had many years ago, and that he shared with me, (with what I perceived was both anger **and** pain), immediately after it occurred. Joe's story was essentially the following, "Laurie, I just came back from Wal Mart, buying oil for my car. As I walked down the main, center aisle of the store, a white woman was walking in the other direction, toward me. Now, mind you, it was the middle of the day, with hundreds of people around in a big store, and **the second** that lady looked at me, she clutched her purse and moved way over. Laurie, I'm so tired of people responding to me like that! This is how God made me. I can't **look** any better than this. I'm a good person, Laurie." Even though Joe shared that story with me years ago, I remember very clearly that he was dressed, as he did frequently, in meticulously ironed pants with a crisp crease, a polo shirt and loafers. Joe is dark brown-skinned so it's possible that the woman's fear was exacerbated for that reason. All I could say to Joe, a young man of deep religious faith who lives his life consistent with his faith, was, "I know, Joe. I know, man." In that moment, I hurt for him. My heart **ached** for my young cousin.

The following was the story of the young woman, an employee of a large Federal agency in Denton, Texas:

> When I was growing up, people used the "N" word all the time, they talked about Black People really negatively and had all the stereotypes. Then, once when I was in elementary school, we moved and for a little while right after the move, I had to go to a school that was mostly black. I'll never forget the classrooms in the school. They had no world globes. They didn't have the clocks on the wall that teachers use to teach kids how to tell time. The alphabets that were hung above the blackboard were hand made by the teachers. There wasn't an abacus in my classroom. We had no record players, no science table, no maps. We had no reading corner. Other than the old textbooks, there weren't even any **books** in the classroom. I remember, even as a kid, thinking that there was no way these kids could compete against white kids because they had nothing. How **could** they compete?
>
> While I was at the school, I made friends with a little black girl. One day after school, I walked her home. When we got to her house, I went in. I noticed the floors. They were beautiful, shiny hardwood. There was a very nice piano in one corner of the living room. The furniture, the curtains,

---

The irrationality of the fear that many European Americans have of African American men and other Americans of Color becomes crystal clear when seen through the lens of American crime statistics. Those statistics demonstrate **conclusively** that in the history of the United States, many tens of thousands more Americans of Color have been beaten, tortured, lynched and in other ways murdered by European Americans, than the other way around. American history demonstrates **irrefutably** that many more synagogues, more Muslim temples, and more African American churches have been defamed and bombed by European Americans, and far more homes and businesses of Americans of Color have been burned by European Americans, than the other way around.

> everything looked perfect. My little friend's mother came out, and she was dressed so nice and her hair looked so pretty. She introduced herself, made iced tea for us and then played the piano for us.
>
> After that, whenever I would hear one of my relatives, their friends or one of my friends use the "N" word and say racist things about Black People, I didn't say anything, but I would always think to myself, "Wow. They're saying those things and they believe those things because they've never seen what I saw. They don't know what I know. They just don't understand." I'm **so** glad that I had that experience. Going to that school for a few months and especially that **one** afternoon at my friend's house saved me. They saved me from a closed mind that would have really limited my thinking, my understanding, and my whole life. I'm so thankful for that.

Those are the kinds of stories that can **deeply** touch our hearts and in so doing, help all of us to understand each other on a level much deeper than we almost **ever** do. If we could learn how to both share our **own** stories **and** with neither judgment **nor** defensiveness, listen to those of **others**, we would grow in wisdom at a rate that I don't think we even believe is possible. In listening, for example, to an Irish American friend re-count the story of his immigrant great grandparents and the discrimination and harassment they faced upon their arrival in Boston in the late 1800's, I want to be able to experience curiosity about their experience, ask questions and learn about their experiences, about which I formerly knew virtually nothing. I want to be able to hear my friend without feeling resentment, without thinking, "Well at least they weren't slaves." I want to be able to give my friend the great human gift of my full presence as he tells me his story, and to listen to him compassionately, with a clear mind and open heart.

Similarly, I would hope that my friend would be able to listen without antipathy, to my stories of Gramzie's formative years, of my parents' experiences and of my own experiences of racism, growing up in New Orleans. I would hope that s/he would be able to hear me without thinking, "Why do they always have to play the race card? They weren't the only ones who had it hard. My great grandparents had it hard when they came over here too." I hope that my friend would also be able to ask questions about our experiences, hear my stories with empathy and compassion, and as a result, have opened to them, a **world** of understanding of an experience which before our conversation, may have been virtually unknown to them in any significant way.

Through **all** of that sharing, through all of that **listening**, in those workshops that I facilitate outside of employment settings, I want the European-Americans in the room to "get it", to truly **emotionally** comprehend the following five things:

1. The actual history of racism both in the United States **and** internationally;

2. The pain and suffering that racism, including the unconscious and thus insidious racism of low expectations has historically caused and continues to cause, in the lives of Americans of Color;

3. The magnificent diversity within populations of Americans of Color;

4. How racism has **dramatically** mentally and emotionally disabled many millions of European Americans and that as a result, **their** lives have been limited in ways that they simply cannot imagine. I want them to see what is possible for their lives were they to begin the long and while difficult, also exceedingly rewarding journey of unlearning racism, of being able to see themselves as **equal**, not **superior** members of the human family. I want them to want that tremendous **personal growth** for **themselves** and the **results**, for their **children**;

5. The incredible awareness of racial issues and empathy toward Americans of Color that some European Americans have. I want them to know of the many, many thousands of European Americans who are working to help themselves and other European Americans become more aware of racism both within themselves and society-at-large. I want them to become aware of how they may become effective anti-racist allies to Americans of Color. I want them to feel deeply motivated to become an ally in their personal lives.

I want the Americans of Color to understand that while contemporary European Americans on a practical level **are** and historically **have** been the **benefactors** of racism, they are **also** its innocent victims, albeit in a **radically** different way from the way in which Americans of Color have been.[74] Specifically, I want the Americans of Color in the room to see that the average European American who grew up in the United States had virtually **no** chance of escaping the chains of racism that have mentally and emotionally enslaved them for centuries. In coming into that awareness, I want them to experience a level of sincere compassion toward European Americans who were raised to have both racial bias and unconscious feelings of racial superiority. I want them to deeply understand that had **they** been raised in the same way, they **themselves** would very likely harbor the exact same prejudices, the exact same unconscious feelings of superiority.

I **also** want the Americans of Color in the room to truly understand that we **also** have both conscious and unconscious biases, (sexism, homophobia, anti-Semitism, classism, colorism, and others), that can be **enormously** hurtful to others. I want them to understand on a deep level, that "isms" that **they** don't experience, significantly impact the lives of millions of **others**. I

---

74 To suggest that the difference in the ways in which racism has historically impacted European Americans and does so today, compared to how it has historically impacted Americans of Color and does so today, as anything **but** "radically different", would be a dangerously false equivalency.

want them to understand that skin color privilege does not make life a "cake walk" because those who **enjoy** the privilege can **still** experience tremendous pain in their lives in **other** ways. I want the Americans of Color in the room to be aware of the **many** thousands of European Americans who are **sincerely** committed racial allies. I want them to see the possibility of allyship among themselves and others who experience not only **racial** but also **other** forms of oppression, as well as those who experience none.

I want the heterosexual people in the room to understand in a **profound** way, how both heterosexism and homophobia impact the lives of lesbian, gay, bisexual, transgender and inter-sexed people as well as people whose manner and style are atypical of their gender. I want the heterosexual people in the room to understand what it would feel like if they lived in a predominantly LGBTQ world and had to pretend to be an LGBTQ person at **every** turn, with family, friends and all day, five out of seven days per week at work. My desire is for them to understand the discomfort of being in an office conversation about everyone's weekend and not being able to talk about the get-together of several of their heterosexual friends that they attended Saturday night. I want them to know what it would feel like to be a heterosexual person of deep faith and hear at their worship service on a regular basis, how immorally bankrupt they are for being heterosexual. I want them to understand what it would feel like to have to prepare for family visits by having their partner assist them in totally "sanitizing" their home, removing all pictures and every other trace of their relationship, having their partner leave, entertaining their family, then upon their family's **departure,** calling their partner to return home, after which they replace all of the pictures and other evidence of their shared lives. I want them to understand the threat of physical violence with which many LGBTQ people live every day, sometimes for just being who we are and at other times for engaging in an act as simple as holding the hand of our partner in public. I want them to understand the discrimination that we face on a regular basis, in every life context, education, housing and employment. I want them to understand what it feels like to experience what may be the most common discomfort for many LGBTQ people—simply others' personal discomfort with us as human beings. I want them to see, understand and acknowledge the magnificent, rich diversity that exists within the community of people who are LGBTQ.

I want the people in the room who are Christian to gain an **intense** awareness of the ways in which religious exclusion, even the most subtle and unconscious, affects their workplace colleagues who are **not** Christian. I want them to understand what it would feel like to live in a culture that is predominantly Jewish, for example, and to experience being a religious minority in that society, a society in which the majority knows very little **about** their Christian faith, and has historically been unwelcoming of people **of** their faith. I want them to understand how it would feel to live in a society in which hate groups exist which target Christians for unspeakable violence, including lynchings, a society in which Christian churches are defamed and bombed, simply because they **are** Christian. I'd like them to truly comprehend the feelings associated with living in a society in which Christians have been historically excluded from social clubs, from neighborhoods, from jobs and even entire professions. I want them to understand the feelings of being a religious minority in the workplace and the experiences of their children at school, during the Chanukah season.

I want **all** of us, those of us who have religious/spiritual faith, of **all** faiths and spiritualties, as well as those of us who are atheist and agnostic, to see, understand and acknowledge the magnificent, rich diversity that exists within both religious and spiritual communities, as well as those which gather in observance of non-religious, non-spiritual, ethical, humanistic principles. I want people of faith to understand that there are millions of people who do not believe in God, who are decent, ethical, compassionate and deeply caring about the lives of their fellow human beings

I want the able-bodied people in the room to **deeply** understand the stories told by people with physical, mental, emotional and learning disabilities. I want them to understand, to the extent that it is possible, their experiences of being patronized, the experience, for example, of having others assume that because they have a **physical** disability, they are also **intellectually** challenged; of having the restaurant wait person ignore them and ask their able-bodied dinner partner, "And what would s/he like?"; of having others assume that because they have a **learning** disability, they are not **intelligent.** I want the able-bodied people in the workshop to understand the experience of a blind person who reports that because s/he is **blind**, people of ten speak very loudly to them. I want them to know what it feels like to have well-meaning people give them unsolicited help in performing the simplest of tasks of which they are fully capable of doing for themselves. I want the able-bodied people in the room to **understand to every extent possible**, the ways in which both low expectations and patronizing attitudes and behaviors, **even the most unintentional**, impact the quality of life, including the career opportunities, of people living with physical, mental, emotional and learning impairments. I want them to see, understand and acknowledge the magnificent, rich diversity that exists within the community of people with disabilities.

I want the people in the room who didn't grow up poor, to deeply understand that people who are living in poverty are **not** genetically "lazy, shiftless and trifling", that as children, they have the **same** dreams as all other people. I want them to understand what living in poverty can do to the human spirit. I want them to know that as a group, people who are born into poverty have the same intellectual ability and human potential as all other people.[75]

---

[75] Dr. Maya Angelou once told Melissa Harris Perry, host of a political cable TV show, the story of her encounter some years prior, with a young high school student who was in an urban school for kids who had been involved in the criminal justice system. In introducing herself to Dr. Angelou, the young woman could do no more than mumble in a thick urban dialect. Years later, that same young woman met Dr. Angelou, again, this time by happenstance. During this later encounter, the young woman was extremely articulate, had earned B. A. and M.A. degrees and was a student in a Ph.D. program. About her, Dr. Angelou said the following: "That young woman was just waiting to become herself." **With opportunity**, people

I want them to see, understand and acknowledge the magnificent, rich diversity that exists within communities of people who are poor.

I want any harassers in the room to deeply understand how sexual and all other forms of harassment impact the person who is the target of the harassment. I want them to "get" on a deep level, how emotionally debilitating workplace harassment can be on the targeted person, and how it can severely impact the targeted person's physical, mental and emotional health **and** their life outside of work.

I want the people in the room who do not experience the daily indignities[76] of "the isms", (racism, sexism, anti-Semitism, heterosexism, ageism, ableism, etc.), to understand on a deep level what it feels like to experience the double blow of first **living** through the indignity, then upon **talking** about it, to be met with one of the common responses: [77] "You're being too sensitive"; "You're looking for it"; "That's happened to me too so it couldn't have happened to you because of your race"; "Maybe the cashier was just having a bad day"; "Why are you always playing the race (or gender, etc.) card"; "Yeah but that happens to everybody"; "Well, if I went to the black, (or Latino, or Native American, or Asian, etc.) part of town and went shopping, the same thing would happen to me"; "The police see all those teenagers the same. Race has nothing to do with it." I want the people in the workshop who respond in that way, to understand that one of the results of those common responses is that they erect cement walls of deep emotional distrust among people, distrust founded in the knowledge that the other person in the conversation isn't even open to **learning** about the

born into poverty whose lives reflect the negative consequences of their economic hardship, **like all other people who are given opportunity**, can "become themselves."

76 See Note Three for more information on the daily indignities.

77 See Notes Four for more information on the common responses.

indignities and about the emotional and practical consequences of the indignities in the lives of those who experience them.

My goal in **all** of my diversity training, is to have participants leave the session with a true understanding of the subject matter. If the focus is race, I want them, at the end of the workshop, to understand the fundamentals of race and racism. In sessions done in the workplace, I want participants to fully grasp the racial dynamics at play in their work environment and specifically how they may improve those dynamics for the benefit of their team and perhaps, the entire workforce. If the focus is gender, or disability, age, issues of gender identity/gender expression/sexual orientation, or any of the other "isms", the same is true. I want the participants to "get it" on a deep level.

In **all** of my diversity work, I want the participants for at least a few hours, to walk, to whatever extent it may be possible, in each other's shoes. My goal is for those who are members of majorities, racial, sexual, ability, gender identity/gender expression/sexual orientation, religious and other majorities, to leave the session with greater understanding **of** and compassion **for** those who are members of minorities; and, for those who are members of **minorities**, to leave with greater understanding **of** and compassion **for** those who are members of majorities.

Finally, and perhaps most importantly, I want the participants in my workshops to understand that it is possible for them to be powerful, effective allies to people who are the targets of racism and all other isms.[78]

---

[78] In my diversity workshops, we discuss the fact that there have **always** been human beings of dominant groups who have been allies to people of oppressed groups. Mrs. Barbara Henry, Ruby Bridges' European American teacher who, despite numerous threats to her life and safety, showed both tremendous courage and compassion by continuing to teach Ruby for the entire school year, is one of the most powerful examples of true ally ship of which I am aware. The example of the Quakers, who helped African Americans escape slavery through the

Over the course of my twenty-three year career as a trainer, I have been fortunate to have trained with a number of very talented European American diversity trainers who not only train, but also live their lives with great insight about diversity issues, specifically, team members of the firms Strategic Interactions of Fairfax, Virginia, Tom Finn Associates of Reston, Virginia and Annapolis Professional Resources of Glen Burnie, Maryland, among others.[79] I feel **particularly** fortunate to have formed precious friendships with three European American trainers who are now among my very dearest friends—Theresa, Jack, and Tom. If asked, they would be the **first** to acknowledge that they still carry somewhere within themselves, the vestiges of many of the negative racial messages which, over the course of their lives, they have received from other European Americans, both in their families, and from society-at-large. That fact notwithstanding, Tom, Jack and Theresa have a depth of understanding about race, our racial history and present experience of race, that I have often wished **all** European Americans and indeed all other **human beings**, could truly share. I fantasize about doing a Vulcan mind meld with Jack, Tom and Theresa, making a copy of whatever it is in their minds that has allowed them, as European Americans, to overcome many of the negative messages they have received about People of Color. In that fantasy, I duplicate that mysterious substance, reproduce it hundreds of millions of times, and make it available to all who wish to live a more intentional, more conscious, more compassionate life.

Underground Railroad, and who adopted the first formal anti-slavery resolution in Germantown Pennsylvania in 1688, is, of course, among the most well-known of many instances of powerful allyship.

79 Tom Finn's Book, *Are You Clueless,* provides many valuable stories of cultural diversity "cluelessness" in the employment context.

Finn, Tom. *Are You Clueless*. Reston: Kells Castle, 2007. Print. www.areyouclueless.com

My childhood experiences of growing up under segregation is a history that I share with Oprah Winfrey, with Condoleeza Rice, with Morgan Freeman and with many, many other well-known African Americans. **All** of us who grew up black, in the south and at that time, lived through it **ourselves** and saw our parents and grandparents endure it as well. I will end my racial memoir, however, fully acknowledging that as painful as my life experiences with racism have been, I have in comparison to **millions** of others, experienced little of the **potential** pain of racism. In New Orleans, I experienced the hardships of integration but hundreds of thousands of African American kids who grew up at that time in Birmingham, Alabama and other parts of the South, experienced actual domestic terrorism—the bombing of their churches, meeting places and for some, their homes, night rides through their communities by the Ku Klux Klan, and much more. Millions of black children who grew up during my childhood years under apartheid, in the ghettos of Johannesburg, Soweto and all over South Africa, experienced **much more** than I. **Millions** of African-American children who grew up in **rural** areas of the American South at that time, who lived through physical violence and night raids of the Ku Klux Klan in their communities, experienced **much** more than I. (In one of my diversity workshops, an African-American woman, **my age**, who grew up in a small rural Alabama community, privately shared with me at the end of the session, that during her childhood, her best friend's father had been lynched—for a reason that I do not remember—by an angry white mob). Unlike millions of black kids who lived in either the rural South or in Birmingham, for example, I was filled with all of the hope but none of the terror of the Civil Rights Movement, the terror of its children demonstrators who faced the full wrath of racist Mississippi and Alabama police forces. Thousands of black kids who grew up in the projects of New Orleans and/or were dark brown skinned, suffered far more than I did. Hundreds of thousands of African-American children who grew up at that time in the northern ghettos of Newark, Detroit, St. Louis and Chicago and in ghettos **all over the country**, in L.A., and Baltimore, in Washington, D. C., and Atlanta, and in so many other American "hoods", suffered the results of the long history of racial oppression in the U.S. **far** more than I. Dark brown skinned African-American children who grew up in New Orleans suffered far more than I. All over these United States, millions of Latin American children who grew up in barrios, Asian American children who grew up in poverty—in Chinatowns, Koreatowns, Japantowns and pockets of Asian American poverty all across the country, and of Indigenous children who grew up in poverty at that time, both on and off reservations, suffered the social consequences of racism **much** more than I. For that reason, I am **very** well aware that the pain of **my** experiences **pales** in comparison to many who had either the same **or much more** God-given intelligence and creativity than I, but who, **due only to the circumstances of their birth, tragically**, became statistics. My heart bleeds for those millions of innocents. I honor their stories.

Beginning in my mid-teens and continuing through my 20's, in New York City, in Ithaca, New York, in Philadelphia and in Washington D.C., I participated in marches and, demonstrations for freedom and equality, and volunteered in non-profit organizations which worked on peace and justice issues. In my thirties, I devoted myself to continuing to help humanity to reach those goals through the vehicle of education. I am, at heart, an educator. I am a trainer. It is my sincere hope that over the course of my career as a facilitator of adult learning, I have inspired at least one person to either begin or continue their path of gaining increased racial awareness.

Lauren Training

Every single person on Earth enters this world in the **exact** same way. We **find** ourselves in our bodies. We just find ourselves in them. **All** of us. **None** of us asked to be born into the racial group into which we were born. None of us chose to be born into the gender group into which we were born. No one chose to be born with a physical, mental, emotional or learning disability. None of us chose our national origin. None of us chose our parents. We just **found** ourselves in our identities, whatever identities we happen to have.[80] Furthermore, each of us has on average, less than ninety years on the planet. If I am fortunate enough to live until I **am** ninety, I am at this point in my life, entering its third and final stage. I hope that over the past sixty years, in the many relationships that I have had with family, colleagues and friends and the even more numerous interactions that I have had with

80 It is appropriate to note here, however, the belief in pre-birth planning, i.e., the belief that prior to birth, we do **indeed** choose our parents, and thus, many of the circumstances of our lives. That concept will be more fully explored in *Religion: Different Paths Same Journey – The Fundamental Truth About Faith and Spirituality.*

many strangers, I have helped at least **a few** of my fellow human beings to see the profoundly deep connection that exists among us all. I hope that I have helped at least a few of us to both see ourselves in each other and the Divine in us all.

So now you know my story, my racial story. Let's begin now, our astonishing journey from the very dawn of our racial past, into our racial history of the last several hundred years, then into our racial present, on to an unimaginably wondrous racial future for us all, and finally, to humanity's racial bottom line which we will have to cross in order to get there. Our starting point is our conventional view or race . . . . our very simple story.

II. The Conventional View of Race: Our Very Simple Story

For the past several centuries, there has been one story regarding race which has surpassed all others, the world over. It is a quite straightforward story. Indeed, it is **exceptionally** simple. The following, is that story:

There is a hierarchy of human worth based upon race. At the **top** of the hierarchy are **Caucasians**, the most intelligent, ambitious, industrious and historically accomplished of all human beings. All other races are inferior to Caucasians, **especially** in intelligence, but also in drive, determination, and in every other positive human characteristic. Next in the hierarchy are Asians, (although some Asian cultures have historically considered **themselves** to be on top, with **Caucasians** in second place). T**hen**, sharing third place, are the Indigenous Peoples of North, Central and South America, and all non-African island-based people. Finally, in last place, at the very **bottom** of the human hierarchy, **far** below all other human beings, are Africans.[81]

---

[81] In this hierarchy, I consider Aboriginal Australian People to be African. Latin People are not mentioned in the hierarchy because there is no biological Latin "race" within the customary understanding of the word, "race". "Latin" or "Latino", are terms, rather, which often refer to people, frequently of different races and many countries, who share certain cultural and in some instances historical connections. Indeed the word, "Latino" often refers to a cultural and linguistic category which is not a biological construct at all. The term, however, is not acceptable to all people who fall within the group. Because it **is** such a diverse group, there is no fully accurate or acceptable word to describe it. Finally, I was not, in this list, attempting to identify all the peoples of the Earth, only our major historical biological racial constructs.

[Indeed, the most **racist** schools of thought representing the cruelest form of racism against people of African descent, have historically contended that Africans are not even **actually** fully human. That tall tale was the very beginning of what is now a long history of likening people of African descent to monkeys, apes and gorillas.

The tragic story of Ota Benge, the young Congolese Pygmy boy who in 1906 was brought to the United States and exhibited for months in the Monkey House of the Bronx Zoo, is perhaps the saddest and most extreme example of the historic dehumanization of an African person. Mr. Benge never recovered from the ordeal and committed suicide at the age of 32.][82]

The Cover of the Jan/Feb, 1981 edition of Science Digest magazine illustrates the point. It displayed the faces of four men in an ascending line. At the bottom of the line is a man of African descent. Slightly above him is a man of Asian descent. Slightly above him is a man of European descent, and slightly above **him** is the face of a man that, according to the magazine's article on the subject, was a member of a new race that was going to emerge in the future. I shared that magazine cover with a number of people, each of whom **without exception**, commented that in their view, the picture quite clearly implied that Africans were at the bottom of a chain of human evolution. I agreed.

Cover, "Science Digest", Jan/Feb, 1981 http://www.amazon.com/gp/product/images/B005STP9H2/ref=dp_image_text_z_0/192-2064822-5965255?ie=UTF8&n=283155&s=books,]

In essence, our racial "**science** story" is that in comparison to all other human beings, Caucasians are the most **genetically**

82 See Note One and National Public Radio's report at the link below for additional details on Mr. Benga's tragic story: http://www.npr.org/templates/story/story.php?storyId=5787947

evolved. Our racial "**history** story", is that they are the most historically accomplished, and thus, the most socially evolved.

While our racial story is, of course, much more complex than I have described above, the preceding description of the human hierarchy constitutes the **crux** of our story about race. It is the racial story which for the past several hundred years, has been both consciously **taught** and even in the absence of an intentional message, unconsciously **believed**, by many billions and perhaps even **the majority** of people on the planet. It **is** our racial story. That racial story, however, is a fairly new phenomenon in the entire history of our species, having originated rather recently, just about 600 years ago in the early1500's with the first known contact in this millennium of Europeans with Africans, the Indigenous People of the Americas, Indians,[83] Aboriginal Australians and other island-based People of Color. Nonetheless, over the relatively short term of its existence, our racial story has lead to one of the most resolute forms of prejudice known to humanity—racism. [84]

Ironically, that story is completely antithetical to our actual story, our true story, our fundamental human truth - the truth that every human being on Planet Earth.........is African.

---

83 The term "Indian" in this work, refers exclusively to people from the country of India.

84 See Note One for other examples of the wretched history of African Americans being compared to monkeys, apes and gorillas.

III. The Fundamental Truth About Race: Africans Are The Parents of Humanity We *All* Began as African

Africans conceived, sired and gave birth to the entire human race. Their DNA is within all of us, within each and every human being on the planet. Whether we hail from the Indigenous People of Asia, of North, Central and South America, of any of the Earth's islands, of Australia, whether we identify as African, Caucasian, Middle Eastern or bi or multi-racial—at the base of **all** of the DNA in **all** of our bodies, is the DNA of our African ancestors. This is equally as true for those of us who, (using traditional physical indicators), appear to be **one hundred percent** Asian, **one hundred percent** Indigenous to the Western Hemisphere, **one hundred percent** Caucasian, and **one hundred percent** Indigenous Islander, as it is for those of us who appear to be **one hundred percent** African. We **all** trace our DNA back to our African roots. **Without** those roots, without our African genetic heritage, we human beings **the world over**, would simply not exist as we do today.

The science which **supports** the universality of our African genes is both overwhelming **and** incontrovertible. Not only **is** it no longer theory, it **hasn't** been for many years. The jury is **in** on this one. The following is a **nutshell** version of that science:

1. The very first humans lived somewhere in southern Africa.[85]

---

[85] Regardless of whether one believes that those first humans were created by a Divine Creator, or that based upon the Earth's archeological record, they evolved from other primates, **or both**, the fact that the oldest human remains ever discovered have been found **only** in southern Africa, makes it scientifically undeniable that our

Eventually, from East Africa, humans migrated to other parts of the African continent. Human beings lived on **only** the continent of Africa, for many millions of years.

2. The skin of our African ancestors was dark. Research conducted by anthropologist Dr. Nina Jablonski, determined that folic acid, which is crucial for embryonic development, is destroyed by too much ultra violet, (UV), radiation from the sun. Thus, the skin of our African ancestors **had** to be dark in order to protect them from over exposure to the powerful African sun's UV rays. Dark skin literally saved humanity from dying out and becoming extinct.

   For more information on the necessity of dark skin in the firswt humans, see the Discovery Channel's:

   "The Real Eve"
   http://www.youtube.com/results?search_query=the+real+eve&oq=the+real+eve&gs_l=youtube.3..0l10.4692.6423.0.7027.12.12.0.0.0.0.260.1540.4j7j1.12.0...0.0...1ac.1.11.youtube.LloHWJUWsqA

3. Eventually, between 90,000 and 180,000 years ago, Africans began migrating out of Africa. Some went by land and then sea to Australia and many of the Earth's islands. Some walked North and East into Asia and then later into North, then Central, and finally South America. Others walked North and West into the Middle East and then into Central and finally Western Europe.

4. The homo sapiens who left Africa were not partially formed humans who developed into full human beings of different

earliest ancestors **lived** there **irrespective** of how one believes they first **appeared** there.

races around the world after **leaving** the continent. When we **left** Africa, we were fully modern African human beings.

5. Those Africans who migrated to the four corners of the Earth, began to slowly physically adapt to their new environments. Over many generations, taking several thousand years, the Africans who migrated to the northern most regions of the Earth began to lose the dark brown color of their skin. The reason is simple—Since the sun was far less intense in the new environments to which humans migrated outside of Africa, our skin no longer required the same degree of protection from the sun's ultraviolet rays.[86] Indeed, as humans migrated north, our skin needed to be lighter to allow for **more** absorption of the sun's UV rays. Consequently, lighter skin was **good** for the Africans who migrated to Europe and other northern locations because it allowed them to absorb **more** vitamin D from the sun, an evolutionary advantage in their new environments where they were exposed to significantly less sun than they had been in their original African environment.

> [Melanin is the color, the pigment in our skin which our cells produce using amino acids. It is this pigment, this melanin, which gives our skin its color. Interestingly, there are only two forms of human melanin, an orange-red pigment called pheomelanin, and a black-brown pigment, called eumelanin. The amino acids in our bodies create **only** those two basic colors. Thus, the immensely diverse variety of skin color that exists among humans, arises from various combinations of only those two pigments. **All** human beings, with the exception of albinos, have a combination of both. Thus, it is literally true that **all human beings on the planet have the exact same two skin colors in our bodies. We just have them in different proportions**.]

86 Conversely, if we do not get **enough** ultra violet light, we develop the potentially lethal disease of rickets.

The hair of the transplanted Africans also began to change. The absence of the environmental factors that resulted in the unique napped African hair texture, caused the hair of the transplanted Africans, over time, to lose its tight texture. Further, the loose European hair can form an oily mat which warms the head in cold climates and thus, may have been helpful to our survival in colder climates.[87]

For **their** survival, Africans required hair that responded very differently. African hair, the **first** human hair, has a coil-like shape and fewer hair follicles than straighter textures and thus, does not respond to perspiration by becoming a thick mat which sticks to the neck when wet, as straight hair does. Rather, it retains its essential bounciness, allowing cool air to more easily circulate on the scalp. For that reason, African hair may have evolved to keep the human body cooler. In essence, the napped texture of African hair likely assisted in the regulation of our body temperature when we lived on hot, open African savannahs. Thus, just as the dark brown color helped humanity survive by protecting our **skin**, napped **hair** likely helped us to survive by protecting our **scalp**.

Finally, in response to the specific environmental and climatic influences of their new habitats, over many generations, the facial features of the transplanted Africans began to change. Their noses became longer in order to warm the air that passes through the nasal passages, protecting the lungs from

[87] The value given to hair in many of our cultures, (often taking on even religious significance in some), is entirely ironic given that our hair is actually excrement, just as are our finger nails, toe nails, mucus, urine and feces. The emotional pain over having "bad", i.e., African hair, as opposed to "good", i.e., straight hair, felt by millions of, (primarily but not exclusively), girls and women of African descent the world over, is particularly tragic in light of that fact.

frigid air. Their lips thinned for a reason which, unfortunately, in all of my research, I was unable to uncover. [88]

6. The dramatic changes to African skin, hair and facial features that occurred over time in all of the new habitats to which Africans migrated the world over, resulted in what we now think of and refer to as the human races—Asians, Caucasians, Australians, Indigenous People of the Western Hemisphere, and the populations of the Earth's islands.[89] Africans, of course, are also considered a "race".

7. The physical changes that the transplanted Africans underwent, were evolutionarily advantageous **adaptations** to their new environments. We did not become Asians, Indigenous People, Caucasians, Aboriginal Australians and Indigenous Islanders through a process of **evolution**. Rather, we became them through a process of relatively rapid and brilliant **adaptation**.

8. Those adaptations took only a few thousand years, an **extremely** short time, evolutionarily speaking. [90]

---

88 Other physical changes also occurred. There is often a difference, for example, between the shape of the calf and the buttocks of many Africans and Europeans. The physiological differences that some people who live in the Arctic Circle have developed that help them live in one of the Earth's coldest climates and that the Moken People of Southeast Asia have developed in response to spending a significant amount of their lives in water, are other examples of our many human adaptations to our environments.

89 In addition, there are some human physical traits, the epicanthic fold of Asian eyes, for example, that may be the benign consequences of other climatic changes.

90 Skin color changes after only a few thousand years, the proverbial "drop in the bucket", evolutionarily speaking. "*The Search for Adam*

9. As a species, we have not had enough time to have developed into **essentially** different kinds of human beings. Such changes (as, for example, a larger brain size, which would ostensibly result in greater intelligence, i.e., arguably **true** superiority), take place **through evolution**, **not adaptation**, requiring a **much** longer time period than has occurred since our migration out of our African homeland.

10. Not only are all modern humans from Africa, we are all from **only one place and one village** in Africa. Perhaps most astounding of all, we are, every one of us, **from the same African woman and man**. There is a **real**, African "Adam and Eve" from whom we are **all** descended. For that reason**, every human being on the planet** is related to every other human being. We are **all** cousins—literally one human family.

The following is **a mere smidgen** of the scientific reports published over the past twenty-five years that support that proposition:

1. Newsweek Magazine, "*The Search for Adam and Eve*", January 11, 1988 was one of the very first articles to report on the subject. In it, the work of a team of geneticists trained in molecular biology was reported upon. Essentially, as a simple way to obtain body tissue, the geneticists had 147 pregnant women agree to donate their babies' placentas to their genetic experiment after giving birth. The 147 women were Middle Eastern, Asian, European, African and Aboriginal Australian. The scientists then put the placentas through a process which

---

and Eve: Scientists Explore a Controversial Theory about Man's Origins", Time Magazine January 11, 1988.

My friend Jack Straton has quite astutely commented that rather than seeing our different skin tones as a reflection of our **differences**, we **could** see our shared human physical ability to darken and lighten our skin in response to climatic changes as an amazing **commonality**.

ultimately gave them a sample of pure mitochondrial DNA, the DNA that we inherit only from our mothers.

After analyzing the DNA, the geneticists came to two conclusions: First, the babies' genes formed a family tree that originated in Africa. Second, the babies' DNA ultimately tracked back to **a single sub-Saharan woman**. **The DNA in <u>all</u> of our bodies originated from that <u>one</u> African woman**.

It was reported in the article that as astonishing as that finding was, it actually wasn't surprising to statisticians who are familiar with the oddities of genetic inheritance.

As a result of their research, the geneticists came to the following "bottom line" conclusions:

A. The human species did not evolve gradually in various parts of the world.

B. Instead, everyone on Earth descended from one woman who lived approximately 200,000 years ago somewhere in sub-Saharan Africa. Her genes are carried in **all** of humankind.

C. Sometime between approximately 90,000 and 180,000 years ago, some of her offspring left sub-Saharan Africa and eventually populated the entire rest of the planet.

D. It takes only a few thousand years for skin color to change. For that reason, if tomorrow, all of the Earth's dark-skinned people moved to Europe, and all of its light-skinned people moved to Africa, in just five thousand years, approximately, Africans would have light skin and Europeans would have dark skin.[91]

---

[91] It is unclear how much their hair and facial features would have changed in such a short time. Those changes may require a longer

E. Although it may seem unbelievable that all human beings alive today came from a single woman, it is actually a quite predictable result of the laws of probability.

Harvard paleontologist Jay Gould is quoted in the article:

> It makes us realize that all human beings, despite differences in external appearance, are really members of a single entity that's had a very recent origin in one place. There is a kind of biological brotherhood that's much more profound than we ever realized.

> **Tierney, John. "*The Search for Adam and Eve.*" Newsweek. January 11, 1988**
> http://www.virginia.edu/woodson/courses/aas102%20(spring%2001)/articles/tierney.html[92]

2. In a November 16, 1994 Washington Post article, "*Forget the Old Labels. Here's a New Way To Look At Race*", Boyce Rensberger, described the genetic unanimity of humanity in further detail:

> "We all descended from black people. Because humans evolved in Africa, the first people probably had dark skin. The white people of Europe descended from Africans who migrated north, between 1000,000 and 2000,000 years ago, and lost their coloring . . . ."

The following are the article's most salient points:

---

period. Skin color seems to adapt faster to climatic conditions than other characteristics.

92 I find it incredible that even in this article in which it is stated that "Eve" was likely a "Black-skinned woman", Eve and Adam are depicted on the magazine cover as medium brown-skinned, and with geri-curled, not napped hair.

A. Questions about why human beings have so many different variations of skin color, or why Africans have napped hair, or why the eyes of Asians are different from the round eyes of the majority of Africans and Europeans, i.e., about why, as a species, we look so different, are honest questions worthy of scientific answers.

B. Today, scientists agree on essentially the following three answers to those questions:

i. There are many more differences among people than the color of our skin and the shape of our facial features. Those differences are biologically deeper than skin color.

ii. The differences have been advantageous to us, helping us to be an evolutionary success. One illustration is the light skin of Europeans. Our African ancestors needed dark skin as protection from the sun's ultra violet rays, but when some of our African forebears journeyed to Europe where there is less sunlight, they would have perished if they had not lost most of the color in their skin . . . .

iii. Races, as we commonly think of them, don't actually exist. For the most part, races are subjective groupings contrived to suit our misunderstanding about human evolution.

C. Human beings have many characteristics that do not correspond to race and each characteristic, when considered individually, demonstrates that two people of different races can be more like each other than two people of the same race.

Human blood perfectly exemplifies that fact. Asian, European and African people may have blood in any of the four human blood types, A, B, AB and O. The blood of an

African Peron with type B blood is much more like that of a **European** Person with type B blood, than it is of another African with any of the other three blood types. Thus, when looking for a blood donor, it is the potential donor's **blood type**, not her/his **race** that determines the donor's suitability. Race is also not considered in the search for organ donors. An Asian Person's closest genetic match for a donated heart or liver, for example, could very well be a Latino, African or European person. It is blood type, not race, that is significant.

While there **are** patterns of certain human characteristics within what we call "races", there are many characteristics that exist within **more** than one race. Millions of Indian People, for example, have black skin that is much darker than the skin of most African People, even though some anthropologists classify Indian People as Caucasian. Some Semitic People have tightly curled hair that closely resembles that of typical African hair. Some European People have noses and lips that resemble those of African People.

Additionally, all of the characteristics that we normally associate with **particular** races, napped hair with African People, straight hair with non-African People, light skin with Asian and European People, dark skin with some South Asian and African People, etc. often exist, simultaneously, in human beings with characteristics that we normally associate with **other** races. Millions of people, for example, have dark skin **and** straight hair. Others have light skin **and** full lips. Millions of others, (many Ethiopians and other East Africans, for example), have dark skin **and** European-like noses and lips.

D. After vast misinterpretations of past years, current science teaches us that:

i. Human beings are the same in all of the areas that are important, and different in a few areas that are unimportant; and,[93]

ii. Our differences arose not because we are essentially different from one another, but in response to the differences in our **climates**.

E. When groups are separated for long periods, they become so genetically different that they can no longer reproduce together. The fact that all human beings can procreate together and have healthy, biologically viable children, is proof that we are all members of the same species.

F. Essentially, anthropologists agree that scientifically speaking, race as we think of it, doesn't actually exist. When we attempt to define race based upon observable characteristics such as facial features and color of skin, we disregard all of the many concealed human characteristics which do not fit into racial categories.

Rensberger, Boyce. "*Forget the Old Labels. Here's a New Way to Look at Race.*" Washington Post. November 16, 1994
http://www.docstoc.com/docs/17682525/%E2%80%9CForget-the-Old-Labels-Heres-a-New-Way-to-Look-at-Race%E2%80%9D

3. Harvard trained geneticist Spencer Wells teamed up with the National Geographic Society and spent more than ten years tracing the source of human DNA. In the project, National Geographic and IBM worked together to collect samples of DNA from human populations across the world. The scientists then followed the small changes that occasionally occur in our DNA as it is passed down through the generations. They use

93 Geneticists estimate that our racial variances account for about only 0.01 percent of all human genetic material.

those changes as genetic markers in essence, because they are easy to identify and never disappear, allowing our family lines to be traced back in history with what is essentially a sort of genetic time clock. Using that scientific method, the genetic researches ultimately followed family genetic lines all the way back to the earliest parts of our genetic record.

The remarkable result of the project is that **the researchers found the actual tribe, the specific African group of people to which the African woman and man from whom we are all descended, belonged**. Specifically, the scientists' research proved that we are all descended from the San Bushmen of the Kalahari Dessert of Namibia in southwest Africa. Dr. Wells explains in his book about the project, *The Journey of Man: A Genetic Odyssey*, that in the entire family tree of humanity, the San Bushmen's branch was the first to split off from the rest of the human family tree, clearly demonstrating that they are indeed the oldest people on Earth. Thus, we now know that it is the San Bushman who began humanity's epic voyage across the planet.

Dr. Wells also makes the following important points in the book, (that mirror some of those referenced in the Time Magazine and Washington Post articles cited above):

A. The phenomenon that we think of as race, originated rather recently.

B. It was probably the Earth's last ice age that resulted in the isolation of people into their different geographic regions that produced the different "racial" groups that we see in contemporary human beings. We did not evolve separately over hundreds of thousands of years . . . . Our information on human DNA proves that all people alive today have a common history.

C. Human beings journeyed from Africa to the entire rest of the world. Eventually, they adapted superbly to climatic conditions that were very different from those of their original homeland on the African continent.[94]

Perhaps the following statements from the book best summarize the results of the project:

"We are a relatively young species . . . . We are in numerous ways, still the same species that left Africa a mere 2,000 generations ago . . . . Now, however, our diversity is combining in ways that were not possible in the past."

Wells, Spencer. *The Journey of Man: A Genetic Odyssey*. Princeton: Princeton University, 2002, Print.
http://press.princeton.edu/chapters/i7442.html

In "The Journey of Man", the National Geographic Society's documentary based on his book, Dr. Wells states:

From them, (the San Bushmen), stemmed every color, creed and nationality alive today.

"The Journey of Man", National Geographic Society
http://www.youtube.com/watch?v=nBJDGzzrMyQ

Finally, Dr. Wells states in the video that the story carried in our blood is undeniable. That story is that every person on the planet, under the skin, is literally African, and that we have been apart for a meager two thousand generations. That story, according to Dr. Wells, makes clear that our former, outmoded notions about race are not only socially harsh, they are also scientifically erroneous.

94 Other animals follow the same pattern as human beings. The farther south they live on the planet, the darker they are. As their habitats are farther and farther north, the lighter they become.

[Information on the San Bushmen and their grand journey across the planet is also available in the Discovery Channel's documentary, "The Real Eve".

4. The June 1, 2007 issue of PLoS (Public Library of Science), included a report of a study done by Cornell University, of the DNA of African-American, European-American and Chinese People.[95]

The scientists in that study found evidence of recent selection on skin pigmentation genes, providing the genetic data to support theories proposed by anthropologists for decades that as anatomically modern humans migrated out of Africa and experienced different climates and sunlight levels, their skin colors adapted to the new environments. However, the study found no evidence of differences in genes that control brain development among the various geographical groups, as some researchers have proposed in the past . . . . 'It is important to emphasize that the research does not state that one group is more evolved . . . . than another', said co-author Carlos Bustamante, a Cornell assistant professor of biological statistics and computational biology.

Rasmus, Nielsen. "Evidence of Very Recent Human Adaptation: Up to 10 Percent of Human Genome May Have Changed." Science Daily. July 12, 2007.[96]

http://www.sciencedaily.com/releases/2007/07/070711134400.htm

95 The latter group of people **were** referred to in the article as "Chinese", **not** Chinese American.

96 Rasmus Nielsen, an adjunct professor of biological statistics and computational biology at Cornell University and now a professor at the University of Copenhagen, Denmark, is the paper's senior author.

5. Among **the** most interesting facts about the genetic relationships of Americans, is that as the result of the approximately two hundred fifty year history of slavery in the United States during which millions of enslaved African American women were regularly and repeatedly raped by their Caucasian captors, their captors' sons and Caucasian male employees, millions and perhaps the **majority** of African Americans are genetically related to European Americans. Indeed, one consequence of that tragic history is that **roughly thirty percent of African American men have Y chromosomes that trace back to Europe**. By contrast, **the mitochondrial DNA of those same men, the DNA that is passed through the female line, is only six percent European**. As Dr. David Reich, Professor of Genetics at Harvard Medical School put it:

Men contributed about three-fourths of the European ancestry that is present in the African American population data. The data speak to a history in which white male slave owners exploited women of African descent—a fact that is well documented in the historical record. That there is evidence of this in the **genetic** data should be no surprise.

Shaw, Jonathan. "*Who Killed the Men of England?*" Harvard Magazine. July-August, 2009.
http://harvardmagazine.com/2009/07/who-killed-the-men-england

Because we share the same biology:

* We can all eat the same food;

* We are all contagious to each other with our illnesses, and take the same medications for them, with most often, the same result;

* Human blood, urine, feces, semen, and intestinal gas are to our senses of sight and smell, all indistinguishable

among our human races, indicating that we are all the same on the inside; and,

* Most importantly, and the **true** test of a species, is that we can all procreate together. The shortest, darkest central African Pygmy and the tallest, whitest Norwegian can have a child together, and that child would be **fully** human. That is possible **only** because the chromosomes of **all** people, even when they look as different as Pygmies and Norwegians, are **exactly** the same. If our chromosomes were **not** exactly the same, we would not be able to procreate **across all races** and produce fully, biologically viable offspring who are **themselves** capable of reproducing other fully human, human beings.

  [Interestingly, because horses and donkeys are genetically so similar, they **can** procreate together, but because they aren't an **exact** genetic match, they produce a mule, a genderless animal, incapable of reproducing itself.]

It is a scientific truth that **all** of the other humanoids which over many eons appeared on the planet and whose skeletal remains are in our musems today, Homo Habilis, Homo Erectus, Peking Man, Neanderthal Man and many others, utterly disappeared. They died out. Had any of them survived and were living with us on the Earth today, **they** would **truly** be a different "race." The essential truth is that of the many humanoids that have evolved on the planet, only one "race" survived. Only one "race" is left on the Earth—Homo Sapien, the family to which all human beings equally belong.

Now, through the wonders of science, we know both that as a species, we were **born** black, and that we survived **because** we were.

We now know that we are all descended, not from the same few African **villages**, not even from a **single** African village.

We now know **beyond any doubt**, that all seven billion of us on the Earth, are descended from **the same two human beings**—a single African woman and a single African man of the San Bushmen People of Namibia's Kalahari desert.

We now know beyond any doubt that all notions of racial superiority and racial inferiority of groups of human beings based upon race, are false. DNA science has proven the unequivocal falseness of assertions that the "races" of humanity are fundamentally different, with Caucasians on top as the superior race, all non-African races in the middle and Africans at rock bottom, inferior to all of the other races. We now know that that assertion is as scientifically false as the notion that children either conceived by or born to unmarried parents are genetically inferior to children whose parents are married. There is absolutely **no** science to it. It is, indeed, pure, utter, unadulterated science **fiction**. In actuality, the **majority** of the racial distinctions that we have historically drawn among ourselves as human beings, as well as the significance that we have **attached** to those differences, are fictional. We know now, that they are fictions with no more fact or science behind them than a child's fairy tale.

We now know that while racial differences obviously exist, our differences are both far fewer and far less **significant** than all the ways in which we are alike. We know, in other words, that as human beings, we are far more alike than we are different.

We have cracked wide open and exposed to the light of day, the secret, indeed **the great truth**, that lies deep within **all** of our DNA, the profound truth that all seven billion of us, every single human being on Planet Earth, every single child, woman and man, share the same great, great, great . . . . grandparents. The profound reality in which we all live is that we are all related. We are all "cousins".

The science is in and the doubt is out. The fundamental truth about race, is that all of humanity is literally one giant family.

IV. Our Racial Past: A Profoundly Tragic Tale

Because until very recently, we have been **completely** ignorant of our common African origin and thus, that as a species, we are **indeed** one family, we have historically dealt with our racial differences with utter dysfunction. We live today with **immeasurable** human suffering **because** of our past racial dysfunction. I narrate this history, not to **wallow** in it, but because knowing and "coming **clean**" about it, is the first and a most important step in our being able to finally, collectively and valiantly walk **out** of that past into a more compassionate, mature, conscious racial future. We can never **heal** from our racial past if we are not aware of and do not **acknowledge** it. That healing is one of the things that I want most **desperately**, for my species that I love so dearly.[97]

The history chronicled here, is of several American groups of color. It is a history that is both brutal and tragic. It is also quite truncated, providing, as it were, a mere **outline** of the **actual** stories for each population discussed. A **comprehensive** list of all of the deeds that as a species we have committed as a result of our historically immature response to our racial differences, would comprise a work of many volumes. Thus, I provide here, no more than **a thumbnail sketch** of some of the most **important** pieces of that history. My attempt in providing this much shortened version of the **actual** history, is to at least spark our thoughts and perhaps even a national **discussion** of how, across the globe, humanity can begin to heal from our wretched racial past. [98]

---

97 While in this section I reference the history of race in a number of places around the world, our focus will primarily be on the racial history of the United States.

98 I have included in this work, a longer account of the history of African Americans than of other Americans of Color with absolutely **no**

A. How It All Began

There may **never** have been a time during which we human beings, the world over, have not oppressed each other. The reality of **regional,** tribal oppression **of** and war **against** people who lived relatively close to each other, has been present throughout our human history. In Asia, for example, there are recorded battles between the Japanese and the Chinese and between the Koreans and the Japanese dating back fifteen hundred years. For **thousands** of years, African tribes, all over the African continent, waged war on other African tribes. During that same time, **European** tribes, across the European continent, waged war on **other** European tribes. Indigenous tribes all across South, Central and North America, engaged in historic war with each other as well. And the people who inhabit the **islands** of the world have also, throughout history, waged war on other tribes of both their **own** and **neighboring** islands. The practice of human beings waging regional war upon, enslaving, oppressing and killing other human beings for any **number** of reasons, to avenge the death of a tribal member, to settle a land dispute, to resolve a contested debt owed to one side, or for a myriad of **other** reasons, has plagued our species, seemingly from our very beginning, in every culture and in every corner of the world.

For the **most** part throughout human history, when we engaged in regional warfare, it was with people who looked like us, people with whom we had a dispute, but **about** whom we held no notions of superiority. Then, about six-hundred years ago, a **totally different** kind of oppression appeared on the planet—an oppression that in a relatively short time period, swept the Earth

intent to be disrespectful to any group. I want, **only and always**, to be equally considerate of **all** human beings. The longer history of African Americans results simply from the fact that because African American history is my family's history, over the course of my lifetime, I have heard more stories about, read, researched and thus **learned** more about the history of African Americans than that of any other Americans of Color.

and took hold of the **entire** human race. It is a form of oppression, many of the results of which plague us **unrelentingly** to this day. That new form of oppression was the European conquest and dominance of most of the world, accompanied by a belief in European superiority **based upon skin color**.

The relationships between European People and People of Color around the world, was tragic from the very beginning of the first large scale contact between them in this millennium.[99] At that time, European explorers began sailing from Europe for the shores of Africa, (and without knowing it initially, because they were unaware of their existence), North, Central and South America, and most of the Earth's islands. It was shortly after those explorations began that the first recorded contact occurred in this millennium between Europeans and many other people around the planet, Indigenous People of the West, the world's non-European Island Inhabitants, Africans and Australians. The Africans, Indigenous People, Islanders, and Australians with whom European explorers first came into contact on those voyages, looked **very** different from them. They **behaved** totally differently. They **lived** extremely differently. The European explorers lacked **all** understanding of them.

> [In *The White Man's Burden: Historical Origins of Racism in the United States*, Winthrop D. Jordan asserts the following about the earliest contact of English People specifically, with African People:
>
> Englishmen found the peoples of Africa very different from themselves. Negroes' looked different to Englishmen; their religion was un-Christian; their manner of living was anything but English; they seemed to be a particularly libidinous sort of people . . . . People much darker than

---

99 Historical reports exist of contact prior to this millennium, in the **ancient** world, between North Africans and the Spanish, between West Africans and the Indigenous People of Central America and between Africans and the Chinese.

> Englishmen were not entirely unfamiliar, but really 'black' men were virtually unknown (to them) . . . . White and black connoted purity and filthiness, virginity and sin, virtue and baseness, beauty and ugliness, beneficence and evil, God and the devil . . . . An adoring (English) nation knew precisely what a beautiful Queen looked like.
>
> > 'Her cheeke, her chinne, her neck, her nose,
> > This was a lillye, that was a rose . . . .
>
> By contrast, the Negro was ugly, by reason of his color, and also his 'horrid Curles' and English standard of ideal beauty was a fair complexion of rose and white. Negroes seemed the very picture of perverse negation.][100]

After the early contacts of Europeans with Africans and Indigenous people, a three-part process then followed.

First, in their lack of understanding of the people they encountered, the European explorers made one **crucial**, erroneous assumption about them. Specifically, the explorers assumed that the non-European people whom they were encountering for the first time, were uncivilized, lacking most, if not **all** of the indices of intelligent human beings. Red, black and brown skin became an **automatic** marker of intellectual and therefore also cultural **inferiority**, while **white** skin simultaneously became just as automatic an indicator of **superiority** of intelligence and therefore also of culture. The explorers became convinced that their assumption was correct. That conviction, in turn, cemented their assumption into their minds as "information", as fact.

---

[100] Jordan, Winthrop D. *The White Man's Burden*. London: Oxford University Press, 1974 Print. While much of Jordan's language and analysis in *The White Man's Burden*, reflect unconscious racial bias, I nonetheless find his historical account of some of the earliest contacts between Africans and Europeans instructive and therefore useful.

> [Those explorers were **totally** unaware of the great ancient civilizations of many of the peoples with whom they came into contact. Africans, for example, developed the advanced and very sophisticated societies of the ancient Egyptian civilization, the Kingdom of Kush, the Timbuktu Empire, and the Kingdom of Aksum, among many others. Indigenous People of the West had the highly developed civilizations of the Incas, the Aztecs, the Mayans and others. Indeed, a number of African and Indigenous civilizations were extremely socially sophisticated and highly advanced in science and technology, long before the **start** of Europe's development, i.e., at a time during which Europeans were far less developed or far less "civilized".[101]]

Second, through the journals of their expeditions, the explorers, (whether intentionally or not), implanted in Europeans, a fear of the People of Color with whom they were coming into contact for the first time. The journals were filled, page after page, with graphic descriptions of Africans and Indigenous People as dark, barbaric, dangerous monsters. Regarding African People **specifically**, some explorers reported that they copulated with monkeys and were **themselves**, therefore, part monkey. [102]

> [In the early 20th century, exhibits of People of Color in "human zoos" were common. The people being exhibited were shown as examples of earlier stages of human evolution.
>
> **Human Zoos Documentary:**
> https://www.youtube.com/watch?v=xedc7pLWyRI]

[101] See Note Two for more information on the history of Africans, African Americans and other Americans of Color.

[102] See Note One for examples of the residue of that horrible story that is still very present with us even today.

Many of those journal entries were then published in newspapers all over Europe. The quite predictable result was that people across the European continent, before ever having even a **single**, personal, first-hand experience with Indigenous and African People, became filled with a deep, irrational fear of us.

European explorers also demonized Indigenous People, widely and intensely, in both stories and pictures. Those portrayals in turn, developed and intensified European fear of Indigenous People as well.

Third, shortly after their first contacts with Indigenous, Australian, African and non-European island-based people, European explorers, based upon their assumption of the intellectual inferiority, cultural inferiority and even minimal humanness, of the people of those groups, began to **treat** them, as radically inferior to themselves.

Later, with regard to European Americans' fear of African Americans, many European Americans who lived with African Americans on plantations in the slavery-based cultures of the southern United States, lived **daily** with the very **realistic** fear that the African Americans whom they held in bondage, were inclined to revolt, making their fear of African Americans even stronger. As a consequence, the clouded lenses through which they initially viewed African Americans as threatening and dangerous, gradually became even thicker, even harder. Over time, for many, that fear escalated into hatred.

Eventually, European-American plantation owners, their wives and employees, began to pass all of the misinformation, fear and hatred of Indigenous People, African Americans and other Americans of Color that **they** had accumulated, to generation after generation of their **progeny,** who in turn, became filled, **themselves**, with the same misinformation, the same fear, and for many—the same hatred. It is a tragic cycle which on **some** level, continues to this day.

B. The Effect of Racism on the Entire Human Race

Over the last 600 years, racism has been no less than **devastating** to the spiritual, mental, emotional and physical health of **billions** of human beings. It has been **indescribably** destructive to the health, in all of those areas, of the groups that have historically been considered racially **inferior—People of Color**. It has also been **utterly** destructive to the spiritual, mental and emotional health of the group that has historically been considered racially **superior—Caucasians**. In addition, racism has totally economically **dis**advantaged People of **Color** around the world, while simultaneously providing a tremendous economic **ad**vantage to **Caucasian** People, the world over. Racism has unquestionably been no less than devastating **to our entire species**.

Our sisters and brothers of color around the planet have suffered from both the psychology and the practice of racism. We have suffered the effects of the **psychology** of racism on the **interior**, i.e., the mental, emotional and spiritual levels. We have suffered the effects of the **practice** of racism on the **exterior**, i.e., the physical, economic and social levels.

C. The Psychology of Racism: Its Effect on Americans of Color

The psychology of racism deprives millions of individual human beings of color of what I believe is our Divinely-inspired, deeply-held feeling of self worth which should be ours simply because we are human beings. Racism has caused **many** People of Color, the world over, to feel and to actually **believe** that we are inferior to Caucasian People. That internalized mental and emotional badge of inferiority has resulted largely from four social messages that as members of the larger societies in which we live, we have received and often internalized **along with** the larger society.

1. Physical Unattractiveness

The first message is that **we are physically unattractive**, i.e., that depending upon which **specific** non-Caucasian group to which we belong, our skin color, eyes, noses and/or lips are ugly. Africans and people of African ancestry have an additional quite undesirable trait—that of "bad", i.e. napped hair. Those messages have caused many millions of children of color to look into the mirror, believe that they are ugly, and wish that they were white. At a very tender age, children of color begin to learn that one's physical appearance affords one either social privilege or social disadvantage.

The message that we are physically unattractive has caused millions of People of Color around the world, as adults, to invest billions of dollars in skin bleaching products, hair straightening products, and blepharoplasty,(eyelid surgery that makes Asian eyes appear more round), all in an attempt to look more Caucasian.

During my month in Ghana in 1976, I was shocked by how many Ghanaian women were wearing straight-haired wigs. I found it totally ironic given that during the same time period, here in the United States, African **Americans** had declared pride in blackness through among other things, wearing our hair in the "natural", or "afro" or "bush" hairstyle. Seeing women **in Africa** wear artificial hair that emulated Caucasian hair was a shock to me as a naïve twenty-three year old who was visiting my ancestors' home continent in order to experience West African culture.

One of the clearest and most entertaining contradictions of that message for little girls of African descent, one which I truly love, is the Muppet song and dance, "I Love My Hair", developed by Muppet Show head writer Joey Mazzarino. Mazzarino and his wife adopted an African American little girl who felt badly about her hair and wanted it to be straight.

"I Love My Hair"
http://www.youtube.com/watch?v=enpFde5rgmw.

The issue of African American women's relationship with their hair is the focus of Chris Rock's 2009 documentary, "Good Hair".

"Good Hair", Chris Rock
http://www.youtube.com/watch?v=1m-4qxz08So

Of course, people of **every** race, **including** Caucasians, engage in such appearance altering behaviors. That behavior is **very** different, however, for **Caucasian People** than it is for People of Color. The difference is as follows: When Caucasians alter **their** appearance, (dye their hair from brunette to blonde, alter their noses to make them smaller, etc.), it is simply an attempt to be either prettier or more handsome—that's it. **Conversely**, when People of Color alter **our** appearance, (lighten our skin, straighten our hair, remove skin from around our eyes to make them more round, etc.), while it is **also** an effort to be more attractive, the specific **picture** of attractiveness which we are attempting to achieve, is inextricably linked to a standard of beauty that is based upon a model of attractiveness found not within our **own** race, but within a **different** one, the Caucasian race, and **within** the Caucasian race, the **Aryan** model, specifically. For People of Color, our appearance altering is based upon the notion that our **racial** characteristics are unattractive. The accompanying internal (and often **totally** unconscious) monologue is as follows: "My dark skin isn't attractive because light and white skin are attractive and dark skin is ugly." "My nose isn't attractive because it's too big, or it's not the 'right' shape, or it's hooked", i.e., **because it doesn't look Caucasian enough**." "My lips aren't attractive because they're too big, i.e., **not Caucasian enough looking**." "My napped hair is 'bad' hair. Straight hair, i.e., everybody else's hair, is 'good' hair." That message has historically lead to a hate/hate relationship between many women of African descent and their hair. During the 1950's and 60's, even many African American **men** straightened their hair. The style was called the Conk. A number of popular black male entertainers and singing groups of the 1950's and early 60's wore their hair in the conk. Perhaps James Brown, Little Richard and Nat King Cole were among the most well-known.

Essentially, when a **Caucasian person** alters **her/his** appearance, the accompanying feeling is that s/he was simply unlucky in the birth lottery by not getting the best of what is characteristic of their **own** race. [103] It is **never** because according to the socially accepted standard of beauty, their **race** has inferior physical characteristics. Caucasian People are **not**, in other words, trying to look more Asian. They are **not** trying to look more like Indigenous People of the Western Hemisphere. Caucasian people are **not** trying to look more African. By contrast, when People of Color alter **our** appearance, it is often in response to what is either a consciously or unconsciously held belief that according to the socially accepted standard of beauty, our race **does** have inferior physical characteristics. It is based upon a belief that we are not attractive because the physical characteristics of our **race** are not attractive. More specifically, the belief is that we are not attractive because we don't look enough like a **different** race, the **Caucasian** race, which **does** have attractive physical characteristics. The associated thought, therefore, is that in order to have a more **attractive** look, we must have a more **Caucasian** look.

As a consequence, while **on an individual level**, both the Caucasian person **and** the Person of Color may feel inferior to those whom s/he believes are more physically attractive than

[103] Interestingly, there **are** particular characteristics of People of Color that many Caucasian People **have** found attractive, some so much so, that they have actually emulated them. The current fad of lip enhancing among Caucasian women for the purpose of having larger lips is such an example. Skin tanning, however, is perhaps the most obvious.

her/himself, the experience of the **Caucasian** person carries no badge of racial inferiority. The experience of the **Person of Color**, however, carries a **huge** one. For that reason, the two emotional experiences of unattractiveness are **entirely** different.

What is **uniquely** emotionally heartbreaking when specifically people of **African** descent engage in appearance altering however, is that we often do so with and in response to the belief that not only are our physical characteristics considered inferior to those of **Caucasians**, they are **also** considered inferior to those of all other People of **Color** as well, i.e., to **all** the Earth's people. Our physical appearance is widely considered, **the world over**, to be **the least** desirable. I believe that it is fair to say that the vast majority of the world's non-African people, (and sadly, a certain percentage of African and people of African descent as well), would prefer **any** other physical appearance—Asian, Polynesian, Indigenous, what many consider to be stereotypically Latin—literally **any** physical appearance, other than African.[104]

Dr. Kenneth Clark's well-known 1950's experiment, (the results of which were used as evidence in the landmark 1954 *Brown v. Board of Education* Supreme Court case in which the court declared state-sponsored segregated schools unconstitutional), clearly demonstrated that even **very young** African American children are **acutely** aware of the presumption of African inferiority. In the experiment, Dr. Clark, an African American psychologist, placed two dolls, one black and one white, on a table in front of very young African American children. Dr. Clark then asked the children the following questions, "Which doll is the pretty doll? Which doll is the nice doll? Which doll is the ugly

[104] My reference to the uniqueness of the experience of African People among People of Color is **not** an attempt to place our experience at the top of a hierarchy of oppression. There **is** no hierarchy of oppression. Human pain is human pain. Every group's experience must be respected equally. Such references, rather, are simply honest descriptions of the ways in which people of African descent are indeed singularly reviled.

doll? Which doll is the bad doll? Why is that doll pretty? Why is that doll ugly? Why is that doll nice? Why is that doll bad? Which doll looks more like you?" When asked, "Which doll is the pretty doll?" the children pointed to the white doll. When asked, "Which doll is the nice doll?", the children pointed to the white doll. When asked, "Which doll is the ugly doll?" the children pointed to the black doll. When asked, "Which doll is the bad doll?" the children pointed to the black doll. When asked, "Why is that doll (the white doll) pretty?" the children answered, "Because she's white." When asked, "Why is that doll, (the white doll), good?", the children answered, "Because she's white." When asked, "Why is that doll, (the black doll), ugly", the children responded, "Because she's black." When asked, "Why is that doll, (the black doll), bad", the children responded, "Because she's black." When Dr. Clark asked the children, "Would you give me the doll that looks more like you?", they handed him the black doll.

Repeat of Dr. Kenneth Clark's famous doll experiment televised during MSNBC's 2008 documentary, "A Conversation About Race"
https://www.youtube.com/watch?v=WG7U1QsUd1g

In order to see whether the results of the experiment would be different approximately some fifty years later, in her 2005 short documentary, "A Girl Like Me", Kiri Davis, an African American teenager, repeated Dr. Clark's experiment with twenty-one African American children. Fifteen of the twenty-one children in Ms. Davis' experiment preferred the white doll.

Ms. Davis' film begins with interviews of a number of young African American teenage women concerning their feelings about the color of their skin and the texture of their hair.

A Girl Like Me, Kiri Davis
http://www.understandingrace.org/lived/video/

The 1961 Ricky Nelson song, "Travelin' Man", which was a gigantic hit on the American Pop charts when I was eight, very clearly illustrates the reality of black undesirability. In it, Nelson describes himself as a "travelin' man" who on his many stops the world over, has a girlfriend, in every port, a "pretty seniorita", a "cute little Eskimo", a "sweet Fraulein", a "China Doll", and a "pretty Polynesian Baby":

Travelin' Man, Ricky Nelson
http://www.youtube.com/watch?v=0janfcZ8LUw.

The absence of **any** reference to African women in those lyrics, is just one of **countless** social messages which over many generations, has communicated the lesson that compared to **all** of the Earth's people, African People, (in this case African **women** specifically), are the least **attractive** and in part for that reason, the least **desirable**. Indeed, I believe that most people can't even **imagine** a verse in the song about a beautiful African woman. Actually at that time, the verse would've referred to a pretty **Negro** girl. All of the women of color in the song were fine, but it was **unthinkable** to include a black woman in such lyrics. [105]

That same message has been present for several centuries **in** many cultures, and **from** countless sources. The story of John Smith's falling in love with Pocahontas is well known. The thought of his falling in love with an **African** woman would, I suspect, be unimaginable to most.

The plot of Rogers and Hammerstein's musical, "South Pacific", in which a European American man ostensibly fell in love and had

---

105 Women of other races are also not mentioned in the song, including Indian women, Indigenous women and Middle Eastern women. Based upon American society's traditional standard of beauty, however, not unlike the women in the song, those groups of women could **also** well have been considered exotic and pretty. My belief, therefore, is that **their** omission did **not** result from bias. Additionally, I fully acknowledge what some may describe as at least the distastefulness of Nelson's descriptions of the women named in the song.

children with a Polynesian woman, was believable even in the 1940's and 50's, when it was written and produced. The thought of a European man falling in love and having children with an **African** woman, however, was at that **same** time, probably absurd.

The unique undesirability of the physical appearance of African People and people of African descent has, of course, been communicated in many more ways than the exclusion of black women from white men's romantic attention. [106] It is present in the lyrics of songs, in television shows, in movies, in art, in literature, in comedy, (in which the message often appears in a particularly ugly, hurtful, variety), and in every **other** genre of cultural communication.

Perhaps the **clearest** message of the distinct unattractiveness of the African face, however, is its persistent portrayal in popular culture, as the face of evil. There **are** many portrayals of evil in popular entertainment that are **not** African, among them Frankenstein and Dracula come to mind; and I've **never** seen a black werewolf, a black witch or a black warlock in either movie or television depictions. But from Star Trek's many dark-skinned non-human monsters, including its humanoid unethical, unscrupulous, money-hungry brown-skinned Ferengies, to the portrayal of the devil as a black man in the 2013 History Channel mini-series, "The Bible", there is an **undeniable** pattern within popular culture, of using dark skin and African facial features as the face of evil. That pattern of portraying evil as African in appearance, which then unfailingly makes its way into all of our subconscious minds, was, not **wholly**, but to a **large** degree, likely responsible for much of the negative response to the depiction of Jesus Christ as a black man in Jean Claude LaMarre's 2006 film, "Color of the Cross." The portrayal in popular culture of evil

[106] The fact that there have historically been many more cultural stories of Caucasian men in relationships with Women of Color, than Men of Color in relationships with Caucasian women, is also worthy of serious analysis, touching as it does, on the intersection of racism and sexism.

as dark in human form, **combined with** the many references to darkness as negative and undesirable in the English language, makes the idea of Christ as a black person, at least for millions of English speakers, not only an oxymoron, but also utterly offensive.

> [Robert B. Moore's essay, "Racism in the English Language", quite clearly describes the many **other** ways in which darkness assumes the connotation of badness, evil and general undesirability in the English language. Quoting Moore, "An integral part of any culture is its language. Language not only develops in conjunction with a society's historical, economic and political evolution; it also reflects that society's attitudes and thinking. Language not only expresses ideas and concepts but actually shades thought.] [107]
>
> **Robert B. Moore's essay, "Racism in the English Language"**
> http://www.femi.pwp.blueyonder.co.uk/race.htm
> http://www.residential-life.unh.edu/diversity/aw_article14.pdf]

Tragically, People of Color in many places **around the world**, among them, India, Brazil, the Caribbean, and the United States, have demonstrated the internalization of the message of our physical unattractiveness in a number of ways, perhaps the most

[107] I do not believe that darkness and evil were **deliberately** made synonymous in the English language in order to demonize People of Color. I **do** believe, however, that: 1. Their being synonymous resulted, over time as the language developed, from a deep-seated, often unconscious view in the minds of many of its earliest speakers, of darkness as both negative and dangerous; and that, 2. Just as the **concept** of darkness became associated with negativity and danger, tragically, dark **people** became unconsciously associated with them as well.

obvious of which is colorism, the same colorism that I experienced at Rivers Frederick Junior High School in the mid-1960's.[108]

In cultures in which arranged marriages occur, the intendeds' skin color is often among the most important considerations in the parents' determination of the suitability of their child's spouse. The lighter her/his skin, the more desirable is s/he. The darker his/her skin, the less desirable. One of what was for me, the most dramatic illustrations of that fact, occurred during the question and answer period of a keynote address that I delivered in the late 1990's at The University of Amman in Amman, Jordan. The subject of the address was multiculturalism and American anti-discrimination laws. Following my talk, one of the first comments came from a female student on my right in the very back of the auditorium, "Well", she began, "Racism is an American problem. We don't have that issue in our culture because our religion, (Islam), teaches us to love each other unconditionally." The **instant** that student completed her sentence, the hand of another young woman on the other side of the auditorium shot up, "Yes, well, we **are** taught that", she remarked, "But you know that when it's time for our brothers to marry, our mothers start looking for a pretty, light-skinned, girl for them."[109]

---

[108] It isn't only People of Color who practice colorism. European Americans do as well. I am noticeably lighter in complexion than Barbara. After eleven years, I can no longer count how many times after Barbara has asked a question of a white person, a store clerk, for example, the person looks at and speaks to me. In those situations, as the person is looking at me, I begin and continue to look at Barbara, essentially **forcing** the person to look at her. It happens consistently. Barbara is somewhat stoic about it, but it hurts me **deeply** to see her, such a good person, treated that way.

[109] Colorism has a definite gender component in that it is often more important for women rather than men, to be light-skinned. Darker skin is generally more acceptable in men than in women. The **consistent** television portrayal of heterosexual African American couples in which the woman is lighter-skinned than her male partner/

The self-perception that based upon one's race, one is ugly, **combined** with the knowledge that most other people **share** that perception, is extremely painful.

2. Intellectual Inferiority

The second societal message of our presumed inferiority that Americans of Color have historically received and that many of us have also internalized in varying degrees, is that **we are intellectually inferior to European Americans**. According to our human racial story, skin color is **inextricably** linked to intelligence. The lighter one's skin, the more intelligent is s/he. The darker one's skin, the less intelligent. Thus, in our racial story, Caucasian human beings, in addition to being more **physically** attractive, are also more **intelligent** than People of Color.

Sadly but not surprisingly, as with the message of **physical attractiveness**, in **this** message as well, Africans and their descendents have a place of **singular** inferiority. According to this message, because Africans and their descendants have some of the darkest **skin** on Earth, we have the least amount of **intelligence** of all of the people on the Earth as well. [110]

---

spouse and the almost **non-existent** portrayal of such couples in which the woman is darker-skinned than her male partner/spouse, unquestionably indicates the gender factor that, is present within colorism. The analysis of the sexism underlying that phenomenon, as well as the intersection of racism and sexism within it, are worthy of continuing study and understanding.

[110] Some people of southern India have skin that is darker than that of the average African, but because (most) Indians have straight hair and often European facial features, in the world's racial story, Africans are considered inferior to Indians, despite the darker complexion of some Indian People.

The story of the intellectual inferiority of one's racial group is one of **the** most negatively destructive messages possible to the human psyche, to human self-confidence and to human self-esteem. Psychological studies that demonstrate that teachers' low expectations of students' intellectual abilities immediately and dramatically affect students' academic performance, clearly tell the story. When groups of people are told over a long period of time, in a myriad of ways and from a variety of sources to which they are regularly exposed, that they are much less intelligent than other human beings, over time, they unfailingly both perform and behave consistently with that expectation. That "Pygmalion Effect" is certainly in large measure responsible for the achievement gap between American Children of Color and Caucasian American children."[111]

I can no longer count on two hands, the number of African American adults who, in a diversity workshop, have shared with the group during the session that in seeking help from their high school guidance counselor with the college application process, were told that they were probably going to "wind up" doing some kind of blue collar, manual labor job so there was no point in their even **thinking** about college. All of the people who shared that story with me were college-educated professionals.

I am not sure it is possible to make one whose group does **not** carry the badge of intellectual inferiority, **truly** understand what that badge feels like, and what it can do to the **soul** of an intelligent human being born into brown or black skin.

3. Historical Irrelevance

The third societal message of our presumed inferiority that Americans of Color have historically received, is that **we have contributed nothing of significance, nothing of value, to the**

[111] The Pygmalion Effect is the theory that human beings perform and behave in the way that others **expect** us to.

human species. The underlying tenet of this message is that **Caucasians** made the world what it is today. They made all of the major discoveries and all of the significant inventions that took the human species from the pre-Industrial to the Industrial Age. They and they alone discovered electricity, mapped the globe and then circumnavigated it, invented radio, television, cars, airplanes, space ships, computers and virtually everything else of value to the world. As the story goes, People of Color have merely existed on the sidelines and are now simply the **benefactors** of at least a century of Caucasian genius. That belief is held by both many millions of Caucasian People, and even more sadly by many millions of People of Color around the world as well.

All of us, those of us who are not of European ancestry as well as those of us who are, have received that message all our lives in history books, in Hollywood films in television shows, in art, in literature, and in a host of other genres,

Fortunately, it is simultaneously true for a number of groups of color, that even if they **have** been the victims of horribly racist portrayals in history books, in Hollywood films and many other sources, **the people themselves**, have a history of cultural traditions and achievement of which they are proud and of which they teach their **children** to be proud. Many Indigenous People, for example, as well as many people of Asian and Australian cultures, know that they have a very rich past of both cultural traditions **and achievements**, knowledge of which has been passed down to their children, through their oral histories.

It is a tragic reality that with respect to this third message, the message of historic insignificance, (just as is true of the first two messages of physical ugliness and intellectual inferiority), African People and people of African descent carry a unique burden. It is the burden that **unlike** various **other** People of Color, many millions of us are **totally** ignorant of the fact that we **too** have a cultural history, both an **African** and an African **American** history, of which we can be exceedingly proud. The "slave curtain" that came crashing down on us in the early 16th century, cut us off from information about the achievements of the great civilizations of our African forbears. Our history, as far as many of us know, can be summed up by the following sentence: "We were savages, then slaves." We have invented nothing, discovered nothing, and generally speaking, have **contributed** nothing to the human species." **That**, tragically, is the overall picture that **many** (but I sincerely hope a diminishing number of) African Americans have of our history.

> [Sometime in the 1970's, I watched a television show in which a small group of African American and European American middle school students were having a conversation. At some point, the conversation became heated. The first verbal jab thrown out with a smirk by one of the European American kids to the African American kids was, "What have your people ever contributed to the world except fried chicken and grass huts?" The African American kids were **totally** unable to answer the rhetorical question, and thus absolutely incapable of verbally responding to the implied insult. Their hurt, however, was obvious. One of them simply reacted by dropping his books to the ground and physically attacking the European American kid who asked the question. That was **one** scene in a television show that I saw **over thirty years ago**, but which I've never forgotten. It has remained very clearly etched in my memory over these many years because **in that moment**, in the very moment in which I heard the question, I felt the pain. While in truth, I could very well have answered the question with, "Well you got a few hours so I can at least **start** the list?", followed by a substantive, content-rich response, I felt the same pain that was portrayed in the scene by the African American kids. It is a pain, I believe, which is familiar to **millions** of people of African descent. Despite the fact that I now know enough about both African and African American history to be extremely proud of both, the knowledge that our achievements are so widely viewed through a lens which in the minds of many **may** be summed up as "fried

chicken and grass huts", can be at most, painful and at least, frustrating.]

There is an agonizing mental ache that results from having been taught, largely through omission, that people of your race have contributed nothing to human history, that your race has no famous engineers, no accomplished architects, no creative inventors, no brilliant scientists, no gifted physicians, no notable attorneys. The ache stems from both your **own** belief, and your knowledge that the majority of people in the society in which you **live**, believe that people of your race have not contributed to the family of humanity in **any** way. The ache stems from being a member of a group which is widely regarded as unintelligent, lacking in any historical achievements and indeed, uncivilized prior to their exposure to Europeans.

4. Social Deviance

When many, and I believe perhaps the majority of Americans hear the words, "black neighborhood", or "Hispanic neighborhood", whether the neighborhood is in the U.S. or the Caribbean, they are accompanied by the thoughts, "poverty", "welfare", "food stamps", "drugs", "crime", "high school drop outs", "teen pregnancy", "sexual promiscuity", "domestic abuse', "absent fathers" and the list goes on and on. What is for many either denied or unknown as direct causes of much of the dysfunction of black and brown neighborhoods racked by such challenges, is the bright, arrow straight line between our history of slavery, the history of employment discrimination against black and brown people, the history of housing discrimination against black and brown people, the history of discrimination in education against black and brown people, the role played by white flight out of cities in the 1960's and 70's,[112] the fact that beginning in 1973 when the draft ended, the hundreds of thousands of young brown and black

---

112 An internet search of the phrase, "The role of white flight in urban blight" results in much enlightening information in this area.

men who had formerly been drafted into the military no longer had that "ticket out", and the drugs which were shipped into the United States, taken off the ships and brought into black and brown neighborhoods by non-black and brown people. In the minds of millions of European Americans, our communities that are dysfunctional in those ways **are** so, not in part due to **any** of those factors. In their minds, they are that way because the people who **reside** in them, are of low intelligence, lazy, criminally inclined, sexually promiscuous and irresponsible. Furthermore, we **are** all of those things because we are **genetically** inclined to be.

The result of having received the four specific messages over the course of one's lifetime that:

1. You and your group are both **physically unattractive and genetically inferior**—and in the case of Africans and people of African descent, you aren't even as **human** as other people;

2. You and your group are intellectually inferior to other human beings;

3. Your group has **contributed** nothing to the human race, and;

4. Your group is socially deviant in every measurable way,

is that **millions,** (although I do not believe the majority) of Americans of Color live with a lack of self-confidence and a lack of respect for their racial group. This is the Person of Color who, sadly, has in his/her mind, a lot to prove to the world—that they are not dumb, or lazy, or violent, or angry, or ill-mannered. It is a tremendously heavy psychological burden. In its most extreme variety, the four messages result in a deep-seated self-hatred.

That self-hatred has historically manifested in many, as shame in being a member of one's race. With regard specifically to many African Americans, in order to make the case that we have **some** degree of human legitimacy, the shame sometimes takes the form of a claim that we have a white grandmother or a white great grandfather, or some other white ancestor.[113]

"Internalized oppression" is the term often applied to that self-hatred. It is the psychological effect of being a member of a group which is considered physically undesirable, intellectually inferior, historically irrelevant, and socially deviant. It is one of **the** most crippling consequences of racism for Americans of Color.

The fact that internalized oppression **is** one of the most powerful effects of historical racism for Americans of Color, makes it **incredibly** ironic that it is also **the** aspect of racism about which I believe **most** European Americans are least aware. That lack of awareness of both the **existence** of internalized oppression and the **effect** that it has both **historically** had and **continues** to have in the lives of millions of Americans of Color, has, I believe, significantly impacted how millions of European Americans have viewed, felt about and judged Americans of Color. Specifically, the lack of awareness of the reality of internalized oppression, while not being exclusively **responsible** for, has in large measure, **contributed**, to what I believe is for **many** European Americans, a sometimes utter lack of compassion for the experiences of their sisters and brothers of color.

D. The Practice of Racism Against People and Americans of Color

On the exterior, practical level, the practice of racism over the past six hundred years, has been largely responsible for three

---

113 Interestingly, the American history of slavery makes quite likely, the possibility that the African American person making the claim may **indeed** have an ancestor, most likely a **male** ancestor, of European descent. The topic is discussed in further detail in Section III above, "The Fundamental Truth About Race: Africans are the Parents of Humanity. We *All* Began as African.

phenomena which have had a radical effect on our human culture the world over:

1. Slavery

Slavery has existed within the human species for thousands of years, and much more often **within** races than **between** them. Perhaps the most well-known history of slavery in the **ancient** world is that of the enslavement of Jewish people in Egypt that lasted for four hundred years, accompanied by much of both the kind and level of cruelty and inhumane treatment as were practiced in the institutions of slavery which have existed in the **present** millennium.

The most well-known institution of slavery **within the past six hundred years**, is the Trans-Atlantic Slave Trade in which West African People were shipped to North and South America and to islands all over the Caribbean and enslaved for life. While in much of my discussion of slavery, I am referring to the **entire** trans-Atlantic slave trade; my **concentration** will be on the institution of slavery which existed specifically in the United States. Many variations of human slavery have existed the world over, throughout our history as a species. The Egyptians, the Romans and the Greeks, all practiced it. In the modern era, the 17th century, specifically, a number of African and Indigenous cultures accepted slavery as a legitimate social institution. Within their cultures, they exchanged slaves, (often members of rival tribes caught in battle), as commodities. The treatment and status of the enslaved varied greatly among societies. In some, the captive was enslaved for only a pre-determined period of time. In others, the enslavement lasted for life, but was not passed on to the captive's progeny.

In the 17th century, however, Europeans introduced into the institution of slavery, two very distinct phenomena, both of which **drastically** changed how it was practiced. First, they made slavery inheritable. For what may have been the first time in four thousand years, since the slavery of the Jews in Egypt, a human being could be **born** a slave. Second, they introduced what the world had never before seen—**an international market economy for labor.** That market was the product of a voracious demand for workers required by the colonial plantation societies of the era. It was that enormous demand for free labor all over the Americas that caused the enslavement of African human beings to be one of the most intractable institutions in American history. Meeting that same voracious demand for free labor was what millions of European American men were both **willing to** and indeed **did** die for—to have the South secede from the United States and form a new nation—a slave nation.

2. Colonization

With few exceptions, most notably China among them, almost **all** of the places on the Earth in which People of Color lived, North America, Central America, South America, all of **islands** of the Americas,(i.e., the entire Western Hemisphere), the entire continent of Australia, vast parts of Asia, the entire sub-continent of India and almost the whole continent of Africa, were violently invaded, conquered declared to be the property of and subsequently colonized, (i.e., unilaterally ruled), by a handful of European nations, and under their rule, the colonized people were horribly oppressed.

The United States' acquisition of the Hawaiian Islands is no exception. It was achieved through a violent, military campaign lead by Captain James Cook in which hundreds of thousands of Indigenous Hawaiian People were killed. Today, of all of the islands' many and very multicultural inhabitants, it is the Native Hawaiian people who by far, lives in the poorest and most squalid conditions.

Tragically, what occurred in Hawaii was not uncommon. The vast majority of the Earth's islands were invaded, and taken over by European colonizers, all, of course, against the will of their indigenous inhabitants.

European colonization of much of the world began near the turn of the 16th century. With respect to Africa specifically, European colonization of the continent is often referred to by historians as, "The Scramble for Africa." During that scramble, which occurred in the latter half of the 19th century, the large European powers, England, France, Portugal, Germany, Belgium and Italy, made what was essentially a mad dash for the continent. At the conclusion, Europe's formal holdings included the entire African continent with the exception of Liberia, Ethiopia, and Saguia el-Hamra, the latter being eventually integrated into Spanish Sahara. By 1914, only Liberia in West Africa and Ethiopia in East Africa, were independent of European control. Between 1885 and 1914, Britain had taken **nearly thirty percent** of Africa's population under its control.

By the end of the nineteenth century, Europe had added to its overseas colonial possessions, almost nine million square miles—**one-fifth of the land area of the Earth**. The well-known adage, "The Sun never sets on the British Empire", was the result of colonial Great Britain's hold of the entire sub-Asian continent of India, much of the continent of Africa, the entire continent of Australia, and scores of islands around the world. It was literally true that the sun was always shining **somewhere** in the British Empire. Britain was to the seventeenth, eighteenth and nineteenth centuries, what Rome was to ancient Eurasia and North Africa. With respect to the many civilizations they overthrew, occupied, annexed and ruled, England and much of the rest of Europe was, during this period, akin to the 1980's Pac-Man video game.

When the British began their colonization of Australia in 1788, the Aboriginal People of Australia lived throughout the entire continent. The majority. however lived along the coasts. Upon their invasion of the continent, the British, under the principle of Terra nullius, (a Latin expression meaning "land belonging to no one", or "no man's land"), claimed the extremely desirable coasts of the continent for themselves, proclaiming essentially, that Australia's coastal regions were largely uninhabited and belonged to no one. Subsequently, the British pushed the Aboriginal People into the Outback, the continent's interior, desert areas, then took over and occupied the entire rest of the continent. Additionally, in order to diminish Aboriginal culture, the British government, for decades, removed Aboriginal children from their parents and placed them in either mission schools or with white families. Today, the Aboriginal People of Australia, **in every measurable category**, live a quality of life that is **remarkably** lower than that of white Australians. Of all of Australia's inhabitants, it is the Aboriginal People who live in the worst conditions, with the highest rate of infant mortality, the lowest rate of educational achievement, the highest unemployment, the highest illness, the highest incarceration, and the lowest life-expectancy rates. In essence, it is the Aboriginal People, overwhelmingly, who live, **in their homeland**, in poverty with all of its accompanying results.

> [On June 3, 1992, in a landmark decision, the High Court of Australia overturned the legal fiction of terra nullius. The ruling has enabled **some** Aboriginal People to reclaim limited amounts of territory which had been stolen from them under the terra nullius doctrine. The court's 1992 ruling has led to numerous lawsuits seeking either the transfer or restoration of land ownership rights to the Aboriginal People. As a consequence, Aboriginal People have regained their former lands in approximately 3,000 agreements. The Noonkanbah people, for example, were recognized in 1994 as the traditional owners of a 699 square mile plot of land in the Western part of the continent. Aboriginal People have also regained significant sections of their continent's Northern Territory, including much of its coastline.]

The Maori, the indigenous people of New Zealand, share the same tragic history of European invasion and conquer. Like the indigenous Hawaiians, the Aboriginal Australians, the indigenous and black people of the Caribbean islands and the indigenous people of most of the **other** islands across the planet, the Maori people are their nation's poorest and most politically, socially and economically disenfranchised.

Portugal colonized what we know today as the country of Brazil. Spain colonized the totality of the remainder of Central and South America, while England and France colonized most of what is now Canada, and the United States.

The European invaders divided among themselves as they wished, the lands they conquered, and then assigned them names. Most of those nations remained colonized **for more than two hundred years**. [114]

Among the most devastating consequences of colonization, were the economic and psychological tolls that it took on the people of the colonized lands.

Colonized people lost **all** of their economic autonomy. Throughout the centuries of colonization, the colonized lands' immense resources—salt in India, diamonds in South Africa, cocoa in Ghana, sugar in the West Indies, and in those and other countries, gold, silver, copper and ivory, were mined, stripped from their lands and shipped to England, France, Spain, Portugal, Holland and all of Europe's other colonial powers. The colonizers often used the forced labor of the colonized people themselves, to mine and strip their own lands. Throughout the centuries of colonization, the **colonizing** nations became richer and richer, while the **colonized** nations became poorer and poorer. That history of the abject pillaging of nations of color was as significant an economic **ad**vantage for the European colonizers as it was an economic **dis**advantage for the colonized nations of color. That history continues, **to this day**, to account, in large measure, for the severe imbalance of wealth which presently exists between the former European colonizers and their former colonies.

---

[114] Indonesia, invaded by the Dutch in 1600, was colonized for over 350 years, one of the longest periods of colonization in history.

The **psychological** toll of colonization was internalized oppression. The internalized oppression resulted from the people of the colonized countries having been taught that European culture represented the apex of human achievement, and thus, that their **own** culture was grossly **inferior** to European culture. Furthermore, those who were colonized received the message that **as human beings**, they **themselves** were grossly inferior to Europeans. They were taught that for that reason, European colonization was in their best interest because their European colonizers were bringing civilization to them.[115]

At the end of the colonial era, while the indigenous people of the formerly colonized nations had regained **political** control of their countries, much of the ownership of **their physical lands**, as well as control of the vast majority of their nations' **wealth**, were still in the hands of the former colonizers' descendants, their countries' Caucasian citizens.

As a species, we were as late as the 1990's, **still** trying to "de-colonialize" the planet. The nation of Namibia did not gain its independence after years of colonization by the government of South Africa until 1990. European colonialism in Africa did not end until 1994, when black South Africans overthrew the Dutch-controlled South African apartheid government. In 1997, England returned Shanghai, by population, the largest city in the world, to Chinese control. At the turn of the 21st century, in 1999, Portugal returned Macau to China, one of China's two special administrative regions which had been under Portuguese colonial rule since the 1800's. That same year, the government of Zimbabwe was also still attempting to undue the wrongs of **its** colonial past. Its specific objective was to redress much of the loss of land and resulting economic injustice suffered by its African

[115] The indigenous people of Africa and India **eventually** regained control of their lands. The indigenous People of Australia, of North, Central and South America, and of many the world's islands, however, including Hawaii, lost their lands, and thus their geographical autonomy, sadly, perhaps, forever.

citizens throughout the country's long history of colonialism. It initiated what was referred to as the "fast track land reform" program, the objective of which was to transfer from Caucasian farmers to African citizens, 4,000 farms located on prime farmland, covering over forty-two thousand miles.

In view of the **centuries** of colonialism during which nations of brown and black people around the world were stripped of much of their countries' natural wealth and the people themselves languished in poverty and lack of education, it is absolutely not surprising that when in the second half of the twentieth century, the developing world's formerly colonized, newly independent nations of color attempted, for the first time, to join the world community of nations on an equal footing, they were **severely** disadvantaged in **every** imaginable way, socially, educationally, technologically and of course, economically.

Having acknowledged the tragic history of **colonialism**, it is important to **also** acknowledge that both India and much of the African continent have tragic **post**-colonial histories as well. India's era of colonization was followed by a war between Hindus and Muslims and the ultimate separation of the nation into two **separate** nations, India for Hindus and Pakistan for Muslims. The amount of human pain and suffering that resulted from both the war **and** the separation, is unfathomable.

On the African continent, colonization was followed by an era in which many **totally** corrupt leaders of some of the newly independent nations kept their countries in **insufferable** poverty decade after decade, (by among other things, either squandering or stealing billions of dollars of foreign aid), during which real progress **could** have been made for their people. The unequivocally **devastating** impact of the misconduct of those African leaders on the present-day, relative lack of economic development of their countries cannot be understated. It is **truly** deplorable, especially since, **unlike** the colonizers, **it was their own countries, their own people,** whom they were oppressing. The malfeasance of those African leaders is **undeniably** a chapter of their nations' histories which intellectual honesty requires that we **fully** acknowledge.[116] **However**, if we are to **truly** understand the present-day extreme inequality in the distribution of wealth among the world's Caucasian nations and its nations of color, intellectual honesty requires, additionally, that we both are aware of **and acknowledge** that the European colonization of nations of color which existed for centuries **before** the era of their corrupt native leaders, is also a **significant** contributor to the present enormous economic inequality between the world's nations of color, and its Caucasian nations.[117]

3. Discrimination—Harassment—Violence

Immediately following the one hundred seventy-five years of American slavery, **ninety-nine years** of abject, often **state sanctioned** discrimination **agains**t, harassment **of**, and violence **toward** Americans of Color began. Those ninety-nine years were 1865 to 1964. In 1865, the 13th amendment, which outlawed human slavery, was passed. In1964, the Civil Rights Act, which outlawed discrimination based upon race, color, national origin, gender and religion, was passed.

During those ninety-nine years, millions of extremely hard working city-dwelling European American immigrants and their descendants began to reap the benefits of all of their hard work

---

116 The many African droughts of the 20th century also contributed significantly to the current poverty of a number of African nations.

117 If we are either unaware of or in denial about the history of colonization suffered by many nations of color around the world, we are left to unconsciously assume that the people of those nations are today poor only because their leaders are corrupt and the people themselves are unintelligent, lethargic human beings who innately lack both the intelligence and the will to live a better life. Sadly, I believe that millions of people around the world do indeed, at least unconsciously, believe just that.

in the cities. They made steady progress from one generation to the next, many moving by the middle of the 20th century, out of city slums and poverty, into the suburbs and middle class. A small minority even moved into wealth.

Immediately after slavery, during the era of reconstruction, numerous African American communities also made tremendous gains. A number of African Americans were even elected to Congress during the time.[118] Many African American inventors had been issued patents for their inventions. [119] The residents of many African American communities were building schools for the education of their succeeding generations, and a number of African American communities were beginning to thrive economically.

Then, **even before the end of reconstruction**, an **unrelenting** campaign of discrimination, harassment and violence against black and other communities of color soon began. It was a campaign of among other things, intimidation, threats, burnings, lynchings, laws which restricted the physical movement of African Americans, laws requiring African Americans to work for European American plantation owners, and then **only** in agriculture, laws requiring segregated schools, laws requiring segregated public accommodations, and practices which segregated neighborhoods At the beginning of that reign of terror, the significant progress that was being steadily made by newly-freed African Americans,

---

118 More African Americans, some of whom were formerly enslaved, were elected to the U.S. House of Representatives in the years immediately following the Civil War than at any other time until the 1960's.

119 The work that African Americans performed during slavery, assisted them, in all likelihood, in developing the considerable number of inventions for which they received patents after the Civil War. They had done the work, thus it was they who knew what was needed to make that work faster and more efficient. See Note Two for additional information on African American inventors.

was beginning to come under attack. That oppression lasted another **ninety-nine** years until the passage of the Civil Rights Act of 1964. The tragic result was that during that period, 1865 to 1964, the progress of African Americans and other Americans of Color, **paled** in comparison to that made by European Americans. As Americans of Color, we lost **a full century** of educational, employment, and political progress. As a **nation**, we lost a full century of potential racial healing and thus, social progress. I can only try to **imagine** the progress that African Americans and other Americans of Color would have made, **but for** the abject oppression under which we lived during that ninety-nine year reign of terror. I can only imagine where, **as a nation**, we would be today in race relations and social maturity.

The following is but a thumbnail **sketch** of the history of the discrimination, harassment and violence that were visited upon various American populations of color from the time of the arrival of the earliest European explorers to the Western Hemisphere in the 1500's, to the present [120]

a. All People of Color

Under the United States Naturalization Law of 1790, **no** People of Color of **any** race were allowed to be citizens of the United States. The original law allowed only immigrants who were free white persons and of good moral character to become naturalized citizens. It excluded from citizenship, **all**, Indigenous People, all **enslaved** people of African descent, all **free** people of African descent, and all **Asian** People. The law even prohibited indentured servants of **European** descent from being naturalized.

---

[120] The histories of the American groups of color provided in this section are exemplary, not exhaustive, representing only a small snapshot of the actual histories.

b. Indigenous People of the Western Hemisphere

> [With reference to the term, "Americans", people who are indigenous to the Western Hemisphere are truly the very **first** Americans. Many of the West's Indigenous People think of themselves as Americans and are indeed, **loyal** Americans. I refer to the people who are indigenous to the Western Hemisphere as "Indigenous", however, because **some** Indigenous people do not refer to the West as "the Americas". "The Americas" were named for Italian explorer Amerigo Vespucci, who was the first to identify North, Central and South America as separate land masses from Asia. (Christopher Columbus thought, until the end of his life, that North, Central and South America were the eastern edge of Asia.) Since it was the ancestors of Indigenous People who **actually** "discovered" the Western Hemisphere, however, it Indigenous People who are arguably more "American" than all other Americans.]

Before the arrival of Christopher Columbus to the Western Hemisphere, the population of human beings that were indigenous to what we now refer to as North, Central and South America, developed three of the most highly advanced civilizations in human history—the Aztecs, the Mayans and the Incas. Each had accomplishments in science, mathematics, astronomy and engineering that demonstrated a **highly**—advanced level of intellectual sophistication. Extremely advanced **pre**-Incan civilizations also existed, such as the Cahokia and the Tiwanaku, among others. For four hundred years, between 500 and 900 AD, Tiwanaku, (the name of both the people and their largest municipality), was the capital of one of the largest, most commanding kingdoms of the southern Andes.

Information on the Tiwanaku culture
http://whc.unesco.org/en/list/567

When Columbus arrived in the Western Hemisphere, **millions** of Indigenous People lived in North, Central and South America and on many of their islands. They lived in communities on land which they had occupied for thousands of years,[121] providing for all of their food, clothing, shelter and medical needs, and practicing their rich cultural and spiritual traditions. Prior to the arrival of Europeans to the Americas, its Indigenous People were independent and totally self-sufficient. They were autonomous and free.

After the arrival in the Western Hemisphere of Columbus, **then**, of hundreds and perhaps thousands of other European explorers, **then**, of thousands upon thousands of European immigrants, **then** of the subsequent founding of the United States, Indigenous People eventually lived on their land in only those places that had been designated or reserved for them by the American government, land we now refer to as "reservations". Since the land on which they were placed was frequently desert land, to provide for their food and clothing needs, Indigenous People from then on no longer hunted. They no longer fished. They no longer grew crops. Instead, on the reservations, they were provided government food rations. In the final analysis, after the arrival of Columbus and other explorers from Europe, Indigenous People were stripped of their self-sufficiency and with it, their dignity. Most important of all, perhaps, they were stripped of their geography autonomy—they lost dominion over their land, their home.

"Over the last 200 years, Indigenous People have been forced-marched onto reservations, their cultures deliberately eradicated, and their quality of life impoverished. Over the last **150** years, the government has tried a series of conflicting methods of dealing with Indigenous People—declaring war on them, **making** treaties with them, **breaking** treaties with them, sending them to Oklahoma, forcing them **onto** reservations, forcing them **off** of reservations, permitting them to own land collectively, forcing them to divide the land into individual plots, dispatching their

[121] Expert estimates of how long Indigenous People had occupied the Americas prior to the arrival of Columbus, range from 14,000 to 20,000 years.

children to boarding schools hundreds of miles from home, closing the boarding schools and sending the children home, outlawing the practice of their religions, and legalizing practice of those religions."

Washington Post magazine Sunday July 18, 1999

Genocide

Sources vary, but researchers have estimated that from six to twenty five million Indigenous People lived in the United States before the arrival of Christopher Columbus**. After** his arrival, millions of Indigenous People were killed by Europeans in all three Americas and many Caribbean islands in massacre after massacre. According to the most recent census, there are now less than three million Indigenous People in the United States. The documentary, The documentary, "The Canary Effect" focuses on genocidal practices aimed at Indigenous People.

The Canary Effect:
http://topdocumentaryfilms.com/canary-effect/

Many European colonists wanted for themselves, the land which they had newly found, and thus wanted Indigenous People out of their way. They hunted them with dogs. They killed thousands of them by mass poisoning. They destroyed Indigenous People's fishing villages and canoes. They went miles up from their communities and blocked their supply of water from brooks and streams. They burned to the ground, their corn and other agrarian fields.

In **their** attempt to exterminate Indigenous People, the British used starvation and massacre as their primary weapons. During part of the 18th and throughout the majority of the 19th centuries, thousands and by some accounts **hundreds** of thousands of Indigenous People were the victims of such massacres, often referred to as, "The "Indian Wars". The following is but a small representative sample of those wars:

* **The Arawak Massacre—1492**
The Spaniards, under the direction of Christopher Columbus, slaughtered tens of thousands of Indigenous People of the tribes collectively known as the Arawaks, who inhabited the islands which later became known as the Bahamas. Those whom they did not kill, they took from their home lands, re-settled them in other locations, and separated their families. That treatment, combined with the arrival of smallpox and other diseases from Europe, nearly wiped out the entire Arawak population. A very small number of Arawak People are alive today, and are passing on their traditional culture to their children.

* **The Napituca Massacre—October, 1539**
After defeating their resistance, Hernando de Soto had two hundred Napituca People executed in a large-scale massacre of Indigenous People by Europeans on what later became American soil.

* **The Tiguex Massacres—1541-1542**
Spanish invaders seized the homes, food and clothing of the Tiguex People and raped Tiguex women. The Tiguex resisted, in response to which the Spanish burned fifty Tiguex People at the stake who had already surrendered.

* **The Cazcanes Massacre 1541-1542**.
The Cazcanes People of Mexico attempted to drive the Spaniards out of Mexico's Nueva Galicia area. In response, Spanish Viceroy Mendoza assembled some 450 Spanish and approximately 30,000 Aztec and Tlaxcalan troops and snuffed out the Cazcanes' rebellion.[122] The reported result was the

---

[122] It was common in both the Americas and Africa, for the European invaders to recruit Indigenous and African People to assist them in battles against other Indigenous and African People. Those recruited

deaths of thousands of Cazcanes People and the enslavement of thousands of others who were forced to work in mines.

* **The Acoma Massacre—January, 1599**
Spaniard Juan de Oñate led a military expedition to retaliate for the killing of eleven Spanish solders by Indigenous People in New Mexico. During the three-day excursion, approximately 800 Acoma People were massacred. The King of Spain later punished Oñate for his actions.

* **The Pamunkey Peace Talks—May 12, 1623**
The British poisoned the wine that they gave to the leaders and other members of the Powhatan Tribe—at a Peace Conference. Approximately 200 Powhatan People died. The British then killed another fifty Powhatan by hand.

* **The Mystic Massacre—May 26, 1637**
British colonists, with assistance from the Indigenous Narragansett and Mohegan People, launched a night attack on a large village of Pequot People who lived on what is now Connecticut's Mystic River. The villagers were burned alive. Some 600 to 700 Pequot People were killed.

* **Phipps Proclamation—November 3, 1755**
The Proclamation read:

"Whereas the Tribe of Penobscot Indians have repeatedly in a perfidious manner acted contrary to their solemn submission unto his Majesty, long since mad and frequently renewed., I have therefore at the desire of the House of Representatives with the advice of his Majesty's Council, thought fit to issue the Proclamation and to declare the Penobscot tribe of Indians to be enemies, rebels, and traitors to his Majesty King George the Second."

---

were often members of tribes which were "enemies" of the tribes under attack, and were promised rewards, (usually goods of some kind), for assisting the invaders.

And I do hereby require his Majesty's subjects of this Province to embrace all opportunities of pursuing, captivating, killing and destroying all and every of the aforesaid Indians . . . ."

The proclamation continued by offering a bounty for the body of every Penobscot man woman and child brought from their territory in Maine which the English wanted for themselves. It read:

> "For every male Penobscot Indian above the age of twelve years that shall be taken within the time aforesaid and brought to Boston, fifty pounds.
>
> For every female Penobscot Indian taken and brought in as aforesaid and for every male Indian prisoner under the age of twelve years taken and brought in as aforesaid, twenty five pounds.
>
> For every scalp of such female Indian or male Indian under the age of twelve years that shall be killed and brought in as evidence of their being killed as aforesaid, twenty pounds.
>
> Given at the Council Chamber in Boston this third day of November, 1755 and in the twenty ninth year of the reign of our Sovereign Lord George the Second by the Grace of God of Great Britain, France and Ireland, Kind Defender of the Faith."

European bounty hunters began by transporting the bodies to Boston to get payment. The physical difficulty of transporting bodies that distance, however, soon became obvious, as a result of which the proclamation was changed to require the presentation of only the scalps of the Penobscot People for payment. The bloody red scalps became known as "red skins."[123]

---

[123] In view of the Phipps Proclamation and the scalping of an unknown number of Indigenous men women and children in which it resulted,

* **Gnadenhutten Massacre—March 8, 1772**
  Pennsylvania militiamen attacked, killed and scalped nearly one hundred peaceful Lenape People. They were Christian, and most, women and children. Only two young boys were spared.

* **The Chehaw Affair—April 22, 1818**
  Federal troops attacked a peaceful village of Muscogee People, killing approximately ten to fifty adults and children.

* **The Bloody Island Massacre—May 15, 1850**
  In retaliation for the killing of two Europeans who had been abusing and murdering the Pomo People near Clear Lake California, U.S. Army Officer Nathaniel Lyon and his U.S. Army unit murdered sixty to one-hundred of the Pomo People on Bo-no-po-ti Island near Clear Lake.

* **The Klamath River Massacres—January 22, 1855**
  European immigrants engaged in a "war of extermination" against the Indigenous People of Humboldt County, California. The war was in retaliation for the murder of six Europeans and the alleged theft of several of their cattle, by Indigenous People.

* **The Wiyot Massacre—February 26, 1860**
  During three simultaneous assaults on the Wiyot People, European immigrants of Humboldt County, California killed approximately 188 Wiyot People. The majority were women and children.

* **The Bear River Massacre—January 29, 1863**
  U.S. Army Colonel Patrick Connor, leading a contingent of U.S. Army troops, killed at least 200 Indigenous People near Preston, Idaho, men, women and children.

---

it is **extremely** ironic that it is **Indigenous** People who have the historical reputation of being scalpers.

* **The Sand Creek Massacre—November 29, 1864**
  At Sand Creek, Colorado, members of the Colorado Militia attacked a peaceful village of Cheyenne People, and killed at least 160 women, men and children.

* **Wounded Knee Massacre—December 29, 1890**
  128 Sioux children, men and women were killed at Wounded Knee, South Dakota by members of the U.S. 7th Calvary.

Slavery

When many Americans think of slavery, our minds create images of African People inhumanely crowded aboard ships and dying by the tens of thousands in passage from West Africa to the Americas. Others think of African Americans with bended backs, picking cotton in Southern fields. Our minds usually do not invoke images of **Indigenous** People chained in coffles and marched to ports, Boston, Massachusetts, Charleston, South Carolina and others, and subsequently shipped to other Atlantic ports. Yet, both the **enslavement** of Indigenous People and an Indigenous **slave trade** were quite pervasive in the early years of the United States. From ocean to ocean, and from Canada to Louisiana, tens of thousands of Indigenous Peoples were enslaved. Many were transported to lands distant from their homes. Significantly more Indigenous People were exported as slaves from Charleston, South Carolina, (to the West Indies, primarily), from 1670 to 1717, than were African People imported from West Africa to be enslaved. More than either disease or war, it was **slavery** that destroyed specifically, South Carolina's small coastal Indigenous tribes.

Attempts to Convert Indigenous People to Christianity

Over several centuries after the arrival of Columbus to the Americas, Europeans and European Americans made numerous attempts to change Indigenous Peoples' spiritual belief systems.

The goal was to convert them to Christianity. The history of Christian missionaries that engaged in such attempts is both long and sordid, complete with consequences of refusal to convert which included the cutting off of limbs and other physical torture, and the deprivation of food and water to entire villages. The history of the treatment that Indigenous People received in Christian missions and from missionaries in the 17th, 18th and 19th centuries, is one of the most painful stories of their post-Columbian fate.

The Taking of Indigenous Peoples' Land

* Indian Removal Act—signed into law by President Andrew Jackson on May 28, 1830. Indigenous American removal was supposed to be voluntary. The **practice**, however, was to put great pressure on Indigenous leaders to sign removal treaties. The result of the Indian Removal Act was the inevitable removal of the vast majority of Indigenous People from their homelands. Under the act, the Choctaw, Creek, Seminole, Cherokee, and Chickasaw people were all taken from their homelands. The ensuing relocations of Indigenous People were to primarily desolate locations which afforded them no viable means of self-support.

* The most infamous removal and relocation of Indigenous People that followed the Indian Removal Act was the Trail of Tears. The Trail of Tears was the movement and relocation from the Southeastern United States to the West, of thousands of Indigenous People. They were walked through several states, with thousands dying along the way from exposure, starvation and disease. The reported length of The Trail of Tears varies but it is documented to have been at least one thousand miles.

* The breaking by the United States government, of treaty after treaty with numerous Indigenous tribes for the **purchase** of their land.

* The subsequent wholesale and outright **taking** of Indigenous Peoples' land which they had occupied in both small and large communities for many thousands of years.

* One of the most recent relocations of Indigenous People was that of the Inuit People, commonly known as Eskimos, who, in the 1950's, were pressured by the Canadian government to leave their homes in northern Quebec. The Canadian government, without providing them adequate food, water and shelter, then transported the Inuit to the forbidding and isolated high Arctic in order to to declare Canadian dominion over the region. In essence, the government of Canada used the Inuit as "human flagpoles". In 1992, the Canadian government admitted that it violated the rights of the Inuit People in that incident, and officially apologized to them. In my research, I was unable to find any information on reparations to the Inuit People for that relocation.

Attempts to Assimilate Indigenous People

* In the late 1800's after all of the "Indian Wars" were over and almost all Indigenous People had been forcibly relocated to reservations, the United States government created boarding schools for Indigenous children. The schools were originally either principally run by or affiliated with Christian missionaries. It was commonly accepted at the time, that Indigenous children should be socialized to live in the general American society, i.e., taught to think and behave like European Americans. At the boarding schools, the children were forbidden to speak their native languages. Both boys and girls were required to cut their hair and wear it in the European style for children. The children were taught Christianity and simultaneously denied the right to practice their Indigenous religions. They were instructed in only European and American history, and forced in a number of other ways, to abandon their Indigenous American identities. The goal was for Indigenous children to adopt European-American culture as their own.

Many cases of physical, mental and sexual abuse at the schools were documented in the twentieth century. Tragically, some boarding schools remained in operation until the 1960's, even though abuse of students had been documented as early as the 1920's.

Discrimination

* Over the past sixty years, Indigenous communities, chiefly in the West, have been persistently exposed to low doses of radiation. The majority of all uranium deposits in the United States are located under the reservations on which Indigenous People live. Uranium enrichment, uranium mining and even the testing and production of nuclear weapons, all occur on Indigenous land. As a result of that amalgam of activities, radioactive waste disposal has occurred either on or near many reservation lands. Information on the possible effects on radiation exposure was often either incomplete or inaccessible to the Indigenous People in the affected regions.

* Indigenous People suffered at the local, state and Federal levels, the effects of "separate but equal" segregation **laws,** as well as the effects of **de facto** discrimination which resulted from discriminatory local, state and Federal **practices.** Thus, not unlike other American populations of color, until the passage of the Civil Rights Act of 1964, Indigenous People could not eat at segregated lunch counters, could not use segregated restrooms, could not drink from segregated water fountains and indeed in many instances, could neither be **in** nor travel safely **through** particular locales. The "White Only" signs and a "White Only" society-at-large, applied fully to Indigenous People.

Present Day Struggle for Dignity

* Indigenous People have historically been **dreadfully** depicted in art and stereotyped in American movies, television shows, and literature as stupid and backward, aggressive and dangerous, heathens and "noble savages". They were always "the bad guys." Such movies and television shows which aired for decades, provided to **millions** of Americans, their **only** view of Indigenous People. The psychological and emotional pain of Indigenous People that resulted from having other Americans exposed, over many decades, to those stereotypes, is immeasurable.

* Indigenous People have fought numerous legal battles for the return of what are for them, sacred artifacts that, over hundreds of years, were taken from them and put into museums, including funerary objects and remains of their ancestors.

* For many years, Indigenous People have been challenging laws that prohibit specific practices of their traditional religions.

* Indigenous People have had to continually fight to protect their religious grounds that have been threatened by mining companies, timber companies, tourism, the proposed construction of ski resorts, backpackers and other intruders.

* Indigenous People have had to protest the ways in which aspects of their cultures have been disrespected through their use as sports mascots in schools both at the K-12 and the university level. In **professional** sports, they have protested the use of the names, "Indians,", "Chiefs", "Braves", "Warriors" and especially, "Red Skins", which is undeniably a racial epithet equivalent to the word, "Kike" for Jews, "spic" for Latin Americans, and "Nigger" for African Americans. The Atlanta Braves' Tomahawk Chop tradition has been a particularly egregious insult to Indigenous culture, tradition and history. Ms. Charlene Teter is an Indigenous woman who actively

works on the issue of the use of images of Indigenous People and Indigenous Culture as mascots.

Ms. Charlene Teter's Work:
http://www.youtube.com/watch?v=lEUl2keJK-w
http://www.youtube.com/watch?v=8lUF95Thl7s
http://www.pbs.org/pov/inwhosehonor/film_description.php#.UcSWPlbn99w

Today, Indigenous People are the nation's poorest, with the highest unemployment rates and levels of what some may consider to be overall "social dysfunction" of any ethnic group in the United States.[124]

c. Asian People and Asian Americans

While the experience of only two Asian American populations in the United States—the Chinese and Japanese communities—have been primarily considered in this work, many other Asian American communities, Indians, Koreans, Vietnamese, Cambodians, Thai, Filipinos, Laotians and others, share a similar history of persecution. In 1907, for example, European American race riots drove Indian People out of both Bellingham, Washington and Live Oak, California.[125]

[124] For much more information on the experience of Indigenous People, (and other Americans of Color), after European explorers arrived on the shores of their land, see Harvard-trained sociologist, Dr. James Loewen's book, *Lies My Teacher Told Me: Everything Your High School History Textbook Got Wrong.*
https://www.youtube.com/watch?v=wjeHlgtahkE

[125] The first race riots that took place in the United States were white race riots. Asian, Latin and African American communities have all been brutally victimized by white race riots.

Chinese People and Chinese Americans

* **1854**—People vs. Hall—The California Supreme Court ruled that both Chinese immigrants **and** Chinese Americans were forbidden from testifying in court against European Americans.

* **1862**—California imposed a "police tax" of $2.50 per month on every Chinese person. It was an act to protect free white labor against competition with Chinese labor, and to discourage Chinese People from emigrating to California.[126]

* **1870**—The Naturalization Act limited American citizenship to "white persons and persons of African descent." The Act barred Chinese People specifically from becoming American citizens.[127]

* **1871**—Purportedly prompted by the death of a European American rancher killed in the cross-fire of a gun battle between two Chinese cliques, Anti-Chinese riots of over 500 European American men broke out in Los Angeles' Chinatown. The riot took place on Calle de los Negros (Street of the Negroes), also called "Nigger Alley" at the time.

  Buildings were plundered, vandalized and pillaged. While eighteens Chinese People were confirmed dead, there are estimates that up to eighty-four lost their lives during the race riots.

---

126 Fortunately, the law did not stand for very long, as it was declared unconstitutional by the California Supreme Court shortly after its enactment.

127 It is interesting that in this specific instance, African Americans were accorded the same right as European Americans, a right that was being denied to people of Asian descent.

During this time, a widespread fear of "cheap Chinese labor" caused European American mobs to raid and destroy Chinese communities both in California and other states.

* **1882**—The Chinese Exclusion Act—excluded Chinese, "skilled and unskilled laborers employed in mining", from entering the United States for ten years under penalty of being either imprisoned or deported.

  Asians who had already settled in the United States and left the country temporarily, had to obtain certification before being allowed to return. The law also excluded Chinese immigrants from becoming American citizens.

  Short Video Clips on The Chinese Exclusion Act:
  https://www.youtube.com/watch?v=hMXrdCNvL04
  https://www.youtube.com/watch?v=GwAhYUgg_uU

* On the Transcontinental Railroad, Chinese laborers were frequently subjected to significantly harder labor than European American laborers and often performed the most dangerous tasks, using dynamite, for example, to blast pathways through the mountains.

* **1885**—Throughout the West, Chinese miners were paid significantly less than European American miners. Mining companies therefore, often hired Chinese miners before hiring European immigrant miners. Mining companies also hired Chinese miners as strike-breakers. The result was serious anti-Chinese sentiment over what was called, "cheap coolie labor". In 1885, the Union Pacific Railroad Company hired Chinese strikebreakers in Rock Springs Wyoming. In response, 150 armed European American men rioted, attacking the Rock Springs Chinese community. In the violence, the community's property was destroyed and twenty-to-thirty Chinese People were killed and several hundred expelled from the community.

After Rock Springs, Anti-Chinese violence spread rapidly to Coal Creek, Wyoming where eleven Chinese People were attacked on September 11, 1885; to Seattle Washington's Chinatown which European American rioters burned down on October 24, 1885; to Tacoma, Washington and several smaller towns in Washington State. Then, beginning in November of that year, mobs of European Americans expelled hundreds of Chinese People from the towns in which they lived. Responding to a request for Federal help from the governor, President Cleveland sent the U.S. military into both Seattle and Tacoma to quell the violence. Anti-Chinese harassment and attacks also occurred in the 1880s in Nevada, Alaska, South Dakota, Colorado and Oregon.

* **1888**—The Scott Act expanded the Chinese Exclusion Act, initially applicable to only Chinese **laborers**, to "**all** persons of the Chinese race". It is estimated that some twenty-to-thirty thousand Chinese People were stranded outside of the United States when the certification requirement for Chinese People who had settled in the country but had temporarily left, went into effect.

* **1889**—The Anti-Miscegenation Act prohibited Chinese and Chinese American men from marrying European and European American women.

* **1889**—In *Chae Chan Ping v. U.S.* the U.S. Supreme Court **upheld** the constitutionality of the power of Congress to exclude groups of people from the right to immigrate to the United States.

* **1892**—The Geary Act—The Act did three things. First, it required all Chinese residents to carry identification papers at all times. Failure to do so could result in either a year of hard labor or deportation. Second, the Act prohibited Chinese Americans from testifying in court. Third, it prohibited them from receiving bail in habeas corpus proceedings.

* **1901**—In *Sung v U.S.*, the United States Supreme Court ruled that unreasonable search and seizure, trial without jury, and cruel and unusual punishment are acceptable in deportation proceedings.

* **1902**—Chinese exclusion was extended for another 10 years.

* **1910**—The U.S. Supreme Court extended the 1870 Naturalization Act from being applicable to only Chinese People, to **all** other Asian immigrants, making **all** Asian People ineligible for citizenship.

* **1917**—The Immigration Act of 1917, Affecting Many Nationalities of Asian Immigrants—The law restricted the immigration of 'undesirables' from other countries, including prostitutes, people suffering from tuberculosis, anarchists, polygamists, criminals, "imbeciles", "idiots", epileptics, alcoholics, the poor, beggars, **and people from "the Asiatic Barred Zone"**, i.e., "any country not owned by the United States adjacent to the continent of Asia".

* Many anti-Chinese laws remained in effect until the 1950's.

* **1982**—Murder of Vincent Chin—Mr. Chin was a young American man who was beaten to death in Highland Park, Michigan, by Ronald Ebens and Michael Nitz. Ebens and Nitz were respectively, present and former employees of the Detroit Michigan Chrysler Auto Plant. The Detroit Auto Industry was experiencing at that time, growing layoffs which were widely believed to have been the result of the increasing competition from Japanese automakers. Ebens and Nitz are alleged to have shouted at Mr. Chin, "It's because of you little motherfuckers that we're out of work", as they delivered blows to his head, beating him to death with a bat. On June 23, 1982, after several days in a coma, 27 year old Mr. Chin, who was soon to be married, died from his wounds.

Mr. Chin's killers killed him because they were angry about the competition that the Japanese automobile industry had become to the American automobile industry. Mr. Chin was Chinese American.

Who Killed Vincent Chin:
http://www.youtube.com/watch?v=lvZ60qRmSGw

Many and perhaps the average American's lack of awareness regarding Mr. Chin's death is dramatized in the video, "Vincent Who." I suspect that it is probable that most Americans are equally as unaware of the **majority** of race-based and other hate crimes that occur in the United States.

Vincent Who:
http://www.youtube.com/watch?v=l_rwnyM1vtE[128]

Japanese People and Japanese Americans

* **1894**—In *re Saito*: A Massachusetts Circuit Court declared that people of Japanese ancestry are ineligible for naturalization because they are "Mongolians", neither white nor black.

* **1913**—The California Alien Land Law—banned "aliens ineligible for citizenship", from owning land in the United States. While the law applied to Indians, Koreans, Chinese, and Japanese People alike, it was **principally** targeted at the **Japanese** population as a result of the much greater rate than other groups, at which they were immigrating to the U.S. Those affected by the law were allowed to lease land only, and in no more than three-year increments. The California Supreme Court reaffirmed the law in 1946. In 1952, the same

[128] Sincere thanks to my friend Susan Hua for informing me of the importance of including information on Mr. Chin's death in this section.

court. determined that it was a violation of the Equal Protection Clause of the 14th Amendment to the Constitution.

* **1922**—In *Ozawa v. U.S.*, Takao, Ozawa challenged the Naturalization Act of 1910 which limited naturalized citizenship to white persons and persons of African descent. In his lawsuit, Mr. Ozawa did not challenge the law as unconstitutional. Instead, his attempt was to have Japanese People classified as white. The court denied his request, ruling that only Caucasian persons were white.

  Interestingly, anthropologists, at that time, classified Indians as Caucasian. Not surprisingly, a few months after the Supreme Court's Ozawa ruling, Bhagat Singh Thind, an Indian Person from India's Punjab region, petitioned the court to allow **Indian** People to become naturalized citizens under the Naturalization Act. The case was *Thind v. U.S.* The court denied Mr. Thind's request, ruling that although all white people were considered Caucasian, all Caucasians were not necessarily considered white.

* **1924**—National Origins Quota Act (Immigration Act)—While the Act placed quotas on the number of immigrants that would be allowed into the United States from certain European countries, it totally banned the immigration of Asian People into the country.

* **1942**—Executive Order 9066—Signed by President Franklin Roosevelt during World War II, the Executive Order authorized the United States military to declare certain parts of the country as "military areas" for use of the military only. Additionally, the military was authorized under the Order, to exclude "any and all persons" from such areas. Military areas were designated primarily in the western section of the United States. People of "Foreign Enemy Ancestry" were ultimately relocated from such areas and detained in what were called, "War Relocation Camps". Far more than any other group, however, it was people of **Japanese** ancestry and nationality, (which also included Korean People as Korea was under

Japanese rule at that time), who were targeted for relocation. During the war, **over one hundred thousand** Japanese Americans were detained in relocation camps in the western United States. **Thousands** of Japanese Americans lost their homes and businesses in the process, requiring them to start over with nothing, after the war.

Japanese/Japanese American Internment during World War II:
https://www.youtube.com/watch?v=6mr97qyKA2s

Digital History of the Internment of Japanese People and Japanese Americans during World War II:
http://www.digitalhistory.uh.edu/learning_history/japanese_internment/internment_menu.cfm

Like Indigenous People, Asian Americans have historically also been dreadfully stereotyped on both the large and small screens, as well as in literature and art. Japanese Americans specifically, were the targets of **extremely** vicious stereotypes during World War II, their faces often depicted on billboards as more monstrous than human. As is always the case with this specific form of victimization, the psychological pain of the target group, as well as the fear and often utter hatred stoked **toward** the group in the hearts and minds **of non-members** of the group, is incalculable

* **1943**—In *Hirabayashi v. U.S.*, the United States Supreme Court found constitutional, curfews imposed by law upon any group of people who had originally come from a nation with which the United States was at war. The ruling was used to authorize the enforcement of curfews aimed at Japanese People.

* **1945**—The all Japanese-American 442nd Regimental Combat Team which fought in Europe during WWII, was awarded 18,143 decorations, including 9,486 Purple Hearts. As a result, the team became the most decorated military unit in American

history. It has been reported that the 442nd Nisei Field Artillery Battalion was the first unit to liberate Jewish People at the Dachau, Germany concentration camp. Members of the 442nd volunteered and served during the second world war at the same time that their families were subject to being sent to relocation camps.

Videos on the Japanese American 442nd Regimental Combat Team:
http://www.youtube.com/watch?v=pu390kDDbi8
https://www.youtube.com/watch?v=lIZC9ihafVs
https://www.youtube.com/watch?v=NOcnz9gvWaI

* **1988**—The United States government issued an official apology to Japanese Americans for their internment in relocation camps during World War II.

* **1999**—The U.S. Department of Justice completed a reparations program in which $20,000 payments were made to roughly 82,000 Japanese Americans or their heirs, who had been interned during the second world war.

* **2010**—October 5—The Congressional Gold Medal was awarded to the 442nd Regimental Combat Team as well as the six thousand other Japanese Americans who served in the Military Intelligence Service during World War II.

All Asian People and Asian Americans

Asian People and Asian Americans also suffered the effects of local, state and Federal segregation laws and discriminatory practices which affected all other People of Color in the United States. They were entirely subject to the discrimination of "White Only" signs, and a "White Only" society-at-large.

d. Latin People and Latin Americans

While Latin Americans who either themselves or whose families are originally from **many** different countries, among them, the Dominican Republic, Cuba, and the countries of Central America, Mexico, Guatemala, Nicaragua, El Salvador, Belize, Honduras, Costa Rica and Panama, have historically been discriminated against in the United States, our focus will be on the history of the discrimination experienced by two of the **largest** Latin/Spanish Speaking groups in the U.S.—Puerto Rican Americans in the East and Mexican Americans in the West. [Puerto Rico is not a country, of course, but an American territory. Thus, native born Puerto Ricans are native born Americans.] The following is but a brief description of those histories:

History of the Indigenous People of Puerto Rico and Puerto Rican Americans

* **In the beginning**—At the time that Christopher Columbus arrived in the Western hemisphere, the Indigenous Taino People inhabited what are now Puerto Rico, Jamaica, Haiti, the Dominican Republic, and Cuba. All but Jamaica, (which was colonized by the French), were conquered by Spain, their land taken and the people themselves, colonized. Many of the Indigenous populations of the Caribbean islands were violently driven to near extinction, with many of their communities having experienced population decreases of over 95 percent well before the end of the 19th century. Subsequently, the Spanish brought in to the islands and then enslaved millions of West African people to provide free labor on thousands of sugar and other plantations.

* **Colonialism**—Ponce de Leon conquered the Indigenous inhabitants of Puerto Rico in 1508. Subsequently, the Spanish used Puerto Rico as a strategic base of trade for almost 400 years. In 1898, Spain ceded Puerto Rico to the United States.

* **Slavery in Puerto Rico:** Museo de la Raiz Africana https://www.youtube.com/watch?v=dh-2E1KReBY

  Images of slavery in Puerto Rico: http://www.google.com/imgres?imgurl=http://www.loc.gov/rr/hispanic/1898/img/slaves.jpg&imgrefurl=http://www.loc.gov/rr/hispanic/1898/slaves.html&h=317&w=500&sz=33&tbnid=58i6cFzg9ZH1yM:&tbnh=90&tbnw=142&zoom=1&usg=__TD7zi42B-l7nCOJ-H6sheaVLcsM=&docid=nNYQ078N7jHcOM&hl=en&sa=X&ei=MIAPUqyvDqrhygGFwoDgDg&ved=0CFAQ9QEwAw&dur=191#imgdii=58i6cFzg9ZH1yM%3A%3BhmY0VgTzGmKtoM%3B58i6cFzg9ZH1yM%3A

* **End of Slavery**—March 22, 1873

* **World War I**—The United States military segregated Puerto Rican American units from European American units. Puerto Rican Americans of African descent were **further** segregated into the 375th Regiment, a regiment of specifically black Puerto Rican American soldiers.

* **World War II**—Puerto Rican American soldiers were used as human guinea pigs by the United States military. Puerto Rican American soldiers on the San Jose Island of Panama, were deliberately exposed to mustard gas in an attempt to determine whether they reacted the same as or differently from the way in which European American soldiers reacted to the gas. The same mustard gas experiments were also done on Japanese American and African American soldiers during the war.

  > [At least eight separate experimental programs in the United States focused specifically on Japanese American and African American soldiers and one focused on testing Puerto Ricans on an island off Panama. The researchers were searching for evidence of race-based differences in the responses of the human body to mustard gas exposure. No differences were found.

The New York Academy of Medicine Report on Mustard Gas Experiments:
http://www.nyam.org/news/press-releases/2008/3096.html]

Social Discrimination—Puerto Rican Americans are comprised of a number of "races", Indigenous People, African, European and Asian.

During the Jim Crow, i.e., the segregation era, Puerto Rican Americans of color were fully subjected to the same segregation, "White Only" laws, as other Americans of Color. Discrimination against Puerto Rican Americans in the New York City area and other parts of the Northeast where millions of Puerto Rican Americans immigrated during the 20th century, was rampant. It has been reported that in New York City, for example, there were signs in many restaurants and other establishments which read, "No dogs and Puerto Ricans allowed".

* **Internalized Oppression**

Puerto Rican Americans are not immune from the psychological impact of being the target of historic racism. Iinternalized oppression affects Puerto Rican Americans as it does other Americans of Color. I have been told by Puerto Rican Americans that it is a common practice in Puerto Rican culture to "marry according to color."

In 1976, I did a two-day recruitment trip to Puerto Rico in order to recruit Puerto Rican high school seniors to Wesleyan University at which I was then employed. Over the course of the two days, I visited six schools, three public schools on the first day and three private schools on the second. On the first day, I saw that in the public schools, the skin color of the students ran the gamut of the human complexion spectrum, with only a small minority being in the light brown-skin range. Knowing nothing about the demographics of the island, I assumed that those kids were representative of the Puerto Rican population as a whole. I therefore began day two of my recruitment trip with the assumption that I would see at the private schools, kids that resembled those I had seen in the public schools the previous day. To my utter surprise, **the vast majority** of the students in the **private** schools, were either white or very light-skinned. Racism and colorism, i.e., white and light-skin privilege were clearly both institutionalized and alive and well in Puerto Rico.

History of the Indigenous People of Mexico and Mexican Americans

Upon the arrival of European explorers to Mexico in the early 1500's, Mexico's Indigenous population suffered widespread displacement by the explorers. In brutal crusades, Nuno Beltran de Guzman and other European explorers and their contingents terrorized the Indigenous People of parts of Mexico with murder, torture and enslavement.

After his conquests, Guzman ordered that the conquered Indigenous People of the area, the Jalisco, be dispersed among the area's Spanish conquerors. Under the order, individual Spanish persons who took ownership of tracks of land, also received the free labor of the Indigenous People who lived upon them. Those who controlled the land were expected to both provide for the needs of and to Christianize the Indigenous People who lived on it. Not surprisingly however, under this system, many Indigenous People became slaves. In 1536, Guzman was arrested and imprisoned for his inhumane actions.

* At the end of the Mexican-American War, (1846-1848), the U.S. annexed a sizeable portion of Mexico onto what was then the Southwestern region of the United States. [129] Mexican People who were residing in that territory when it was still Mexico, i.e., before it was annexed to the U.S., were subsequently subjected to **severe** discrimination.

---

[129] The annexation of that part of Mexico to the United States is what is referred to by the statement sometimes used in social protests by Latin people, "We didn't cross the border. The border crossed us."

* **Lynching**

From the mid-19th century through the early 20th century, **hundreds** of Mexican People and Mexican Americans were lynched across the United States. Mexican People and Mexican Americans were lynched at rates that have at times been second only to the rates at which African Americans were lynched.

* **Illegal Deportation**

During The Great Depression of the 1930's, the U.S. government sponsored The Mexican Repatriation Program. The program was intended to encourage Mexican immigrants to voluntarily return to Mexico. Many, however, were removed against their will. In total, up to **one million** persons of Mexican ancestry were deported under the program. Approximately, **sixty percent** of those deported, were American **citizens**. With its Apology Act, the State of California became the first to officially acknowledge and apologize to Mexican Americans for, ""the fundamental violations of their basic civil liberties and constitutional rights committed during the period of illegal deportation and coerced emigration."

Expulsion of (Mexican) American Citizens
https://www.youtube.com/watch?v=RZ5pvg5-4Nk

* **Social Violence**

"The Zoot Suit Riot of 1943 was a shocking incident of racial violence perpetrated against Mexican American People in Los Angeles in 1943. For some time prior to the incident, conflicts had broken out between Caucasian American U.S. Naval servicemen stationed in a Latin neighborhood and Latin youth in the area, Finally, the frequent conflicts intensified into several days of non-stop rioting. During the riot, mobs of European American servicemen entered business establishments intending to attack Mexican American men, some of whom were wearing zoot suits, the signature and quite popular attire of some groups of Mexican Americans during that era. Over several days, the violence spiraled out of control until **thousands** of servicemen joined the attacks. They walked shoulder-to-shoulder down streets, entering public place after public place, attacking Mexican American men and boys. A witness to the attacks, journalist Carey McWilliams, wrote the following account:

> "Marching through the streets of downtown Los Angeles, a mob of several thousand soldiers, sailors, and civilians, proceeded to beat up every zoot suiter they could find. Pushing its way into the important motion picture theaters, the mob ordered the management to turn on the house lights and then ran up and down the aisles dragging Mexicans out of their seats. Streetcars were halted while Mexicans, and some Filipinos and Negroes, were jerked from their seats, pushed into the streets and beaten with a sadistic frenzy."

The local police officers who were called to the scene were ordered to not arrest **any** of the servicemen. After several days, the police did, however, arrest, more than 500 **Mexican Americans**, charging them with vagrancy, rioting and other crimes. It was reported that the police even **assisted** in the unrestrained, multi-day assault in which more than 150 people were injured. The race riot finally stopped when base commanders declared the affected areas off-limits to servicemen. The Zoot Suit Riot was only one of countless acts of violence against Mexican Americans in American history.

The Zoot Suit Riots:
http://www.laalmanac.com/history/hi07t.htm
http://www.pbs.org/wgbh/amex/zoot/eng_peopleevents/e_riots.html
http://www.youtube.com/watch?v=dwINn5DEL1c

* **Segregation**

Mexican Americans have been subjected to segregation in every aspect of life. They were, in every state, officially excluded from neighborhoods and segregated in public school systems. In some states, Mexican Americans were also excluded from serving as jurors in court cases, especially in those in which there was a Mexican American defendant.

* "White Only" signs and the "White Only" larger society in which those signs existed, applied **fully** to Mexican Americans.

* **Internalized Oppression**

Mexican Americans, not unlike other People of Color, have also fallen victim to internalized oppression in the form of colorism. In the 1994 documentary, "The Color of Fear, "Roberto Almazan commented that when a baby is born in the Mexican American community, the family is happy if the baby is born light-skinned, declaring delightfully, "Es rubio! Es rubio!" meaning that the baby is pretty. Additionally, I have noticed that what appears to be a majority of Mexican American actors do not represent the actual physical diversity of Mexican Americans, but are, to the contrary, more often light-skinned and with a noticeably European appearance.

e. African People and African Americans

i. Slavery

The Transatlantic African slave trade resulted in nearly two hundred fifty years of slavery suffered by African People in North, Central and South America and throughout the Caribbean. The following is but a **skeletal** outline of what happened to African human beings in that slave trade.

- African human beings were hunted and captured, often in gigantic nets, in West African open fields while either planting or gathering vegetables, hunting, either going to get or carrying water back to their village, walking down to the nearest stream for a bath, travelling to a neighboring village to effect a trade or visit a friend, and otherwise carrying on their daily lives. Those caught were snatched out of their lives and ripped away from their families.

  [This aspect of slavery is rarely focused upon, but the pain of a man whose wife never returned home after going out in the morning to get the family's daily water supply, or of a parent whose child never returned home after going out in the afternoon to play, or of a woman whose husband never returned home after going out on an evening hunt for a small animal for the family's dinner, or of a child whose parent never returned home from a visit to a friend in the neighboring village, was surely **excruciating**. Family members simply disappeared. Once the people of the villages in the area in which disappearances were occurring learned that they were being hunted like animals, it must have been absolutely harrowing.

  The image of African People living at that time in the jungle like animals, was no more than a cruel stereotype, believed, tragically, by millions of Americans of all races, including, sadly, many African Americans. The dramatization of an African village of civilized human beings in the opening scene of Alex Haley's 1977 TV miniseries, "Roots", was for millions of Americans, likely their very **first** experience of seeing African People living in that way. Some undoubtedly did not believe the depiction, thinking that it was no more than a Hollywood portrayal which for the sake of the film, was intended to make African People appear to be more civilized than they actually were. Like Indigenous People of the Western

Hemisphere, however, Africans, at the time of the slave trade, were and for thousands of years **had** been, living in highly organized villages and societies, in nuclear and often extended families, as fully civilized people with established social traditions, religious rituals, political systems, and in some, advanced technology.

All of the sources that I have read about the Transatlantic Slave Trade refer to the "slaves" that were taken from Africa. One "sea change" in our understanding of the slave trade that I **sincerely** wish would occur, is for us to comprehend that no "slaves" were taken from Africa. **People, human beings** were captured and taken, people who were members of nuclear families, extended families and larger communities, husbands, wives, sons, daughters, grandchildren, sisters and brothers, aunts and uncles, nieces, nephews, cousins, neighbors and friends. It was human beings who were living normal human lives who were taken.]

Millions of other African people were also sold to the Europeans slavers by the chiefs of their historical tribal enemies.[130]

- The captured were chained to others who had been caught on that particular "hunt" and marched in line to a holding

[130] Slavery was practiced at that time among many African tribes. Members of a warring tribe captured in battle were often taken by the victors as slaves. In the form of slavery they practiced, however, slavery could not be passed down from one generation to the next. In other words, a person could not be **born** a slave. Additionally, one could often work themselves out of enslavement. I have often wondered whether the African chiefs who sold their tribal enemies into slavery were aware of the specific form of slavery into which they were selling them—generational slavery that was based on skin color, (the color of their **own** skin), and that was meant to be perpetual.

place, sometimes referred to as a "slave castle". Those "castles" were actually dungeons where captured people were kept, often for weeks, awaiting the next slave ship to the Americas. The conditions in the dungeons were utterly inhumane. Temperatures frequently approached and topped 100 degrees in the various dungeon rooms or chambers. There was no method of disposing of human waste. Those in the dungeons had no ability to bathe and clean their teeth. They lived in the constantly present putrid smell that accompanied those conditions. Food, often only bunches of bananas, were literally thrown into the dungeon chambers. Those in the dungeons often suffered constant and severe thirst as the result of being given insufficient water. Those who "misbehaved" were shackled to the dungeon walls by either their necks or their ankles.

[In July of 1976, I toured St. George's Slave "Castle" in Cape Coast, Ghana, the oldest and largest slave "castle" in the Trans Atlantic Slave Trade.[131] I walked into the chambers where people, some of whom, I was painfully aware in that moment, may very well have been my ancestors, were held in such conditions. I saw the neck and ankle shackles that were still attached to the walls and felt the extreme slickness of the black floors under my feet. I listened as the tour guide explained that the slickness was the residue of the mixture of banana peels, human feces, urine, vomit, and in the female dungeons, menstrual blood, that remained more than three centuries later.

It was sunset when we completed the tour. All of us, Americans, Europeans, Africans, and people from

[131] The irony of naming a slave castle in honor of someone who is revered for his holiness, a person referred to as St George, is amazing.

St **George's Slave Castle** http://www.youtube.com/watch?v=Ow2rItUTQtY

many other places in the world, strangers to each other for the most part, after exiting the dungeons, stood in a large circle in the castle's great, outdoor center courtyard to listen to the tour guide's roughly three-minute closing remarks. After a few seconds of silence, we spontaneously grabbed each other's hands. After about a full minute of silence during which most of us stood with closed eyes and bowed heads, someone in the circle quite unexpectedly began to sing an "old Negro spiritual", one that we sang on our Canal Street picket lines that hot summer of 1972.

"Oh oh oh oh freedom. Ooooooh ooooooh freedom. Ooooooh Ooooooh freedom over me. Over me. And before I'll be a slave, I'll be buried in my grave, and go home to my Lord and be free."

After the first few words, several of us joined in, singing the verse several times. At the end, there was another minute or so of silence. Then suddenly, out of the quiet stillness, someone else, quite extemporaneously, again began to sing. This time, it was, "Amazing Grace", and this time, **most** of us joined in. When we finished, I didn't see a single dry eye, not in anyone who was **not** of African descent, and not in the many of us who **were**. Some of us shed tears. Some of us sobbed.]

- Upon arrival of the next slave ship that came sometimes days, sometimes weeks later, the people who had been captured and held in the dungeons, were marched in chains from the slave castle, down to the awaiting ship. **On** that ship, still chained together, they were laid down in rows, like sardines, in the ship's lower decks. Chained together in those rows, they again lived, **for weeks** during the trip across the Atlantic, in their own excrement, urine, vomit and menstrual blood. The men were often chained at the ship's oars and forced to row. The only possible movement for the women, children and the men not rowing, was, perhaps the ability to sit up to eat. It is estimated that between two and four million African people did not survive the journey, the "Middle Passage," that most treacherous of voyages across the Atlantic from Africa's west coast to the Americas. Those that did not, and often those who were still alive but **chained** to the deceased, were tossed overboard. The skeletal remains of those millions of African human beings, today, pepper the floor of the Atlantic from West Africa to the Americas.

- **1619**—The arrival in the United States of the first enslaved African People.

  Some captured African People were also shipped from ports in West Africa to ports in South America and all over the Caribbean.[132] Upon arrival in the Americas, they were:

  - Doused with cold water to dilute the stench of their bodies after the weeks-long journey across the Atlantic;

  - Still in chains, marched to an auction block which was often a stage or platform that stood several feet higher than the surrounding ground, affording an unobstructed view of them to the European Americans who were there to view and possibly purchase them;

---

132 Brazil, unlike the United States which has a black population of only **twelve** percent, has a black population of more than **forty** percent. People of African descent are also in the majority in most of the Caribbean islands. Nonetheless, despite their large numbers, I have personally witnessed that in Brazil as well as in the islands, it is consistently people of African descent who have the lowest paying jobs and are consequently at the bottom of their nations' economic ladder. That fact is an undeniable, poignant, present-day vestige of the history of African slavery throughout the Western Hhemisphere.

- Inspected like livestock by the spectators and plantation owners, their hair, teeth, skin, strength, apparent overall health and ostensible age;

- Sold to the highest bidder and taken away in chains to his plantation;[133]

- Either kept on **that** plantation till death, or sold over the course of her/his life to one or more plantation owners, living enslaved on the **last** plantation, until death. In being sold away to other plantation owners, families were permanently stripped apart, spouses from each other, children from their parents and parents from their children;

  [I have often wondered whether the millions of African human beings who were captured, transported and sold into slavery, perhaps every night in their dreams, experienced themselves in their former existence, living a normal human life in their village, with their parents and siblings as a child, and later with their spouse and children as an adult. Perhaps in their dreams, they saw themselves as a child, back in their village, climbing a tree, picking berries, or playing a game with other children. Perhaps they saw themselves as an adult, attending their daughter's wedding, or their adolescent son's initiation into manhood, or simply walking through the woods to the nearby river for a bath. I have often wondered whether they escaped every night, to the freedom and dignity of being a human being. Tragically, those **born** enslaved, never knew freedom, never knew and thus had no **memory** of ever having lived a normal human life. Unlike those who had been captured and transported

[133] In an effort to keep the enslaved people as powerless as possible, those who spoke the same language were intentionally not sold to the same plantation owner.

across the Atlantic, they could not even **dream** of freedom. We **know**, from the historical record, what their daily lives were like. It is tragic that not even their **dreams** were likely any better.];

- Physically tortured, through among other things, repeated beating of their bare backs with leather straps until the resulting scars resembled a map of the Los Angeles freeways and the cutting off of their feet to punish runaways;

- Repeatedly raped;

- Worked in the fields six days a week, usually from sunrise to sunset in the harshest of weather conditions, blazing heat and bitter cold, even when sick and often when very pregnant. often with the child of one of the European American men who lived and/or worked on the plantation;[134]

  Those who worked in the house, (usually the light-skinned African Americans who were frequently the children of the plantation owner, his sons or employees), worked well after sunset, until the plantation owner and his family went to bed;

[134] When I ponder that fact, I think about Gramzie, of course, and am simply overwhelmed by the hundreds of thousands of times African-American women held in slavery did not know until their child was born, whether the father was her African American male partner, if she had one, or one of the white men on the plantation. Many times, African American young girls knew that their baby was fathered by a European American man on the plantation because no African American man had ever been sexual with her. There were undoubtedly many instances, however, in which the young girl did not know **which** European man on the plantation was her child's father, the plantation owner, one of his sons, or one of his employees.

- Given only the simplest and worst food to eat, often only either beans or rice and scraps of meat;

- Psychologically humiliated, often by being forbidden to look any white person in the eye, i.e., being required to look at the ground when either speaking to or being spoken to by a white person; being required to call their male captors "Master" and the women and little girls of the captor's family, "Ma'am", while themselves being called "Gal", "Boy", and "Niggah"; being kept ignorant by being forbidden to learn to read and write; being prohibited to legally marry; and surely most psychologically painful of all, living with the constant knowledge that at any time, their spouse, mother, father, sister, brother or any of their children could be sold away to another plantation owner; and,

- Killed as an example to other African Americans as punishment for running away, for trying to learn to read, or for breaking other rules.[135]

> [When I think about this utterly nightmarish history of slavery, I think about the fact that I was born exactly **ninety** years after the passage of the 13th amendment which outlawed it. Ninety years. One lifetime. One lifetime separated me from slavery. I think about the fact that when I was born, **there were still people alive** who had been born as slaves. I think about the fact that this history is Oprah Winfrey's history. It is Sidney Poitier's history. It is Dr. Maya Angelou's history. It is Dr. Mae Jamison's history. It is General Colin Powell's history. It is Dr. King's history. It is Gramzie's and Grandpa Jim's history and the history of my father's parents, Gramps and Grandma Emma. It is the history of all of my neighbors and friends in

135 Killing an enslaved African American as punishment, however, was a tactic of last resort, as each enslaved person was a highly valuable "commodity" to the plantation owner for whom he had often both **paid** a handsome sum, and could **sell** for one.

Pontchartrain Park, as well as that of all the kids from the Desire Project who were my elementary school classmates. It is **my** history. When I think about the horror of American slavery, I think about the fact that **but** for the Union's Civil War victory, **all** of us, Angela Bassett, Eleanor Holmes Norton, Geoffrey Canada, Will and Jada Smith and their two children, Bernice and Derek King, my family, neighbors, friends and millions of other people like me . . . . we could all have been born and lived our entire lives as slaves. It is haunting.]

- In sum, for approximately **two hundred fifty years**, (the 246 years from 1619 when the first African People arrived in the United States, until 1865, when the 13th amendment abolished slavery), African Americans provided **millions** of hours of free agricultural labor to European American plantation owners, often making both them and their progeny extremely wealthy. We planted and tilled their fields, cleaned their homes, washed their clothes, cooked their food, and took care of their children, including even breastfeeding their babies. In all of that, we were required to show total and complete obedience, respect and deference to the plantation owner and all other white people.

  In essence, the extreme physical cruelty, sexual abuse and psychological humiliation that we endured during slavery, resulted in our being treated as if we were not even human. Indeed, I have heard reports that plantation **animals** were often literally treated better than the enslaved African American **human beings** who took care of them.

- **1787**—On July 12, with the enactment of the Three-Fifths Compromise, enslaved African Americans were formalized into the United States Constitution as three-fifth human. The legislation attempted to settle the question of whether for the purpose of determining their number of U.S. Representatives, states would be permitted to count enslaved African Americans as residents. The Northern states did not want us to be counted. The Southern states, ironically but not surprisingly, did. The compromise allowed states to count every enslaved African American human being as three-fifths of a person.

[Dr. Khalil Gibran Muhammad, Director of the Schomburg Center for Research in Black Culture, commented on MSNBC's January 5, 2013 Melisa Harris Perry's show that, ". . . . If you take the value of slaves in 1860, it exceeded the entire banking industry, [and] the entire railroad industry, ... If you take all of the commerce of our internet age, and translate it back to the railroad period, as well as all of the manufacturing in the country, that's how valuable slavery was, not just in the United States, but in the Western world.". In response to a question from Ms. Harris Perry, Dr. Muhammad went on to state that it was absolutely the labor of enslaved African Americans that made the United States the economic power that it ultimately became.

When I hear, as I have many times, an African American comment that the United States was "built on our backs", I believe that it is the facts articulated by Dr. Muhammad, to which s/he is referring. While the majority of African Americans may not be aware of the **specific** economic facts elucidated by Dr. Muhammad, I believe that many of us know **intuitively**, that the two-hundred fifty years of free labor of our great, great grandparents and their predecessors, was a **singularly** significant contribution to the development of the tremendous economic engine of the United States. It is for that reason that I have always been fascinated by discussions about and analyses of the issue of reparations for African Americans.]

- **1820**—The Trans-Atlantic slave trade was made illegal in the United States. Slave trading was declared an act of piracy punishable by death.

- **1857**—The enslavement of African Americans was legally condoned by the highest court of the land, the United States Supreme Court. In its infamous decision, *Dred Scott v. Sandford*, 60 U.S. 393, Dred Scott, an African American enslaved person, sued for his citizenship. The Supreme Court of the United States declared in the case that, "The authors of the Constitution had viewed all blacks as beings of an inferior order, and altogether unfit to associate with the white race, either in social or political relations, and so far inferior that they had no rights that the white man was bound to respect." In addition, the Court made four significant declarations in the case:

  1. Mr. Scott was not a citizen of the United States;

  2. African American people being held in slavery, were the private property of their European American captors;

  3. No African American, free or slave, could be a citizen of either the United States or of the state in which they live; and,

  4. The section of the Missouri Compromise of 1820 that prohibited slavery in the Federal territories was unconstitutional.

- **1865**—The 13th amendment to the United States Constitution outlawed slavery.

- When slavery ended in 1865, three to four million newly freed African Americans literally walked off of thousands of plantations with nowhere to go and nothing but the clothes on their backs. Many immediately began searching for loved ones, children spouses, parents, grandparents and siblings who had been sold and taken away to other plantations. Many began to look for work on other plantations. Some stayed on the plantations on which they had been enslaved, and worked for “slave wages”.

- After being freed, the formerly enslaved African Americans kept the last names of their former captors, Washington, Henderson, Myers, Johnson, and others, and passed those names on to their children.

- African Americans, in 1865, no matter how long ago their ancestors had arrived in the country, after **generations** of totally unremunerated hard labor by their **ancestors** and years of their **own** unpaid labor, started off in 1865, as if they were, “fresh off the boat”, as if they had just arrived in the United States from West Africa. It was as if their forbears had never paid the tremendous dues that they **had** paid; as if they had never worked for more than two centuries for literally millions of hours in the United States, receiving absolutely no remuneration. In 1865, just eighty-eight years, before my birth, African Americans started building their lives in the United States from literally nothing.

- **1865—The Black Codes**—On the heels of the abolition of slavery, **all** of the former slave states passed the Black Codes. The codes varied from state to state, but the objective of all of them was the same—for European American plantation owners to regain control over African Americans formerly held in slavery.

  The codes **severely** restricted the lives of recently emancipated African Americans. They regulated the movement of, the marriages, the right to own and sell property and all other life activities of newly freed African Americans. They denied us the rights to vote, to testify against European Americans in court, and to serve on juries and in state militias. More than all else, however, the Black Codes were an attempt to control the **labor** of newly freed African Americans. They defined African Americans as agricultural laborers. In South Carolina, African Americans were required to have a special license and certificate from a judge to pursue anything **but** agricultural work. Plantation owners feared that African Americans would not work without coercion and for that reason, commonly **compelled** freed African Americans to work. The codes regulated African Americans' duties and hours of labor. They **required** freed African Americans to sign annual labor contracts with European American land owners, compelling us to work on their plantations. African Americans who refused, could be arrested and hired out to European American plantation owners. The Codes also discouraged African American self-sufficiency, even prohibiting African Americans from growing our own crops. The Codes of some states even allowed judges to assign African American children to work for the owners of the plantations on which they were formerly enslaved, **without the consent of their parents**. In essence, the Black Codes were an attempt, after slavery, to both create a steady supply of cheap African American labor, and to continue the inferior social status of African Americans. They were in essence, the South's way of creating a form of quasi-slavery to negate the results of the Civil War.

- **1868**—Fortunately, on July 9th, 1868, three years after slavery was abolished, the U.S. Congress passed the 14th Amendment to the Constitution. The Amendment's Equal Protection Clause prohibited the Black Codes from being introduced in the future in southern states.

ii. Segregation

In 1876, eight years after the repeal of the Black Codes, southern and border states began passing laws which required the separation of black and white Americans. They mandated, "separate but equal" schools and public facilities, including eating establishments, water fountains, restrooms, waiting rooms, public seating areas, and **every** other aspect of public life. The law required that **all** facilities be "separate but equal." The reality, however, was that the facilities were **never** equal. Facilities that were assigned to African Americans were always **vastly** inferior—vastly . . . . and always.

[**1895**—My grandparents, my father's mother and father are born, exactly thirty years after slavery was abolished.]

My Father's Parents Emma and Alcibiades Joichin

➢ **1896**—State laws requiring segregation were challenged in *Plessy vs. Ferguson*, a landmark United States Supreme Court case which specifically challenged a Louisiana law that required railroads to seat black and white passengers in separate cars. **By a vote of 7 to 1, the United States Supreme Court upheld the constitutionality of segregation**. The case institutionalized state sanctioned segregation in southern states. Segregation remained the law of the land in the South for another sixty eight years until it was outlawed by the Civil Rights Act of 1964 when I was in junior high school.

[Ironically, in the midst of all of the abject oppression in which African Americans lived in the post Civil War era, two African Americans, Hiram Revels and Blanch Bruce, a former slave, both Republicans and both from Mississippi, were elected to the United States Senate. Senator Revels served from 1870 to 1871. Senator Bruce served from 1875 to 1881. During the period of reconstruction, twenty-one African Americans also served in the United States House of Representatives, all from Southern states.]

iii. Lynching

Decades of lynchings of **scores** of African Americans followed the Civil War. For African Americans, particularly for the millions who lived in rural parts of the south, the period of lynching was a time of fear and terror second to only that which we experienced during slavery. Lynchings of African Americans were often very public events, with a party atmosphere, sometimes referred to as "bar-b-ques". According to the records of the Tuskegee Institute, 3,446 African Americans, both women and men, were lynched for nearly a century, between 1882 and 1968, my junior year of high school.

"Although the practice of lynching had existed since before slavery, it gained momentum during Reconstruction, when viable black towns sprang up across the South and African Americans began to make political and economic inroads by registering to vote, establishing businesses and running for public office. Many whites—landowners and poor whites—felt threatened by this rise in black prominence. Foremost on their minds was a fear of sex between the races. Some whites espoused the idea that black men were sexual predators and wanted integration in order to be with white women."

Lynching in America: The American Experience—People and Events
http://www.pbs.org/wgbh/amex/till/peopleevents/e_lynch.html

It has been theorized that in the South, lynching replaced slavery as a means of control of African Americans.

Without Sanctuary: Photographs and Postcards of Lynching in America:
http://withoutsanctuary.org/main.html

Anti-lynching legislation that was supported by President Harding in the 1920's and passed in the House of Representatives was filibustered in the Senate several times and thus, never passed. On June 13, 2005, Senators Mary Landrieu of Louisiana and George Allen of Virginia sponsored a resolution in which the U.S. Senate issued a formal apology for never passing the nearly 200 anti-lynching laws that had been introduced into the Congress and supported by seven Presidents between 1882 and 1968.

Senate Apologies for Not Enacting Anti-Lynching Legislation
http://www.democracynow.org/2005/6/14/senate_apologizes_for_not_enacting_anti

iv. **White Race Riots**

The history of white race riots with their accompanying shocking violence perpetrated against African Americans is well documented. The 1906 Atlanta race riot, the 1917 East St Louis Riot, the 1921 Tulsa Oklahoma riot and the 1923 Rosewood Florida riots are among the most well-known of the white riots.

The Atlanta Riot of 1906 was the consequence of fabricated stories printed by two Atlanta newspapers, the Atlanta News and the Atlanta Georgian, which at the time, were rivaling for readers. Both publications falsely printed stories a number of times, reporting that white women in Atlanta had been raped by black men. The situation climaxed on September 22, 1906, when both papers reported that four white women had been raped by black men. That same day, roughly ten thousand European American men converged on downtown Atlanta's Decatur Street and began killing African Americans. Estimates are that the mob murdered a total of twenty-five to forty African Americans. Two European Americans were killed in the African Americans' defense.

[The reported rape of a European American woman by an African American man was, historically, perhaps **the** most often used fabrication to justify European American violence against African American communities. Perhaps it was the many stories of reputed rapes of white women by black men that resulted in the stereotype of the sexual promiscuity of African Americans and other people of African descent.

Although no allegation of rape was involved, the story of Emmett Till is the most well-known incident in which white men allegedly felt the need to defend the honor of a white woman against what they considered was inappropriate attention by a black male. Emmett was a fourteen year old black boy who, in 1955, depending upon the particular report consulted, was said to have either whistled at or otherwise flirted with at a twenty-one year old white woman in a section of the Mississippi Delta. In response, two of the woman's male relatives took Emmett from his family's home, drove him to a barn, beat him, gouged out one of his eyes, shot him in the head, tied a cotton gin fan to his body and threw him into the nearby Tallahatchie River.

Tragically, such incidents, instigated by both the Ku Klux Klan and by individual groups of White Americans, were common in the rural South during that time of our nation's history. Emmett Till's torture and murder was one of several events that spawned the Civil Rights Movement.

[1906—Gramzie is born on December 12th, forty-one years after slavery was abolished.]

The East St. Louis Riot of 1917—The riot was a "bloody outbreak of violence in East St. Louis, Illinois, stemming specifically from the employment of black workers in a factory holding government contracts. It was the worst of many incidents of racial antagonism in the United States during World War I that were directed especially toward black Americans newly employed in war industries. In the riot, whites turned on blacks, indiscriminately stabbing, clubbing, and hanging them and driving 6,000 from their homes; 40 blacks and 8 whites were killed." Encyclopedia Britannica:

East St. Louis Race Riot of 1917:
http://www.britannica.com/EBchecked/topic/176788/East-Saint-Louis-Race-Riot-of-1917

The Tulsa Race Riot of 1917—The riot grew out of black resistance to the attempted lynching of Dick Rowland, a nineteen year old shoe shine man. White mobs set fire to the economically successful black Greenwood district of Tulsa, known as the Black Wall Street, destroying 1,256 black homes and as many as 200 black businesses. Fires leveled 35 blocks of residential and commercial neighborhoods. Black People were then rounded up by the Oklahoma National Guard and put into several internment centers, including a baseball stadium. White rioters in airplanes then shot at and dropped improvised kerosene bombs and dynamite on them. Thirty-nine people (26 black, 13 white) were confirmed killed. Recent investigations suggest that the actual number of casualties is actually much higher.

The Rosewood Florida Massacre of 1923 is perhaps the most well-known of the white riots, its story having been told in the 1997 movie, "Rosewood" directed by actor and director, John Singleton. The riot was the result of allegations by Fannie Coleman Taylor, a young white woman, that she had been raped by a young black man. Sarah Carrier, a black woman who worked for the Taylor family, reported that on the morning of the alleged rape, Ms. Taylor and her boyfriend had argued, after which he abused her. Rosewood's African American residents thought that Taylor made up the story of being raped by a black man in order to save herself from a scandal.

The following is the chronology of events that then lead to the Rosewood riot:

August 5, 1920
Four black men in McClenny, Florida are removed from the local jail and lynched for the alleged rape of a white woman.

November 2, 1920
Two White People and at least five Black People are killed in Ocoee in a dispute over voting rights. The black community of Ocoee is destroyed, twenty-five homes, two churches, and a Masonic Lodge.

February 12, 1921
A black man in Wauchula is lynched for an alleged attack on a white woman.

December 9, 1922
A black man in Perry is burned at the stake, accused of the murder of a white school teacher. A black church, school, Masonic Lodge, and meeting hall are burned.

December 31, 1922
On New Year's Eve, a large Ku Klux Klan Parade is held in Gainesville.

January 1, 1923
Early morning: Fannie Taylor reports an attack by an unidentified black man.

January 2, 1923
Armed white men begin gathering in Sumner. Approximately 200-300 white men from nearby Levy and Alachua counties, many of whom were members of the Ku Klux Klan, begin to converge on Rosewood. The African American section of the town is destroyed by fire, every home, every business, every church. Every**thing**.

February 12, 1923—To investigate the massacre, a special grand jury was empanelled. The jury concluded that there was no evidence to issue a single indictment.

Atlanta, East St. Louis, Tulsa and Rosewood are only four of the many white race riots that took place in the United States in the late 19th and early 20th centuries. Many occurred in financially thriving African American communities. Those communities were terrorized and then often totally destroyed.

"Rosewood"—Movie Trailer
https://www.youtube.com/watch?v=ZoroUDTSY70

[**1923**—My father is born in the same year, on September 21st, fifty-eight years after the end of slavery.

1924—My mother is born on November 10th, fifty-nine years after the end of slavery.]

v. Other Discrimination, Harassment and Violence

➢ **1932 - The Tuskegee Syphilis Experiment**

Initiated by the U.S. Public Health Service, the Tuskegee Syphilis Experiment was done on roughly 400 African American men. The men were primarily illiterate sharecroppers from a poor, rural Alabama county who were in the late stages of syphilis. The subjects were unsophisticated, trusting, and happy to receive free health care which for some, was the first medical attention they had ever received in their lives. The goal of the study was to determine whether syphilis had the same or a different effect on African Americans and European Americans.[136] The men were told neither from what disease they were

[136] The Tuskegee Experiment done on African American men and the mustard gas experiment done on Puerto Rican American men, represent what are possibly the most heinous deliberate acts by trained, licensed American medical professionals ever recorded. The **abject evil** of those experiments, however, **pales** in comparison to the experiments that were done on Jewish People in extermination camps during World War II.

suffering, nor of its seriousness. Their physicians told them only that they were being treated for "bad blood." All of the data from the experiment was to be collected from the men's autopsies, thus the doctors had absolutely no intention of curing them. Instead, they intentionally allowed the men to physically deteriorate from the effects of the illness - heart disease, paralysis, blindness and insanity. The experiments continued until 1972, my sophomore year in college. James Jones, author of an historical account of the experiments, labeled them, "the longest nontherapeutic experiment on human beings in medical history."[137]

- **1934 - Housing Discrimination**

The practice of **informally** engaging in housing discrimination and segregation has **always** existed in the United States. In the mid-1930's, however, housing discrimination became **legally sanctioned** by the Federal Government.[138]

The practice of "redlining" neighborhoods began through the 1934 National Housing Act. Redlining, also known as mortgage discrimination, began when the Federal Housing Administration allowed the Home Owners'

---

137 The Tuskegee Experiments were done within the broader context of the false science of eugenics, the internationally accepted practice of categorizing groups of "undesirable" people as inferior and degenerate. That categorization was then used as justification for segregating the 'inferior' groups from the rest of society, sterilizing and even exterminating them, as Hitler attempted to do to Jewish People during World War II.

138 For additional information on the history of how the Federal government discriminated against Americans of Color in housing, see, "How We Got Here: The Historical Roots of Housing Segregation", at http://www.civilrights.org/publications/reports/fairhousing/historical.html.

Loan Corporation to create "residential security maps", outlining the level of security for real-estate investments **in 239 cities** around the country. On such maps, areas that were labeled "high risk", were outlined in red. Many neighborhoods populated primarily by People of Color were redlined on the maps, indicating that **banks would deny all mortgage capital to the residents of those areas.**

The practice of redlining contributed greatly to the decay of many communities of color since a lack of loans for either buying or making repairs to homes in those areas made it extremely difficult for them to attract and keep families. **Many urban historians point to redlining,** (which was made possible **only** through the assistance of the Federal government which gave permission to real estate agencies to engage in the practice), **as one of the main initial factors for urban disinvestment and the resulting decline of urban areas throughout the mid-twentieth century**[139] The subsequent influx of drugs into inner city neighborhoods in the 1970's was a second serious blow to inner city communities.

Housing discrimination against African Americans also occurred through the discriminatory implementation of the 1944 Servicemen's Readjustment Act, commonly known as the GI Bill. The bill guaranteed cheap mortgage rates to millions of returning World War II veterans. When **African American** veterans attempted to use the GI Bill to purchase homes, however, they were met with discrimination. Many European American realtors believed that they would lose future business by working with African Americans. Convinced that the presence of a black

---

139 Ironically, it was the Federal Housing Administration through which many residents of Pontchartrain Park, including my parents, financed their homes. I suspect that the fact that it was an all-black community made the financing in this instance, more palatable.

family in predominately European American neighborhoods would drive down the white residents' property values, some realtors believed that it was **unethical** to sell homes to African American families in white communities. Some real estate agents wouldn't even **show** African Americans homes in such areas and when they **did,** would attempt to talk them **out** of buying the home, often with stories of how unwelcomed they'd be in the neighborhood, complete with sharing their "concern" for their safety. Thus, although the GI Bill was by law, **available** to all World War II veterans, **actual** opportunity to be home owners, was disproportionately **afforded,** to white GIs and their families.

- **1936 – Publication of *The Negro Travelers' Green Book: The Guide to Travel and Vacations*.**

  The guidebook informed African American travelers where they could eat, sleep and get their car repaired while traveling. The book had a dual purpose – to help African Americans stay safe and to avoid humiliation while travelling.

  The Negro Motorist Green Book
  http://www.autolife.umd.umich.edu/Race/R_Casestudy/Negro_motorist_green_bk.htm

- **1939 – The Daughters of the American Revolution refused world-renowned African American opera singer Marion Anderson, permission to sing in Washington, D. C.'s Constitution Hall.**

  In response, first lady Eleanor Roosevelt assisted in having her sing one month later, on Easter Sunday, on the steps of the Lincoln Memorial. Ms. Anderson's audience included more than 75,000 people at the Memorial, and millions of radio listeners. There, on the steps of the Lincoln Memorial Ms. Anderson sang the words, "My country tis of thee, sweet land of liberty, of thee I sing."

Marion Anderson singing at the Lincoln Memorial
http://www.youtube.com/watch?v=mAONYTMf2pk.

- **Sundown Towns**

Sundown towns, (sometimes called "sunset towns"), were all-white by design. The towns derived their name from posted signs saying that People of Color had to leave the town by sundown. Some towns had signs placed at their entrance with statements such as the following:

"Nigger, Don't Let The Sun Set On You in Hawthorne".

That **very** sign was posted in Hawthorne California in the 1930's. The "Only White People in Town After Dark" rule was enforced officially, through restrictive covenants, in some towns, and informally through intimidation in others.

- **1948 – July 26th** The first crack in the American iron curtain of segregation occurred with President Harry Truman's signing of Executive Order 9981, ending segregation in all U.S armed forces. By then, my father had completed most of his military service during World War II in a segregated United States \Army.

  [Although **the Armed Forces** were integrated, when African American and other troops of color returned home after the war, they still faced a very segregated **society**. After returning from Europe, my father and the other African American GIs who served in Europe during World War II, upon arriving at the Mason Dixon line on the train ride home from New York to New Orleans, were required to leave the front cars of the train and move to the back. My father told me that as he and his buddies were moving themselves and their gear to the back cars, they asked each other, rhetorically, "What the hell did we just go over there, fight and die for? To come back home to **this** s__t?!"

Daddy once told me that over the course of his entire life, it was only during his two years in Paris in the war that he felt like a man and not a black man.]

August 14th – Unanimous Adoption of the Dixiecrat, (or States Rights Democratic Party) Platform

The Dixiecrat Party was a short-lived national American political party formed by southern Democrats in response to President Truman's integration of the American armed forces and to the call by the Democratic Party to end racial discrimination. Their official 1948 party platform read in part, as follows:

We stand for the segregation of the races and the racial integrity of each race; the constitutional right to choose one's associates; to accept private employment without governmental interference, and to earn one's living in any lawful way. We oppose the elimination of segregation, the repeal of miscegenation statutes, the control of private employment by Federal bureaucrats called for by the misnamed civil rights program. We favor home-rule, local self-government and a minimum interference with individual rights. We oppose and condemn the action of the Democratic Convention in sponsoring a civil rights program calling for the elimination of segregation, social equality by Federal fiat, regulations of private employment practices, voting, and local law enforcement. We affirm that the effective enforcement of such a program would be utterly destructive of the social, economic and political life of the Southern people, and of other localities in which there may be differences in race, creed or national origin in appreciable numbers.

1948 Platform of the States Rights Democratic Party
http://www.presidency.ucsb.edu/ws/?pid=25851

[**1953** – My birth on August 15th, almost five years to the day, after the Dixiecrat Party Platform was adopted, and eighty-eight years after slavery was ended.]

- **1954 – May 17th – Brown vs. Board of Education Decision The Supreme Court's landmark decision declaring that racial segregation was unconstitutional**
  https://www.youtube.com/watch?v=TTGHLdr-iak

- **1955 – Murder of Emmitt Till**
  https://www.youtube.com/watch?v=GU1wuqyOP98

"The Untold Story of Emmett Till" – Movie Trailer
http://www.biography.com/people/emmett-till-507515

The Civil Rights Movement – Selected Highlights

[I am enormously proud that the Civil Rights Movement was a non-violent crusade. I am proud that **thousands** of the African American activists in the movement, on many Sunday afternoons after church, attended workshops in which they studied the principles of non-violence, made a commitment to them and practiced controlling their emotions and reactions to verbal and physical provocation. I am **infinitely** proud that many of those who did so, were young African American high school students, college students, and even children. The most well-known organization of children active during the movement was, of course, the Birmingham Children's Crusade.

It was Mahatma Gandhi's non-violent movement in India against British colonialism, that was Dr. King's inspiration to lead a non-violent movement for civil rights in the United States.

Dr. King speaking on Mahatma Gandhi's influence on him.
https://www.youtube.com/watch?v=-JsbbFHpfSc

Dr. King's Paper, "My Trip to the Land of Gandhi", July, 1959
http://mlk-kpp01.stanford.edu/index.php/encyclopedia/encyclopedia/enc_kings_trip_to_india/

Description of Dr. and Mrs. King's Trip to India
http://mlk-kpp01.stanford.edu/primarydocuments/Vol5/July1959_MyTriptotheLandofGandhi.pdf

I admire and am inspired by Mahatma Gandhi and Dr. King more than any other public figures For a very inspiring depiction on the life of Mahatma Gandhi, see the movie, "Gandhi" at http://www.imdb.com/title/tt0083987/]

1955 - Early Bus Boycotts, Montgomery, Alabama
http://www.history.com/topics/rosa-parks/videos#bet-you-didnt-know-rosa-parks
(This url may have to be copied and posted into your internet browser.)

December 1st - Arrest of Mrs. Rosa Parks, Montgomery, Alabama

Mrs. Rosa Parks was arrested and booked in Montgomery, Alabama for refusing to give up her seat to a white man and then stand on a public service bus. Her action led to the historic Montgomery bus boycott which Rev. Dr. Martin Luther King, Jr. was asked and reluctantly agreed to lead. It was perhaps more than any other, **the** event that spawned the beginning of the American Civil Rights Movement

Rosa Parks: Taking a Stand
http://www.youtube.com/watch?v=49ALwDsUzrk

1957 - September 4th - Desegregation of Central High School in Little Rock, Arkansas
http://www.youtube.com/watch?v=RGjNqrQBUno

http://www.youtube.com/watch?v=75dhe5Zsy8k

1960 – February 1st - Woolworth Lunch Counter Sit-In – Greensboro, North Carolina which spawned sit-ins across the South
http://www.youtube.com/watch?v=iw_Jn-uqWaA

1961 - The Freedom Riders Begin Their Work
http://www.youtube.com/watch?v=DcvsWXrS2PI
http://www.youtube.com/watch?v=6T50Ym94k8Y

1963 – April 16th - Dr. King writes his famous "Letter from a Birmingham Jail"
http://www.latinorebels.com/2013/01/15/audio-recording-of-letter-from-birmingham-jail-by-dr-martin-luther-king-jr/
https://www.youtube.com/watch?v=XIpfCVt2eb4

May 2nd – Beginning of Birmingham Children's Crusade Mighty Times: The Children's March
https://www.youtube.com/watch?v=5c113fq3vhQ

June 11th - President Kennedy Announces The Civil Rights Act
http://www.youtube.com/watch?v=-srOvwG81lw

June 12th - Murder of Civil Rights Activist Medgar Evers, Jackson, Mississippi

Mr. Evers was shot and killed by white supremacist Byron De La Beckwith, a member of his local White Citizens' Council.
http://www.biography.com/people/medgar-evers-9542324

August 28th - March on Washington

A pivotal event in the movement which helped spur the passage of subsequent national civil rights legislation that forever changed the nation.

http://www.youtube.com/watch?v=ZA9TJCV-tks

Dr. King's "I Have a Dream" Speech delivered at the march
http://www.youtube.com/watch?v=smEqnnklfYs

September 15th, 10:22 A.M. Bombing of the Sixteenth Street Baptist Church, Birmingham, Alabama

Robert Chambliss, a member of a Ku Klux Klan splinter group, bombed the Sixteenth Street Baptist Church, the sanctuary of an African American congregation and a meeting place of local civil rights leaders in Birmingham. Twenty-three people were injured and four young African American girls were killed, Denise McNair, 11, Cynthia Wesley, 14, Addie Mae Collins, 14 and Carole Robertson, 14.

A few days prior to the bombing, Alabama governor George Wallace told the New York Times in an interview that in order to put a stop to integration, Alabama needed, "a few first-class funerals."

Robert Chambliss was identified by a witness as the man who placed the dynamite under the steps of the church. On October 8th of that same year, Chambliss was found not guilty of the murder of the little girls, but was fined one hundred dollars and given six months in jail for the illegal possession of the dynamite.

In reviewing the original Federal Bureau of Investigation files on the case, Bill Baxley who in 1971 began serving as Alabama's Attorney General, ascertained that significant evidence collected by the Bureau against Chambliss, had never been used in the original trial.140

[140] Based upon the newly exposed evidence, in November, 1977 Chambliss was re-tried for the bombing. At age 73, he was found

Bombing of 16th Street Baptist Church
http://www.youtube.com/watch?v=q-MuWDsv5pg

1964 – June 21st - Murder of Three Voter Registration Workers - Philadelphia Mississippi

The party was organized in order to challenge Mississippi's all white, anti-civil rights delegation to the 1964 Democratic National Convention. Ms. Fannie Lou Hamer was elected the party's Vice Chair.

Fannie Lou Hamer Documentary Part 1
https://www.youtube.com/watch?v=TC4CPv1yXaQ

July 2, 1964 President Lyndon B. Johnson Signs The CivilRights Act
http://www.youtube.com/watch?v=Bygv9u1G6Xo

The Act which outlawed segregation and other discrimination, in education, employment and public accommodations, among other areas. The Act was announced by President Kennedy, but he did not live long enough to see it passed and to sign it into law. President Johnson did both.

1965 – February 1st – Assassination of Malcolm X

Malcolm X Assassination Part 1
https://www.youtube.com/watch?v=imV4kqJNP_0

> [While Malclom was not active in the Civil Rights Movement in the **traditional** sense, his evolution as a human being so exquisitely exemplifies its spirit, and indeed its very **essence**, makes acknowledgement of his assassination during the movement, more than fitting. Malcolm's transformation was from a man

---

guilty and sentenced to life imprisonment. He died in prison, eight years later.

whose words at the beginning of his public life were **dripping** with hatred for Caucasian People, to one who, upon his return from his trip to Mecca, was able to see the brother and sisterhood of all humanity, who was therefore able to understand American racism within a larger, global context and who, as a result of his experiences abroad, ended his life aware that true love among people across **all** racial lines is indeed possible. **That**, is the **very** conversion about which Dr. King spoke so passionately, as being possible in the hearts of southern white Americans.

I have always found travelling abroad as an African American **very** interesting because, ironically, it is when I have been **out** of the country that I have most felt like an American and not a **black** American.

I was in London on the day of and in the days immediately following the September 11th tragedy in the U.S. In attending a commemorative ceremony outside of Buckingham Palace that took place on one of those days, I was asked by one Caucasian British person after another, "You're an American, aren't you?" (I'm still not sure what it was about either me or the way I was dressed that made that so apparent.) Then, upon my telling them that I was, I consistently received the following comment or a very similar one, "We're so sorry. We're just so very sorry." That verbal expression of sorrow, which was obviously sincere and heartfelt, was then followed by a hug. While I would never imply that racism does not exist outside of the United States, there really is **something** categorically different about being abroad as an African American. In my **personal** international experiences, it is that I am related to as an American, not as a black person. It is a feeling of freedom that I rarely have at home. Since the early 20th century, famous African American intellectuals and entertainers including Josephine Baker, James

Baldwin and Richard Wright, all of whom became French citizens, and others who lived abroad for many years, Dexter Gordon, Langston Hughes, Charlie "Bird" Parker, Paul Robeson and Nina Simone(who lived in the South of France for the last eleven years of her life), shared my experience. Additionally, thousands of ordinard African American citizens became ex-patriots in the 20th century. As reported by Bio.com:

> "There were four all-Black regiments during World War I: the 9th and 10th Cavalry and the 24th and 25th Infantry. The men who served in these regiments were considered heroes in their communities, sewing the seeds for equality in the U.S. military. However, still facing insurmountable segregation in the United States at the time, many soldiers opted to remain overseas where they experienced greater freedom and acceptance. " http://www.biography.com/people/groups/african-american-expats/photos][141]

March 7th - "Bloody Sunday"

The stampede and brutal beating by police officers on horses, of hundreds of peaceful, non-violent Civil Rights marchers on Selma Alabama's Edmund Pettus Bridge. The marchers were protesting Alabama voting authorities' statewide practice of denying African Americans the right to vote. The incident is commonly known as Bloody Sunday.

Videos on Bloody Sunday
http://facedl.com/fvideo.php?f=aqauqaoeqoaonokui&selma-alabama-1965-edmund-pettus-bridge-o

http://www.history.com/shows/mankind-the-story-of-all-of-us/videos/bloody-sunday-1965#

[141] I also find it interesting that when I have been abroad, European Americans seem to have been much more comfortable with and friendly toward me than they are when I am at home.

March 28th – Dr. King on NBC's Meet the Press
https://www.youtube.com/watch?v=fAtsAwGreyE

August 6th - Signing of the Voting Rights Act – President Johnson Gives Pen to Dr. Martin Luther King, Jr.
http://www.youtube.com/watch?v=Bygv9u1G6Xo

Voting Rights Act of 1965
http://www.youtube.com/watch?v=vQ2j8zSxPgU

September 4th - Signing of Executive Order 11246 Creating Affirmative Action

The Act required Federal contractors and sub-contractors which do a certain minimum dollar amount of business with the Federal Government to take "affirmative actions" to ensure that equal opportunity is provided in all aspects of their employment.[142]

Affirmative Action and White Privilege – Session One
http://www.youtube.com/watch?v=vw7ZUAQsHXg

1968 – February 4th - Dr. Martin Luther King Jr.'s Sermon – "The Drum Major Instinct"
https://www.youtube.com/watch?v=BcuifZJdyaY

April 4th - Assassination of Rev. Dr. Martin Luther King, Jr.
https://www.youtube.com/watch?v=fAtsAwGreyE

Report of Dr. King's Assassination:
https://www.youtube.com/watch?v=cmOBbxgxKvo

142 Executive Order 11246 was not the first to require affirmative actions to ensure equality of employment opportunity by Federal contractors. President Roosevelt signed the first such order, Executive Order 8802, in 1941. President Kennedy signed one, Executive Order 10925, twenty years later in 1961.

April 11th - Signing of the Fair Housing Act

Fair Housingt Act: Looking Back, Looking Forward
http://www.youtube.com/watch?v=wdKzxSC7DTU

LBJ Signs Fair Housing Act
http://www.youtube.com/watch?v=IDo9mb6-su4

One of the best compendiums of the history of the Civil Rights Movement is the Public Broadcasting Service's documentary series, "Eyes on the Prize".
http://www.youtube.com/watch?v=9Yd78uDXskQ
http://www.pbs.org/wgbh/amex/eyesontheprize/about/fd.html

The Republican Southern Strategy

Just as on the heels of emancipation, the Southern states took to every extent possible, a hard tack back toward slavery, so too, on the heels of the tremendous gains of the Civil Rights movement of the 1960's, the Republican Party, with the election of Richard Nixon in 1968, took a hard tack back toward racial animosity - its Southern Strategy. That strategy relied on courting the Southern and white working class vote by playing directly to the animosity, fears and prejudice that millions of European Americans within that demographic held toward African Americans. Th strategy, specifically, is to convince that population that they cannot get ahead because the government makes them pay, through their tax dollars, for the welfare check and food stamps of millions of lazy, sexually permiscuous, criminally inclined African Americans who swindle the government of of millions of dollars.

More Recent History

1976 – Ronald Reagan uses the Southern Strategy, in Presidential Campaign

Ronald Reagan used the Southern Strategy, in his now infamous story of the South Side of Chicago's "welfare queen" during his 1976 presidential campaign:

> She has eighty names, thirty addresses, twelve Social Security cards and is collecting veteran's' benefits on four, non-existing, deceased husbands, and she is collecting Social Security on her cards. She's got Medicaid, getting food stamps, and is collecting welfare under each of her names. Her tax-free cash income is over $150,000.

In my research, I was unable to find either any video or audio of President Reagan's welfare queen speech.

1980 - President Reagan kicks off his second Presidential campaign in Philadelphia, Mississippi

Four years after receiving the 1980 Republican presidential nomination, Ronald Reagan again employed the Southern Strategy, kicking off his second campaign in Philadelphia, Mississippi, where, sixteen years earlier in 1964, for attempting to help African Americans to register to vote, James Chaney, Andrew Goodman, and Michael Schwerner were murdered by the Mississippi White Knights of the Ku Klux Klan. In his campaign kick-off speech, Reagan used the term, "states' rights", widely employed by the Southern states prior to the Civil War as a reference to their right to do what they wished at the state level, including continuing the institution of slavery.

1981 - Explanation of the Southern Strategy in Republican strategist Lee Atwater's 1981 interview with political scientist Alexander Lamis:

"Here's how I would approach that issue as a statistician or no, as a psychologist, which I'm not, is how **abstract** you handle the race thing. In other works, you start out in 1954, now ya'll are going to quote me (inaudible), by saying, 'Nigger, nigger, nigger.' By 1968 you can't say 'nigger'—that hurts you, backfires. So you say stuff like, uh, forced busing, states' rights, and all that stuff, and you're getting so abstract, now, you're talking about cutting taxes, and all of these things you're talking about are totally economic things and the byproduct of them is, blacks get hurt worse than whites. And subconsciously, maybe that **is** part of it. I'm not saying it. But I'm saying that if it **is** getting that abstract, "We want to cut this," is **much** more abstract and that coded, then we're doing away with the racialproblem one way or the other. You follow me? Cause obviously sitting around saying, we want to cut taxes, we want to cut this and we wanna, is much more abstract than even the busing thing, uh, and a hell of a lot more abstract than "Nigger, nigger, you know. So anyway you look at it, race is coming on the back burner."

New York Times' November 14, 2012 Article on the Release of the Audio of Atwater's Interview with Lamis, with the Audio Recording Embedded
http://www.thenation.com/article/170841/exclusive-lee-atwaters-infamous-1981-interview-southern-strategy

1988 - Perhaps among the most well-known components of the Republican Strategy are two political commercials. The first was used by President Ronald Reagan in his1988 Presidential Campaign. In the ad, the face of Willie Horton, an African American murderer and rapist, was shown as the viewer listened to the soundtrack in which it was explained that the viewer should vote for Reagan because he supported the death penalty for such individuals while Governor of Massachusetts, Michael Dukakis, his Democratic opponent, did not. The use of a picture of an African American as opposed to a European American convict was widely thought by many to be a direct appeal to the fears that millions of European Americans have of African American men.[143]

Willie Horton Commercial of the 1988 Ronald Reagan Presidential Campaign

https://www.youtube.com/watch?v=EC9j6Wfdq3o[144]

1992 – The second very famous commercial of the Southern Strategy, was Republican Senator Jesse Helms' 1992 re-election campaign commercial depicting the hands of a European American man tearing up what is apparently a notice that he had been turned down for a job for which he had applied, accompanied by the following sound track:

---

143 It was her awareness of that fear of African American men that caused Susan Smith, who murdered her two young sons in 1994, to announce to the media and the public, that a black man had robbed she and her husband and then kidnapped and killed the children. Her full description was of a black man in a dark knit cap. Ms. Smith knew that her story would be both more credible and more emotionally compelling if the alleged perpetrator was African American.

144 Shortly before his death from a malignant brain tumor, Mr. Atwater expressed remorse for his role in the development of the Willie Horton ad. In a February, 1991 letter published in Life magazine, he said to Michael Dukakis, "In part because of our successful manipulation of his campaign themes, George Bush won handily." In 1988, Mr. Atwater said, "In fighting Dukakis, I said that I 'would strip the bark off the little bastard' and 'make Willie Horton his running mate.' I am sorry for both statements: the first for its naked cruelty, the second because it makes me sound racist, which I am not......... My illness helped me to see that what was missing in society is what was missing in me: a little heart, a lot of brotherhood.......I don't know who will lead us through the '90s, but they must be made to speak to this spiritual vacuum at the heart of American society, this tumor of the soul".

> You needed that job, and you were the best qualified, but they had to give it to a minority because of a racial quota. Is that really fair? Harvey Gantt, (Helms' African American opponent), says it is. Gantt supports Ted Kennedy's racial quota law that makes the color of your skin more important than your qualifications. Your vote on this issue next Tuesday: For racial quotas, Harvey Gantt. Against racial quotas, Jesse Helms.

Jesse Helms' 1992 "Hands Commercial"
http://www.youtube.com/watch?v=KIyewCdXMzk

President Reagan's launch of his second Presidential campaign in Philadelphia, Mississippi, his welfare queen speech, his Willie Horton television commercial and Senator Helms' "Hands" commercial are probably the most well-known examples of the Republican Southern Strategy. The strategy was used, however, in campaign after campaign, hundreds and perhaps thousands of times in state after state, all across the country.

1997 – The United States Department of Agriculture, until 1997, denied loans to many thousands of African American farmers while granting them to European American farmers with similar financial circumstances. The National Black Farmers Association sued the Department in 1999 and again in 2009, resulting in settlements to the black farmers in the amounts of $1.25 billion and $1.15 billion respectively.

1998 - Murder of James Byrd – June 7th,

Mr. Byrd, an African American, accepted a ride home from three European American men in a pick-up truck, John King, Lawrence Brewer and Shawn Berry. Instead of taking Mr. Byrd home, however, the three men drove him to an isolated area where they severely beat him, urinated on him, chained him by his ankles to the back of the truck and dragged him along an asphalt road for more than two miles. The dragging ultimately severed Mr. Byrd's head and right arm. The autopsy of Mr. Byrd's body revealed evidence that he was conscious and trying to keep his head up during most of the nightmare. An FBI investigation determined that Mr. King and Mr. Berry were well-known white supremacists. Following Mr. Byrd's brutal murder, Texas passed a hate crimes law. Years later, a Federal hate crimes law was also enacted, The Matthew Shepard and James Byrd Jr. Hate Crimes Prevention Act.[145]

Mr. Byrd's son Ross, with help from the organization, Murder Victims' Families for Reconciliation, an organization that opposes capital punishment, campaigned to have spared, the lives of those who murdered his father.

2002 – December 5th - Use of the Republican Southern Strategy by Senator Trent Lott

Repbulican Senator Trent Lott of Mississippi, speaking at the 100th birthday party of Senator Strom Thurmond of South Carolina, praised Senator Thurmond for his 48 year Senatorial service. Senator Thurmond, one of the Senate's most consertative members, ran for President in 1948 on the Dixiecrat, (States' Rights) ticket. The Dixicrat party advocated the perpetuation of racial segregation.

145 Matthew Shepard was a 21 year old European American man who in early October, 1998, was brutally tortured and left to die, tied to a fence by Aaron McKinney and Russell Henderson. It is believed that Mr. McKinney and Mr. Henderson targeted Mr. Shepard because he was gay. The legislation that resulted from Mr. Byrd and Mr. Shepard's murders, the Matthew Shepard and James Byrd Jr. Hate Crimes Prevention Act, is widely referred to as "The Matthew Shepard Act". I am both deeply troubled and saddened by that fact. It leaves me feeling that Mr. Byrd's life and horrific death are just not as significant as Mr. Shepard's. Neither man deserved what happened to him. They both died as the result of hate. Both deserve equal recognition.

Of Thurmond, Lott said: "When Strom Thurmond ran for president, we voted for him. We're proud of it. And if the rest of the country had followed our lead, we wouldn't have had all these problems over the years, either." Senator Lott later resisgned from his position as Senate Republican Leader as a result of the controversy in which his comments resulted. He later apologized for his remarks.

2004 - Two white teenagers were arrested and charged with criminal mischief for etching racial profanities on Mr. Byrd's grave.

2013 – June 25th - Supreme Court Takes Huge Blow to Minority Voter Registration Rights
http://www.youtube.com/watch?v=2Vt9-bXP3Uo

August 7th - Outside of Coney Island's MCU Baseball Park stands a statue depicting the moment Pee Wee Reese, on a day on which Jackie Robinson was facing more than usual racisttaunts and jeers from the crowd, walked over to Mr. Robinsonand put his arm around him. The statue is a symbol of racialequality and human compassion. On Wednesday, August 7th, the statue was defaced with a swastika and the following words, "Heil Hitler", "Die Nigger", and "Fuck Jackie Robinsonand all niggers."

> [The Southern Poverty Law Center, which tracks both the movement and activity of American hate groups, has reported a dramatic escalation of white supremacist groups since the 2008 election of President Obama. Groups that self-identify as neo-Nazi, neo-Confederate, White Nationalist, Skinhead, Christian Identity and others, are reputedly growing in both numbers and internet visibility, having literally hundreds of websites. The 1988 murder of Ethiopian student Mulugeta Seraw in Portland Oregon by three white supremacists was the among

the most publicized hate crimes that have occurred within the last thirty years, but it is only one of many other acts of racial violence targeted at Americans of Color that could have been reported in the national media. Interestingly, hate groups of brown, black and Asian Americans that target European Americans for personal and collective violence are virtually unknown.]

September 12th - U.S. Senator Ted Cruz' Speech to the Heritage Foundation

The Rebublican Strategy continues to be used today. It was more than apparent in both of President Obama's presidential campaigns. The consistent lack of response from many Republican politicians to their constituents' racist comments about the depictions of first **candidate**, then **President** Obama, clearly speaks to their desire to allow the strategy to work in their favor. Even if they didn't **personally** engage in the racist politics, they were happy to accept whatever political advantage they may have been able to acquire by allowing **others** to do so. Some Republicans, however, did indeed engage in racist politics themselves, as evidenced by their references to the President as, "The Food Stamp President", and claiming that the President is a Kenyon and not American, that he is a Muslim and a terrorist. The objective was to play on the fear that millions of European American have of black men and to make them, in turn, afraid of the President.

One of the most recent uses of the Southern Strategy was the September 11, 2013 keynote address to the the conservative Heritage Foundation made by Senator Ted Cruz. In his remarks, Senator Cruz praised Senator Jesse Helms for being brave enough to say the "crazy things" for which he was widely challenged during his career in the Senate from 1973 to 2003. Those "crazy things" were Senator Helms' many and frequent racist comments and statements. During his thirty-year Senatorial career, Senator Helms championed the continuation of racial segregation, opposed the Civil Rights Act, (which he called, "the most dangerous piece of legislation ever introduced into the United States Congress."), and the Voting Rights Act, and conducted a 16 day filibuster to prevent the Senate's approval of a federal holiday in honor of Dr. King. Senator Helms was throughout his political career and indeed until the time of his death, an avowed segregationist racist. In his address, Senator Cruz said that we need a 100 more Jesse Helms' in the U.S. Senate.

The Heritage Foundation's program during which Senator Cruz spoke is named the Jesse Helms Lecture Series.

"Ted Cruz: We Need 100 More Like Jesse Helms in Senate"
https://www.youtube.com/watch?v=ZvR2BX7IJeU

> [I learned of Senator Cruz' speech, in a news report, of course. I wonder what it would feel like to be able to read newspapers and magazines and watch television news without **constantly** seeing stories of my race being disrespected and hated. It takes a toll on one's soul.][146]

The Republican Southern Strategy has contributed **exponentially** to the intensification in American society, of the twin sibling of racial prejudice – racial resentment. Playing as it does, on the fears and for some the hatred that millions of working class and millions of Southern white Americans have historically harbored

---

146 As a professional in higher education, most mornings I read the publication, *Inside Higher Ed.* Stories describing the harassment of African American students at colleges and universities across the country, are common. Recently, on a single day, (November 25, 2013), the following three stories were published:
http://www.insidehighered.com/quicktakes/2013/11/25/fourth-student-suspended-san-jose-state
http://www.insidehighered.com/quicktakes/2013/11/25/3-colleges-party-themes-or-costumes-offend-many
http://www.insidehighered.com/news/2013/11/25/ucla-grad-students-stage-sit-during-class-protest-what-they-see-racially-hostile

and which some **continue** to harbor toward African Americans, the strategy has impeded racial understanding and harmony in a way that few other things have. The Republican Southern Strategy is to racial **prejudice,** what the Black Codes were to racial **discrimination.**

Note on the Question: Why Haven't African Americans Accomplished As Much As European Americans?

I have not heard this question raised in a number of years. Perhaps there is a concern in contemporary American society that the act of doing so may be perceived as racist. I believe, however, that the question may not even **occur** to many, and perhaps **most** Americans of **all** races because of a subconsciously held a belief in the intellectual inferiority of African Americans, and that belief, provides the answer to the question.[147]

Whenever the question was raised in the past, it was often in two parts, "Why haven't black people accomplished as much as white people in the United States? They've had over twenty years of Affirmative Action." **Every single time** the question was posed, my emotional response was always the same—both exasperation **and** understanding. My **exasperation** resulted from the fact that in my experience, most Americans lack the fundamental historical knowledge that **results** in the question. My **understanding** stems from my full awareness that many and I believe **most** Americans lack that knowledge simply because we are not **taught** it in our American history courses, none of us, not Americans of Color, not European Americans. In responding to the question, I would inform the questioner of the following five "bottom line" facts:

[147] I also believe that the question doesn't even **occur** to millions of **other** European Americans, because of an unconscious belief in the inherent intellectual inferiority of African Americans relative to European Americans.

1. African Americans were enslaved from the time of our arrival in the United States in 1619, until 1865, i.e., for 246 years, approximately two-and-a-half centuries.

2. We have now, in 2013, been free for 148 years, just a little over half the time that we were enslaved.

3. For the first 99 of those 148 years, i.e., from 1865 until the passage of the Civil Right Act of 1964, the vast majority of African Americans lived, by law, as second class citizens under segregation and other state sanctioned discrimination in all aspects of life, including housing, education and employment, **coupled with** extreme violence in the forms of lynchings, white race riots and hate crime.

4. Thus, African Americans have been on the same "legal playing field" with European Americans for less than a half-century, specifically for only the last 49 years.

5. The bottom line numbers of African American history can be summarized as follows: 1964 – 1619 = 345 years of abject oppression. 2013 – 1964 = 49 years of full civil rights under the law. The bottom line math—We have lived in slavery and under wretched oppression **six times longer** than we have lived in freedom and legal equality.

    [Of course the 1964 Civil Right Act made discrimination illegal, not extinct. While African Americans have had full civil rights **under the law** for the past 49 years, we and other Americans of Color have throughout that time lived with and continue into the present, to live with racial discrimination in all aspects of our lives.]

We don't know this history because we don't teach it as the integral part of the American story that it is. In my experience, African American children of my era were taught about our history, **almost exclusively**, within the context of the subject of slavery. During what was initially Negro History **Week**, and then later Black History **Month**, we were taught about the institution of slavery itself, about emancipation, reconstruction, and the most historically notable figures of that period—Harriet Tubman, Frederick Douglas, Sojourner Truth, and a few others, George Washington Carver, Booker T. Washington and W.E.B. DuBois come to mind. **That** was the sum total of our history that we were taught. We were, almost exclusively, a people who were slaves and then struggled against it. Period.

It is vitally important to the self-esteem of African American children that in addition to our history of slavery, they be taught about both our many contributions to American culture, and about the greatness of many of our ancient African civilizations. Children of African descent must know that just as in pre-Columbian times, there were great ancient civilizations in the Western Hhemisphere, the Mayans, Aztecs, Incas and others, just as there were great **Chinese** and **Japanese** empires, there were **also** great ancient **African** civilizations—Timbuktu, Kush, Nubia, and the great Nile Valley Civilization, among others.[148] The message that I want our children to not only **know** beyond the shadow of any doubt, but to also **feel in their very bones**, is both that as African Americans, not only are we not inferior to anyone, but that indeed, we have a place on the world stage of which they can be enormously proud.

But **all** children must be taught about the great civilizations of People of Color around the world. Children should know, for example, that with respect to the ancient Indian civilization, and the Hindu religion which it spawned, the distinguished late astronomer Carl Sagen wrote that, "The Hindu religion is the only one of the world's great faiths . . . . in which the time scales correspond, no doubt by accident, to those of modern scientific cosmology. Its cycles run from our ordinary day and night to a day and night of Brahma, 8.64 billion years long, longer than the age

148 See Note Two for more information on African and African American history and the history of other People of Color.

of the Earth or the Sun and about half the time since the Big Bang. And there are much longer time scales still." [149]

Children should know, quoting Sagen, again, that, "The dates on Mayan Inscriptions . . . . range deep into the past and occasionally far into the future. One inscription refers to a time more than a million years ago . . . . A millennium, [a thousand years] before Europeans were willing to divest themselves of the Biblical idea that the world was a few thousand years old, the Mayans were thinking of millions and the Indians of billions."[150]

In essence, children should be taught the **true** chronology of humanity's great civilizations. They should be aware of the time period during which the great ancient Indigenous, African, Asian and South Asian civilizations existed and flourished. If children **were** aware of that chronology, they would know that **long** before Europeans achieved dominance in the world, People of Color had **the** most advanced civilizations on the planet. They would understand how the full human story **actually** developed and unfolded. That insight may in turn, I believe, **significantly** decrease the likelihood that children of all races, would develop unconscious feelings of the **superiority** of Caucasian human beings and the **inferiority** of all others.

The question, "Why haven't African Americans accomplished as much as European Americans after being here for so long?" is deserving of its answer.

---

[149] I do not believe that it is an accident that the ancient Hindu time scales correspond to those of modern scientific cosmology. I discuss this topic more fully in Fact Five of We *Are One*, Religion: Different Faiths Same Journey - The Fundamental Truth About Faith and Spirituality.

[150] Sagen, Carl. *Cosmos*, New York: Random House, 1980, Print

f. Muslim People and Muslim Americans

Muslims are not a race. Muslims are a religious community comprised of **all** of the races of humanity. Since the tragedy of 9/11, however, discrimination against, harassment of and violence perpetrated upon Muslim People and Muslim Americans have increased to the point at which they now approximate racism and anti-Semitism. In the United States, Muslim human beings are the targets of both hatred and hate crimes in many of the same ways that Jewish Americans and Americans of Color have historically been. It is often the case that Muslim women wearing the hijab receive negative looks and have been physically attacked in public and that Muslim American men now live as African, Latin and other American men of color have for decades, experiencing the constant look of fear on the faces of others.

> [Indeed, in the United States of 2013, one need not even **be** Muslim to be targeted for anti-Muslim violence. In the minds of some Americans, a number of religious groups who wear articles of clothing similar to those worn by Muslims, are indistinguishable from them. Thus, men of other faiths, Sikh men, for example, who wear the Dastar, (a turban-like garment), are **also** targeted for such violence. While the actual motive of the gunman behind the August 6, 2012 shootings which took place at the Wisconsin Sikh Temple, during which six Sikh people lost their lives, is unknown, it is possible, if not likely, that anti-Muslim sentiment could have been at the root.
>
> **Alleged Gunman in Wisconsin Sikh Temple Attack ID'd as Army Veteran: FBI Explores Links to White Supremacist Groups**
> http://usnews.nbcnews.com/_news/2012/08/06/13141505-alleged-gunman-in-wisconsin-sikh-temple-attack-idd-as-army-veteran-fbi-explores-links-to-white-supremacist-groups?lite]

As a consequence of the many stereotypes of Muslim People that have emerged, **particularly since 9/11**, millions of both Muslim Americans and those who are **assumed** to be Muslim, now understand in a very **real** way, the pain of losing one's individuality to the insanity of racism.

4. Lack of Adult Role Models in Positions of National Power and in the Entertainment Industry

A. Positions of National Power

One of the consequences of historical racism for children of color, is that it robbed us of role models of adults in positions of national power, **respected** at the national level, who looked like us. (We also did not see leaders on the local, parish/county and state levels as well.)

Throughout my childhood and well into my adulthood, those who held political power in the United States were with few exceptions, of neither my race nor my gender. Edward Brooke, the African American attorney elected to the U.S. Senate from Massachusetts in 1966, and Thurgood Marshall, the esteemed African-American attorney appointed by President Johnson to the Supreme Court in 1967, were the only two people of my race of whom I was aware, who held any political power during my formative years. [151] There were **none** in such positions, of both my race **and** gender. During my lifetime, until I was in high school when Senator Brooke and Justice Marshall emerged onto the national scene, **all** of the Presidents, all of the **Vice** Presidents, all of the **Senators** and all of the **Supreme Court Justices**, were white men.

I have wondered, from time to time, how little white boys my age may have been emotionally and psychologically affected had throughout

151 Mr. Brooke was the first African American elected to the Senate since the elections of Senators Revels and Bruce in the 1870's.

their formative years and indeed continuing into their **adulthoods**, (with the exception of two white women who broke through the racial iron curtain), the President, Vice President, the Supreme Court Justices, the Senators and U.S. Representatives had **all** been African American women. I wonder if they would have been discouraged about their prospects of future success. I wonder how many would even have **tried** to do well in school. If the little white boys of my generation had seen on the national stage, **only** African American women in positions of power and leadership, I wonder how they would have felt about their possibility of achievement as adults.

> [I've also wondered how it may have affected those same little boys if they had grown up thinking that even **God** was black.]

During the years of my childhood, I saw **only** white men in the news industry. I had **no** role models of either African Americans or women in that field. None. The first time I saw an African American newscaster, **I was twenty five years old**. He was Max Robinson, who in 1978, began co-anchoring ABC's nightly "World News Tonight" broadcast. We can't even **imagine** a world in which European American men saw only African American women as news reporters and news anchors for the first twenty five years of their lives.

B. The Entertainment Industry

During my formative years, I and millions of other kids grew up watching more television than we should have, on a steady diet of shows such as Lassie, Leave it to Beaver, My Three Sons, The Donna Reed Show, Father Knows Best, Ozzie and Harriet, The Andy Griffith Show, Make Room for Daddy, The Courtship of Eddie's Father, Gidget, the Munsters, The Adams Family, Bewitched, the Dick Van Dyke Show, Petticoat Junction, Gomer Pyle, and The Beverly Hillbillies, to name just a few. As a kid, I enjoyed all of those shows to no end. A few, (Lassie, The Andy Griffith Show, Leave it to Beaver, Father Knows Best and the Courtship of Eddie's Father come to mind most readily), sometimes had valuable moral lessons for children.

Most if not all of the sit coms of that time had a kind of innocence which I wish we still had in popular entertainment today. Still, in **none** of those shows do I remember seeing **any** People of Color. If from time to time there **were** a few, I never saw them.

I remember Asian Americans in only two roles when I was growing up—Hop Sing, the Cartwright family's subservient cook on the Bonanza Show, played by actor Victor Sen Yung and later, the character of Mrs. Livingston, the nanny, on the show, "The Courtship of Eddie's Father", played by actor Umeki Miyoshi. I don't remember **a single** Latin American actor as a child. Indeed, I remember only one **portrayal** of a Latin person, the Ed Sullivan show's Jose Jimenez character, played by the comedian, actor and screenwriter Bill Dana. That portrayal, unfortunately, was an extreme stereotype. My only memory of any portrayals of Indigenous People on television was in Westerns, in which they were depicted as uncivilized savages who were always both the "bad guys" and the losers. By comparison, **surprisingly**, African Americans fared somewhat better. I actually saw African Americans depicted in six regular TV shows, four of which, for the time, were quite positive roles—Bill Cosby as Alexander Scott, an international spy for the American government on the "I Spy" show, Greg Morris, as Barney Collier, an electronics expert, (of whom I was **very** proud), on Mission Impossible, Nichelle Nicholls as Lieutenant Uhura, the Chief Communications Officer in the original Star Trek series, and Dianne Carroll, as a nurse and Vietnam widow on the show, "Julia". The only other African Americans I remember seeing on television were the cast of characters on the Amos 'n Andy show, (Kingfish, Sapphire, Mama, Andy, Calhoun and Lightnin') and Flip Wilson, on his own comedy variety show. There were so few African Americans on television in the 60's, that Jet magazine listed on its back cover, all of the African American actors who were appearing on television the following week. [152] Our representation **behind** the scenes in the television industry was almost totally non-existent.

---

[152] I was also too young to remember Nat King Cole's variety show which aired from 1956 to '57. It was the first television show with a black host.

In all of the television commercials that were aimed at kids for Slinkies, Silly Putty, Chatty Cathy, Mr. Potato Head, and dozens of other toys, in all of the commercials aimed at adults for Twenty Mule Team Borax, Timex watches, and those that told them that "Winston tastes good like a cigarette should", in **none** of them, in not a **single** commercial of all the hundreds that we watched, do I remember **any** People of Color. There **were**, however, two advertisements that had images of African Americans on their products' packaging—those of Uncle Ben for Uncle Ben's rice and Aunt Jemimah, for Aunt Jemimah's pancake syrup. Judging from their clothing, I assumed as a child that both were servants.

Regarding the movie industry, to my knowledge, People of Color were virtually, if not **totally**, absent behind the camera as writers, producers and directors. As for those in **front** of the camera, Sidney Poitier was the only African American actor I remember seeing at the movie theater. The actor, (whose name I don't know), who played the maid, and Bill Robinson who played the butler in the Shirley Temple movies, were the only African American actors I remember seeing in movies that I watched on television.[153]

> [Many years later, in listening to the audio book of Sidney Poitier's Autobiography, *Measure of a Man: A Spiritual Autobiography*, my heart **ached** when I listened to Mr. Poitier relate the story of his experience in an upscale Atlanta restaurant in1955. Upon entering the restaurant, Mr. Poitier requested a table from the African American man who was the restaurant's maître d. The maître d responded by apologizing and then explaining to Mr. Poitier that while he **could** give him a table, a "screen" would have to be placed around it so that the restaurant's

[153] I was too young to have been familiar with Dorothy Dandridge, Lena Horne, Hattie McDaniel, the Nicholas Brothers, Cab Calloway and the few other African American movie stars of their era. I **did**, however, see Hattie McDaniel play the maid character in the re-runs of two or three movies that had been produced before I was born.

white guests could not see him. The gentleman explained that it was the restaurant's practice. It was the law. Rather than suffer that indignity, Mr. Poitier chose to leave the restaurant.[154]

My heart aches when I think about the experiences of Mr. Poitier and **so** many African American movie stars of that era, **who despite tremendous fame and wealth**, regularly faced humiliating discrimination. Dorothy Dandridge, for example, sometime in the 1950's, was told that she was not allowed to swim in the pool of the hotel at which she was staying because if she got into it, it would have to be drained, cleaned and re-filled for the use of the hotel's Caucasian patrons. Following that conversation, Ms. Dandridge, in defiance, dipped one of her toes into the pool. Later, upon passing through the pool area, she saw an African American man in the bottom of the drained pool, scrubbing it with a brush.[155]

I am deeply saddened when I think about the horrible indignities suffered during the pre-Civil Rights era by Ms. Dandridge and all of the other entertainers of color who travelled for a living, great musicians, Duke Ellington, Ella Fitzgerald, Louis Armstrong and so many others, great actors such as Paul Robeson and Ethel Waters, great athletes, among them, Jackie Robinson, members of The Negro Leagues and the Harlem Rens. I grieve that they had to experience the indignities through which they lived.

---

[154] I have **tremendous** respect for Mr. Poitier, who upon seeing in the face of the maître d, how painful it was for him to have to inform him, Mr. Poitier, of the necessity of the screen, more than his own personal anger, felt **compassion,** in that moment, for that African American gentleman.

[155] The irony of the fact that it was a **black** man who was in the pool, cleaning it, is almost unbelievable. Irrationality is one of **the** hallmarks of racism.

"On the Shoulders of Giants"—Movie trailer about the Harlem Rens
http://kareemabduljabbar.com/osg/

Tragically, I have over many years, heard stories of **contemporary** African American celebrities regarding their experiences of daily indignities. I have heard African American male actors describe how difficult it is for them to get a taxi in New York City. I have read stories about African American celebrities' experiences of the "shopping while black" phenomenon—being followed by salespeople and security personnel in retail establishments. All presumably had enough money to buy not only anything **in** the store, but indeed, **the store itself**.

The most recent such incident about which I read in the news, occurred just last month, July, 2013, and involved Oprah Winfrey. Oprah was in Zurich, Switzerland for the wedding of her longtime friend, musician Tina Turner, who lives in Zurich. While shopping in Zurich, Oprah asked a store clerk to show her a black bag that was behind a screen. The clerk refused to show her the bag, allegedly saying to Oprah, "You will not be able to afford that." Oprah reports that she asked the salesperson a second time to see the bag, and again, she refused, offering to show Oprah other, less expensive bags. The bag was priced at thirty-eight thousand American dollars. Forbes magazine estimates that Oprah earned 77 million dollars over the past year. Her net worth is well over two billion dollars. In that moment, (in which the sales clerk presumably did not recognize her), despite her unparalleled worldwide fame **and** her fortune, Oprah experienced what has been referred to as the soft bigotry of low expectations.]

I sincerely do not believe that without experiencing it, one can **truly** understand the psychological and emotional impact on children of having virtually **no** adult role models in important societal positions who are of either their race and/or their gender, and especially if those children **also** have no such positive adult role models in their **personal** lives. I'm **fully** aware of how fortunate I am to have had the African American adult role models that I had in my early life. I'm also well aware of how fortunate **all** American children of color of my generation are to have grown up during The Civil Rights Era, for many of us were **convinced** that by the time we grew up, American society was going to be **completely** changed. We **knew** that as adults, we were going to have opportunities of which our parents could have only dreamed. The Civil Rights struggle was a struggle that we were **convinced** we were going to win. We felt in our **core,** that we were on the just side, the side of good, the moral side, the side of righteousness. We were on the right side of **history**, and we knew it. It was a time of **incredible** hope and amazing optimism. My generation is the **extraordinarily** fortunate benefactor of the success of that movement. That profound truth is not lost to me. [156] We may not have **had** role models in politics and business on the national level, but we knew that we were destined to **be** those models for our children.

---

[156] It was **undeniably** the Civil Rights Movement of many thousands of Americans, led valiantly by Dr. King, that finally took the United States out of its ninety-nine year old, post-Civil War racial cesspool, as a result of which the lives of Americans of Color were changed forever. It is for that reason that my heart sank when Lambert told me some years ago about the following conversation that he overheard between two African American teenage girls on the Washington D.C. Metro: "Tomorrow's MLK Day. I'm glad we have it off from school." "Me too, but I don't know **why** we have it off. Martin Luther King never did nothin' for me." As utterly repulsive as the statement of the second young woman may be to many, she is not to blame, for if we do not **teach** young people - of **all** races- about our racial history, they **cannot** know it. The fault lies with us, the adults, who fail to teach them.

5. Eurocentrism

In addition to slavery, colonialism, discrimination, harassment and violence, the practice of racism has historically taken the additional form of Eurocentrism. The following is my personal experience with this form of racism.

The history that we were taught throughout my education, from elementary school on, was **entirely** Eurocentric.

In high school, between the four Shakespeare plays that we were required to attend, ("A Midsummer Night's Dream" and "Twelfth Night" are the only two I remember), we had to read Charles Dickens' Great Expectations, George Eliot's Silas Marner, and Herman Melville's Moby Dick.

We had to learn about the great European and American explorers—Christopher Columbus, Hernan Cortes, Vasco de Gama, Amerigo Vespucci, Captain James Cook, Lewis and Clark, Thor Heyerdahl's voyage on the Kon-Tiki and others.

We learned all about the famous and infamous European and American political and military figures—Julius Caesar, Napoleon, all of "the Georges" and other kings of England, George Washington, Thomas Jefferson, James Madison, Abraham Lincoln, among many others.

We learned all about the famous European and American authors, Homer, Geoffrey Chaucer, William Shakespeare, Ernest Hemingway, Edgar Allan Poe, Nathaniel Hawthorne, Herman Melville, Walt Whitman, Mark Twain and others.

We had to learn about the great European classical composers, Beethoven, Bach, Brahms, Chopin, Handel, Tchaikovsky and others.

We were taught about many of the great European scientists, Galileo, Copernicus, Newton, Pasteur, Darwin and Mendel.

All of those figures, in addition to all of the **miscellaneous** characters, both real and fictional, about which we had to learn, (Johnny Appleseed, Rip Van Winkle, Huckleberry Finn, Paul Bunyan, Daniel Boone, and Davy Crockett are the ones I remember), were white and all were male. I can literally count on one hand, the number of white women about whom I remember learning—Joan of Arc, Betsy Ross, Marie Antoinette, Francis Nightingale, and Madame Curie.

The little, handheld cardboard fans with wooden sticks that we were handed in church every Sunday, had a picture of Jesus in which he literally looked more like the stereotype of a California beach boy than a Jewish man from a Middle Eastern climate. Yes, as the result of having seen **that** image of Jesus all our lives, in the minds of most African American, (and African), Christians and other Christians of Color, Latin, Indigenous and Asian People both in the U.S. and abroad, Jesus was white, and therefore His Father, **our** Father, **God** the Father was white. He **definitely** didn't look like us.[157]

During the years of my education, at the same time during which I was being taught all about the achievements of European People and their descendants, I was being taught very little about the history of People of Color, and much of the history that I **was** taught about People of Color, was both inaccurate and incomplete.

We actually **did** study **one** great African civilization, the ancient Egyptian civilization, believed by many historians to be the most advanced civilization on the Earth during the height of its power.

---

[157] 143As a little girl, one of my very favorite Christmas Carols was, "Some Children See Him". Even as a child, I cried every time I heard it. It's message, while not at all true, touched me deeply. While I am fully aware of what the order of the lyrics represents, unintentionally, I assume, ("Lilly white" is first and "dark as they" is last), they still bring tears to my eyes, even to this day.
http://www.youtube.com/watch?v=s49gEmTlOTk
http://www.youtube.com/watch?v=_1gZuabWfb8

We were taught, however, in both words and **pictures**, that the Egyptians were white. Metro-Goldwyn-Mayer's 1963 blockbuster movie, "Cleopatra", (in which Cleopatra, played by Elizabeth Taylor, and all of the other Egyptian characters were portrayed as white), was perhaps the **quintessential** lesson to us all that the ancient Egyptians were indeed Caucasian.[158] I find astounding, the fact that that myth was so widely believed, and for so long, since among several other reasons, the Egyptian People aren't white today!

When I was a young child, perhaps nine or ten, Gramzie gave me a book entitled, *A Child's History of the World,* by V.M. Hillyer.[159] She had only a third grade education and therefore could neither read nor write, but seeing the book's pictures, which were clearly for children, wanted me to have it. Because Gramzie couldn't read, she had no idea what I, a 5th or 6th grader at the time, was about to read in it.

The ancient Egyptians depicted themselves in their paintings on the pyramids, as both dark and medium brown in color In *A Child's History of the World*, Hillyer explained the color of the Egyptians on the pyramids in the following way:

> When they painted a picture they used any color they thought was pretty, usually blue or yellow or brown. Whether the person or thing was **really** that color or not made no difference.

Hillyer explained the fact that one of the greatest ancient civilizations on the planet was a black, African civilization, by simply claiming that the Egyptians weren't black. They were white.

---

158 Images from the 1963 movie, "Cleopatra": http://www.youtube.com/watch?v=fkRZTil4ges

159 Hillyer, V.M. *A Child's History of the World.* New York: D. Appleton-Century Company, Inc., 1935. Print

Concerning the origin of People of Color, Hillyer stated only the following:

> All of the people who lived in the country of the Tigris and Euphrates were white. We don't know how nor when nor where colored people first lived, though it is interesting to guess.
>
> [The grandness of African history stands in stark contrast to that historical falsehood. The subject of African history is dealt with in much more detail in Note Two, however, since Hillyer mentioned the Egyptians specifically, a short video illustrating Egyptian self-portraits and some of their artifacts is appropriate here.
>
> **Self-Portrayals of Ancient Egyptians on Pyramids and Other Egyptian Art (Be sure to scroll down the page.)**
>
> http://www.tuttartpitturasculturapoesiamusica.com/2011/03/ancient-egypt.html]

I still have among my books to this day, that *Child's History of the World* that Gramzie gave me so many years ago.

The history that we were **all** taught, American Children of Color **and** European American children, was a history of selectivity and omission. It was a story which was almost completely Eurocentric.[160]

All of the birthday cards that I received as a child, had a picture of a little white girl on the front, always with blonde hair and blue eyes.

---

[160] See Note Two for more information on African and African American history and the history of other Americans of Color.

A Few of My Childhood Birthday Cards

I didn't play with dolls, but among the dolls that my friends had, I don't remember seeing a single doll of color, not Chatty Cathy, not Thumbelina, not Barbie and her crew—Ken, Midge, Allen, Scooter, and Skipper, not G.I. Joe, not Johnny West.

The kids on the boxes of **all** of the toys with which we played, Twister, Candy Land, Spirograph, Lemar Jr. and Lambert's Lionel train, electric football game and race car track, were **all** white.

All of the characters in the Archie comic books that I loved and read all summer long, were white.

The only television cartoon characters of color that I saw were the Congolese in a cartoon in which Popeye had gone to the Congo to rescue Bluto, who was missing. The Congolese were portrayed as savage cannibals who wanted to boil Popeye in a big black cauldron, and eat him. That was the very first image of Africans that I remember ever receiving.

Women's makeup was available in only tones that matched the hue of Caucasian skin. "Flesh colored" band aids were somewhat pink in color.

The weddings of African Americans that I attended as a child, **all** had a little Caucasian couple on the top of the wedding cake, **and**, no one thought anything of it. It was totally normal. I've tried to imagine a wedding of a Caucasian couple at that time, (and even now), in which the cake topper was a little African American bride and groom. I cannot.

In those and in countless other ways, American culture was **entirely** Eurocentric. I believe, however, that most European Americans were, at that time, as unaware of our nation's Eurocentrism as a fish is of water. It was like the air we breathe, and for those in the majority, as status quo and as natural as honey to a bee. **But,** if you were in the **minority**, and you **didn'**t look like the kids on television shows, in the commercials, in the movies, on cereal boxes, on your birthday cards, in the comic books that you read; if the dolls and soldiers that you played with didn't look like you; if whenever you used a band aid, it stuck out on your skin like a sore thumb; if your teachers and the women in your family always had a very noticeable powder line at the base of their jaw line, American Eurocentrism had a kind of "in your faceness" that **constantly** communicated to you that you don't count, you don't matter, that you're unimportant and irrelevant, indeed, that you're **invisible**, that you **are** all of those things, because you are so **undesirable,** and that you are **undesirable** because of your race. In other words, the message from the larger society in which we lived, was that except for the labor which it wanted to extract from us, and the money that it wanted us to spend as consumers, it didn't **want** to see us, and that **despite** our numbers in the millions, we were to be utterly ignored. The message from the larger American society, in essence, seemed to be, "Give us the work we want to get from you, buy the goods and services we want to sell to you, and then we're going to pretend that you don't exist in our country." That message, combined with the often suffocating legal, financial and social oppression in which we lived at that time, coalesced as an affront to **the very humanity** of millions of Americans of Color.

E. The Psychology of Racism: Its Effect on European Americans

In order for us to gain a **full** and thus an **accurate** understanding of our racial history and its impact on our entire species, in addition to understanding the psychological impact of racism on Americans of **Color**, we must both realize and acknowledge the **enormous** impact that racism has had on our **European American** brothers and sisters as well. The insanity of racism has over time, (just as it has done to millions of Americans of Color), mentally and emotionally disabled many millions of European Americans.[161] It has resulted, for those millions, in the loss of their ability to **truly** see themselves as being **equal** and not **superior** to Americans of Color. In the process, they lost their compassion for their fellow human beings of color and in so doing, also lost an **enormous** part of their **own** humanity. The psychological poison of racism has left millions of European Americans entirely incapable of living their lives freely, i.e., without the fear of People of Color which they needlessly experience in a variety of ordinary life circumstances. It has left those millions utterly unable to even **imagine** the fullness and richness that a diverse circle of friends would bring to their lives.

I believe that for millions of European Americans who are truly good people, who have not a single **conscious** racist thought about **any** group, who **treat** all people respectfully, who would **never intentionally** engage in behavior that is biased in any way and who may even very sincerely self-identify as having a deep spiritual and/or religious orientation for which racism in any form

---

161 While racism is not categorized by the mental health profession as a mental illness, the manner in which and depth of the extent to which it has negatively impacted our view of each other based upon race, may indeed have resulted in our living in a kind of alternate racial reality that is as "alternate" to humanity's true racial reality as is any alternate reality experienced by the most certifiably, severely mentally ill person.

is abhorrent, **unconscious** racism, like a thief in the night, has stolen their ability to experience a deep feeling of the absolute equality of humanity. With even their conscious antipathy toward racism, those millions are unable to see African Americans, Latin Americans and other People of Color as their true intellectual and cultural equals.

The spiritual, emotional and psychological effect which racism has historically had and **continues** to have on European Americans, is in several significant ways, radically different from that which it has had and continues to have on Americans of Color. It **is**, nonetheless **also** an incalculable human tragedy, one which, if as a species, we are to ever mature beyond the ravages of racism, we must both bring into sharp focus and deeply understand.

F. The Practice of Prejudice Against European Americans[162]

1. All European Americans

Anti-Semitism, anti-Irish, anti-Italian, anti-Polish, and anti-Catholic sentiment, as well as bias against Southern and Eastern Europeans, are as much a part of the American story as is the history of racism against Americans of Color. There is one enormous difference, however, between the historical bias and resulting discrimination experienced between Americans of Color and European Americans. That difference is that European Americans, irrespective of whether their families were Catholic, or originally from Ireland, Italy, Poland, Southern or Eastern Europe, **over time**, eventually, all became "**white**" and **with** that designation, were granted rights and privileges that Americans of Color were **never** accorded. Being **white** became their significant social classification. **Eventually**, with few exceptions that applied primarily at the very top of society, (e.g., admittance to exclusive social and sport clubs), whether any particular white person was Catholic, or of Italian, Irish, Polish, Southern or Eastern European background, did not matter.[163] They were "white". **That** is what mattered.

We in American society will have moved a long way on our journey of becoming more racially aware and compassionate

---

[162] Since the bias which European Americans practiced on each other was based not upon their **race**, but rather, upon their national origin, and/or religion I believe that it is more historically accurate to refer to that form of bias, not as racism, but as prejudice.

[163] Indeed, many Eastern European immigrants changed their names to more Western European sounding names. In so doing, many totally left behind any identification with whatever formerly "less desirable" European ethnicity they may have had, allowing them to then fully blend into "**white**" America.

when a critical mass of European Americans have gained the awareness that their experience of ethnic discrimination is **significantly**, **qualitatively** different from the racial discrimination experienced by Americans of Color because of that **one** fact—they enjoy white privilege.

That said, the prejudice and discrimination that have been practiced against **European** American groups based upon ethnicity, are just as morally bankrupt as the prejudice and discrimination that have been practiced against Americans of Color. They are just as wrong. It hurts **every** and **anyone** who is its target, including human beings of Caucasian descent. Irish immigrants, for example, **endured serious and sustained** discrimination when they began to enter the United States in appreciable numbers in the 19th and early 20th centuries. The same is true for many other European immigrant groups. Their stories, their human experiences with the pain of prejudice and discrimination, whether or not it is based on their ethnicity, also deserve and need to be **listened** to deeply and **responded** to with great respect and sincere compassion.[164]

2. Jewish Americans

The history of Jewish Americans is **very** different from that of other European American groups.

Outside of the United States, Jewish People have a unique and heartrending history of being subjected to discrimination,

---

[164] One of the most compelling stories of non-race based prejudice I have ever heard was shared by a participant in a workshop that I facilitated many years ago for the National Association of Women Judges. The judge, a European American, described her experiences of religious bigotry as a child of the only Catholic family in a small rural Pennsylvania community. The kind and depth of pain the judge clearly experienced in just **recounting** the story, were deserving of great compassion in that moment.

harassment and violence in country after country, living through pogrom after pogrom, the world over. The attempt of Germany's Third Reich during World War II to totally annihilate Jewish human beings from the planet, is perhaps the most horrific injustices committed against a group of people during the 20th century.

[The following three films about The Holocaust are highly recommended:

Shindi's List
http://www.imdb.com/title/tt0108052/

Oskar Schindler on The Holocaust
http://yearslaterwewouldremember.com/the-memoir-an-excerpt/media/

The Diary of Anne Frank—The Movie
http://www.imdb.com/title/tt0052738/?ref_=tt_rec_tti

The Diary of Anne Frank—The Television Miniseries
http://www.imdb.com/title/tt0246430/]

Within the U.S., although most Jewish Americans are white, and therefore share the significant privilege that white skin grants in the United States, of all of the "white" groups in the country, Jewish Americans have suffered, by far, the **most** discrimination, and for the longest time, even into the present. Sephardic and other Jewish Americans of Color are, of course, subject to the same skin color discrimination as are other Americans of Color.

Additionally, Jewish Americans experience the "otherness" of being a very small religious minority in the United States, with all of its associated challenges.

Historically, American Jews were subject to anti-Semitism from the moment they arrived at Ellis Island, where they largely arrived from Europe. Jewish American communities have been terrorized and attacked by the Ku Klux Klan and other white supremacist groups. **Individual** Jewish Americans have been lynched by the Klan. Synagogues have been vandalized, bombed and burned by hate groups across the United States. Throughout American history, while other European Americans were allowed membership in exclusive social clubs, employment in elite law firms and other benefits of being white, Jewish Americans were often excluded. During the Jim Crow era, many establishments in the South that were "White Only" forbade Jewish Americans from entrance and membership as well.

Perhaps it is that history that resulted in Jewish Americans being among the strongest allies of African Americans during the Civil Rights Movement during which, in many peaceful demonstrations, they were beaten and even killed right alongside us. Rabbi Abraham Joshua Heschel, Michael Schwerner and Andrew Goodman are perhaps the three most famous Jewish Americans who were active in the movement. Dr. Cornel West and Rabbi Michael Lerner, in their book, *Jews and Blacks*, elaborate on the history of the complex relationship between the two groups.[165]

Tragically, anti-Semitism is still very much present in various aspects of American life. Additionally, the results of the tracking of hate crimes against Jewish Americans by the Anti-Defamation League and the Southern Poverty Law Center, are disturbing.

G. A Final Comment on Our Racial History

What pain we have caused based upon what we perceive to be our racial differences. What mind-boggling pain. In order to heal from it, we **must** understand both that history and the tremendous human suffering in which it has resulted over several centuries.

165 Lerner, Michael, West, Cornel. *Jews and Blacks.* New York: Grosset/ Putnam, 1995. Print

I have been very **sorely** reminded of that history on trips to Alaska, Mexico, Costa Rica, Panama, Brazil, Peru and to the islands of St. Thomas, Puerto Rico and Kaua'i. It was the very **powerful** juxtaposition of golfers, resort, hotel and restaurant guests, scuba divers, snorkelers, souvenir buyers, photograph takers, night club goers, kayakers, and those on sail boats and catamarans, who are almost exclusively of **Caucasian** descent, **against** the hotel maids, the hotel bell hops, the resort grounds keepers, and the restaurant cooks and dish washers, who are almost exclusively of **African** descent.[166] I was reminded of it when I took guided tours of San Diego, Los Angeles, Santa Fe and many other locales within the United States. The explanations of how Indigenous People lived in all of those places in the "pre-Columbian" and "pre-Captain Cook" era, and what happened to them upon and then subsequent to the arrival of the Spanish, the Portuguese and the British, have left me somber, each and every time I have heard them, **when** they are discussed.[167]

In summary, an important facet of our nation's racial healing is our awareness of three important histories:

1. The history of the achievements of the many great ancient civilizations of People of Color on the continents of Africa, North, Central and South America, and on the sub-continent of India;

2. The unfettered history of racism in the United States; and,

3. The history of the many contributions that Americans of Color have made to the United States, **despite** slavery and

---

166 Adding to that hurt, is my knowledge that a large percentage of the **owners** of those businesses are also Caucasian, even on black-majority islands.

167 On many tours that I have taken, the history of Indigenous People prior to the arrival of Europeans is given only a passing mention.

> debilitating discrimination, harassment and violence—our accomplishments in science, medicine, engineering, law, music, and virtually every other field of human endeavor.

The history and effects of racism in the United States are indescribably ugly, painful and repulsive. Being honest about that history, however, is one of the first steps toward moving **beyond** it. Our nation's racial history must no longer be denied and callously minimized through unsympathetic and absolutely false equivalences drawn between the oppression suffered by European American immigrants and Americans of Color. We must collectively recognize that while on the **individual** level, there is **absolutely** no hierarchy of human pain, on the **group** level, there are **dramatic** differences in both the amount and the kind of societal oppression that Americans have endured, and that many of those differences are based upon race.

If we are **not** honest about what has taken place in the United States and the rest of the Western Hemisphere with regard to race, we risk the continuation of the false belief that the **majority** of the unemployment, the poverty, the alcohol and other drug abuse, the crime and other socially aberrant behaviors of many of the residents of America's inner cities, its barrios and Indigenous reservations, as well as the levels of poverty and crime which exist in the Caribbean Islands, are the direct result of the laziness and bad morals of People of Color.[168] The **danger** of that belief is

---

168 In a recent conversation with a European American friend in which the topic of favorite vacation spots was being discussed, s/he commented that s/he preferred Hawaii to St. Thomas because there is a lot of poverty in St. Thomas. My friend went on to state that for that reason, while there on his/her last vacation, s/he didn't want to go anywhere on the island outside of the resort at which s/he and his/her family was staying. This person is originally from a small American city in which there is a large, predominantly African American community which is racked by poverty. In the instant my friend commented on the poverty of St. Thomas, I wondered whether s/he had an understanding of the historical causes of the poverty

that it both sews and prolongs feelings of hostility and resentment toward and fear of People of Color, contributing to a complete lack of understanding **of** and compassion **for** communities of color, making racial healing improbable, if not impossible.

> [I have presented here, what is literally just a thumbnail sketch, a **smidgeon** of the history of People of Color in the United States. Information on the history of the **accomplishments** of Americans of Color is available in Note Two.]

Having provided a **very** brief outline of the history of what, in the United States has been done in response to our racial differences, I feel **compelled** to declare that those of us who were born to parents of color in the United States should **never** use our history as an excuse to not attempt to live our best life consistent with our very highest purpose. I believe **deeply** that regardless of **whatever** experiences we have had as a result of having been born into the racial group to which we belong, whether we are in the majority or a minority group, it is our responsibility as human beings to do our best to live a responsible, conscious, examined life of principal. Failure to do so condemns us, both individually and collectively, to perpetually live the results of a very tragic racial history and prevents us from moving into the future in a more positive and **empowered** way.

That said, if we are to be intellectually honest, we must **also** both acknowledge and understand how the history of racism, with its iron curtain of abject discrimination, harassment and violence, have impacted the lives of Americans of Color. We must begin to

---

of both the island and her/his native city. I wondered if s/he had the **unconscious** belief that poverty and being of African descent are somehow just inextricably linked. I don't actually know. S/he may have been **very** well aware of the ways in which our history of oppression has significantly contributed to our present status. I do not believe, however, that the majority of Americans are.

understand both the full extent and the impact of the damage that has been done.

Finally, to those who would criticize my call for a deep acknowledgement and understanding of our racial history by characterizing it as, "wallowing in the past", and blaming Caucasian People for all of the world's ills, I say the following: Educating oneself and others about the past is **extremely** different from "wallowing" in it. "Wallowing" is **not** the objective of acknowledging and understanding the past. Rather, it is to help in the process of racial **healing**. Not **a single** European American alive today had **anything** to do with the discrimination, harassment and violence that were practiced against Americans of Color in the past, **absolutely nothing**. The social, legal and economic systems which are the foundations of that oppression, were established long before a **single** contemporary European American was ever born. We **all** inherited this madness, **all** of us alive today. Blaming contemporary European Americans for that history, is therefore illogical, insane, and on a practical level, utterly counter-productive. I intend my **call** for acknowledgement and understanding of it, to be neither an indictment of contemporary European Americans nor an attempt to make them feel guilty. Indeed, I am fully aware that guilt makes it exceedingly difficult for us, as human beings, to learn and grow, which in turn, makes it impossible for us to be clear, effective allies to each other.[169] I **do** hope, however, that a deep understanding of our racial past will do the following for our European American sisters and brothers:

[169] The article, "*Beyond Guilt: How to Deal with Societal Racism*", which my friend Jack Straton and I co-authored, explores in detail, the topic of how responding to racism with guilt, emotionally paralyzes the person experiencing the guilt, and as a result, prevents him/her from being able to be an effective ally in anti-racism work. The article is available at
http://rise.pdx.edu/GuiltMultEdNileStraton2.pdf

1. Help them to deeply understand what Americans of Color have experienced in the past; and,

2. Help them to fully comprehend how all of the discrimination, harassment and violence that we experienced in the past, continues to impact both our present and theirs.

That acknowledgement of the past, combined with a genuine and concerted effort to dismantle all of its present-day vestiges will, I believe, make it possible for the majority of Americans of Color to truly forgive. **All** of us who have been seriously hurt by prejudice, whether we are Jewish American, Muslim Americans, Indigenous American, African American, Latin American or Asian American, **must** forgive, for without our forgiveness, humanity, as a species, cannot heal.

[The forgiveness that I reference in this context is not forgiving present-day European Americans for slavery and other wrongs of the past since as previously stated, they had nothing to do with that past. For the vast majority of present-day European Americans, it is forgiveness, rather, for the following:

* The heretofore general denial on the part of many European Americans, of the true history of racism in the United States.

* The general denial on the part of many European Americans, of the present day **effects** of that history on the lives of Americans of Color.

* The deep-seated and unconscious belief by many European Americans, of their genetic, intellectual and social superiority to Americans of Color.

* The deep-seated and unconscious favoritism generally given to European Americans in education, employment and housing, in which those beliefs often result.

* The countless ways in which that favoritism and those feelings of superiority have a significant negative impact on the lives of Americans of Color.

* For a small number of European Americans, it is forgiveness for the conscious acts of racism which they have committed against us in education, in employment, and housing, in denying us the right to vote, in minimizing the **impact** of our vote, and for acts of physical violence carried out against us by both individuals and white hate groups.]

Dr. King said it in the following way:

> We must develop and maintain the capacity to forgive. He who is devoid of the power to forgive is devoid of the power to love. There is some good in the worst of us and some evil in the best of us.
>
> Martin Luther King, Jr.

With respect to our tragic human racial history, we must get to it, in order to get **through** it. We must **acknowledge** it, and have a critical mass of human beings be on the same page, sharing the same historical **awareness** of it. We must do so because that acknowledgement and shared awareness of our racial past are **crucial** to our ability to avoid in the future, many of the ways in which our racial **past** has impacted our racial present. Using the lens of that past, let us look now, at four of the most significant realities of our racial **present**.

V. The Impact of Our Racial Past on Our Universal Racial Present

I have often wondered what our planet would today be like if not for our horrific racial history. Doing so is **exceedingly** difficult. What is clear, however, is that the three results of historic racism - slavery, colonization, and discrimination/harassment/violence directed at People of Color the world over, have resulted in the following four present-day racial realities:

A. Two Worlds Within a World

"Two Worlds Within a World" refers to the reality that on this planet, there is a "developed world" which, with the exception of South Africa, is comprised almost **exclusively** of "white" majority nations, and a "developing world" which is comprised **exclusively** of countries inhabited primarily by People of Color.

> [A world in which Dr. King, Anne Frank, Harvey Milk, Daniel Pearl, Matthew Shepard and Prime Minister Yitzhak Rabin had lived beyond the dates of their assassinations, is portrayed in the video, "Imagine a World Without Hate", produced by the Anti-Defamation League.]

B. Two Worlds Within Nations

"Two Worlds Within Nations" refers to the dramatic difference in the social statistics of Caucasian People and People of Color in **every** single country on the planet which they cohabitate, statistics on factors, including the occurrence of low birth weight, teen pregnancy, high school completion rates, college completion rates, functional illiteracy, unemployment, under-employment, depression, alcoholism and other drug abuse, crime, incidence of incarceration and recidivism, mental illness, physical illness, emotional violence and life expectancy.

With respect to my home, **the the United States,** specifically, I wonder what our American culture would today be like had we, as a nation, worked earnestly for the ninety-nine years from 1865 to 1964, to truly heal from the national nightmare of slavery. I wonder where we would be today with regard to both racial equality and race relations, if during that time, we had made a genuine and concerted effort to achieve racial justice, understanding and reconciliation for **all** American numerical minorities, Indigenous People, i.e., Native Americans, Hispanic Americans, Asian Americans, Jewish Americans and African Americans. I wonder if the increasing number of hate groups in the U.S. would now not only **not** be increasing, but indeed, if they would exist at all. Tragically, I cannot imagine that alternate reality.

I cannot count how many times I have wondered where we would now be as a nation, had Dr. King lived to successfully wage the Poor People's Campaign which he had begun to organize near the end of his life. The prospect of getting European Americans and Americans of Color working together in one massive coalition for economic and social justice, would have transformed this nation in ways that we are incapable of imagining. It is my fervent belief that if there **is** a next great American leader, **that** is the movement s/he will lead. S/he will be the leader who will successfully demonstrate to European Americans living in poverty, that right-wing pundits and conservative politicians whose dog-whistled message that they cannot get ahead because the government is supporting millions of People of Color using their tax dollars, have sold them a bill of goods that results in keeping powerless, **all** people who are poor, including them. S/he will be the leader who opens their eyes to the reality that many wealthy, European American right wing politicians and radio and TV pundits do not care **one iota** about them, and indeed, that their agenda is to keep poor people, **all** poor people, **including** them, politically disenfranchised by keeping them separated, and that they do so, by using race. The next great American leader will be s/he who is able to convince European Americans who are poor, that it is squarely, solidly and undeniably in their best interests to work together with Americans of Color who **also** live in poverty, to address the issue of systemic economic inequality in our country. That next great leader will be s/he who unites across racial lines, Americans living in poverty and their allies, to form a powerful movement for economic justice in the United States. S/he will be the next Bobby Kennedy, the next Dr. Martin King, Jr.

[I have often wished that **some** charismatic European American politician, religious leader or secular humanist could get through with the following messages to a critical mass of European Americans who live in poverty and to those who are working and middle class:

To European Americans who live in poverty:

> First, according to the U. S. Department of Commerce, only **one percentage point** separates the total percentage of whites from the total percentage of blacks in the United States who receive welfare benefits. The statistics, specifically, are that of those who are on welfare, 38.8 percent are white and 39.8 percent are black. What that means is that almost the same **number** of whites and blacks receive welfare;
>
> [Obviously, those same statistics also indicate that based upon the fact that only 12% of the American population is African American, we receive a greatly disproportionate percentage of welfare benefits, i.e., much more than some may say is our "fair share". Many of the historical reasons for that fact are elucidated in this work.]
>
> Second, since only one percentage point separates the number of blacks and whites who receive welfare, there may very well come a time in the **near** future when whites will be receiving more welfare dollars than blacks;

Third, there are currently, **today**, more than **twice** as many white Americans on welfare, as Hispanic Americans. The Department of Commerce reports that of Americans who are on welfare,15.7 are Hispanic;

Fourth, the same government programs that help to lift **minorities** out of poverty also help to lift **you** out of poverty. Specifically, when aid to education is cut, and when job training and placement programs are cut, it hurts almost exactly the same number of poor **whites** as it does poor **blacks**. The same is true for the programs that support you until you are **able** to work your way up and out of poverty, the WIC program, the SNAP program, the Head Start program.[170] When **they're** cut, **that as well** hurts poor whites just about as much as it hurts poor blacks; and,

Fifth, there's only **one** Federal treasury. **All** of our taxes, **regardless** of our race, go into the very same bucket. That means that many **millions** of working class, middle class and wealthy blacks and Hispanics pay many **millions** of dollars in taxes to support the many **millions** of poor whites who are on welfare.

To working and middle class European Americans:

When you vote against the rights of workers to organize and form unions to represent them, when you vote for those who oppose providing quality health care to every American, when you vote for politicians who oppose the extension of unemployment insurance benefits at specific and appropriate times, when you vote for those who want to give enormous tax breaks to corporations while simultaneously denying you

---

170 **WIC:** Women, Infants and Children—A supplemental nutrition program for women, infants and children.

SNAP: Supplemental Nutrition Assistance Program—the old food stamps program.

Head Start: a Federal program that enhances the school readiness of children from low income families from birth to age five.)

comparable advantages, when you vote for politicians who oppose funding for public higher education, if you do so out of fear, in other words, if you do so because you have been taught that "lazy minorities" are getting government benefits that you are paying for with your tax dollars that you **yourself** are not receiving, you have been snookered. You have been sold a lie that causes you to vote, time and time again, against your own best interests, specifically, against your own **financial** best interests. You have been sold ten pounds of garbage by those who benefit from **instilling** that fear in you, those who financially benefit from your voting against all the things that would economically help you, those who would have absolutely no problem financing their kids' education.

As Americans, we will have come a long way when a critical mass of European Americans who live in poverty and who are working and middle class, understand those messages.]

C. An Incalculable Tragic Waste of Human Potential[171]

The historic practice of racism has deprived our species of the potentially brilliant contributions to humanity that **could** have been made by the millions of American children of color who were born and grew up on its reservations, in its barrios, its inner-cities and in rural poverty, children who were not able to escape the dysfunction of their surroundings. They are the millions of children who **but for the circumstances of their birth**, would have grown up to become exceptional teachers, brilliant scientists, trades people, nurses, social workers, clerical workers, mathematics geniuses, medical researchers, gifted artists, outstanding

[171] While in both this section and Section D below, my analysis is specific to the United States, the focus of both sections, the twin realities of an incalculable waste of human potential and the existence of the daily indignities, are applicable to People of Color around the world.

engineers, creative architects, excellent attorneys and talented doctors. We have lost **millions** of them over many years and as a tragic result, have today, been deprived of their gifts.[172]

Among exceptional Indigenous People that come to mind are Frank Howell Seay, Maria Tallchief, Leslie Marmon Silko, N. Scott Momaday, Winona Laduke, Ben Nighthorse Campbell, Robbie Hood, Charles Curtis, Diane Humetewa, and Rupert Costo. Tragically, we will never know how many more there may have been if the first contact between Indigenous People and European People had been different from what is our actual tragic history.

When I think of Latin Americans of distinction—Ellen Ochoa, Franklin Chang-Dìaz, Hilda Solis, Maria Hinojosas, Sandra Cisneros, Luis Miramontes, Nilo Cruz, Carlos Santana, Bill Richardson and Sonia Sotomayor, among many others, I wonder how many millions of other Latin Americans of equal brilliance and talent we have lost through centuries of discrimination against them.

---

[172] Hundreds of thousands and perhaps millions of children on reservations, in barrios, inner cities and in rural poverty, however, **do** beat the odds, complete high school and go on to have productive careers and healthy adult lives.

I also mourn, however, those who are the drug dealers, the pimps and the gang members of their communities for while they may live with large sums of money, dress the part and drive fancy cars, we have lost them too. They started out just like my elementary school friends at Moton, indeed, just like **all** of us, tiny and innocent, most likely in a hospital nursery, only to later make choices that ruin their lives and gravely hurt dozens and perhaps hundreds of others. Yes, their actions are their choices, choices for which they must be fully accountable. I can't help but wonder, though, how many would have followed a different path had a broader, fuller range of life choices been more apparent to them. I mourn them **and** their victims.

The number of Asian Americans who have contributed so significantly to our country, among them, Minoru Yamasaki, Miné Okubo, Elaine Chao, Leyna Nguyen, Ut Huynh Cong, Ellison Onizuka Subrahmanyam Chandrasekhar, Lisa Ling, Deepak Chopra, Thomas Tang, Tammy Duckworth, and Jay Kim would surely have been significantly larger **but for** the years of discrimination suffered by their ancestors in the United States.

And sadly, I can only wonder what the United States would now be like if African Americans had never been enslaved. What would our country be in the present, if for example, the parents and grandparents of all of the kids of The Harlem Children's Zone had in **their** formative years, the same educational opportunity that their progeny now enjoy? I wonder how many Gwen Ifills, Daniel Hale Williamses, Gordon Parks, Marian Wright Edelmans, Elijah McCcoys, Regina Benjamins, Thurgood Marshalls, Toni Morrisons, Oprah Winfreys, and Barack Obamas we have lost. Had they been free to follow their true passions, I wonder if Fannie Lou Hamer would perhaps have been an artist, or if Mrs. Rosa Parks would have been an inventor and engineer. I wonder if perhaps thirty years ago, Dr. King would have been our first African American president.

It is a **great** human catastrophe that we shall never know how many children of color we have lost **due to racism** and what contributions they would have made to American society and to the human species.

> [Let me be clear that it is **undeniable** that we **also** lose the potential contributions of millions of **European** American children as well, who are born into and remain in a cycle of poverty. That Appalacia and many other parts of the United States are **filled** with poor European American kids and adults who but for the circumstances of **their** birth, would have made **tremendous** social contributions, is **absolutely incontrovertible.** Their potential contributions are of no less value than those of poor American children of color. My point in highlighting the loss to our nation of

poor Americans **of Color,** is that **as a percentage of the American population**, we lose many, many more Americans **of Color** to poverty, than we do **European** Americans. That undeniable fact is, I believe, due to a large extent, to the legacy of racism which impacted our forebears and has in smaller but nonetheless significant measure, been passed on to us.]

D. A Social Structure of Unearned Privilege for Some and Daily Indignities for Others

1. Unearned Privilege

An unearned privilege is a right, benefit or advantage that is bestowed upon an individual based solely upon his/her membership in a group, **not** upon anything that the individual has done to **earn** the right, benefit, or advantage.

[See Note Three for learning points about Unearned Privilege]

Two of the most significant unearned privileges of being European American in the United States, are:

a. Not triggering an automatic **fear** response in others simply because one is white; and,

b. Not triggering an automatic **suspicion** response in others, (e.g., being suspected of shoplifting and other socially aberrant behavior), simply because one is white.

Those two benefits bestow the simple but precious human right of individuality. They allow one to live one's life not as an Asian Person, or a Black Person, or a Brown Person or as any other **color** person. They allow one to be seen, rather, as a "regular" person, as a human being, as the individual human being which s/he was born. It is the **tremendous** privilege of being thought of, viewed as and responded to, as an **individual**. It is the privilege, in most life circumstances, of being given the benefit of the doubt as opposed to being immediately suspect. Living **with** the advantage of individuality, is an emotional **universe** apart from living **without** it. It is **entirely** different from never knowing how you're going to be responded to in **every** new situation in which you must interact both with the majority of **people** in society, as well as with the majority of people **in positions of power** in society, those with the power, among many other things, to offer or not offer you a job, to approve or not approve your home loan, or to admit or not admit your child to one of the best schools in your community. The former feels like emotional freedom. The latter, a kind of emotional prison, one from which it is impossible to escape.

[I know how dramatically different the two realities feel because:

1. I experience what it is like to be responded to neutrally and even pleasantly, nearly every day when I speak to strangers by phone who may be unaware that I am black; and

2. Those telephone conversations are **dramatically** different from the in-person meetings which often follow, in which I'm often responded to, not negatively, but with surprise that I'm black. The surprise is then immediately followed by what I refer to as the "Oh . . . Oh . . . Hi black person" nervous handshake and then an interpersonal dynamic which feels **noticeably** less relaxed than the preceding telephone conversation.]

I have said in many training sessions that being on the receiving end of the "Oh, hi black (or Latin, Asian, Indigenous) person" response provides one the opportunity to do consciousness or awareness work in that moment. It is a growth opportunity for the other person. What I have said to the person on the receiving end of the nervous behavior is the following:

Judging from the person's nervous response to you, you think that you know at least some of what the person may think about you. But you know that what they **think** they see in you, is **not** you. It is **not** who you are. And you also know that they don't know that. Thus, as between the two of you, you are the more conscious person. So if the dynamic is going to shift, you are the one who is going to have to shift it. Now does that mean that you have to engage in a kind of, "But I **am** a good person. You **don't** have to be afraid of me. I don't like that rap music that has all that foul language **either**. I **don't** play the race card. I **am** intelligent . . . ." dance? **Definitely** not. There is absolutely **no** dignity in that. That is **not** what I'm advocating. What I **am** advocating, is that when you experience the nervous, "Oh . . . . I see. Well now I'm a lot less comfortable with you" response, you maintain your dignity and just stay true to who you are as a person. Try to not become frustrated or angry, and definitely don't engage in an effort to disprove what you believe are the person's stereotypes for that is no more than a 21st century step-'n-fetch it routine. Just stay true to who you are and know that **in time**, that person will see who you really are. If the other person is just an acquaintance, know that due to the temporary nature of your relationship, this may not be a learning opportunity for the other person, but in simply staying true to who you are, you are at the very least maintaining your dignity.

The person to whom I give that advice often responds to it by saying something similar to, "Why should I always be the teacher, the consciousness raiser? It's exhausting to always have to put people at ease or **prove** that I'm a responsible person". I then respond in the following way, "You **don't** always have to be the teacher. You **don't** have to always be the consciousness raiser." Whether or not you play that role is a choice. It's always **your** choice. Sometimes, if you've just recently been in the same situation, it's a **totally** legitimate choice to simply disengage from the situation gracefully. In order to not burn out from the effects of the daily indignities, it is important that you choose your battles wisely. You don't have to fight every single one. Just know that when you see the uncomfortable "Oh hi_____person" response, you are the more conscious person and thus you are the one with the ability to turn the dynamic into a learning opportunity for the other person when you choose to do so.]

Merely being responded to neutrally, (if not pleasantly), in most social settings by the majority of people, is a **tremendous** privilege which **on the basis of race alone**, European Americans most often **do** have and Americans of Color most often do **not.**

> [The 1991 ABC Primetime Live video, "True Colors", demonstrates the dramatic difference in the way African Americans, specifically, are often responded to by some European Americans.]

"True Colors"
http://www.youtube.com/watch?v=YyL5EcAwB9c

The economic advantages that accompany unearned racial privilege have built a middle class for European Americans that, in proportion to their population, is **enormously** larger than the middle class that has developed in American communities of color. As the preceding historical sketch illustrates, Americans of Color have been the targets of relentless, historic and systemic discrimination in both education and employment. It is housing discrimination, however, that has perhaps contributed most to the disparity in wealth between Americans of Color and European Americans.[173] The intentionally erected barriers that Americans of Color have historically faced when attempting to purchase a home in a desirable neighborhood, have made it impossible for hundreds of thousands, and perhaps millions of us, to become homeowners in such neighborhoods. Thus, we have generally been able to neither build and then use home equity to put our children through college, nor pass a home on to them. Thus, while

173 The symbiotic relationship of education, employment and housing is explored in Note Five.

it is true that since the end of slavery, each succeeding generation of young Americans of Color has generally attained a higher level of **education** than preceding ones, **financially** speaking, each generation has essentially started off from scratch. The experience of a large proportion of European Americans, however, is **very** different. Many have **for generations**, passed on ownership of either land and/or a home to their children, providing them an **enormous** economic advantage with which to begin adulthood.

In order for humanity to racially heal in the future, those who are the benefactors of both historic and contemporary racial privilege, must both be aware of **and** acknowledge that privilege. Doing so does not nor **can** it make anyone guilty of racism. It **does**, however, confer a very important responsibility to at the very **least**, not, **collude** in the American system of racial privilege, (to the extent that it is possible), and furthermore, if one is courageous enough, to actively work to dismantle it.

> [Peggy McIntosh's article on unearned racial privilege, "White Privilege, Unpacking the Invisible Knapsack", remains one of the seminal works on the issue of racial privilege.
>
> **Unpacking the Invisible Knapsack**
> https://www.youtube.com/watch?v=DRnoddGTMTY]

2. The Daily Indignities

Racially-based indignities impact the lives of millions of Americans of Color each and every day, the indignity, for example, of being profiled by law enforcement and store clerks to name only two. Based as they are on one's physical appearance, and specifically on the race that one appears to be, racially-based daily indignities are **deeply** hurtful. I wish that as a society, we understood how it impacts many Americans of Color to read and hear news stories, (as I have countless times), about young European Americans who are charged with a serious crime, including sometimes heinous murder, **and yet**, are described in the media as "angel-faced" or as looking like "the kid next door", or called, "The Barbie Bandit", or described as looking like "the typical American kid", or as "the kind of person who could live in our neighborhood", or when a witness says that the suspect "just didn't look like the kind of person who would do such a thing." It is all based on looks. The image of who does **not** look like a criminal is so clear in the minds of many only because the image of who **does** look like one, is equally as clear. It is a kind of pervasive, often unconscious bias that **profoundly** affects the lives of millions of innocents who "fit the profile".

It is because our image of what a criminal **does** look like, (a Person of Color), and does **not** look like, (a Caucasian Person), that two shoplifter partners, one African American and the other European American, reported on a national news show several years ago, that their very successful strategy was to walk into a store together and have the African American browse around while the European American stole hundreds of dollars of merchandise. To paraphrase the European American, "We knew who they'd be watching."

The ABC television show, "20/20 What Would You Do?" did a 2009 episode focused on the different reaction that European Americans have specifically to European and African American teens engaged in the exact same criminal activity. A follow-up was done in 2012. In the experiment, two groups of three teenage boys were vandalizing a car. One group was African American. The other, European American. Not only were the two groups of boys engaged in the exact same behavior, however, they were also the same approximate age and were dressed the same. The results of the experiment were not surprising. More 911 calls to police were made in response to the black teens than to the white ones, two to three **times** as many.

In the 2012 follow-up, the situation was changed. This time, three white teens were again **vandalizing** a car but in this experiment, the black teens were **asleep** in one nearby. Incredibly, twice as many 911, (i.e., **emergency**), calls were made in response to the black teens **who were sleeping** in a car, than in response to the white ones who were **vandalizing** one. One passerby told the police dispatch person that the black teens "seemed like they were up to something."

ABC's 20/20 What Would You Do: Racism in America—Part 1
http://www.youtube.com/watch?v=_cCQU0jt4cs

ABC's 20/20 What Would You Do: Racism in America—Part 2
http://www.youtubpe.com/watch?v=VQHdbW36XjE

At times, an indignity comes in the form of being denied a simple acknowledgement that others, in the same instant, receive. An experience that I had while walking into a supermarket with my two European American friends, Jack and Theresa, illustrates this specific indignity. As the three of us began walking from the parking lot toward the entrance of the market, I noticed a young European American woman with a tablet and pen in hand standing just in front of the door. I watched as she asked every person in front of me who passed by her, whether they were a registered voter. She was clearly attempting to get signatures on a petition. I was in front of Theresa and Jack. As I passed the young woman, I assumed that she was going to ask me the same question that she was asking of all the shoppers entering the store, so, with a smile, I looked at and prepared to respond to her. She did not, however, make eye contact with me. A second later, as Theresa and Jack passed her, she looked at and spoke to them, "Hi. Are you guys registered voters in Multnomah County?" In that moment, I was not, "looking for it". I wasn't even expecting it. It was a beautiful Spring day and I was enjoying my friends' company. Then suddenly, out of the blue, right in that moment, coming out of nowhere, there it was, that all-too-familiar message that I had received all my life, the message that the person experiencing me was so uncomfortable with the prospect of interacting with me, that they simply ignored me. I made the decision, in that moment, to not bring it to the young woman's attention. I just didn't have the emotional energy at the time. It was a beautiful Oregon morning and I just didn't want to deal with it. Upon entering the store, however, I asked Jack and Theresa if they'd noticed what had just occurred. Even though both are **very** conscious of racial dynamics, in **that** particular instance, neither had. Upon bringing it to their attention, they decided to take a moment to very simply and quickly bring the incident to the young woman's attention. When they then walked outside the store and described to the woman in their very gentle way, what had just occurred, she seemed to be shocked, declaring several times, "Race had nothing to do with it. I just didn't see her. I'm not racist." Theresa and Jack's intention in bringing the incident to the young woman's intention was not to embarrass her, guilt her or accuse her of being racist.[174] Their intention, rather, was to simply use the episode as a learning opportunity, a chance to make her be perhaps just a little more self-aware in the hope that she will be more conscious in her future interactions with People of Color. In that moment, Theresa and Jack were my allies. They demonstrated then and there, what it means to live consciously with regard to race, as European Americans. Doing nothing in such circumstances, simply allows the irrational, unfounded fear of People of Color to continue and to be repeated time and time again.

Often, an indignity comes in the form of different and preferential treatment being **accorded** to a Caucasian Person **in the same instant** that it is **denied** to a Person of Color. One of the many occasions on which I experienced this specific indignity was as a member of a government-contracted team of approximately ten trainers who were traveling the country conducting diversity training for the U.S. Department of Health and Human Services, in the mid 90's. We were a diverse group of Latin Americans, African Americans, European Americans, Indigenous People and Asian Americans. San Francisco was one of the many destinations on our itinerary. After checking into our San Francisco hotel the

[174] That young woman was indeed, quite possibly **not** racist. She may very well have had friends of color at school or in her neighborhood with whom she may have been quite comfortable. That fact, however, often does not translate into a **general** comfort level with Americans of Color.

evening of our first day of training, a number of us on the team decided that after putting our luggage into our rooms, we would meet in the lobby to go to dinner. I, along with three other team members, one of whom was one of our two European American colleagues, arrived first in the lobby. As we talked, we discovered that unlike the rest of us, our European American teammate's room had a microwave and jacuzzi bathtub. Upon learning of the difference in our rooms, everyone but our European American colleague laughed loudly. It was just such a blatant example of the kind of unearned privilege that we had discussed in numerous workshops which were routinely, roundly denied by many of the European American participants. We laughed, not because the privilege given to our colleague and denied to us was in any way funny. It was more of an "of course" response. Our European American colleague, however, finding absolutely nothing humorous in the situation, promptly went over to the registration desk, and with his voice quaking with utter furor, spoke to the attendant who had just checked us all in:

> These people, (pointing to the three of us who were sitting nearby), are my friends. They're my colleagues. We're trainers. We all work for the same training organization. The exact same logistics company made all of our reservations. They paid the exact same rate for all of our rooms. We all checked into the hotel together, about fifteen minutes ago. Yet, I now learn that for some unexplained reason, I got an upgraded room, a room that's better than all of my colleagues' rooms. I want you to move me. I want the same kind of room my friends got, and I want you to take care of it right now.

Having overheard the entire conversation, we all told our colleague that he really didn't have to do that. We told him that it was enough that he had brought the situation to the attention of the establishment, that changing his accommodation wouldn't accomplish anything, and to just take a nice hot bath in the jacuzzi later on and enjoy the room. But our colleague was **furious**. He was **adamant** that he should **not** have the deluxe room and required the hotel to indeed move him into a room that was comparable to ours. [175]

Upon hearing our colleague and friend's demand, the hotel desk clerk's first and **immediate** response, was, "Sir, I assure you that race had nothing to do with it. We honor all of our patrons and we treat them all equally." To those of us listening, the clerk's "Race had nothing to do with it" response, was both predictable and expected. It's the automatic denial response that's given, usually in an almost spontaneous, knee jerk fashion, in the **vast majority** of such situations. Indeed, the response was so **very** predictable, that we would probably have laughed at **it** as well, had we been less conscious of being "appropriate" in that moment. After repeating his, "Sir, I can assure you that we do **not** discriminate in this hotel" response several times, the clerk changed our colleague's room.[176]

Our colleague's bringing the blatantly unequal treatment that we had received to the attention of the hotel employee and

[175] This incident is characteristic of so many in which European Americans are given preferential treatment when they **themselves** aren't even aware of it.

[176] It is often the case that after experiencing the double whammy of an indignity followed by the rapid fire, adamant **denial** of it, the person who has received the indignity must then, (frequently in the heat of feeling high emotion), attempt to give a very measured, mature response to both the indignity **and** it's denial. The consequence of expressing frustration, or even **annoyance** in that moment, (particularly for African Americans, for whom the stereotype of being "angry" largely still exists), is that of appearing to be yet another "angry black person who thinks the world owes them something and who's just playing the race card," and thus underscoring another stereotype—that African Americans are **indeed** hostile and angry. I cannot describe, in a way that does justice to the truth, the emotional toll of having to navigate those kinds of situations over and over again, throughout the course of one's life.

demanding that he be assigned the same kind of room to which the rest of us had been assigned, was one of the most powerful examples of allyship I have ever seen. [177]

I had yet **another** experience of seeing a European American colleague being given different and preferential treatment within a relatively short amount of time that it was **denied** to me, on yet another training trip. I was travelling with just one other colleague this time, a European American man,[178] After checking into our rooms, I went down to the hotel coffee shop to buy a bottle of water. After purchasing the water, I began heading back to my room only to discover that I had left it without my room key. Naturally, I immediately went back downstairs and to the concierge desk to request assistance getting into my room. Upon doing so, very politely, the concierge requested that I show him some form of identification. I explained that I didn't have any identification on me at that moment, as it was in my bag, which was on my bed, in my room, **of which I was locked out.** As if not having heard me **at all**, the concierge told me that he would be unable to let me into my room unless I could show him

[177] My friend and colleague Tom Finn demonstrated true allyship in a conversation in which the two of us were discussing with a potential client, the possibility of our providing sexual harassment training for his organization. The client, who was aware that I am a lawyer, began the discussion by asking a number of legally-based questions. As he did so, he'd look at Tom each time, which is not a lawyer, and did so even though **I** was answering his questions. After the third or fourth time it happened, Tom said to the client, "Lauren's the attorney. You really should be asking her those kinds of questions." In that moment, Tom became my ally. He responded just before I was about to.

[178] In facilitating diversity training, I have often worked as one of a two person, mixed race, mixed gender training team in which my training partner has most often been a European American man. The learning for participants as they watch us model deep mutual respect **for** and obvious equality **with** each other, can be as powerful as any lecture or any exercise on the agenda.

identification. **Once again**, I informed him that my ID was in my bag on my bed, and then **went on** to tell him that I'd be happy to show it to whomever would let me into my room as soon as they opened the door. **Incredibly**, he responded once again by telling me that it was hotel policy to not allow anyone into any guest rooms without proper identification. At that point, I asked to speak to the hotel manager. The concierge then looked at me with both suspicion and anger, then instructed an employee to let me into my room and to be sure to check my ID after doing so.

Needless to say, I was in that moment, as I **often** was in such situations, both furious and curious. I was furious about having received what was at least extremely rude, and I suspected, also racist behavior. [179] I was **curious** about whether I would have been treated the same or differently had I been a similarly-dressed white woman of my age in the same circumstance. I devised a plan to both test my assumption and satisfy my curiosity.

Sometime later that evening, I told my colleague about the incident and asked him if he'd do an experiment with me. I asked him if he'd put his business casual clothing back on, (as I had been dressed when the incident occurred), go down to the lobby, speak to the same concierge with whom I'd spoken, tell him that he'd locked himself out of his room, and ask his assistance in being let back in to it. He wholeheartedly agreed to do so.

As my colleague spoke to the concierge, I inconspicuously watched from a nearby vantage point as the following conversation took place:

> My colleague to the concierge:
>
> > Excuse me. I just came down to the lobby to get a bottle of water from the coffee shop and I seem to have locked myself out of my room. I wonder if

[179] I suspected that the behavior was racist because I doubted that I would have received the same treatment but for my race.

My colleague **was unable to complete his sentence** before the concierge interrupted:

> Of course sir. I'll get someone to help you right away.

The concierge then called a hotel employee who accompanied my colleague to his room, opened the door and said, "Good night sir." He was never asked for Identification, not by the concierge and not by the employee who opened the door for him.

My colleague and I then both went down to the lobby to inform its management of what had just occurred and how differently we had been treated, by the same person, in the same evening, in the very same situation. The manager's response was as predictable as the concierge's behavior:

We have a strict policy of non-discrimination. It's against the law for us to discriminate and even if it weren't, we would never do such a thing. We value all of our customers and treat them all with the same respect and professional courtesy.

I then replied, very clearly telling the manager that the concierge had indeed behaved toward me in the way that I had described and that in view of how differently my colleague had been treated, the concierge's behavior was clearly based on bias. My colleague and I then walked away.

This was once again, the extremely familiar pattern that I had seen throughout my adult life, of a perpetrator **engaging** in racist behavior, and then adamantly **denying** that s/he had done so. [180]

---

[180] The action followed by the subsequent **denial** of the action are also often accompanied by a third affront—accusing the person who is the **target** of the discrimination, of being "overly sensitive" or of "playing the race card." I have not seen that accusation in an actual conversation which follows an indignity; rather, it is frequently the analysis of "indignity situations", offered by a European American attendee in a diversity workshop.

It is for that reason that I and I believe many African Americans and other Americans of Color, sometimes feel anger or at least frustration in situations which may appear to many **European** Americans to not warrant that response. The anger and frustration felt when you've just been treated **badly**, result from the feeling that you may have just been treated **unfairly**. It is a feeling which results from a **lifetime** of being treated unfairly based upon your race, causing you to suspect that racism may be at play **yet again**, in the present situation.

Many Americans of Color, in addition to often being, (with differing frequency based upon one's geography, complexion and other variables) in situations in which we are unsure about whether we have just received treatment that is racially biased, also live with **another** painful reality. That reality is the awareness that there are many times during which you may be receiving racially-biased treatment of which you **are** not and cannot possibly **be** aware.[181] You may be paying the same price for a hotel room or anything else for which someone else has paid **the exact same price**, and **yet**, you may be receiving an inferior product, good or service. You may not have been offered the complimentary room upgrade. You may not have received the gratis birthday dessert that the restaurant offers. In **any** situation in which it is up to another's **discretion** to offer you a courtesy, that courtesy may or may not be extended to you based usually not upon whether or not the person is a racist, but based, instead, upon that person's personal comfort level with you.

> [When an American of Color is on the receiving end of a racially-based indignity, it is often not conscious racism or conscious bias which is the source. Rather, it is often a matter of the other person's personal comfort level which is at play. It is their lack of personal comfort with an American of Color that results in their response to the person, often

---

[181] When one **is** aware of that kind of discrimination, however, it is **imperative** that it be challenged whenever one has the emotional energy to do so.

> putting the person at a disadvantage in whatever the situation is in which they are engaged.]

That is an utter unfairness with which, as an American of Color, if one is to live a centered, graceful, dignified, indeed **sane** life, one must simply learn to live.

About three years ago, I experienced a daily indignity that was actually quite similar to Trayvon Martin's, the African American teenager who on February 26, 2012, was shot and killed in Sanford Florida by George Zimmerman. Months after that tragic shooting, I sent the following letter to the New York Times editorial division and several television talk show hosts, describing my experience:

> I am an African American woman who works as Director of the Office of Equity and Diversity at a major California university. About 18 months ago, I left my office for a lunchtime walk. I was dressed in a business suit and sneakers. When I reached a residential neighborhood several blocks from campus, a European American man came literally running out of his house, and across his lawn to confront me. "What are you doing here?! Do you live around here?!" My immediate response was, "No. I **work** around here, at the university." The second I responded, I regretted that I had done so because I didn't owe that man an answer to his question. I should not have had to explain my presence in his neighborhood. I doubt seriously that he would have responded with the same suspicion of a **European** American woman walking in his neighborhood in the middle of a sunny day, dressed in a business suit and sneakers. My point is that while the attention in the Trayvon Martin case is on African American men, it should be known that some of us who are **not** African American men, i.e., who are African American **women**, are **also** profiled, although admittedly not nearly as often as African American men.

There are many crucial issues in the Trayvon Martin case. The irrational fear of African Americans is certainly among the most important. One afternoon in 1964, two months after the passage of the Civil Rights Act, I sat on the front of a city bus on my way home from my junior high school. It was one of the first times that by law, I was allowed to do so. Two European-American girls who appeared to be a couple of years older than I, were sitting in the seat beside me talking. At one point during their conversation, I heard one girl say to the other, "I'm not afraid of the ones that look like her, (pointing to me . . . . I'm light brown skinned), I'm afraid of the really dark ones." I **know** that that young white girl wasn't lying. I **know** that her fear was real. I know that it's real because I **see** the fear reaction in so many European Americans when I walk toward them on a sidewalk in cold weather, wearing a hooded overcoat and from a distance, my race is apparent but my gender is not . . . .

In discussions about unearned privilege, the following three things almost without exception, come up as among the largest unearned privileges that many people have: First, not living with an understanding of the pain of constantly being profiled, (which I feel to this day, sometimes, when I'm in a high-end department store); Second, living without even an awareness that **other** people experience it; and, Third, living totally unaware that one's **own** unconscious reactions may contribute on a regular basis to others' experience of the pain. It is the pain of losing one's individuality and thus, by necessity, the major part of one's humanity.

It is because I know the reality of the fear of African American men that I make it a point to make eye contact with, smile at and say, "hi" to young black men whose paths I cross in public. It's such a simple gesture, yet it is **extremely** powerful. The surprise on their face and delight in their voice when they respond with, "Hi", (although the non-verbals that I often perceive from them cause me, in my mind's ear, to actually hear, a delighted, "***Oh*** . . . Hi!"), is simply priceless. I wish I could get a critical mass of people to acknowledge the humanity of young black men in that same very simple but very profound way. It just **might** make a real difference.[182]

---

[182] Later, on the day of the incident that I described in that letter, I attended the monthly meeting of a small women's contemplative dialogue group of which I was a member. After the communal reading of the passage for that session, and doing our individual contemplation on it, we'd share our thoughts about the passage with the group. All of the group's readings were from the writings of Thomas Merton. That week, it included the theme of forgiveness. After my individual contemplation, during which I had sat in silence and meditated on the concept of forgiveness, I described for the women in the group, my experience earlier that day of being racially profiled in the university neighborhood. I then shared with them that the passage served as a very timely, helpful and on some level, **healing** reminder for me, of the need to forgive **and to love** the gentleman who had stereotyped and profiled me earlier that day. The moment I finished, one of the other participants, (all of whom were European American), responded, "Well I didn't know we were going to come here and talk about **that** tonight." Even though **forgiveness** was the theme of my comments, hearing about my experience had clearly made my fellow participant uncomfortable. What I felt in that moment was both the outrage of the still fresh experience of that afternoon, **coupled with** the sting of the very familiar response to the sharing of such an experience, the response, essentially, of, "Look, stop looking for racism around every corner. Race had nothing to do with it. I'm uncomfortable hearing about this stuff and I resent you for **making** me uncomfortable." I have never **heard** shared out loud the, "Look, stop looking for racism around every corner", and the "I'm uncomfortable hearing about this stuff and I resent you for making me uncomfortable", comments, however, I **feel** them in the verbally expressed, "Race had nothing to do with it" comment as strongly as if they **had been** actually said.

My letter continued with the story of the young African American man's experience in the Florida convenience store.

I continue**,** in present time, to experience a particularly insulting daily indignity. It occurs, from time to time after I have shaken the hand of a European American. It happens so quickly, so unconsciously, that if I dared bring it to the person's attention, s/he would be **completely** horrified and undoubtedly, with much emotion, go into immediate denial. If it is a man, after shaking my hand, he will wipe his hand that touched mine, on his right pant leg. It's a very quick, single, downward swipe. If it is a woman, she will rub her hands together—also most often a quick single swipe. It happens seldomly, but often enough for me to notice. Interestingly, on most of those occasions, it is the white person who has extended their hand to me, being quite affable and warm in doing so.

I have never assumed that the person who has just wiped her or his hand after touching mine is a racist. In fact, I very rarely make that assumption about **anyone**. I am fully aware that rather than racism, it is **unconscious bias** which is more likely at play, especially since the European American person is the one who **initiated** the handshake. The assumption that the person who just wiped his/her hand is a racist, is therefore totally ludicrous. That said, this "hand**shake** followed by a hand **wipe**" phenomenon, is one of the clearest examples of the many events which occur in the lives of Americans of Color, the source of which **could** be racism or bias, but could also **no**t be. Some people are germ phobic, and are therefore uncomfortable shaking **anyone's** hand. It could also be possible, however, that what **may** be at play, is **unconscious discomfort** with a Person of Color, or perhaps with an African American specifically. In the moment in which the hand swipe occurs, it is impossible to know.

> [Those kinds of situations, in which one does not and cannot know whether either racism or bias is the source of another's negative behavior toward them, depending upon the circumstances, **can** be as stressful as those in

which racism or bias is apparent. Upon moving from the East Coast to Redlands, California in 2001, several things occurred shortly after I moved into my neighborhood. My trash was overturned on my front lawn, someone was repeatedly calling me and then hanging up after I answered, and twice, I noticed a car stopping in front of my house, after which the driver took a picture of it. It turned out, thankfully, that each had a non-threatening cause. My trash had been turned over by an animal, the phone calls were being made by a non-English speaking person who was trying to locate the person who had my telephone number before me, and the man taking the pictures was a realtor who wanted to show one of his clients, a home that was comparable to the one the client was considering purchasing. When the incidents occurred, I called my realtor, Judy, to discuss the matter. She advised me to call the Redlands Chief of Police, who was a friend of hers. After listening to my account of events, the Chief then informed me that he was taking the matter seriously because there had been Klan activity in the vicinity in the recent past. Before I knew the actual source of the incidents, for about two weeks, in addition to the events themselves, I was also **extremely** disturbed by the Chief's concern. I was greatly relieved, of course, that each of the three situations had an innocent cause, but the not knowing felt almost as stressful as if my concerns had been verified.[183] My Redlands experience exemplifies

[183] I am fortunate that throughout my **entire** career, I have had only one difficult relationship with the person who was my supervisor. Her reaction to me was **so** extreme, (assuming ill intent on my part, speaking to me disrespectfully, never once talking with me about our many miscommunications regarding assignments), that while I didn't **know**, I did **wonder** if perhaps either I reminded her of another black woman whom she may have previously known whose work ethic she didn't respect, **or** if she may have unconsciously harbored racist stereotypes of African Americans in general. I wondered about both possibilities because our relationship went so negative so quickly after we began working together. She made negative assumptions about me and treated me harshly before ever getting to

why for millions of Americans of Color, the issue of race is almost always present.]

The story of the young Florida man and many similar stories that numerous other African Americans have shared with me over my career as a diversity trainer, Trayvon Martin's story, and my own numerous life experiences, have caused me to state that living life as a Person of Color in the United States is often like living life as if one has plastered squarely onto the very **middle** of one's forehead, the message, "Dangerous . . . . Fear and Suspect Me." It is the emotional and psychological experience of living, everyday, with the constant reminder on the faces of strangers that when they look at you, it is **that** message that they see, whether you are on your way to work, or to the barber shop, or to church, or as in the case of young seventeen year old Trayvon Martin, on your way home from a convenience store to watch a basketball game, carrying a pack of candy and an iced tea.

The two phenomena of the **unearned racial privilege** of which European Americans are the daily **benefactors**, and the **daily indignities,** of which Americans of Color are the daily **recipients**, are among the realities of race in the United States that most

---

know me as a person. While it is true that her treatment of me was tremendously unpleasant, **irrespective** of the source, the **possibility** that racism may have been the cause, was quite troubling. She eventually improved her demeanor toward me, and rather drastically, but to this day, I remain totally unaware of the reason for her initial behavior with me. In this case, the "not knowing", as it often does, has left as residue, an unpleasant cloud of suspicion. Nonetheless, throughout the time that we worked together, while I felt and in all likelihood displayed a low level of "emotional coolness" toward her, (i.e., always smiling and saying "Hi Karen", {not her real name}, when I saw her, but not engaging in any other friendly informal conversation), I continued, as I had to, to treat that person with the respect, professionalism and dignity that my mother taught me so well, so many years ago. I continue to this day, to work on not letting my disappointment in a person impact how I respond to them and to instead, be "big" enough to remain warm toward them. As was true with respect to my law school locker mate thirty years prior, I wish that I had been able to do so in this situation as well.

impact the everyday lives of us all. The continued unawareness, denial and minimization of them by millions of European Americans, are among our nation's largest barriers to racial understanding and healing. The acknowledgement of both, and of the pain which they cause to millions of Americans of Color, is critical to our ability, as a nation, to evolve beyond racism.

In the final analysis, the four present-day realities of two worlds within a world, two worlds within nations, an incalculable waste of human potential and a social structure of unearned privilege for some and daily indignities for others, **all based upon race,** is the world which every human being alive today has inherited. **None** of those phenomena, however, are naturally-occurring. There is absolutely nothing **natural** about, putting it simply, People of Color living "beneath" people of European descent **every place** on the planet. It is **not** the result of less intelligence or a lower work ethic or a lower incentive for progress in People of Color. The utterly unjust reality of People of Color being on the bottom and White People being on the top of every social structure around the word, is a totally artificially-constructed phenomenon based upon gross misunderstandings about our human origin, our **abundant** similarities and indeed, our ultimate unity.

Let us look now at how and where we **have** and have **not** made, **are** and are **not** making progress in advancing beyond those catastrophic present-day states of racial affairs.

VI. Our Racial Present: Mixed but Encouraging

The United States

The long march of history is comprised of periods of progression followed by periods of regression in various combinations of longevity. For all of the reasons elucidated above, I believe that in several ways, we in the United States, are presently in a period of racial regression. Thus, today, fifty years after Dr. King delivered his "I Have a Dream" speech on the steps of the Lincoln Memorial, **despite** the election of our first African American President, his dream of racial equality is still only that—a dream.

Unearned racial privilege, daily indignities, and the structural racism at the root of the educational and economic disparities that have been historically present between European Americans and Americans of Color, both still exist and continue to cause tremendous pain and suffering for Americans of Color.

A number of extreme forms of racism surfaced during President Obama's presidential campaigns and continued throughout his first term. Among the **most** offensive, were the many pictures that surfaced of the President and First Lady as monkeys and Arizona radio host Barbara Espinosa's June 17, 2012 reference to the President, made live on air, as the nation's "first monkey president".

The Southern Poverty Law Center, (SPLC), which tracks hate groups and the occurrence of hate crimes in the United States, has reported for the past several years, and particularly since the 2008 election of President Obama, that the number of hate groups in our nation has increased at an alarming rate. SPLC has warned federal authorities that such groups constitute a growing threat.[184] Hate **speech** by officials elected to local, state and even **national** office, has spiraled to a level that I never thought I would see in my lifetime.

Over the past several years, Congressional districts in several states have been **intentionally rigged** to minimize the voting power of Americans of Color in those states. In our last presidential election, we witnessed the implementation of a number of new voting **practices** that were **also** intentionally designed to minimize the voting power of Americans of Color. They include the shortening of early voting times, the alleged placement of inadequate numbers of voting machines in primarily districts of color, resulting in shockingly long lines and waiting times to vote, attempts to require identification for the purpose of voter registration that would overwhelmingly disenfranchise voters who were likely to vote for President Obama, and even billboards that **deliberately** gave voters in neighborhoods of color, incorrect information about the identification required to register to vote.

Despite all of those troubling redistricting and discriminatory voting practices that occurred during the past two presidential elections **and** thousands of pages of other compelling, irrefutable evidence of its absolute continuing necessity, Section V of the 1965 Voting Rights Act has recently been dismantled by the United States Supreme Court.

Affirmative Action in higher education continues to be challenged at the **level** of the Supreme Court. Additionally, attempts are being

---

[184] The Southern Poverty Law Center's March 5, 2013 report on hate crime in the U.S. is available at: http://www.splcenter.org/home/splc-report-antigovernment-patriot-movement-continues-explosive-growth-poses-rising-threat-of-v

[A] Southern Poverty Law Center report on hate incidents in general: http://www.splcenter.org/get-informed/hate-incidents?page=11&year=&state=TX

made to either cut or severely limit student loan programs that will overwhelmingly impact Students of Color.

In the nation's recent housing crisis, Americans of Color were **disproportionately** targeted by predatory lenders for tricky sub-prime home loans that were likely to ultimately result in the loss of their home. Many Americans of Color targeted for such loans had incomes, and credit and mortgage payment histories that were equal to and on par with European Americans who, at the same time, were being regularly qualified for standard mortgages.

The sentencing structure of the justice system, which has much harsher sentences for crimes that are more often committed by Americans of Color than comparable crimes committed by European Americans, has resulted in the incarceration of **massive** numbers of American men of color. [185]

In the United States, we very clearly have a **long** road to travel before reaching the goal of racial understanding, compassion, justice and unity.

It is **all**, on one level, **deeply** disturbing.

> [In addition to the **intentional** ways in which Americans of Color are discriminated against in current American

185 In her book, *The New Jim Crow: Mass Incarceration in the Age of Colorblindness*, civil rights attorney and legal scholar Michelle Alexander makes a compelling case that a new kind of segregation exists in the United States today—the mass incarceration of a heretofore unparalleled percentage of African American men (and increasingly women as well). http://newjimcrow.com/

In declaring that the U.S. has progressed racially even with the continued existence of certain racial inequalities, such as the mass incarceration of African American men, I do not intend **in any way**, to minimize the seriousness of those inequalities.

> culture, we are **also** disproportionately impacted by what is on its face, a race-neutral phenomenon—the country's loss of working class jobs through outsourcing and technological advancement.]

Even in view of all of those troubling realities, however, over the past nearly fifty years since the signing of the Civil Rights Act of 1964, the United States has made **tremendous** progress toward the goals of racial equality and justice. This is not the same country into which I was born nearly sixty years ago. The following are some of the most apparent indices of that progress:

The proportion of Americans of Color who are college graduates and solidly middle class is **significantly** larger today than it was in my childhood. Pontchartrain Park may well have been an anomaly "in its time", but today, there are middle class black neighborhoods in **many** parts of the country.

Our nation's progress in the legislative branch of government at the national level is mixed. Today in 2013, there are no African American, Indigenous, or Asian American Senators. Not one. In terms of People of Color in the United States Senate, our nation has two Latin American members. Twenty-eight Latin Americans, forty-four African Americans and thirteen members who are either Asian American or Native Hawaiian serve in the House of Representatives. Only one Indigenous American serves in the U. S. Congress today, Representative Tom Cole, Republican from Oklahoma and member of the Chickasaw Nation.

It is at the national level, in the executive branch of the government, however, that we can quite vividly see the most dramatic progress. The nation's top **lawyer**, **Attorney** General Eric Holder, is African American. The nation's top **doctor**, **Surgeon** General Dr. Regina Benjamin, is African American. The President's National Security Advisor, Susan Rice, is African American. The former Administrator of the Environmental Protection Agency, Lisa Jackson, (who grew up in Pontchartrain Park), is African American. And of course **the President, Barack Obama, is African American**. The President and the first lady,

Michelle Obama, also African American, are both Harvard-trained attorneys. In 2007, just a little more than six years ago, I **never** thought, **in my wildest dreams**, that I would see **any** of that in my lifetime, and **certainly** not an African American **President**—not in my lifetime . . . . and **not**, in my wildest dreams.

President Obama seemed to come out of nowhere, politically. There were **no** People of Color in the pipeline to the presidency when he emerged. No one. Barack Obama just almost literally **appeared** on the American political scene. Now, **just five years later**, we look at Deval Patrick, Governor of the state of Massachusetts, we look at Cory Booker, Mayor, Newark, New Jersey, we look at U.S. Representative Joaquin Castro from the 20th district of the state of Texas, and his twin brother Julian Castro, mayor of San Antonio, Texas and we see, today, a clear and undeniable pipeline. We see a pipeline for each of them that **could** lead directly to the halls of the White House, straight into the walls of the oval office.

There are news reporters, news anchors, meteorologists and sports reporters of many races and both genders on the majority of local television newscasts in every city I have visited across the country over the past several years.

Considering the television entertainment industry, People of Color are routinely portrayed in television shows as physicians, businessmen and women, as diverse human beings of every educational level and economic class, and with full and complex lives. The 1980's situation comedy, "The Cosby Show", centered on an affluent African American family in which the mother was a lawyer and the father, a doctor, remains, in syndication, one of the most popular television shows of all time. Oprah Winfrey is widely considered to be one of the most powerful women in the television industry, both having had the number one daytime television talk show for many of the twenty-five years during which it aired, and now, having both her own television **network**, **and** satellite radio station. Television commercials feature actors of color so regularly, that when on occasion a commercial does **not** have a Person of Color in it, the absence is noticeable.

In the **movie** industry, now, more than forty years after the Civil Rights Movement, there is a growing number of **highly** successful actors of color, some of whom are considered Hollywood "leading" women and men. While their numbers are still far from representative of their **presence** in the industry, many more and indeed, a **growing** number of Americans of Color are now working **behind** the camera in the movie industry as well, as writers, producers, and directors. There are even several African American-owned movie production companies, of which Tyler Perry's is perhaps the most well-known. Overall, in every genre of entertainment from the page to the stage, a growing number of **highly** successful Americans of Color are making their mark on American culture.

Today, in department store displays of special event and holiday cards, people of **various** ethnicities are depicted on them. Every kind of doll from babies to Barbies, are available in colors that span the human complexion spectrum. The pictures of kids on toy, cereal and diaper boxes represent wonderful human diversity. Comic book and cartoon characters are racially diverse. At makeup counters in most department and cosmetic stores across the country, women's makeup is available in colors that match all skin tones.[186] Even cake toppers are now racially diverse![187]

Oprah Winfrey, due to her ability to disseminate her message of self-awareness and empowerment to tens of millions of people around the planet—perhaps to more people than anyone else

---

[186] I leave to the segment of *We Are One* that is focused on gender, my analysis of the phenomenon of women's makeup itself.

[187] I am aware that the availability of such products in diverse representations is in addition to altruism, as likely the result of the many billions of potential dollars that their manufacturers may earn by marketing to Americans of Color.

currently alive—is arguably the most influential **woman** in the world. If one assumes that **President Obama**, as the leader of the most powerful nation on Earth, is the most influential **man** in the world, the reality in which we now live, in 2013, is that **the two most powerful people on Planet Earth**, are a man and a woman, both of whom are of African descent. [188]

I am encouraged by the continuation of diversity training in both educational settings and in the employment arena where I hope that my work and that of others is making a considerable difference.

Communities across the country are actively working on being inclusive and fully welcoming to all. Among the first was the city

---

188 One of the areas in which I wish we had made **more** progress over the past half century is science. Today, there are still too few People of Color in the sciences. I am proud, however, of two particular scientists of color. One is astrophysicist Neil deGrasse Tyson. Among the country's most prominent and well respected scientists, Dr. Tyson is African American. Since 1996, Dr. Tyson has served as Director of the Hayden Planetarium at New York City's American Museum of Natural History, and since 2006, has been a regular host of the Public Broadcasting Network's program, NOVA scienceNOW. The other is Dr. Mae Jemison. Dr. Jemison, also African American, is an astronaut, physician and college professor who holds nine honorary doctorates in science, engineering, letters, and the humanities. In September, 1992, Dr. Jemison flew on the Space Shuttle Endeavor, serving as co-investigator on a bone cell research experiment during the mission.

I also take particular delight in the fact that Morgan Freeman, an African American actor whose work I greatly admire, is the host of one of my favorite science shows, the Science Channel's "Through the Wormhole". Mr. Freeman was born in 1937 and spent his early years in segregated Charleston Mississippi. He explained on one of the early segments of the series, that as a little boy, he had a fierce curiosity about all manner of scientific mysteries.

of Billings Montana. In 1994, Billings citizens joined together to fight hate crimes and intolerance. Each time a hate crime occurred in Billings, nearly the **entire** Billings community with the support of local media, the police department, governmental officials and religious and secular humanistic groups, took a collective stand against the crime. Using the Billings example, communities **across the country** have begun working to create hate-free work environments, towns and cities.[189]

Additionally, I am inspired by the Hope in the Cities (HIC) initiative.[190] HIC is a program in which attendees participate in a dialogue series entitled, "Honest Conversation on Race, Reconciliation, and Responsibility", and in which trained facilitators lead groups through a series of six, two-hour dialogues. Participants also are led through a curriculum in which both didactic and experiential learning about our racial past that has resulted in our racial present, takes place. The program's stated goal is the creation of just and inclusive communities. Cities across the nation, including Portland Oregon, Selma Alabama, Baltimore Maryland, Hartford Connecticut, Natchez Mississippi, and Dayton Ohio, as well communities in Europe, Australia, South Africa, Brazil and India have replicated HIC's model of racial healing through dialogue.

Equally promising are programs such as Portland Oregon's "Uniting to Understand Racism", a community-based group (in which my friends Jack and Theresa have been active for years), which sponsors a six-week long dialogue series for schools, businesses, and governmental agencies. The goal of the program

---

189 The documentary, "Not in Our Town", profiles the courageous work against hate crime done by the Billings Montana community.
http://www.niot.org/niot-video/not-our-town-billings-montana-0
http://video.pbs.org/video/2137348207/

190 Hope in the Cities Project
http://www.us.iofc.org/hope-in-cities-iofc

is for participants to develop trust, engage in deep dialogue and gain clarity on the vision for their community in the future.

Portland Oregon also has an Office of Equity and Human Rights. Its mission is to, "provide education and technical support to City staff and elected officials, leading to recognition and removal of systemic barriers to fair and just distribution of resources, access and opportunity, starting with issues of race and disability." [191] Among the office's resources is its equity training and education program. Other cities across the nation have similar offices.

There is good, solid, meaningful anti-racism work such as that being done in Billings Montana, by Hope in the Cities and in Portland, Oregon, taking place in towns and cities across the United States. Americans are coming together to find creative and successful methods of standing up to intolerance in our communities, and of creating organizations in which a critical mass of people are conscious, intentional, respectful and courageous with respect to our human differences. Many of those efforts focus not only on race, but on **all** forms of oppression, sexism, anti-Semitism, Islamophobia, prejudice against people with disabilities, ageism, homophobia and heterosexism, and all of our other phobias, prejudices and "isms".

I have a deep passion for compassionate action, and I am **profoundly** heartened by all of that **tremendously** exciting, **compassionate** work.

In all of those and other ways, we have evolved to a place which just fifty short years ago, perhaps even **Dr. King** could not have dreamt. While Dr. King's fifty year old dream today remains a dream deferred, I have nonetheless often wished that he were here today to see all of the ways in which our country **has** progressed toward the goal for which he worked so courageously and ultimately gave his life. I wish that Dr. King had lived to see

---

[191] Portland Oregon's Office of Equity and Human Rights http://www.portlandoregon.gov/oehr/

President Obama. Perhaps it was President Obama's presidency that The Creator allowed him to see from the mountain top the evening before his death.

> [The night before his assassination, Dr. King made his last public speech at the Mason Temple, Church of God in Christ Headquarters in Memphis, Tennessee, during which he stated the following: "Like anybody, I would like to live a long life. Longevity has its place. But I'm not concerned about that now. I just want to do God's will. And He's allowed me to go up to the mountain. And I've looked over. And I've seen the Promised Land. I may not get there with you, but I want you to know tonight, that we, as a people, will get to the Promised Land. So I'm happy, tonight. I'm not worried about anything. I'm not fearing any man. Mine eyes have seen the glory of the coming of the Lord."]
>
> **Dr. King's Last Speech**
> http://www.youtube.com/watch?v=Oehry1JC9Rk

Clearly, the United States has both an enormous and ironic double helix of both a horrid history of racial **oppression** and simultaneously, encouraging **progress** in maturing beyond it.

The Planet

Equally as encouraging as the racial progress which we have made over the past half-century here **in the United States**, is that noticeable racial progress **may** now be gradually beginning to occur across the planet. Consider:

> This [Barack Obama's] election is resonating right across Europe . . . . It has really resonated with the black and other minorities that make up the populations of France, of Germany, of Italy, of Britain. In Germany for instance, of the three million or so people of Turkish origin, there is barely one in public service. Just one in fact this year,

> was elected head of the Green Party—the only significant member of a minority in German politics. In France when in 2005 there were race riots . . . . in Paris' out-of-the-city ghettos, as Interior Minister back then, Nicolas Sarkozi called them scum, but standing with Obama when Obama visited Paris again in July, he . . . . as President, has nominated and named three people of migrant status to his Cabinet. Since Obama's election, Sarkozi himself has talked about increasing minorities in civil service, in politics and the media, of which there are literally almost none right now. So these are big deals in Europe where they're hoping for their own Obamas. France for instance, has something like ten-to-fifteen percent black people of French origin who're not at all represented in politics. So this is a very big deal for the people around the world who're looking for their own empowerment . . . .

Source: MSNBC's Rachel Maddow Show, January 19, 2009

And later, from the same show:

> Among the people gathering together tomorrow to watch the inauguration of Barack Obama, will be a group of African-Iraqis . . . . A group of African Iraqis were in DC for the Inauguration. Fifteen hundred years ago, East Africans were brought to Iraq as slaves. There are now about three hundred thousand of them (less than one-percent of Iraq's overall population). The African-Iraqis have had a very hard time of it. They're discriminated against. Most live in extreme poverty. Not one of their number holds political office. But that may be about to change. A slate of eight black Iraqi candidates is running for office in the provincial elections in Basra at the end of this month. They say they are inspired by the outcome of our election here. The Secretary of their political party told USA today, "We heard Obama's message of change. Iraq needs change in how they see their own black-skinned people. We need our brothers to accept us." It is going to be an

uphill climb. The slate of eight black candidates, calling themselves the Free Iraqi Movement, will be among about eighteen-hundred people vying for just thirty-five seats in the provincial government of Basra down in southern Iraq. In the meantime, in their Basra neighborhood, the black Iraqi candidates will host a feast tomorrow to watch and to celebrate the swearing in of the man who is their electoral inspiration.

Source: MSNBC's Rachel Maddox Show, January 19, 2009

The fundamental good news of **both** stories, is that President Obama's election is making a positive change in not only how we "do" politics **in the United States,** but indeed, how it may be practiced from this point forward **in nations across the globe.**[192] Specifically, his election may be making politics noticeably more inclusive of People of Color who have historically

---

192 In view of the historically unprecedented level of absolute vitriol of President Obama's political opponents, that assertion may be understandably difficult to trust. My belief, however, is that the bitterness, the venom, the downright contempt that have characterized the manner in which President Obama's political opponents have responded to him, (both politicians and private citizens), play the very important historic role of creating a very bright "red line in the sand" that illustrates in no uncertain terms, just how bad our politics can get, and in so doing, demonstrates to us in the clearest terms, the place to which we must never, in the future, return. That bright red line is a crucial piece in the puzzle of our evolution.

A tremendously significant **second** lesson for us all, is the absolute grace, dignity and maturity with which President Obama has responded to the vitriol of his opponents, consistently being the "adult in the room." That powerful double lesson, the lesson of how **to** be and how **not** be in the world, is available for us all to learn from President Obama's presidency. It is yet another true learning opportunity of which these human lives that we live, provide to each and every one of us, virtually all of the time.

been systematically shut out of political participation not only in the United States, but in nations the world over. That shift in inclusiveness, I believe, is slowly leading us to a time during which we are finally beginning the process of coming into racial balance on the Earth - a balance in which there is an equal sharing of power of people of all races around the globe.

Final Thoughts on Our Racial Present

Nothing is stronger than an idea whose time has come. When an idea or a reality's time has come, nothing, **nothing** can stop it . . . . The following are just four examples:

After two hundred fifty years of living in enslavement, African Americans could simply **not** continue to live as slaves. By the late 19th century, slavery had ended in many other countries in the Western Hemisphere and it was just too late in our history for the United States to continue to be one of that institution's last hold-outs. In 1865, the end of American slavery was an idea whose time had come. The thought of African Americans living as slaves **in the 20th century,** is unfathomable.

By 1920, when we received the right to vote, women, for **seventy-two years**, had fought valiantly for it. The beginning of the third decade of the 20th century was the time at which women **had** to get the right to vote. We had already gained the right to vote in a number of **other** developed countries. It was the 1920's and our nation could simply continue no longer with **half** the country, women, living in total political disenfranchisement.

Segregation **had** to end when it did in 1964. It simply could **not** have continued any later in the 20th century. The thought of "men, women and colored" restrooms, of "white and colored" water fountains,of "white and colored" seating areas in movie theaters, at lunch counters and in all other public facilities **in the 1970's, '80's** and **'90's**, in the United States, is simply unimaginable.

[It is for that reason that the continued existence of segregation in South Africa during those same decades was no less than an utter abomination. Had I lived in South Africa, I would have been approaching my 40th, rather than my 11th birthday when segregation ended, just as my parents were when it ended in the United States. I would also have had to carry a pass at all times, showing that I had the right to be wherever I was. I would have had to have done so until I was 33 years old when South Africa's pass laws ended.]

And in 1981, President Reagan could **not** have appointed another man to the Supreme Court. For the President to have appointed yet another man to the highest court of the land, i.e., to **continue** to have **no** women sitting on the nation's highest court, **in the 1980's and '90, approaching the 21st century**, was simply inconceivable.

Of course all of those things, the end of slavery, women's gaining the right to vote, the end of segregation and the first woman being seated on the Supreme Court, were the result of significant societal pressure and on a **practical** level, each very well could **indeed** have failed at the time that they actually succeeded. It is on a **different**, a higher, a **metaphysical** level, I believe, on which such historical events take place at inescapable times. It is on that **same** level, the metaphysical level, on which I believe humanity **will** racially mature. I believe that our maturing beyond racism is an idea whose time has come and that for that reason, **nothing** will be able to stop it—nothing. [193]

---

193 The lists of laws passed in countries **the world over**, that prohibit discrimination give me tremendous hope for the human species. While laws prohibiting discrimination based upon sexual orientation among other characteristics are often still lacking in many countries, the start that we have made is encouraging. For more information, see: http://en.wikipedia.org/wiki/List_of_anti-discrimination_acts and, http://www.whatishumanresource.com/anti-discrimination-laws

VII. Inverse Realities: Walking in Another's Moccasins

"Oh Great Spirit, keep me from ever judging a man until I have walked a day in his moccasins."

Indigenous Prayer of Unknown Origin

Science has proven that race as a phenomenon, is nothing more than an arbitrary system of categorizing human beings based upon false demarcations.

By logical extension, it is obvious that prejudice **based upon race** is also utterly arbitrary. Indeed, prejudging people based upon **any** physical difference is arbitrary. Using greater intelligence as a standard for determining human superiority, we **could,** for example, believe that men who **keep** their hair are superior in intelligence to men who **lose** it. We could believe that tall people are more intelligent than short people. We could believe that right-handed people are more intelligent than left-handed ones. [194] We could believe that "early birds", people who wake up early and energetically, are superior in intelligence to "night owls", people who upon waking early, are groggy and lethargic and whose natural bio-rhythm causes them to sleep late.

Based upon those beliefs, we could have first enslaved and then enacted social and economic policy that would by either design or effect, have kept the "inferior" groups, bald men and their families, short families, left-handed people and "night owls", less

---

[194] Some cultures actually **have** historically held beliefs about left-handedness that we now know to be utter nonsense. Perhaps the most extreme, was the belief that left-handedness is a demonic curse. As a result of that belief, in some cultures, left-handed people were both forced to use their right hand, and also discriminated against, sometimes severely.

well educated and less lucratively employed than the "superior" groups. As a result, the inferior groups would live in the "bad" areas and seriously lag behind the superior groups in education, in employment, and in every other way.

But in reality, we don't believe **any** of that foolishness . . . . Thank God! We **know** that as a group, men who retain their hair are no more intelligent than men who are bald, that tall people are no more intelligent than short people, that right-handed people are no more intelligent than those who are left-handed and that early birds are no more intelligent than night owls. What a nightmare of a world this would be for men who have male pattern baldness, for short people, for left-handed people and for night owls if we **did** hold such ridiculous beliefs. Fortunately, we understand that **all** of those things, hair vs. baldness, height differences, hand dominance, and bio-rhythms are simply **differences** among us, none of which result in differences in intelligence. We know, in other words, that those physical characteristics are not physiologically linked in any way, to intelligence.

But there is literally no end to the kind of arbitrary distinctions that we human beings can draw among ourselves. We could, for example believe that men who have sired one or more sons are more masculine than men who have sired only daughters. The abundantly clear resulting societal message would be that men who have only daughters are **inferior** to men who have sons. Both the sexism **and** the idiocy of that message are unambiguously apparent. Nonetheless, in a society **based** upon that belief, men's social clubs could be established in which only men who had sons were allowed to join. Several of our most recent American presidents, Lyndon Johnson, Richard Nixon, Bill Clinton, George W. Bush and our present President, Barack Obama, would all be barred from membership.

Similarly, we **could** believe that blonde, blue-eyed Caucasian People are more intelligent than those who have brown or black hair and brown eyes (and that Caucasian People with red hair and who have green, hazel, or gray eyes are just genetic oddballs).[195] Under **this** theory, then, blonde, blue-eyed Caucasian People are the only "**true**" Caucasians because Caucasians who have brown or black hair and brown eyes are **obviously** closer to People of Color. They are simply not **as** Caucasian as blonde, blue-eyed Caucasians. A world in which Caucasian People with brown or black hair and brown eyes, i.e., the **majority** of Caucasian People, are both **considered** to be and in every aspect of life, **treated** as if they are inferior to blonde, blue-eyed Caucasian People, is simply unthinkable. Can we even **imagine** an American society in which there are schools for blonde, blue-eyed Caucasian children and **different and entirely inferior** schools for all other Caucasian kids?[196]

In that society, based upon having received a superior education **in** those schools, only blonde, blue-eyed men and women would have access to society's best and highest paying jobs. Based upon the salaries they're **paid** in those jobs, only **they** could afford

---

[195] Mrs. Jane Elliott's work shown in the ABC network 1970 video, **"The Eye of the Storm"**, and her subsequent videos on eye color distinctions are the inspiration behind this hypothetical.
http://topdocumentaryfilms.com/a-class-divided/
http://www.janeelliott.com/

[196] As unthinkable as such a world is, the ABC News video, **"The Ugly Truth"**, (a preview of which is available at http://www.employeeuniversity.com/videos/ABC_News_Discrimination_Series.htm), quite clearly illustrates that among European Americans, as well, "attractive" people often have an advantage over people with "average" looks. To whatever extent attractiveness is associated with blue eyes and blonde hair, it is to **that** extent that eye and hair color remain sources of unearned privilege in our **actual** world when unconscious bias is at play in employment, housing and other selection processes. Other studies have established a similar advantage for tall men. The phenomenon, overall, is that people who others experience as "attractive", have advantages in the form of a host of unearned privileges that others do not.

to live in the "best" communities. And because they **do** live in those communities, (where the real estate tax base which funds public schools is highest), only they, blonde, blue-eyed Caucasian People would have quality public schools for their children. (Of course those who wished, could also afford to send their kids to private schools). That quality education would, in turn, allow their children to get the best jobs, and as a result, live in the best neighborhoods, continuing the cycle of **total** social and economic advantage to the society's blonde, blue-eyed Caucasian people, generation after generation, going back, perhaps, for 350 years.

The society, recognizing that dark-haired, dark-eyed Caucasian People's poverty and other enormous social challenges are the direct result of many generations of discrimination, harassment and violence against them, would perhaps put into place, programs to help the dark-haired, dark-eyed people to catch up with blonde, blue-eyed people in education, employment and housing. They might enact Affirmative Action programs and dark-haired, dark-eyed set asides for them.

In this society, the dark-haired, dark-eyed Caucasian People would adamantly declare, "But this isn't fair . . ." Blonde, blue-eyed people are **not** better than us! They **think** they are because that's what they've been taught all their lives. It's what they **want** to believe. But for the last three hundred fifty years they've set up the whole society to their own **total** advantage. Blonde, blue-eyed people have been steadily economically advancing while deliberately keeping us far behind, **for over three centuries**. **That's** why their schools and neighborhoods are better. It's **not** that they're superior to us!"

Undoubtedly, the blonde, blue-eyed people would say that the dark-haired, dark-eyed people should stop whining about the past and just pull themselves up by their bootstraps the way **they** all did. They'd say that the dark-haired, dark-eyed people should just stop playing the hair/eye card. They would resent the programs designed to help the dark-haired, dark-eyed people catch up and deeply feel that such programs are "reverse discrimination against them". Despite the undeniable history of the discrimination against, harassment of and violence toward dark-haired, dark-eyed people, the vast majority of blonde, blue-eyed people would, at least **unconsciously**, continue to hold the same view—that they are superior to dark-haired, dark-eyed people and that as a group, dark-haired, dark-eyed people are simply not intelligent, and are lazy, criminally inclined, and all together inferior to them.

But in even **that** society with its deeply entrenched hair and eye color prejudice, there would be some, **a minority** of blonde, blue-eyed Caucasian People who **would** truly understand. They would understand how their society's history has put dark-haired, dark-eyed Caucasian People at total social and economic disadvantage. They would know that dark-haired, dark-eyed people are indeed their **full** equals, and not **only** intellectually, but in every other way as well.

Further, there would be a minority of blonde, blue-eyed people who would be active in civil rights organizations and civil rights demonstrations **on behalf** of dark-haired, dark-eyed people. Despite their best efforts, though, that minority of conscious blonde, blue eyed Caucasian people would not be able to convince the majority of the other blonde, blue-eyed people that their attitudes and beliefs about dark-haired, dark-eyed Caucasian people are totally wrong. The unconscious blonde, blue-eyed people would remain marred in ignorance, not knowing, (indeed being virtually **clueless** about), what they don't know and not being in any way open to learning it.

Such would be a sheer nightmarish, hellish world be for dark-haired, dark-eyed Caucasian People.[197]

---

197 Hitler's failure to universalize the idea that only blonde, blue-eyed Aryans are the "true Caucasians", is a blessing to the majority of Caucasian People, in proportions of which I do not believe most can and do comprehend.

In yet a **different** world, we **could** believe that People of Color, and especially African people, are inferior to Caucasian People. In **that** world, our physical characteristics, our skin color, facial features and hair texture, would be considered both undesirable and inferior.

In such a world, we could believe that of **all** the Earth's people, Africans and their descendants most physically resemble and thus are closer to monkeys and other non-human primates. **Based** upon that belief, we could have a long and cruel history of **comparing** African People **to** those animals in all media forms, literature, still photography and video. As incredible as it sounds, that history could even include instances of placing African people and other People of Color into "human zoos."

In **this** world, we could believe that our physical characteristics are intricately linked to our intelligence, making us **intellectually** inferior as well.

We could believe that African people are genetically prone to criminal activity and to personal and social irresponsibility. On the **basis** of those beliefs, we **could** have a multi-century history of the enslavement of, discrimination against, harassment of and practice of tremendous violence toward African People and other People of Color. We could have taken over their continents and islands all over the Earth and used them to exploit their **own** land, all for the benefit of European People.

In this world, we'd point to all of the achievements made by Europeans. We'd say, "Just look at the evidence. It was **us,** after all, who was able to oppress **them**. They couldn't oppress us. They weren't intelligent enough to either strategize as we did or to invent the gun, both of which allowed us to end up on top. That **alone** tells the story. We invented the ships to travel the world. We invented guns which their bows and arrows couldn't compete with, and were able to do so **because** we we're more intelligent. Who invented electricity? The white man. Who invented the telegraph? The white man. The telephone? The white man. The car? Trains?

Airplanes? The white man? Who invented movies and television? Who invented every instrument in the orchestra? Us. It was just natural for us to develop as the superior race. In the climate that we evolved in, we **had** to be hard-working and industrious in order to survive. Their climate made them lazy and lackadaisical. It's not their fault and it's not our fault. It's just what naturally happened."

"Just look at the sophistication of our music, classical music, compared to that jungle music they make, if you can even call it music", the conversation would continue.

"And look at the refinement of the dancing we developed, all the ballroom dances like the Waltz, the Rumba, the Mambo, and the Samba, as opposed to that disgusting gyrating that they do that they **call** dancing", the speaker would say.

As the conversation continued, we could hear, "Which race took humanity into the Industrial Age? Who took us into the space age? Who invented computers? **Who made the entire modern world what it is today**? The white man—Europeans. What have **they** done? Nothing. They're nothing more than the benefactors of our genius. Their contribution to the world? Fried chicken, grass huts and gangsta rap. We're superior. It's obvious. Period".

In this world, Caucasian People would be absolutely **convinced** that they are superior to People of Color, and especially to African People.

That world is nothing less than a complete, hellish nightmare for African People.

> [It is interesting that even in **this** world in which the assumption of African inferiority is the norm among perhaps the **majority** of human beings, I have on a few occasions, heard an African American assert that when the educational opportunity playing field begins to level, African Americans are going to excel intellectually. In such conversations, the speaker usually gave examples of African American

intellectual achievement often on the part of African Americans who came from poverty. They point to examples of black intellectual achievement such as Public School 318 in Brooklyn, New York. Seventy percent of the school's students live below the federal poverty line, yet, over the last ten years, its chess team has won more chess championships than any other school in the United States.]

In such conversations, I have heard, African Americans point, among others, to the following examples of black achievement:

* The Dance Theatre of Harlem, the country's **only** national black ballet theater is among the top ballet companies in the entire world. http://www.dancetheatreofharlem.org/

* Marion Anderson and Jessye Norman, two of a very small number of African American opera singers, both became world renowned and were widely considered to be among the world's top opera singers.

* "After all those years of them singing it, who recorded **the** most moving and popular version of "God Bless America"? Ray Charles. Same thing with the National Anthem. After all those years of them singing it, who recorded the most moving and popular version of it? Whitney Houston."

* Dr. Ben Carson, neurosurgeon and Director of Pediatric Neurosurgery at Johns Hopkins Hospital, was raised by a single mother with a third grade education. Dr. Carson developed and thus, was the first surgeon to perform both the intrauterine procedure to relieve pressure on the brain, and the hemispherectomy, the procedure in which he successfully removed one half of the brain of a young girl who suffered from uncontrollable seizures. The seizures were stopped by the surgery. Dr. Carson made medical history in 1987 by also being the first surgeon in the world to successfully separate conjoined twins joined at the back of the head.

* Dr. Vivien Thomas—Dr. Thomas was born in 1910, in New Iberia, Louisiana, the grandson of a slave. In 1930 as a nineteen year old carpenter's apprentice with only a high school diploma, he was hired by the European American doctor, Alfred Blalock, as his laboratory assistant. In Dr. Blalock's lab, in two-hundred operations on dogs, **Mr**. Thomas first created then surgically cured the "blue baby syndrome". Because he did not have a medical degree at that time, however, Mr. Thomas was not allowed to perform the surgery on a human being. Dr. Blalock, therefore, at Johns Hopkins Hospital, performed the first "blue baby" operation on a human baby. Before doing so, however, he requested that Mr. Thomas stand over his shoulder on a step stool during the operation in order to instruct him, step-by-step, on what to do during the procedure. Mr. Thomas did and the baby's life was extended by several months. By 1946, Mr. Thomas became John Hopkins' highest paid lab technician, going on to train many dozens of surgeons during the 1940's. In 1976, still with only a high school education, he was awarded an honorary doctorate by Johns Hopkins Medical School. Dr. Thomas was then appointed to the faculty of Johns Hopkins Medical School as Instructor of Surgery. The 2004 HBO film, "**Like Something the Lord Made**", (http://www.youtube.com/watch?v=18pPecSv-kw), based on Katie McCabe's 1989 award-winning Washingtonian article by the same name, (http://pdf.washingtonian.com/pdf/mccabe.pdf), is based on the life of Dr. Vivien Thomas. The article's title, "Like Something the Lord Made", is based on Dr. Blalock's description of Dr. Thomas' surgical skills as **being**, "like something the Lord made."

[In this same context, over many years, I have heard the following comments from a few African Americans, all put together here in a single conversation, a conversation which will no doubt be disturbing to some, myself included:

"They, (European Americans), may not be **consciously** aware of it, but that's **really** why they feel they have to keep us and other People of Color down. On some level, they **know** we're superior to them. Yes, we're physically superior. After all, they could **never** have physically survived what **we've** been through; they're not strong enough. But we're **intellectually** superior to them too, and subconsciously, they **know** it. Did you see the movie, 'Stand and Deliver'? Just look at what those Hispanic kids did. Once they had access to good education, they outscored **all** those rich white suburban kids on that math test. Now, who is this country's most eloquent speaker **of all time**? Martin Luther King. You think a **white** southern Baptist preacher could speak the way Dr. King did, with his eloquence and his passion? No way. They just don't have what it takes, the fire and that particular kind of genius. And did you know that Dr. King skipped two grades in high school and started college when he was fifteen years old? And look at what Barack did. He was the new kid on the block and **yet**, he out politicked them **at** their own game. He was brilliant, masterful, really. When's the last time you saw a young **white** politician do that? See, once the educational playing field is leveled, that kind of achievement won't be the **exception** for our kids. It'll be the **rule**. I mean, look at all the thousands and thousands of black people who started out in the projects and in rural southern poverty and became doctors and lawyers. How many stories do you hear about white people from Appalachia going to medical school and law school? And who's the highest paid man in Holloywood? Tyler Perry. And you and I both know what would happen if all those young drug-selling brothers in the hood would go to college and start legitimate businesses. Right. They'd show this country what real entrepreneurism looks like. Wall Street would be backing those young bloods left and right. They did it with the gangsta rappers. They poured millions and maybe even billions of dollars to promote gangsta rappers. That's just another of **many** examples of how they can hate you and even hate what you're doing, but if they can make money off of you, they'll still do it, while hating you the whole the time. Amazing.

And look at what Caucasians have done to the environment. Everybody else on the planet, American Indians, Africans and other People of Color, we understand, respect and value nature. Them? Nature's the enemy to be defeated. Just look at what they've done, not only to the **planet**, not only to damn near all the other **people** on the planet, but to all its **non**-human life too. Hundreds of thousands of species—gone. They're ruining this Earth, and unfortunately, not only for them, but for **all** of us, including the animals and plants. It's scary what they're doing to the Earth and the animals. **We** can see it, but them? Because of how they think about and relate to nature as something to conquer? They're totally blind to it.

They're just not like other people. They're natural predators. Take gun powder. The Chinese invented it and used it in celebrations for **two-thousand years** when Marco Polo went to China and saw it for the first time. Them? They saw it and thought, "Oh, we can kill people with this." Then what'd they do? Took it back to Europe and invented the gun. They're **having** the gun is what allowed them to take over most of the planet. They defeated everybody else not because they were smarter, but because they had guns. Look what happened in Viet Nam when the Vietnamese were equally armed. The Vietnamese won because they had guns just like the whites, **and also** because they were on their home turf. If Africans and Hawaiians and Indians and Aboriginal Australians and all of the island people around the world who were attacked and defeated by Europeans had had **guns** during those first contacts, they would've beat the crap out of them and we'd have a very different world today. If the playing, or in this case the **fighting** field is even, you can't fight people on their home turf, (which they know **intimately** and you don't know at all), and win. The home turf advantage is just too great. Europeans were able to oppress other people around the world because they had guns, **not** because they had superior intelligence. They did not.[198]

But the story **they** tell is that they defeated every other race and ethnic group on the planet because of their intelligence. What they've done to history, how they've distorted it, is incredible. Look at the Southerners. They wanted to keep us as slaves so badly that they even declared war **against their own country**. **They actually wanted to leave the United States**. It was treason. They were **all** traitors, all of them. But according to **their** history, those same traitors were heroes, patriots. They reenact their Civil War defeat every year, over and over again. Now they even want to teach "Confederate History" in public schools. They hated the United States and wanted to leave it. They were traitors to this country they say they love so much, not patriots. Look, you lost. Get over it. Move on.'

It's obvious why Caucasians are so different from other human beings. It's because first, they mated and mixed with the Neanderthals, and that's just a proven fact,

---

[198] Jared Diamond, in his book and accompanying documentary, *Guns, Germs and Steel: The Fates of Human Societies*, provides a detailed discussion of the role of guns in the European conquest of most of the cultures on Earth. While I disagree with Diamond's timeline for the development of particular human civilizations, his analysis of the role of guns within this context, is quite interesting.

Guns, Germs and Steel PBS Video: http://www.youtube.com/watch?v=cLJfZOyFpZo

which actually makes them less human than everybody else, and second, because they ate so much red meat all winter long when they were living in those caves in Europe. **That's** why no other people on Earth have done as much harm to so many other people on the Earth as Europeans. Think about it. Eskimos' climate is even colder than theirs but **they** didn't turn into worldwide enslavers and killers. Why? Because they ate mostly fish, not red meat. That's why they didn't become as aggressive as Europeans did, even in their climate. Just think about it.

And that's why they have all those 'white supremacy' groups. They're insecure because on a deep level they **know** that they're inferior to us. If you really **were** convinced of your superiority, would you have to go around beating your chest about it all the time: 'The white race is superior! We're the most evolved! The white man is better! We're smarter!' It's sort of like, 'Me thinks these people doth protest too much.' If they **really** believed that mess, they wouldn't have to go around thumping their chest about it all the time.

So we know the real deal. We're **clearly** physically superior. And you know we're emotionally and spiritually stronger too, right? I mean, there's **no way** they could've emotionally and spiritually survived what we've been through. Check it out......after they'd enslaved us **for two hundred and fify years**, destroyed our successful communities, lynched us, harassed us unmercifully, segregated us in society, discriminated against us in every possible way, and for millions of them and their progeny, became rich off of our free labor, they're crying like babies about twenty years of Affirmative Action. 'That's reverse discrimination!' It's a joke. They're weak people. That proves it. So in their minds, they **had** to make us intellectually inferior because if not, in other words, if we we're physically, emotionally **and** intellectually superior, we'd be what? Right. Superior people. And they just couldn't have **that**.

But you know what's really pitiful? They're so absorbed in their own self-righteous, self-proclaimed fake superiority that they don't even know how ridiculous that makes them look to us. They have absolutely **no clue** that the more they proclaim their white pride in their "superiority", the more insecure and ludicrous they look to us.

But look, the world is round and what **goes** around **comes** around, and as unbelievable as it may seem to us now, all the stuff that they put us through is going to come back around on them. Just like we were on top in the past with our advanced civilizations while they were in Europe living in caves and eating raw meat, we're going to be on top again in the future. I didn't say it, Einstein said it. For every action, there's an equal and opposite reaction. It's a law of the universe. They can keep this racist bulls--t going if they want to, but just wait. We're going to be on top again. **We** won't live to see it, but our **and their** grandchildren will."

I am thankful both that I have rarely heard those kinds of statements as an adult and that I did not grow up hearing them. Listening to them as an adult made me wonder just how they may have affected me if I **had** been exposed to them as a child. They may have hardened my heart and in so doing, limited both the ability of my brain to clearly think and of my heart to deeply feel. It was then that I began to understand, not just intellectually, but on an **emotional** level, the way in which hearing racist comments about Americans of Color have impacted both the minds and hearts of millions of young European American children. They were doomed from birth, doomed to a life of both unconscious feelings of superiority **to** and irrational fear **of** Americans of Color. I realized that many millions of children of **all** races who grow up hearing such comments about **any** group of people, are doomed from birth to being mentally incapacitated and emotionally disabled.

Fortunately, however, some children who grow up in such environments, **despite the odds**, escape that fate. My friend Tom grew up in a small, white, suburban New Jersey community located about forty-five minutes away from Newark. Tom has shared with me that during the 1960's when he was a child, he saw on the front page of the local newspaper, pictures of African Americans burning large sections of Newark during the riots that followed Dr. King's assassination. In relating the story, Tom explained that in his world, he had absolutely **no** exposure to African Americans, and that for that reason, his only image of us, was as people who riot and burn buildings. That image, Tom explained, was combined with fear. Seeing the newspaper pictures, he was afraid as a child, and wondered if black people were going to, as he described it, "come up over our hill, and burn **our** town." That visual and accompanying fear were combined with his regularly hearing from neighbors, comments about African Americans not wanting to work and being on welfare. Interestingly, even as a child, Tom knew that like him, the adults in his life also had virtually no contact with African Americans. Tom said that while he never **said** anything to the adults, he did **question** whether they actually knew what they were talking about. In his words, "I really don't know why I questioned . . . . but I think it was the mean-spirited nature of their talk. To be that 'anti-black' just seemed ignorant to me because I knew they couldn't know black people well, so how could you be that negative?"

One of the reasons that I **know** that there is hope for humanity to ultimately be **truly** post-racial, is Tom's example as one of the most conscious, compassionate human beings I know, **despite** having grown up with the enormously common "triple whammy" of having a total lack of exposure **to**, hearing constant negative comments **about** and experiencing feeling fear **of** African Americans. Tom's example and that of my other European American friends has convinced me that we are capable of rising above the initial station in life into which we were born and sincerely living the value of accepting all of humankind as equal and thus worthy of equal value.

Tom told me that his biggest lesson from that experience is, "The power of media images overlaid with both a lack of contact and stereotypical chatter, i.e., of segregation and both the ignorance and fear in which it results." The power of those influences, however, were clearly no match for the power of the human heart to find and feel empathy. I believe that the hearts of **billions** of human beings have the very same capacity to feel love for all humanity.]

Or . . . . we could simply invert the history and present day reality of our **actual** world, i.e., use the reality in which European and African Americans **have** lived in the past and **do** live in the present, to imagine yet a **different** world. In this world, the lowest people on the human spectrum, **Africans**, had historically oppressed **Caucasians**, and were, as a result, on top financially and thus socially and educationally. In **this** world, we would believe that people who have **dark** skin are more intelligent and superior in every other way to people who have **light** skin. We would accept that people of African descent are superior to all other people based upon what we would believe is our quite apparent physical and intellectual superiority.

As part of the history of this society, Africans would have sailed to the Americas, claimed and then taken over the land of their Indigenous People and drove them onto reservations.

That history would also be one in which Africans had also sailed to Europe, and over time, taken over all of it, colonized and subjugated all of the European people and maintained total control of the continent of Europe for centuries. In this history, Africans used European people in slavery-like conditions, to mine the natural resources of their lands and then, for many decades, sent those resources, those minerals and diamonds mined from Europe, to African countries, making African countries wealthy at the total expense of the European people from whose lands they were taken.

In this alternate reality, while in Europe, Africans would also have hunted and caught Europeans in large nets, transported them to the Americas and its islands and for two hundred fifty years, enslaved them for life. The children of the enslaved Caucasians would be born slaves.

In the history of this world, Africans would have built "human zoos" and displayed Caucasian People in them. The history would even include an instance in which a young Caucasian boy had been displayed in the monkey house of a national zoo.

As a result of the rape of hundreds of thousands of European women during the two hundred fifty years of slavery, European Americans in this world would have many different skin colors and hair textures, with the majority actually being mixed-race. People who have straight hair and/or are mixed-race in appearance, however, would definitely **not** be considered African. In this world, one has to have the physical appearance of a "pure" African to have black skin privilege.

After their long period of enslavement, European Americans would no longer have European names. Instead, they would have the last names of their former African captors and after more than two centuries of African enslavement, would give their children African first names as well. Although Caucasian Americans would be **aware** that Europeans living in Europe have European names, at the end of slavery, most would not change their names back to European names, feeling that they could no longer identify with those names because too much time had passed since their ancestors lived in Europe. Thus, little Caucasian **boys** would have names, for example, such as Adebayo Appenteng and Bobo Okeke and little Caucasian **girls** would have names such as Jahzara Fofana and Kianga Mandela.

Their 250 year period of enslavement would have not only wiped out European Americans' **connection** to their original cultures, it would also have utterly erased any **knowledge** that they could have had about their cultures. They would know only that their ancestors came from **somewhere** in Europe. They wouldn't know, however, whether they were Italian, Irish, Spanish, British or any other **specific** European nationality.

Those two-and-a-half centuries of the enslavement of Caucasian Americans would be followed by an additional one hundred years of discrimination against, harassment of and violence toward them. Beginning just after the end of slavery with the "White Codes" and for a full ninety-nine years following slavery, Caucasian Americans in this alternate reality would be oppressed and discriminated against in **every** aspect of life. They would be segregated from African Americans in all public accommodations. Caucasian Americans would not be allowed to drink from the same water fountains as African Americans and other black people. They would not be allowed to use the same restrooms as black people. Caucasian adults would be allowed to work in only menial jobs. Caucasian children would be sent to their own, very inferior schools. They would live in their own very deprived communities.

This world's history would include Sundown towns, where no Caucasian person would be safe after dark. In this society, there would be entire states through which Caucasian families would be nervous about traveling. In order to save travelling Caucasian families the humiliating experience of being turned away from motels, restaurants and automobile garages, a travel guide would exist which would inform them where there were sleeping accommodations, places to eat and available car repair services along their route that would accept them.

The history of this world would be **replete** with black lynch mobs that for more than a half century after slavery, by final accounts, would have lynched **thousands** of European Americans, **both** men **and** women. Many of the lynchings of European Americans would have been done in a party-like, celebratory style and referred to by African Americans as "bar-b-ques."

In this world, numerous black supremacist groups would exist. The members of those groups would dress up in black robes and hoods, terrorize Caucasian communities, fire bomb Caucasian churches and burn the homes of Caucasian citizens. They would use the symbol of Christianity, the cross, as their emblem.

In this society, medical experiments would be performed on Caucasian People to see if they responded the same as African People to certain chemicals and diseases. Indeed, two entirely fake sciences, craniology and eugenics, would be devoted to systematically establishing the genetic superiority of Caucasians.

Scientific Racism: The Eugenics of Social Darwinism
https://www.youtube.com/watch?v=-eX5T68TQIo

Police officers would regularly harass and arrest Caucasian men both with and often without cause. In this alternate reality, African judges give Caucasian People **significantly** longer sentences than African People **for the same crime**. In comparison to their population, European men represent a **hugely** disproportionate percentage of the country's prison population. Every European American person, no matter how well educated, how accomplished, how distinguished, how famous, how wealthy, or just plainly **good** they are as a human being, **every** European American person is subject to suffering the indignities of driving while white, shopping while white, or even **walking and sleeping in a car,** while white.

The notion of Caucasian inferiority would be found in every form of entertainment and other cultural expression, including the performance of white face as particularly entertaining.

In this world, as a result of **all** of that unspeakable oppression, the history of the United States would include a peaceful, non-violent Caucasian American Civil Rights Movement of the 1960's in which many thousands of Caucasian Americans would have studied, learned and practiced the principles of non-violence in preparation for their movement, and then successfully utilized, modeled and lived by those principles in facing the racist, African American police forces of southern cities. Those police forces would have responded to the peaceful Caucasian American protesters who were praying, or walking in silence, or singing Old Caucasian Spirituals and Freedom Songs from their days of slavery, with barking, frothing dogs, billy clubs across their faces and backs, and the blunt force of the full strength of fire hoses. Many of those same African American police officers whose job it was to **protect** the peaceful Caucasian American demonstrators who were exercising their constitutional right to protest, would **themselves**, be members of black supremacist and African American hate groups.

This culture would be one in which large wealthy think thanks would name lecture series after famous black supremacist politicians and fifty years after the European American civil rights movement had ended, other black politicians would make speeches in those programs in which they praise the black supremacist politician for whom the series is named.

This society would have in it, a major political party which used a Southern Strategy, (where European Americans had been enslaved), to court the votes of conservative, racist, working class and southern African Americans, the design of which is to intensify the fears and stoke the resentment of those African Americans toward European Americans.

In this alternate reality, many African Americans would see the government's Affirmative Action attempts to help Caucasian American communities overcome some of the present day lasting effects of past discrimination against Caucasian People as "reverse discrimination" against African People.

Internally, on the personal level, millions of Caucasian People would experience internalized oppression and self-hatred. They would absolutely hate the lack of texture in their hair, the lack of color in their skin, the lack of fullness in their lips and the lack of "character" of their noses. Every single one of those characteristics would **unequivocally** indicate their genetic inferiority.

Caucasian American women in this world would support a multi-million dollar hair care industry devoted to making their hair as napped as it could possibly get. There would be a video of a puppet that resembles a little European American girl which was produced to try to teach little European American girls to not hate their hair. And European Americans, as well as people the world over, would tan in an effort to become as dark as possible, undergo surgery to have a larger, more African looking nose, and undergo procedures to have thicker lips.[199] They wouldn't wear certain colors because they had heard all their lives that those colors accent their paleness, of which they would be utterly ashamed.

When looking at two dolls lying in front of them on a table, a black and a white one, European American children, when asked, "Which doll is the pretty doll? Which doll is the smart doll? Which doll is the good doll?" would point, **each time**, to the black doll. When asked, "Why is this doll, (gesturing toward the black one), pretty and smart and good?" the little white children would respond, "Because she's black." When asked, "Which doll is the ugly doll?" they would point to the white one. When asked, "Which

---

199 It is interesting that lip enhancement is now a procedure that many European American women are undergoing.

doll is the dumb doll?" they would point to the white one. When asked, "Which doll is the bad doll?" they would point to the white one. When asked, "Why is this doll, (gesturing toward the white one), ugly and dumb and bad?" the children would say, "Because she's white." When asked, "Which doll looks more like you?" the little white children would point to the white doll.

Because of all the world's people, the physical appearance of Caucasians is the **most** different from African People, their skin the **most** lacking in pigment, their noses, the most different, because it is **their** race which has people who have hair and eye colors that are generally unknown in other human populations, because they generally have significantly more body hair than other human beings, Caucasian People live with the **constant** awareness that of **all** the world's people, they are considered the world over, to be both **the least attractive.**

In this reality, it is **Europe** that would have the world's most ancient civilizations, societies which achieved such greatness, that the method of some of their technological accomplishments, (erecting pyramids **5,000 years ago**, for example, which are still standing today), remains a mystery even into the present. When European American historians attempt to educate African American historians about the greatness of their ancient European civilizations, however, African American historians would deny the history, asserting that Europeans are not intelligent enough to have created such great societies, and posit that it was ancient **Africans** who had actually **travelled** to Europe who were responsible for the great ancient societies that were located on the European continent. Great Europeans of antiquity would be depicted in popular culture as African. Children would either not have been taught about Europe's great ancient civilizations at **all**, or would have been taught that they were really **African** civilizations.

All of the images that everyone would see of **present-day** Europe would be of very poor, starving people in totally under-developed European countries—France, England, Italy, Spain, Holland and others. European Americans would see on television, commercials showing poor, starving European children accompanied with pleas to help feed and educate them. Most people would be totally unaware of the centuries-long history of the African colonization of Europe and its effects. The vast majority of **European Americans** wouldn't be aware of that colonial history either. They **would** know, however, that not only African Americans, but people **all over the world** view Europe as essentially a cultural wasteland filled with pitiful people.

The facts that:

* As a species, we are aware of the great ancient civilizations of the Indigenous People of the Western Hemisphere, of Asian People, of people of the sub-Asian Indian continent, and most aware, of course, of the many great ancient **African** civilizations; and,

* We simultaneously, we know absolutely **nothing** about any great ancient **European** civilizations, those of European descent are also considered to be the world's **least intelligent** people as well.

Finally, because of the primitive conditions of **all** of the places in the world in which they live, no matter what continent, people of European descent are also considered to be **the most socially aberrant people** on the planet—lazy, trifling, shiftless and of low morals.

European Americans know in that this world, that no matter **how** many of them have **outstanding** achievements in the sciences, in technology, in medicine, literature, art and many other fields of human endeavor, those that attain them are always seen as the **exceptions** in a race of people who are otherwise largely perceived through very thick lenses of bias as lazy, criminally inclined, sexually promiscuous and constantly playing the race card.

In this alternative reality, **God** would be depicted as **only** black. Any depictions of God as white would be **highly** offensive, and even blasphemous to many.

In such a world, conversations such as the following would take place: [200]

"Just look at the evidence", the person of African descent in that world would say. "The environment that **we're** best adapted to, is the one that made our very existence **as a species** possible, the one that **gave rise** to human beings. That's why nobody else **on the planet** has the fullness, the thickness, the strength our beautiful hair. Among **all** other people, **our** hair is unique. It's special. Everybody else has that thin, stringy, oily stuff. Their hair is like animal hair—dogs, cats, gorillas, monkeys and orangutans.

And have you ever **smelled** their hair, that greasy, matted mess when it's wet? Phew!

Now in terms of skin color, people are much more attractive and much more human looking with **brown** skin. **They** even look better with brown skin, **and they know it**. That's why they're always trying to **get** it. And they even buy **artificial** tanning products because the sun, the very source of life, is **their** enemy. They can't stay outdoors in the sun for more than a minute without

---

[200] All of the comments used to describe this world, a European American inverse reality, are painfully ugly and perhaps even disturbing to some. They rival many thoughts and comments that are and have been both believed and said about African Americans. What I have done here, is simply applied either those same or similar thoughts and comments to **European** Americans. My intent in giving voice to them is to help European Americans walk in the moccasins of another, moccasins that have been internally lined with thorns. I do so with the knowledge that it is **that** experience above all others, the experience of walking for a time in the shoes of another, which gives rise to the possibility of true understanding and to the deep empathy which then often follows.

burning. When I see them at the beach I'm actually shocked by how pale and colorless their skin actually is. It looks like raw chicken skin. It literally makes me sick to look at. You can't argue it. People are **much** more fit and healthy looking with brown skin.

And, if we were to mate with them all over the world, the world would become **browner**, not whiter, which **proves** that we're genetically dominant, and genetic dominance is **clearly** superior to being genetically recessive. Who but a **fool** would doubt that genetic dominance is superior to genetic recessiveness? It's just common sense. [201]

You want proof? Just look at the difference in how we age. You can see it. It's the melanin and the natural oil in our skin. They don't say, 'Black don't crack' for nothing.

They have no texture in their hair and no color in their skin. They don't even have butts and lips. Some of them have nothing more than a **pencil** line for a top lip.

But not only are we **genetically** stronger, we're also **physically** stronger. In all those months of the year when they were eating nothing but red meat and were huddled up in caves trying to protect themselves from those frigid temperatures, we were eating fruits, vegetables, grains, nuts **and** meat. We were living freely on the Earth, enjoying our environment. All year long, we were

[201] The assertion that African genes are dominant, is scientifically utterly false. The fact is that in **all** races, dark **eyes** are genetically dominant. A blue-eyed gene and a brown-eyed gene will **always** result in brown eyes, **never** blue eyes, and **never** a mixture of the two. Black **skin,** however, is **not** genetically dominant. The mixture of a gene for black skin and a gene for white skin will **not** always result in black skin. Sometimes, it will result in either one or the other. Most often, however, it will result in **a combination** of the two genes, i.e., some shade of brown skin. It is that **combination** of genes that would account for the "browning" of the world, not a **dominance** of the gene for black skin.

hunting, fishing, planting and harvesting and pursuing our cultural traditions, including music and dance. It's no wonder our bodies are stronger."

And you know what they say—stronger body, stronger mind."

The speaker would then probably continue with a long list of African achievements in science, mathematics, technology and other fields that "proved" our intellectual superiority over all other people. In so doing, we would be blind to the fact that our financial advantages gave us social and most importantly, **educational** advantages which **allowed** us to have the achievements that we would have had in those fields. We would point to the achievements **themselves** as proof of our intellectual superiority, likely denying that our historic treatment of European people was in large measure responsible for their **under-**achievement, relative to us. Indeed, we'd think on some level, perhaps at least unconsciously, that the very fact that we were **able** to oppress Europeans, i.e., that we were (in our eyes), the "winners" of history, is one of the most obvious **indicators** of our superiority.

The conversation would continue:

"And look at the mathematical sophistication of **our** music as compared to **theirs**. They did pretty well with their 'classical' music, but except for that, the beats, the rhythms of **our** music (i.e., African beats and African rhythms), are on an entirely different mathematical level than theirs. Compare **any** of our music, jazz, do wop, blues, gospel, **any** of them, to rock, country, folk, heavy metal, i.e., to **any** of their music, and it's obvious—ours is **much** more complex, **much** more advanced. **Nobody** else's musical beat comes anywhere **near** the mathematical complexity of the African drum beat. There's just no comparison. There's just **so** many examples of this.

And look at how we **play** music. When Louie (Satchmo) Armstrong came along, nobody had ever seen **anybody** play the trumpet like that. Satchmo's level of trumpet playing was

totally new in the music world. He blew 'em away. Same thing with Wynton today. Wynton Marsalis by many accounts, is the number one trumpet player **on the planet**, and in **all** genres, not only in jazz and blues, but in "their" musical genre too - classical. There's not a single white boy out there who even comes **close** to Wynton. Even in the music that **they** come up with, like rock, who was and still **is** the best rock guitar player of all time? Jimmy. When Jimmy Hendrix suddenly appeared on the rock scene, those white rock boys were literally in shock. They were in shock. Jimmy . . . . blew . . . . them . . . . out . . . . of . . . . the . . . . water. Jimmy Hendrix **redefined** their understanding of what a guitar could be made to do. And the rock queen is who? Yeah – Tina. Tina Turner took rock performance to a level that no white woman has ever come **close** to. **Tina is bad!** Even in **rock**, the genre **they** developed, the best rock guitarist is a black man and the best female rock performer is a black woman. Now what does that tell you?

Now let's look at how they dance . . . . Wo. It's amazing. It's like they **hear** the music, but they don't **feel** it. How can you hear music, and move your body to it the way they do? They have **no** natural rhythm. None. It never ceases to amaze me. Now, **our** dance, African dance, has taken over in India, Korea, in the entire world. Let's put it this way—the day we see a white James Brown, or a white Michael Jackson is the day it's gonna freeze over in a very hot place that rhymes with "bell". Elvis was the closest thing they had and that was only because he was **imitating** black dancers and even then, he couldn't even **compare** to them, wasn't even in the same league. Now once they **see** us do it, they can **learn** it, but to come up with it on their **own**? No way. They just don't have it.

And singing? Think about it—If you want to win any of those televised national singing competitions, how do you have to sound? Black. Have you ever heard a white singer with the strength, the depth and the **power** of the black voice? I don't think so. They have that distinctly Caucasian nasally sound. That's why we call them 'honkies'.

In a nutshell, they just have no cool, no 'soul', (and the latter may be literally true.) That's why they mimic our art.—our music, our dancing, our singing. You don't see us mimicking theirs.

And then sports? Please. Ok, let's start with the first one—horse racing. **From the very beginning of the sport** in the 1800's, the best jockeys were black, most of whom were slaves at the time. The white jockeys couldn't touch 'em. Black jockeys won thirteen of the first twenty-eight Kentucky Derbys. Look, Isaac Murphy won three of them in the 1800's and was called, 'the greatest jockey of all time', not just the greatest black jockey. Now let's go to the most obvious one today—running. All you have to do is look at the Olympics. That line of sprinters? All black, and of West African heritage. They can't touch us. Same thing in distance running where **East** Africans dominate. Basketball? We own it. Football? We have the best players, hands down. Baseball? A lot of the records broken in the **Major** Leagues had already been broken **years** before in the **Negro** Leagues.[202] Look at Jackie Robinson. In 1947, he broke the color barrier, was the first one in the Major Leagues and look at his record. In '47, **his first year**, he was named National League Rookie of the Year. In '49, he won the batting title and was National League Most Valuable Player. He led the National League in stolen bases in '47 **and** '49. He **led** second basemen in double plays **four years in a row**, from '49 to '52. **In a ten year career**, he led the Dodgers to **six** World Series and one World Series Championship, **and he wasn't even among the strongest players in the Negro Leagues**.[203] We

---

[202] **Short Documentary on the Negro Leagues**
http://www.youtube.com/watch?v=9sa7y4lvl1E

"Soul of the Game" A Home Box Office Movie about the Negro Leagues
http://www.youtube.com/watch?v=LiDULxPh0hU

[203] Of all the players in the Negro **Leagues**, Jackie Robinson was intentionally chosen to integrate the Major Leagues because of his stellar academic, personal and professional histories and his

have the best football players too. I don't even need to go **into** that. And boxing? You'll be in a lot of trouble if you're waiting for a white Jack Johnson, Joe Louis or Muhammad Ali. They showed the world that the Great White Hope is just that—a hope! Even in sports which they've historically dominated, tennis and golf for example, once we start playing them, we rule **them** too.[204] Let's take golf. I have one word—Tiger. Number 1 golfer **in the world**. Now look at tennis. Althea Gibson was the only black professional tennis player in the world and what happened? As **soon** as she turned pro, she won the Grand Slam in 1956, Wimbledon **and** the U.S. Open in '57 and then the U.S. Open **again,** in '58, and was the top-ranked U.S. tennis player both years. Those white girls couldn't **touch** Althea. Now what are the chances that the **only** black tennis player is going to be **the number one** player, **in the world**? If there were three hundred professional female tennis players, the chances were 1 in 300. [205] Now fast forward twenty years. There's **still**, only a literal **handful** of African Americans on the national tennis circuit, and yet who dominated? Arthur Ashe, who won the '68 U.S. Open, and ranked the number 1 tennis

---

temperament. He was judged to have the strong, calm temperament necessary to withstand the emotional abuse of which he would certainly be the recipient in being the first African American player in the Major Leagues.

Short video about Jackie Robinson
https://www.youtube.com/watch?v=Ph2cKXA2Mjs

"42", Movie Trailer about Jackie Robinson's integration of the Major Leagues
http://www.youtube.com/watch?v=tkI3RDL5__Y

[204] In this world, perhaps European Americans wouldn't dominate in tennis and golf, but we'll posit it for the sake of making the sports comparison in this imaginary world.

[205] **Althea Gibson Video**
http://www.youtube.com/watch?v=-O2G3pUNdxU

player **in the world** in '69. He won the U.S. Open again in '75, and **to this day**, is the only person **in the world** to win both the U.S. Nationals **and** the U.S. Open in the same year, and he was still an amateur player when he did so! He hadn't even turned pro yet. Jimmy Connors was their Great White Hope and in 1975, Arthur, ten years older than Connors and at the end of his career, not only beat him, he **embarrassed** him.[206] Now, fast forward **another** twenty years and who dominates world tennis? Three words say it all: Venus and Serena. Look, sports played at the international level, sports on the world stage prove time and time again that African People are faster, stronger and have more physical endurance than Europeans. Once we get in, we break all the records they ever set. That case is established and closed shut.

Even in every genre of **comedy**, from the squeaky clean to the 'bluest', our comedians are funnier—**much** funnier. Every now and then they get a George Carlin, but he's an exception. We put flavor in our food, soul in our song, rhythm in our dance, beat in our music, and a special kind of humor and warmth in our interactions with each other that they just don't have and clearly envy. Need I say more? It's totally clear at this point that **anything** they can do, **we** can do better.

Now let's look at history. What were they doing four thousand years ago when we were building the great pyramids of Egypt? What was happening in Europe at the same time that the great Timbuktu society was flourishing? And the Kush Empire? And the Nubian civilization? Where's the evidence of great, advanced **European** civilizations of four and five thousand years ago? Have you ever heard of any? No. Why? Because it doesn't exist, because they don't **have** any advanced ancient civilizations. The only thing they have is Stonehenge—a burial ground, that's it. Look, human civilization on the planet traveled up from the South. Even **within** Europe, the southern Europeans talked about the infidels of the north. Look, it's simple. Europeans were the last people on the planet to **appear**, and **Northern** Europeans were

---

[206] **Arthur Ashe Video**
http://www.biography.com/people/arthur-ashe-9190544

the last people on the planet to be **civilized**. They're the babies of the species. That's why they're the least collective, i.e., the most individualist in orientation. They're immature.

This is overwhelmingly an Asian, brown and black world. They're just a small minority on this planet for a reason.

Listen, **God** is black. The Bible says it. Jesus' feet were the color of shiny, buffed bronze, (Revelation 1:15), and his hair was like lamb's wool. (Revelation 1:14) [207] What more proof do you need? The thought of God as white is just absurd. Wouldn't he make his original people look like him? Why would he make them look so different from him? It's absurd. The Bible says that we were made in His image and likeness. We know what that means. C'mon."

In summary, in this world, African People would be absolutely **convinced** that they are superior to Caucasian People. Our imagined conversation would end as follows: "Look, I hate to say it, but the doggone bottom line is that yeah, they're people, but they're kind of like "people light". I mean science has proven that, their genes aren't even purely human. After all, they mixed with those Neanderthals in Europe. That's a known fact. That's probably why they're so hairy. No other people on Earth are as hairy as them. They're closer to the other primates. All the pieces fit. We're superior, period."

African Americans of conscience who try their best to **not** be racist, would respond to such a conversation in the following

[207] Gramzie had always told me as a child that, "It says in the Bible that Jesus feet shined like polished brass and that he had hair like lamb's wool." Since she could not read, however, she had probably been told this herself. In many versions of contemporary Bibles. Revelations 1:14 reads, ". . . . His hair were **white like** white **wool**, like snow . . . ." It would be fascinating to speak with a Biblical scholar about the history of that verse. It would be equally as fascinating to speak with the appropriate expert about the probability that Jesus the man who lived in a Middle Eastern desert climate and died at the age of 33, had snow white hair.

way: "Look, have a heart and try to understand. They come from a frigid, unforgiving climate. They lost the melanin and the oil in their skin, (which keeps **our** skin young), the texture in their hair and the fullness of their features because they physically adapted to a **very** hostile environment. The violence in their communities is just a natural outcome of the aggressive tendencies they **had** to develop in order to survive in their unforgiving native climate. Their comparatively low intelligence, (compared to ours), is just the result of the simplicity with which they lived in those caves in Europe—kill or be killed. Eat or be eaten. It's all they knew. **We** come from a climate where **everything**, where **all** life thrives, so it's only **natural** that we've thrived more as human beings. Can't you see that it's not their fault? The way they are? And look at how we've treated them. We enslaved them for 250 years and then **horribly** oppressed them for another hundred years after that. The Civil Rights Act was just passed in 1964. That was just 50 years ago. So after 350 years of slavery and horrific oppression, you think it's fair to expect them to have caught up with us after only 50 years? It's just amazing to me that with **that** history, some of us are going to court claiming that Affirmative Action is 'reverse discrimination.' It makes me feel totally **guilty** and **ashamed** of being black sometimes. It's just racist to blame them for their condition. Can't you see that?"[208]

In sum, this world would be a veritable **nightmare** for European human beings. Fortunately for them, they are not living it, and never have. For African Americans and other Americans of Color,

---

208 In this description of a reality in which European Americans and African Americans have changed places, I have used many "intense" descriptions and characterizations. I hope that in feeling what may be for some, the difficulty of **reading** this description, they may begin to understand and empathize with the psychological and emotional pain of **living** it, i.e. of living in a society in which **the very kinds** of thoughts, assumptions, beliefs, feelings, history and present-day social circumstances **described** in this inverse reality, **actually exist** for one's own racial group.

however, this world is not some terrifying **fictional** horror. It is both our actual **history** and our **present day reality**. [209]

It is dreadfully heartbreaking that the European American **alternate** realty is the **actual** reality of African Americans and other Americans of Color. It is heartbreaking that **for the past six hundred years**, millions of Americans of Color have **lived** that nightmare **despite** the fact that the belief system, upon which it is based, is just as much a science fiction as is the belief that blonde, blue-eyed Caucasian People are genetically superior to dark-haired, dark-eyed Caucasian People. It is heartbreaking that as a society, we have not yet fully awakened from the nightmare. It is tragic that billions of us are still living the effects of the nightmare. It is equally as demoralizing that **many** of the terrifying facts of both African American history and contemporary life are shared by both other **Americans** of Color and by People of Color the world over.

Presumed superiority and inferiority of men based upon whether they are bald or maintain their hair as they age, or upon whether or not they have fathered a son, as well as presumed superiority and inferiority of all people based upon height, hand dominance, hair color, and eye color, is utter science fiction idiocy. It is time for the science fiction idiocy of presumed superiority and inferiority based upon race to end. Too many **billions** of human beings are suffering its effects.

---

[209] This world is actually dramatized in the 1995 film, "White Man's Burden", starring. Harry Belafonte and John Travolta. The film depicts an alternate America in which African and European Americans have reversed cultural roles. In my opinion, however, the film depicted a very **limited** view of this inverted reality. Had it included many of the characteristics of the transposed world described **herein**, the film could have been **significantly** more powerful. It would probably need to be followed by a television mini-series, however, in order to have the time required to do justice to the **actual** history and present day reality. A kind of "Roots Reversed" series would likely be enormously enlightening to most Americans.
http://www.youtube.com/watch?v=23DeZKfXN_A

I sometimes wish that I could stand on a rooftop of every "challenged" African American community in the country and at the top of my lungs, shout out to the residents, **but especially to the children, especially to the kids**, "We are not inferior! **You** are not inferior! We are brilliant and gifted! **You** are brilliant and gifted! You have a history of which you can be very proud. Our **non-violent** American Civil Rights Movement ignited the conscience of this nation and sparked subsequent Civil Rights Movements for many other Americans. Know who we are! Understand who **you** are!" Dr. King gave that same message much more eloquently:

Dr. King's Speech on African American Self-Esteem
https://www.youtube.com/watch?v=HlvEiBRgp2M

Malcolm X's speech on the same subject:
http://www.youtube.com/watch?v=gRSgUTWffMQ

I have described this alternate European American reality in such detail because I am fully aware that it is actually **having** another's experience, i.e., "walking in their moccasins" that may be our most powerful way of **truly** understanding their experience. My detailed description of the alternate European American experience was an attempt to help society's most racially **privileged** group, European Americans, to "walk in the moccasins" of one of its most misunderstood and historically **despised and oppressed** racial groups, African Americans. My fervent hope is that the experience will lead to a level of understanding of the experience of African Americans and by extension, **other** Americans of Color, which many European Americans may previously have never had. If nothing else, my hope is that this chapter will help to make relics of a much less conscious past, comments such as, "You're too sensitive." "That was in the past. Everybody has stuff to deal with. That's life. Get over it." "My ancestors had it bad too when they came over, but they worked hard to get out of poverty." "Stop whining, playing the race card and looking for racism around every corner."

I have often wondered what a person of **any** race who has been blind from birth, would think and feel if faced with the following scenario: Upon beginning college, our blind friend, Brian, gets to know two of his classmates, Lance and Kevin, fairly well. Over the course of Brian's freshman and sophomore years, in walking to class, eating in the dining hall, attending concerts, studying in the library, going to the gym and just hanging out with Lance and Kevin, Brian consistently experienced Lance as a mature, secure, kind, compassionate person. He experienced Kevin, however, as just the opposite—immature, insecure, mean and often callous. At the beginning of Brian's junior year, his parents met Lance and Kevin for the first time and were shocked to find that while Kevin was of their same race, Lance was not. Brian's parents then demanded him to stop associating with Lance immediately. Brian then attempted to explain to his parents that Lance is an upstanding, terrific guy whom he is honored to call a friend, and that Lance is essentially a "jerk" whom he'll never see again after graduation. Brian's parents, however, are unable to hear his message and remain insistent that he end his friendship with Lance immediately. Brian then pleads with his parents, saying to them, "Ok, I've felt his hair. It feels different than mine. I've felt his nose. It has a different shape than mine. I've felt his lips. They're different than mine. So what?! I've felt his skin, and even though you tell me it's a different color than mine, **it feels exactly like mine**. I don't have a clue what color is. Not a clue. His different skin color means nothing to me. Why can't you **see** beyond this color? And I'm the blind one?!"

We must evolve to the point at which when we look at each other, we see beyond our covers, our shells, i.e., our bodies. We must begin to see that no matter into what kind of body we were born, we are all divine souls. We must understand that our bodies are like automobiles. We use them to be and to move around in the world, but we must realize that our bodies are not us and we are not them. Can we even **imagine** the consequences of some intelligent alien life mistaking our cars for us? Equating us who ride inside them as part of their internal mechanics? That mistake is exactly the one we make when we equate each other with our bodies.

I hope is that this chapter on inverse realities will help us **all** to understand the moral imperative of never judging another, **any** other, until we have walked a day in their moccasins.

VIII. Our Racial Future: A Way Forward

In order for humanity to have a realistic chance of maturing beyond racism, we must work on two challenges which to date, have proven to be virtually intractable: **A.** Structural racial inequality; and, **B.** Prejudice.

A. Structural Racial Inequality

1. The United States

Blatant discrimination in public accommodations, education, employment and housing has been against the law for the past fifty years. The lingering effects of our horrifying racial past that are **structural** in nature, disproportionate poverty, crime and the many other social ills in Indigenous and in black, brown American communities are very complex and thus, extremely difficult to solve. There is no one answer to the challenge of structural racial inequality in the United States, and certainly not an easy one.

> [Perhaps it is for that reason that when the question, "What can we do about structural inequality in the United States?" is posed to television political pundits and social commentators, I have only heard the following kinds of generic and thus unhelpful responses: "We have to work on getting beyond it." "We have to make it a priority." "We have to have a national dialogue about it." I do not remember **a single** television pundit **ever** giving a specific, action-based response to the question . . . . and **we need specific responses**!]

I am **personally** convinced, that for every community of color racked by the many social ills elucidated earlier in this work, there is a **specific**, multi-tiered solution to the high school dropout rate.

I know that there is a **specific**, multi-tiered answer to the teen pregnancy rate. **I have no doubt** that for every such community, there is a specific, multi-tiered resolution to the drug infestation challenge, an answer to the health crisis, to the problem of gang involvement by our young people, to the dilemma of domestic violence, to the crime of rape, to the problem of alcoholism, to the issue of low self-esteem and self-confidence, to the fact that our children watch too much television and to the inadequate schools that our kids attend. I know that there is a solution to the need for fresh paint and trash pick-up in our challenged neighborhoods. Every such community would do well to have both a separate committee to work on each issue, and a coordinating committee to manage and support all of the issue-focused committees. What we need in communities of color that are plagued by these challenges, is **serious, long term, sustained** community organizing, **led by the residents themselves,** in which the young people must play an important role.

Second, duplicating New York City's Robin Hood Foundation in **every** challenged community in this nation, from inner cities, to reservations, to the hinterlands of Appalachia, would be of significant assistance to community committees in funding their efforts.

If I had the President's ear, I would tell him that after he leaves office, we need him to return to his community organizing days. We need him to roll up his sleeves and not **lead** a national community organizing movement, but to instead, do the following two things:

- Inspire us all to become **active** in it, especially the residents of challenged communities and,

- Initiate highly successful Robin Hood-like funding foundations In those communities across the country.

I believe with everything that is in me, that in **every** one of our challenged communities, tremendous progress can and will be made that no one, not even the residents themselves, can possibly imagine.

Answers to the crucial issues of unemployment, under-employment and of the absence of grocery stores in communities of color may lie outside of our communities more so than other answers, but even with respect to **those** issues, my resolute belief in the power of intention instills in me a **grea**t faith that once people who live in "challenged communities" begin to work earnestly on them, a way will be made with respect to those issues as well.

Finally, I'm aware that there is **much** excellent community organizing being done all in neighborhoods all across the country that are challenged by a host of social ills. I want to fully acknowledge that wonderful work. My suggestion is simply that the **collective** organizing of such neighborhoods, at the national level may make a significant difference, a kind of United Communities of America.

2. The Planet

Structural inequality at the **global** level (which is not exclusively, but certainly in large measure a result of our international racial past), is being addressed in developing nations around the world by individuals, non-governmental organizations, corporations and governments. Encouraging progress is being made in helping communities in those nations to access clean water, to provide solar-powered light and medical refrigeration, in the provision of nutrition to children, without which they would die of malnutrition, and in the immunization of children and adults against preventable illnesses. That said, much more progress **needs** to be made, of course, in those and in so many other areas, education, housing, infra-structure and others. I am, however, immensely encouraged by the work of the Carter Center, the Clinton Global Initiative, the Bill and Melinda Gates Foundation and similar organizations around the world.

Senior citizens, especially in developed countries, those who have completed their careers with still many years of meaningful contribution yet to give, could make an immense difference, both in the U.S., and in developing countries across the globe. An international campaign to inform seniors in **every** country, of both the opportunity and the personal rewards of international service resulting in many more "boots on the ground" in communities in need around the world, could help tremendously.

It is admittedly as a layperson without any experience working at the international level that I comment that the many efforts to address structural inequality at the international level appear to be quite unorganized. Significant benefit may result from the coming together of the minds of those who have been working on the issue of international structural inequality to think strategically about an organizational structure for their work leading to the formation of a single umbrella organization for their work, a kind of United Nations for International Equality.

B. Racial Prejudice

Prejudice, as the term implies, is quite simply the practice of prejudging. Within the context of race, it is, of course, the practice of prejudging people **based** upon their race. The specific form that such prejudging has historically taken and **continues** to take, is that of having unconscious, negative spur-of-the-moment judgments about Human Beings of Color. Those judgments have been/are made by both People of Caucasian Descent and People of Color, toward both members of our own **and** other groups.

Prejudice is a complex problem because it is often extremely unconscious. It is complicated because it is frequently present in good-hearted, well-meaning, non-racist and even **anti**-racist people, people who because they **are** so consciously non or anti-racist, are unable to see and acknowledge whatever prejudice may reside in their subconscious minds. For some, it is indeed spontaneous, unconscious negative judgments about a Person of

Color, that the person is a shoplifter, for example. For others, it is the unconscious prejudice of low expectations of black, brown and Indigenous People. For still others, it is unconscious feelings of superiority. For still others, it is unconscious feelings of fear. For many, it a combination of all four. It is **an enormous** problem. It is a problem which is the result of an acutely low level of awareness of members of majority groups, majorities of all kinds, racial, gender, gender identity, gender expression, sexual orientation.

Our path beyond prejudice is two tiered. On the first tier is education. It is learning a shared body of fundamental knowledge about the biology of race, about our racial past, about how our racial past has impacted our racial present and about the basic dynamics of our racial present. It is a body of knowledge which we must **all** share. On the **second** tier is action, specific actions that we must take in order to spread that body of knowledge to all Americans.

1. The United States

a. Education—What We Must Know

Tragically, beginning in the late 1970's, the Republican Southern Strategy acquired a partner as a solidifier of racial prejudice—"gangsta" rap music;[210] specifically, the vile, disgusting, violent, misogynist, racist lyrics of what was beginning to come out of the mouths of black gangsta rap artists. For millions of white Americans who already harbored prejudice and/or hatred, and/or resentment toward black Americans, gangsta rap music and its accompanying sexually explicit videos was the thing that sealed the deal. Through the gangsta rap culture, what they had long suspected about African Americans was proven, in their minds, to have been true. Gangsta rap culture then became the lens through which they saw **all** African Americans. As such, the

[210] I acknowledge the clear distinction between generic, value neutral rap music and gangsta rap.

gangsta rap musical genre wielded yet another serious blow to any efforts to increase racial understanding, empathy and compassion in our nation. It was a setback that African Americans, a people who were in general already and historically **had been** widely misunderstood, could ill afford. I can only wonder whether the black gangsta rap artists and super wealthy white music moguls who often funded them with millions upon millions of dollars, may one day look back upon **their** actions, with the same remorse that Mr. Atwater, facing death, looked upon his.[211]

The Republican Southern Strategy and the birth of the gangsta rap culture were **individually**, enormously injurious to our ability, as a nation, to make true racial attitudinal progress. Their **combination**, became a venomous cocktail that has cost us, the entire country, **dearly**.

---

[211] One of the canons of the Civil Rights Movement was that the protesters, (whether they were sitting in at lunch counters, participating in freedom rides, or walking in a march), dressed respectfully and always maintained their poise. In so doing, along with the peacefulness of their protests, they both demonstrated that they were **themselves** worthy of respect **and** modeled for the white Americans who would **abuse** them, a level of maturity and civility that they wanted to **receive** from them. When some ten-to-fifteen years later, I witnessed the dress and actions of gangsta rappers, I had only four words, "What happened to us?" I am indeed aware of at least part of the answer to that question. Nonetheless, I am saddened for the young people who were/are caught up in the gangsta rap culture because they have the same potential as the kids and young adults who were so composed and so dignified in the Movement. They are, tragically, simply unaware of their own inherent greatness. I wonder if gangsta rappers who are African American truly know and understand what their ancestors and the hundreds of thousands who participated in the Civil Rights Movement endured on their behalf. Sadly, their words and actions tell me that they do not.

Here now, is the body of knowledge of which I believe, as Americans, if we are to ever move beyond racial prejudice, we must **all** be aware:

i. The vestigial psychological and emotional scars of our American racial history on both Americans of Color **and** European Americans, are largely still with us today. Among Americans of Color, those scars often take the form of internalized oppression with all of its frequently attending consequences—for millions, low self-esteem and self-respect and a general inability to imagine a life of accomplishment and success. Among European Americans, the scars are often feelings of guilt, and/or subconscious feelings of superiority **to** and fear and/or suspicion **of** Americans of Color. Feelings of racially-based low self-esteem and low self-confidence, as well as either conscious or unconscious feelings of guilt, superiority, fear and suspicion, have mentally and emotionally disabled many **millions** of human beings, as a result of which our lives, **all** of our lives, have been limited in ways that we simply cannot imagine.

ii. Regarding racial, (i.e., unearned) privilege:

a.) A system of racial privilege that is both overt and subtle, hasresulted from of our racial past. That system still exists, of which millions of European Americans are the present benefactors;

b.) That same system still puts millions of Americans of Color at a significant educational and economic and thus overall social disadvantage;

c.) The overall remarkably high standard of living enjoyed by the Earth's Caucasian populations as compared to its People of Color, (many of the conditions of America's inner cities, the way the majority of Indigenous People live in the United States, the poverty in which the black populations of many Caribbean islands live, how the majority of Indigenous Hawaiian People live in Hawaii, the way the majority of Aboriginal People live in Australia, and the economic conditions of many African nations, among other examples), is an unearned racial privilege. It is **not** due to a genetic difference in the intelligence and industriousness of Caucasian People and People of Color. It is, instead, a vestigial effect of the historic geographic disenfranchisement, slavery, and colonization **of**, discrimination **against**, harassment **of** and violence **toward** the Earth's People of Color over the past six centuries.

d.) Both because the system of racial privilege was established long before **anyone** alive today was born, and because we are **all** born into this world in pure innocence, **no one** today should feel guilty about having been born into the privileged group. Specifically, "I feel guilty about what my ancestors did" is a burden that contemporary European Americans should not carry. It is not theirs and it is getting in the way of racial healing. Race relations in the United States would be significantly advanced if rather than having **that** feeling, millions of European Americans would instead, with knowledge of the past, feel as follows, "Our ancestors were utterly blinded by racism. I'm grateful that I wasn't born at that time. I'm doing what I can in **my** time, in **my** life, to end racial privilege."

iii. The nature of the "daily indignities" of racism", specifically that:

a.) Although fortunately not at past levels, many Americans of Color continue to experience the painful daily indignities of racism;

b.) Educational and economic advantage does not shield Americans of Color from experiencing the daily indignities. Having a college degree, working in a high-paying job, living in a nice home in a middle class neighborhood, even being a nice person, **none** of it provides protection from racial daily indignities because the person **engaging** in the indignity does not **see** the college degree of the Person of Color. S/he does not **see** the person at work, in a suit, in their professional capacity. S/he does not **see** their home and neighborhood. Most often, they do not know the person and thus do not know their character. They do not know, (on the many occasions on which it is true), that the person who is the recipient of their indignity, is an honest, good human being. They see one thing—the person's race.

c). The "common responses" that are often given when a Person of Color attempts to describe his/her experience of a daily indignity, have the effect of essentially shutting down communication and in the process, halting what could potentially lead to invaluable insight into the experience of another; [212]

d.) It is possible for **all** of us to learn both how to respond empathetically in **conversations** about daily indignities and in **situations** in which daily indignities actually occur.

iv. Regarding personal racism:

a.) It is possible for people to be prejudiced without being racist. It is possible, for example, upon initially meeting a Person of Color, before s/he has said **one** word, for one to have an unconscious pre-judgment about how the person is going to speak, or about his/her family background, intelligence, education, religion, interests, taste in music, taste in food and level of education, among an entire host of other pre-judgments.

b.) Having those pre-judgments does not **make** one a racist. One can be prejudiced without ever **once** having used the "N" word or other racial epithet. Prejudice is a state of

[212] See Note Four for more information on the common responses.

mind, most often unconscious. It is the state of mind that causes one to clutch one's purse just a little tighter when a Man of Color passes by. It is the state of mind that causes employees in stores to profile Americans of Color. It is the state of mind that causes an innocent seventeen year old kid returning home from a local convenience store with candy and tea, to be assumed to be a criminal and then shot and killed.

c.) Today, it is primarily and most often **not** overt racism, but rather **those very pre-judgments**, in other words, **it is unconscious bias**, the unconscious bias that results in both low expectations and sweeping negative generalizations about People of Color, that regularly disadvantages us.

Specifically, those prejudices disadvantage us, time and time again, in educational, employment, and housing opportunities, in the criminal justice system, and in a host of other areas of life. Additionally, today, it is most often **prejudice**, **not** overt racism, which continues the existence of structural and institutional racism. Both are alive and well today, through the enormously powerful vehicle of prejudice.

d.) The corollary of unconscious **prejudice** against Americans of Color, is in the subconscious minds of many European Americans, an unconscious **preference** for others of their own race, a preference that they unconsciously exercise in making decisions that have a significant impact on the educational, employment and housing opportunities of Americans of Color.

e.) One of the most important things upon which our ability to make serious racial progress in the United States is largely dependent, is the willingness, (or unwillingness), of European Americans to acknowledge their personal racial prejudices and preferences and to make a serious commitment to mature beyond them.

v. Americans of Color can also be **enormously** prejudiced with respect to other human variances, including skin color, race, gender identity/gender expression/sexual orientation and religion, among others.[213] We must understand that when we are in our privileged, or our "up" identities, (i.e., whether we are able-bodied, or Christian, or heterosexual or in any other privileged group), we can be as "dumb up" as anyone else.[214] Our history of oppression does not relieve us **in any way** of our responsibility to work on our prejudices. We have the **exact** same responsibility to unlearn colorism, classism, prejudice against people with disabilities, heterosexism, homophobia, classism ageism and all of our other prejudices, as European Americans have to unlearn racism.

> [I would add, however, that in addition, we also have the responsibility of remaining gracious and poised and as Dr. King would say, even loving, in the face of those who are uncharitable and unloving toward us.]

vi. The facts, (as opposed to the widely-believed fictions), about the government's attempts, including Affirmative Action, to address the surviving, present-day effects of our long history of discrimination.[215]

---

213 I am particularly disturbed by the fact that even with our history as targets of some of the most heinous, inhumane treatment to which human beings have been subjected, many African Americans, including many African Americans of faith, hold a heterosexist and homophobic worldview.

214 See Dr. Robert Terry's "Parable of the Ups and Downs" for information on how, as human beings, we go, "dump up" when we are in our "up" categories.
http://resources.css.edu/DiversityServices/docs/parableupsanddowns.pdf

215 See Note Five for learning points about the government's efforts to address the effects of that history.

vii. **None** of us are responsible for whatever negative racial messages we may have received as children.[216] **All** of us, however, in all of our various racial identities, can, to varying degrees, "unlearn" whatever negative and false racial messages we may have learned as children. It is our responsibility to engage in that "unlearning", that washing, that mental cleansing of our consciousness.

viii. The facts regarding the tremendous diversity that exists within racial and cultural groups. Essentially, we need to learn to experience and to respond to every human being as an individual.

ix. The scientific fact that our wonderful diversity notwithstanding, all of the "races" of humanity have a common origin, and thus, are equally human. The "racial", i.e., physical differences that exist among us and that result in our looking often very different from one another, are primarily cosmetic. Further, the physical and physiological traits that human beings share, are **immeasurably** more numerous than those that differentiate us, and thus, the traits that **do** differentiate us, need not **divide** us. When they do, it is because we have socially **manufactured** such divisions. Essentially, we need to experience every human being with empathy and compassion, as our sister and brother.

Our collective awareness of the nine truths elucidated above, create for ourselves at least the **possibility** that we can all become radical allies to one another across **all** of our racial divisions. Over the course of our history, we have many examples of our having done so, and often at the risk of great personal peril. To name but a few: We have seen Anglo Saxon German families, keep Jewish families hidden in their homes, in safety from the Nazis. We have seen European Americans march and die alongside African Americans, in the American

[216] See Note Six for more information about how, as children, we acquire racial stereotypes and their accompanying feelings.

Civil Rights Movement. We have seen a Men's Movement in the United States which actively works on the issue of men's violence against women. Today, we are seeing in high schools and colleges across the country, gay and straight alliances. In essence, we truly **can** move beyond the false racial divisions that we have constructed to become true allies to one another in the system of racial privilege and daily indignities into which we were all very innocently born. We **can** unite, despite our differences. We have done so, courageously, **many** times in our past.

b. Action—What We Must Do

We must raise awareness. We must dismantle prejudice. Raising awareness is my life's work. **In** that work, I have found that there are a number of awareness models that are particularly effective in helping adults to become more conscious. Dr. Milton J. Bennett's Developmental Model of Intercultural Sensitivity is my favorite.[217] In his model, Dr. Bennett spells out six stages of self-awareness in the area of intercultural sensitivity. Stage I, the **lowest** stage is called the Denial of Difference stage. Sadly, I believe that most Americans live in this first stage of awareness. The following characterize the Stage I level of awareness, the Denial of Difference stage: [218]

217 Developmental Model of Intercultural Sensitivity, Milton J. Bennett, M.D. http://www.library.wisc.edu/EDVRC/docs/public/pdfs/SEEDReadings/ intCulSens.pdf

218 The term, "Denial of Difference" can be misleading since at this stage of awareness, the individual sees almost nothing **but** difference, difference between themselves those who are of a different race. This stage is called, "Denial of Difference", however, because it is characterized **in part**, by statements that **do** deny difference, statements such as, "There's no difference." "We're all the same." "Race doesn't matter." "I don't even see race.".

- It is the default mechanism for many people who grow up in a homogenous environment.
- People at this stage of development have very few and rather simple categories for understanding cultural differences, other people and themselves.
- Stage One individuals use terms such as "foreigners" in reference to entire races and nationalities of people. They may refer to Thai, Japanese. Vietnamese and all other Asian cuisines, as "Chinese food."
- Stage One is generally a benign perspective in that no malice accompanies it.
- The Denial of Difference stage, although not malicious, is still potentially **highly** damaging because it can lead to an extremely inhuman consequence—the denial, (or at least the total lack of awareness) of the possibility that the people who are different from the denier, actually live much more complex lives outside of the denier's very simple categories of understanding.

Those simple categories of understanding lead the person in this stage to for example, ask their Indigenous acquaintance, "So, how old were you when you first learned to ride a horse?" or, "Can you teach me how to make that turquoise and silver jewelry? It's so pretty.", or to a Nicaraguan student, "I love Mexican food. You were lucky to grow up eating it.", or to their Asian friend, "I've been trying to download some software onto my computer, but just can't make it work. Would you have any time tomorrow to help me out with that?", or to their sixty year old African American neighbor, "I just loved the way Michael Jackson danced. Who's your favorite hip hop artist?" The person at this stage of awareness would, (as was true of a famous European American cable news show host), be utterly surprised that in a Harlem restaurant, the patrons have the ability to order tea without shouting profanities at the waiters, and that at a concert, the African American star of the show would establish a norm of no profanity and that her band would be dressed in tuxedos. This person's very simple categories of understanding would cause him to be **completely** surprised that the "gangsta rap" culture is not characteristic of African American culture in general.

It is Stage One awareness that is the source of the daily indignities of "shopping while black", (which I have personally experienced many times in my life), and "driving while black"; of the act of killing Sikh people in response to anti-Muslim sentiment; of New York City's stop and frisk law; of a statement made within the past year by a former governor that, "immigrants are more fertile" (presumably than European Americans); of yet another statement by a member of the U.S. House of Representatives that, "This is a very serious matter because it is our children who are the prize for this, (the LGBTQ) community. They are specifically targeting our children."

If I am correct in assuming that she was referring to African Americans in general, (and I may not be), the response of the Zimmerman Trial's Juror B37 to CNN correspondent Anderson Cooper's interview question, "When she, (prosecution witness Rachel Jeantel) used the phrase, "creepy ass cracker", what did you think of that . . . . and did you see that as negative statement or a racial statement as the defense suggested?" perfectly characterizes this stage. The juror's response was, "I don't think it's really racial. I think it's just everyday life, the type of life that they live and how they're living and the environment that they're living in." Again, **if** my assumption is correct, Juror B37, in her wildest imaginings, is probably **utterly** incapable, of conceiving of a Pontchartrain Park. It is in all likelihood, simply not possible for her, in her present consciousness, to see and really understand that African American communities and other American communities of color are as diverse and as complex as European American communities. Her ostensible Stage One awareness has blinded her and all others who live at the Stage One level of consciousness, to that reality. It is truly an emotional disability, every bit as much so as the kind of emotional disability that blinds millions of Americans who are born and raised in poor neighborhoods, to their inherent value and human potential.

It is this Stage One level of awareness that I believe characterizes, quite tragically, the majority of Americans. At this stage, the person does not really know what it is that they **think** they know, they don't **know** that they don't know, but interestingly, they are often **convinced** that they know. In reality, what they frequently "know" is misinformation. The suggestion that, "Affirmative Action laws were passed in order to lower standards so that minorities and women could get in", is typical of misinformation that results from Stage One awareness. Each time someone has made that comment either to me or in my presence, I responded in the same way, "That's an interesting perspective that I actually happen to disagree with. Have you read the Affirmative Action laws? Have you read the legislative history behind the laws which explain their intent?" **Not once**, in my experience, was the question answered affirmatively. After my discussion partner has said "no" in answer to my question, I then go on to share with them the historical, fact-based, i.e., the **correct** information. What always amazes me, however, is the level of **emotion**, the anger and resentment that so often accompany their misinformation.

If I lived **my** life in Stage One awareness, I would believe that all southern White Americans always **have** been, **are** and always **will** be racists. I would believe that all **other** White Americans are racist as well, and are merely hiding it. But I know . . . . I **know** better than that. As a child raised by a mother who greatly respected and followed Dr. King's message of love and non-violence, I was taught to not think that way, and I certainly couldn't **talk** that way. That message of love allowed me, as an adult, to see the humanity of **all** people, **including** White People, even those who do not see my individuality and **my** humanity. I am **eternally** grateful that although I have, in some very painful ways suffered what is often the great heartbreak of being a Person of Color in the United States, I was spared the added emotional disability of cultural blindness.

In order for people to be moved out of Stage One awareness, they must be introduced to more difference, more complexity regarding the groups of people about whom they think simplistically. In this regard, it would be helpful for teams of experienced diversity trainers, psychologists, teachers and advertising executives to brainstorm how to provide such categories in the most effective way, in the least amount of time, to the largest number of people, for sustained results, over the longest possible period of time.

One mechanism which I have personally witnessed to be extremely effective in providing complexity to Stage One thinking, is deep dialogue. As mentioned earlier, fortunately, about this, there is exceedingly good news—this kind of consciousness work, this kind of dialogue work is already happening. It is indeed being done in community-based groups and organizations such as Portland Oregon's Uniting to Understand Racism. On matters of faith, religion and spirituality, it is being done in the community-based dialogues facilitated by The Faith Club and the Jewish-Palestinian Living Room Dialogue Group, among a number of others. It is being done by professionals in organizations like the Compassionate Listening Project and the Public Conversations Project. This work of "having the conversation" about which we hear so much from progressive television pundits, is being done, and being done well, in pockets all over the country. As I mentioned, however, in "The Grand Trilogy of Truth", Part II to the Introduction, I believe that dialogues on multicultural issues may yield their greatest possible results if they are preceded by good solid training in which participants receive information on the following three essential things:

- The fundamental facts about the biology of race;
- The facts about our racial past; and,
- The facts about how our racial past has influenced and continues to influence our racial present.

When the conversation goes well, it can provide for European Americans, an experience that mirrors that of the young Texas girl who spent an afternoon at the home of her elementary school friend.[219] For Americans of Color, it can provide the awareness of our **own** prejudgments of both ourselves and of European Americans. Most importantly, however, when the conversation is successful, it results in each person**, irrespective of race**, doing within her or himself, serious, sincere soul searching.

With regard to **discrimination**, we **first** needed civil rights laws to make it illegal. We **then** needed Affirmative Action to **accelerate** its demise. With regard to **prejudice**, we **first** needed the kinds of societal changes heretofore discussed, more People of Color as college graduates, in a much broader range of professions, as members of the middle class, in high levels of government, in high-level corporate positions and in movies, television shows, Broadway plays and other forms of popular culture. We **now** need an intervention to accelerate **its** demise. We need "affirmative actions" to hasten the death of prejudice.

The most important of those actions, is education. So, in answer to the question, "What can we do about the fact that so many people make almost **automatic**, negative judgments about black men and other People of Color?" that has been recently raised on several television political panels in response to the tragedy of the killing of Trayvon Martin, the following are my two specific suggestions:

- ❖ For children, it is multicultural education both in every school and in every grade. Children are born innocently,

---

219 The objective of the experience is not to convince European Americans that for example, not all African Americans are poor, or that not all Latin Americans are undocumented, or that not all Asian Americans are mathematically inclined, or that not all Indigenous People are alcoholics. Rather, the purpose of the experience is to illustrate that communities of color are not monolithic, that they are as diverse as European American communities, by class, religion, political ideology and in every other way that human beings **can** be diverse. Essentially, the goal of the experience is to introduce complexity to whatever Stage One awareness any participants may have.

but **we must work to keep them that way**. The following short video showing the reaction of children to a cereal commercial which featured an inter-racial couple is both a perfect and very powerful demonstration of that innocence.

> **Kids' Reaction to Cereal Commercial Featuring Inter-Racial Couple**
> http://www.youtube.com/watch?v=VifdBFp5pnw

❖ For adults, it is learning the basic facts about race and racism either in workshops or online, followed by conversations in families and in workplace-based diversity workshops. It is discussions in public libraries and town hall meetings. It is faith-based dialogues in our many religious communities. It is discussions in secular humanist organizations. All such sessions should, of course, be voluntary, but they should be **available** in those many venues, to all who are interested.

> [In over twenty-three years of conducting workplace training, however, I have learned that those who **most** need a specific kind of training, will very often **not** attend it voluntarily. [220] I believe that with respect to cultural diversity training and conversations being conducted on a large, societal level, the same would be true. For members of that population, both television and online videos should be available, for while they may not ever attend an **in-person** session, they **may** be curious enough to view one privately.

[220] Interestingly, it is sometimes the case that such individuals will approach me at the end of an employer-required workshop and tell me that when they arrived at the session in the morning, they did not want to be there, but that they were now very glad that they had been. They then often go on to say something similar to, "I learned a lot. I didn't know what I didn't know. Thank you."

> Many other methods of massive education are also available, that those trained and experienced in marketing could certainly develop. I am a trainer, an educator, and as such, would rely heavily upon the creativity of those individuals to create an immense groundswell in our national appetite for diversity training.[221]]

In the United States, we have, thus far in our existence as a nation, taken two giant leaps away from our racist past, ending slavery in the 1860's and making racial discrimination illegal in the **19**60's. Nearly fifty-five years have already passed since the 1960's. Our next great step in racial healing **cannot** wait another forty-five years until the **20**60's. Americans of Color will have become the majority in our country several years before. Indeed, the number of American children of color and European American children five years old and under, is now statistically even, with children of color slated to outnumber their European American peers well before the taking of the next census. For that reason, if we do **not** before then make significant progress toward achieving both racial equality and at least improved race relations if not racial understanding and **empathy**, what we risk in the future is one of two things, either:

- Our nation more resembling an apartheid-like country, in which the minority unjustly rules the majority, than the United States we now know and have over the course of its existence been attempting to make a more perfect union; or,

- African Americans and other Americans of Color waging a **second** non-violent civil rights movement which by its very non-violent nature, **will** be successful, the result of which is a nation in which black is the new white, a world of an inverse reality similar in many respects to the inverse world described above.

[221] I think of "diversity" training as the umbrella term for "anti-racism" training, "prejudice reduction" training and "multicultural" training.

Both prospects are unspeakably frightening.

In order to make our next enormous, historic shift away from racism in as short a time as is realistically possible, as we **continue** to actively work against current attempts to roll back civil rights, as we **continue** to struggle to defeat present-day efforts to deprive Americans of Color of voting rights, as we **continue** to strive for equality of education, jobs and housing, in other words, as we continue our very important work on all facets of structural inequality, we must now **also** take on the issue of **prejudice** in the **present**, as affirmatively and with as much fortitude as we took on the issues of **slavery and discrimination** in the past.

This is my fervent belief: If in our nation, we are not working on Stage One awareness, we are not working on prejudice, and if we are not working on prejudice, we are not working on our future.

It has been very wisely said that we change the world when we change our minds. Doing so will be our next great, affirmative racial leap.

2. Prejudice—The Planet

Consciousness raising on the global level is far more complex than that of doing so in the United States alone. Identifying the specifics of **how** that goal is accomplished worldwide, will require the cooperation of people highly experienced at the international level. Perhaps a kind of body loosely patterned after South Africa's Truth and Reconciliation Commission, coupled with a national dialogue somewhat akin to President Mandela's Dialogue for Justice, could be helpful in nations around the world. Perhaps some of the awareness work that I have outlined for the U.S. could also be helpful at the international level. Like the American movement, however, this one must **also** be lead by ordinary people. It must be lead by ordinary citizens who have been working in non-governmental organizations in government, in education, and in corporations, **in their own countries**, the world over.

Eckhart Tolle has said that, "awareness is the greatest agent for change and that suffering has a noble purpose: the evolution of consciousness." Humanity must now awaken from our long international nightmare of racism and prejudice and become aware. We have suffered the horror of racism for far too long.

Having awakened, we must then study, learn and apply the principles of allyship. Just as the civil rights protesters of the 1960's studied and learned both the theoretical principles and the practice of **non-violence**, our cause, **today**, while **continuing** the brilliant tradition of non-violence, is to study, learn and apply the fundamental principles of **allyship**, and we must utilize them with compassion.

The Dalai Lama has told us that,

> World peace must develop from inner peace. Peace is not just the absence of violence, but the manifestation of human compassion.

If we are to ultimately make racial inequality and racial injustice ancient relics of a distant past, we must learn to practice radical compassion on the global level.

> [The Charter for Compassion elucidates brilliantly, I believe, both the kind and level of compassion that as a human species, we must begin to practice toward all other human beings, all other life forms on the Earth and toward the Earth itself. The Charter for Compassion is available at the following urls:
> http://charterforcompassion.org/
> http://www.youtube.com/watch?v=wktlwCPDd94]

IX. Race: Humanity's Bottom Line

Humanity's racial bottom line is that we **must** accept and embrace a compassionate, evolved view or our perceived racial differences. We must **understand completely** that the story of the human racial hierarchy based upon race in which the lighter-skinned people of the Earth are at the top, brown-skinned people are in the middle and black-skinned people are at the very bottom, is a dreadfully simple tale that is an utter science fiction. We must **acknowledge fully** that race, as we have been taught to think of it, doesn't even exist. We must **comprehend deeply** that if, as a species, we do **not** mature beyond racism, we will not, nor **can** we, flourish and prosper in the future. We must come to a profound understanding that resonates deep within us, that just as the contents of a **book** cannot be judged by its cover, so too can the value of a **human being** not be judged by **her** cover. **We must know that all human beings, all around our beautiful planet, are of absolutely equal value**.

We have matured beyond race-based slavery. We have matured beyond colonization. We have matured beyond race-based segregation, apartheid in South Africa and Jim Crow in the United States. We have matured beyond state-sanctioned racial discrimination and harassment in other forms. I know that as far a journey as we still have to travel before we reach true racial healing and world-wide human unity, I know that if we can save the planet, we **will** get there. My confidence is firmly rooted in my knowledge that the long march of history has shown us time and time again, that those who work valiantly for truth and justice are **without fail**, ultimately victorious, **every** time. Mahatma Gandhi expressed that most profound truth in the following way:

> Whenever I despair, I remember that the way of truth and love has always won. There may be tyrants and murderers, and for a time, they may seem invincible, but in the end, they always fail. Think of it: always.

I continue to ask myself, "Where would we be if as a species, we had been more mature, had we been wiser over the course of our history, had we not spent so very much of our time and energy on racial and other forms of oppression?" [222] I wonder if by now we would have invented structures, homes, hospitals, schools and office buildings that are fully capable of withstanding category 5 hurricanes and tornadoes. I wonder if we would have societies across the globe, powered by **totally** clean, renewable energy from the sun, water and wind. If throughout our history as a nation, **all** children, **regardless** of their race, had been able to achieve their highest potential in science, in medicine, in architecture, in engineering, in law, in government, in the social sciences, in the arts, I wonder where our nation, and by extension, our **world**, would today be.

With our young but quite rapidly increasing knowledge of the human genome, we are now becoming aware of what is surely one of the cruelest ironies of human history—that Africans, who became the most misunderstood and despised of **all** the Earth's people, actually **gave birth** to the entire rest of humanity. That profound irony has the power to lead us to a much more compassionate, evolved view of race. It can teach us two very deep lessons. Those lessons are that we are truly **one** race, the **human** race, and that one of our highest callings as a species of sentient beings inhabiting this magnificent planet, is to respect and love each other. What our world needs, at this juncture, more than any other single thing, is more love, more compassion.

From the time we took our first steps out of our African home, we have come a very long way on our most improbable journey across our beautiful, tiny globe. Now, we can and we must go

[222] I pose the same question with respect to the time, resources and effort that we have historically expended on war. Among the Dogon people of the southern Sahara Desert in the African country of Mali, avarice and violence are virtually non-existent. The Dogon and a handful of other peaceful human societies around the planet have much to teach us. Additional information on the Dogon is available in Note Two.

even farther. We are both too brilliant and too divine to be mired in the immaturity of racism.

Mahatma Gandhi once said the following:

> A small body of determined spirits fired by an unquenchable faith in their mission can alter the course of history.

My **fervent** hope is that this work will play at least a **minor** role in the "fire" behind either a small or a large body of such determined spirits; spirits whose mission is to give birth to peace across the planet, a peace founded upon a great, worldwide awareness of our human oneness, a peace that is built upon a rock of compassion and a pillar of love.

Dr. King's words provide a fitting summary to this work:

> I refuse to accept the view that mankind is so tragically bound to the starless midnight of racism and war that the bright daybreak of peace and brotherhood can never become a reality . . . . I believe that unarmed truth and unconditional love will have the final word.
>
> Rev. Dr. Martin Luther King, Jr.

My final word, is that everywhere, all across our majestic Planet Earth, we can all genuinely be in love with one another as the sisters and brothers that we truly are. Doing so, is our clarion call. It **is** in every one of us.
http://www.youtube.com/watch?v=op9sUiANKiE

I wrote this book for the generations of those of **all** races who came before my grandparents and suffered and died for human dignity and freedom.

I wrote this book for Gramzie and for all the members of her generation who succeeded against tremendous odds, in raising my

parents' generation of strong, dignified, wise, compassionate African Americans.

I wrote this book for **that** generation of African Americans, my parents', members of The Greatest Generation, who came before us and gave us so much.

I wrote this book for all of the brave human beings who were active in the Civil Rights Movement,—all those who committed themselves to, learned and **consistently practiced** the principles of receiving violence non-violently, who were beaten, hosed, chased and bitten by dogs, and never lifted **a finger** to strike back; for all those who marched and rallied in peace and in prayer; for those who were arrested and jailed multiple times, and as they were, adamantly filled the police wagons and jailhouses with the sound of freedom songs; for all those who went in and **sat** in; for those who sat **down**; for the Freedom Riders; for those whose homes and churches were firebombed; for all the women who made meals for the demonstrators, prepared their churches for organizing meetings and cleaned their church kitchens afterwards; for all the women, Ms. Dorothy Height, Ms. Coretta Scott King, Ms. Fannie Lou Hamer, Ms. Daisy Bates, Ms. Ella Baker and so many others, who provided leadership in the movement but were not recognized; and for those, children and adults, who made the ultimate sacrifice.

I wrote this book for my mother. I hope you're proud of me, Mama.

Most of all, I wrote this book for our wonderfully diverse and brilliant human species. I wrote it to help us all to see the Divine in ourselves and ourselves in each other.

Reflections from Space
http://www.youtube.com/watch?v=OGdHmaFGVQk

Regarding that which we commonly call "race", I leave you now with a Trilogy of Great Unity of what, here on our beautiful, magnificent planet Earth, we must know, what we must do, and we must be.

X. We Are One
A Trilogy of Great Unity

This We Must Know: The Trilogy of Profound Truth We Must Know That . . . .

1. We are all, seven-plus billion of us, very deeply connected to each other;

2. It is possible for us as human beings to genuinely understand, sincerely value and deeply love each other, all of our sisters and brothers of humanity with whom we share the Earth. In other words, we **can** mature beyond racism. The choice, is ours; and,

3. If we **are** successful in maturing beyond racism, our future will be glorious in ways that are presently utterly unimaginable to us.

This We Must Do: The Trilogy of Transformative Action We Must Unite as One Human Family. We Must . . . .

1. Heal from our painful past of hatred and division and deeply understand both our opportunities of doing so and our risks of not;

2. Evolve out of war into non-violence and out of non-violence into peace; and,

3. Develop compassionate communities, benevolent institutions and judicious nations and in so doing, save our precious planet.

This We Must Be: A Trilogy of Ultimate Being We Must Be In Love . . . .

1. With Ourselves;

3. With Every Other Human Being; and,

4. With The Divine

Notes

[Please note that the urls to the websites contained in these six Notes are not duplicated in the lists that follow of short video clips, documentaries, movies, television miniseries, training videos and websites.]

<u>Note One</u>

The Most Cruel Form of Psychological Racism Practiced Against People of Color—Particularly African Americans

People of Europeans descent have a long history of comparing People of Color of many different ethnicities, to other non-human primates. I believe that it is human beings of African descent, however, who while not exclusively, are **most often compared** to species of higher primates, monkeys and chimpanzees, primarily. Depictions of African Americans as monkeys is an historical and currently still common theme in the literature of hate groups. China's snub-nosed monkeys have white skin, as does Costa Rica's White Headed Capuchin monkey. Many monkeys, gorillas and chimpanzees have thin lips and all have straight hair, neither of which is characteristic of people of African descent. Nonetheless, the literally de-humanizing insult of being likened to monkeys, apes and chimps, is reserved overwhelmiingly, for people of African descent. No human beings of **any** group, no matter **what** physical characteristics they may share with those animals, be it the thin lips, the straight hair the white skin of some primates, or the black skin and broad noses of others, should endure such inhumane treatment.

The most grotesque results of the practice of analogizing people of African descent and other People of Color to non-human primates, were the 19th and early 20th century public exhibits of various

Peoples of Color in what were called, "human zoos", also referred to as "ethnological expositions, or "Negro villages". The exhibits often emphasized the cultural differences between Caucasian and non-Caucasian peoples and frequently included an explanation that non-Caucasian People, Africans in particular, exist on a continuum somewhere between the great apes and Caucasian human beings.

Of course one of **the most egregious**, most tragic examples of the dehumanization of a human being of African descent in this context is the story of Ota Benga. December 13, 1992, Washington Post . . . . "In October 1903, Samuel Phillips Verner, a missionary, scientist and explorer, was commissioned by the director of the Louisiana Purchase Exposition of the St. Louis World's Fair to go to Congolese Africa and 'bring the Pygmies.' The exposition was to offer what no other exposition had: an anthropology exhibit that would 'prove' the intellectual and technological superiority of European civilization by gathering for display, 'types and freaks from every land.' The most exotic 'type' would be the Pygmy, rumored to be a race of **semi-humans, barely evolved from the ape.** Among Verner's Pygmy cargo was **Ota Benga, (a boy from the Pygmy tribe), who was exhibited for several months at the (World's) fair and then, later, at the Bronx Zoo**." After being taken from the zoo, Ota was sent to an orphanage, eventually found himself in Lynchburg, VA., and finally, in early adulthood, committed suicide.

The following are just a very few of many examples of the historic practice of comparing specifically African Americans, to apes, gorillas and monkeys.

Early Nineties, Oprah Winfrey Gets Called a Monkey by Skinhead
https://www.youtube.com/watch?v=lCiqozFWzl0

April 1, 1991, Time Magazine

It was reported in an article from this edition of Time that on March 3, at 12:39 A.M., after intervening in an argument that took place purportedly between two or more African Americans, **police officers** Laurence M. Powell and Timothy E. Wind **of the Los Angeles Police Department** contacted another team of officers who were working on another case and described the squabble they'd just worked on as follows: ". . . . **It was right out of Gorillas in the Mist**. The stakeout team replies: '**Hahahaha . . . let me guess who be the parties**'."

April 21, 1991, Washington Post

"The Washington Post's African-American reporter Gary Lee was asked by a policeman in Svirdlosk **if he lived in a zoo**.

July 10, 1991, Washington Post

"Los Angeles—An independent commission asked to investigate the police beating of motorist Rodney G. King reported today that . . . . computer messages such as '**sounds like monkey slapping time**' . . . . have been exchanged with little review or objection from department supervisors."

September 17, 1993, Washington Post

"**AT & T, the nation's largest long-distance telephone company,** yesterday apologized for a cartoon printed in an employee magazine that company officials characterized as a 'racist illustration.' Complaints arose earlier this week when employees received the magazine with the drawing, which shows people on various continents making telephone calls. **The caller in Africa is depicted as a gorilla**."

January 18, 1994, Washington Post

It was reported in the article that at a bar in Oberhof, Germany, approximately fifteen German skinheads **allegedly made monkey noises** and shouted, "Nigger Out!" to Robert Pipkins, an African American athlete who as a member of the U.S. luge team, was in Oberhof, Germany, practicing for the Winter Olympics. The article then goes on to report that, (Judge) Feld-Gerdes read from a statement that Eschrich. (one of the accused who was charged with and scheduled to stand trial for harassing and attacking Pipkins and his European American teammate who came to his aid), had made to police about the incident. In the statement read by the judge, Eschrich said: "Negroes come from Africa. They come from the bushes. **We wanted to show him he was an ape**."

September, 1994, Atlantic Monthly, "How We Become What We Are"

"In 1992 a firestorm of protest caused Frederick Goodwin, a psychiatrist and the director of the federal Alcohol, Drug Abuse and Mental Health Administration, and the world's authority on manic depression, to resign his job and return to his previous position as director of the National Institute of Mental Health after he drew a parallel between inner-city violence and primate studies (involving rhesus monkeys.)"

March 3, 1996, Washington Post

"**CBS Sports basketball analyst Billy Packer** . . . . referred to Georgetown guard Allen Iverson as 'a tough monkey' during the nationally televised game . . . . The comment came as Packer was describing a replay in which Iverson drove to the basket, switched the ball from his right hand to his left hand, was fouled by Villanova's Alvin Williams and still made the shot. '**You're talking about a tough monkey here**', Packer said."

The article goes on to report that **the late Howard Cosell** also referred to an African American athlete as a monkey. It occurred during ABC's 'Monday Night Football' broadcast of a September 5, 1983 game between the Dallas Cowboy and the team of Washington, DC.[223] When the Washington DC team's African American wide receiver Alvin Garrett caught the ball and then made a particularly dashing run, Cosell, referring to Garrett, commented: "**That little monkey gets loose, doesn't he?**'"

March 6, 1996, Washington Post commentary by Courtland Milloy

"White sportscasters have a sordid history of attempting to undermine the achievements of black athletes. One of the better-known cases involved **Jimmy 'the Greek' Snyder,** another CBS Sports analyst, who said on the air in 1988 that **blacks were superior athletes because of 'breeding from the time of slavery'** and that the only area in sports left for whites was coaching . . . . A year earlier, **Al Campanis** was fired as vice president and director of player personnel for the Los Angeles Dodgers baseball team after saying that **blacks are too dumb to be field managers or general managers**."

The article went on to report:

A. Other characterizations of African American athletes by European American sportscasters in which they, (African American athletes), had been compared to cockroaches and bulls;

B. That people had called to complain about Billie Packer's "tough monkey" comment, not coaches, but people in the audience who had been called a monkey because of their race; and,

---

[223] The name of the Washington, DC team is the "Washington Redskins". I do not use the term, "Redskins", however, as it is an extremely offensive racial epithet which refers to Indigenous People.

C. That former Klansman David Duke's almost successful campaign for governor of Louisiana was rife with depictions of African Americans as apes.

November, 1997, Essence Magazine

"Tiger Woods . . . . **got teased as a child—was even called a monkey**—and couldn't play at some golf courses because of his color."

July 19, 1999, Jet magazine

'A lawsuit recently was filed accusing Microsoft of including a 'racially charged' message linking Black people to monkeys. The message was included in the company's Publisher 98 software, the lawsuit says. The suit . . . . claims that people will see an image of a Black couple sitting on monkey bars when they type the word 'monkey' to get access to pictures of the animals**."**

January 16, 2000, Washington Post

"John Rocker, the Atlanta Braves' relief pitcher . . . . referred to a black teammate as a 'fat monkey'.

July, 31, 2006, WorldNet Daily

"U.S. Secretary of State Condoleezza Rice has been in the Middle East . . . . A cartoon last week in **the PA (Palestinian Authority) controlled Al Quds depicted Rice pregnant with a monkey.** A caption read, 'Rice speaks about birth of a new Middle East'."

July 19, 2013, Inside Higher Ed

The University of California, Los Angeles agreed to pay 4.5 million dollars to an African American surgeon, Dr. Christian Head, to settle a racial discrimination lawsuit which he filed against the university. The university also offered an official apology to the doctor for retaliating against him for his having brought the suit. The retaliation, which appeared in a slide show for new residents, was a portrayal of Dr. Head as a gorilla being sodomized.

http://www.insidehighered.com/quicktakes/2013/07/19/u-californiapays-45m-settle-surgeons-racial-bias-claim#ixzz2Zoy0Ayr6
(This url may need to be copied and pasted into your web browser.)

November, 2013

Grosse Pointe Officers Make Mentally Challenged Man Sing and Make Animal Noises

http://www.youtube.com/watch?v=r5MF96b5ta0

In the following article on the incident, it is reported that, "One video portrayed a voice alleged to be an officer asking black man to do humiliating tasks, including "dance like a chimp." The animal noise the man made appeared to be monkey sounds.[224]

Think Progress: Cop Admits He Ordered Mentally Ill Black Man to Sing, Make Animal Noises

http://thinkprogress.org/justice/2013/11/23/2987931/cop-admitsordered-mentally-black-man-sing-make-animal-noises/

---

224 The reaction of the white woman in this clip exemplifies brilliantly, the kind of European American denial of racism and the pain that it causes that are discussed in this work.

I could certainly have chronicled **numerous** other references to and depictions of African Americans as monkeys and chimpanzees that appeared in publications in many other years after 1991, the year I began collecting them. I could also have chronicled the abundant references to and depictions of President and Mrs. Obama as monkeys which occurred during the President's two presidential campaigns. I chose not to do so, however, because it was simply too painful.

Note Two

History and Accomplishments of People of Color—A Representative Sample

African History

Both African history and African **American** history are rich and impressive. They are histories of major African and African American contributions to human culture of which every person of African descent can be extremely proud. In addition to the history of our **oppression**, all people, especially African American **children**, should be aware of our history of **greatness**. While it is impossible to represent that history in this note, I will provide a small sampling of those largely unknown and generally denied histories:

African history is a story of many ancient sophisticated, trading and seafaring and for some, technologically advanced civilizations. One need only do an internet search of the following kind of phrases to learn about the greatness of so many advanced ancient African civilizations:

- List of African kingdoms
- Ancient African civilizations
- Pre-Columbian African empires
- Early Sub-Saharan African cultures
- Ancient West African societies
- Ancient civilizations of East Africa
- Seafaring African cultures
- Ancient African art
- Ancient African mathematics
- Ancient African astronomy
- Ancient African architecture
- Ancient African engineering
- Ancient African medicine
- Ancient African navigation

A synopsis of many ancient African accomplishments in science and mathematics can be found at the following website:

https://www.asbmb.org/asbmbtoday/asbmbtoday_article.aspx?id=32437

Evidence of an African Presence in the Americas Before Columbus:

The following is Dr. Ivan Van Sertima's July 7, 1987 testimony given to the U.S. House of Representative's Subcommittee on Census and Population of the Post Office and Civil Service concerning a bill to amend the Christopher Columbus Quincentenary Jubilee Act.:

> "People have said the Africans did not have boats. That is not true. Africans invented seven major ships along the Niger. They had the papyrus reed boat, they had the catamaran-type boat, and the double canoe, the power canoe. They had a range of ships on the Niger. They had a range of ships on the Nile. They had 3000 years of ships on the Nile. Even the Phoenician ships made use of the structure of the African boat and introduced several variations. Along the Indian Ocean Coast of Africa, where I spent a year in Tanzania studying, ships that carried elephants to China in the thirteenth century are reported. There are reports of Africans bringing elephants to China two centuries before Columbus." . . . . [225]

---

[225] More information on the voyages of Africans to the Americas is available in Dr. Van Sertima's book, *They Came Before Columbus The African Presence in Ancient America:* http://books.google.com/books/about/They_Came_Before_Columbus.html?id=sPR1AAAAMAAJ

See Dr.Van Sertima speaking about his research on the pre-Columbian African presence in the Americas at: http://www.youtube.com/watch?v=x1ZeK4ecHKU

"Now, the big problem that arises here is people ask where are these people, so-called people who came? What did they look like? How do we know they were there? They have found fourteen stone heads, (in Mexico). They are still finding stone heads. One of them found in 1862 has not only African-type features, it has Ethiopian braids . . . ."

http://www.google.com/search?q=african+stone+heads+in+mexico&rlz=1T4GGLS_enUS494US494&tbm=isch&tbo=u&source=univ&sa=X&ei=eu2qUYqXC6r8igLktIHwDw&ved=0CDwQsAQ&biw=1280&bih=571

"Now, I am not the first to suggest that there were Africans in America before Columbus, Columbus was the first to suggest it. Columbus actually said in the journal of his second voyage when he was in Haiti, then known as Espanola, Native Americans came to him and told him that black people had come in large boats from the south and southeast trading in gold-tipped spears. Probably Columbus did not believe this and that fact in itself would not be enough because the so-called "black" people could be any people. It could be dark, bronze people from south America. However, Columbus actually sent back on a mail boat to Spain, samples of these gold-tipped spears. When the metallurgists in Spain assayed these spears, they found they were identical, not similar, but were identical in their ratio of gold, silver and copper alloys as spears then being forged in African Guinea.". . . . .

"Garcia sighted blacks off Colombia. He says so, 'These are the first blacks we have seen in the Indies.' Vespucci returning home sighted a boat with tall black men. Peter Martyr, the first historian of America cites these black men and calls them Ethiopian pirates shipwrecked on the East Coast. Vasco Nunez de Balboa, after the discovery of the

Since Dr. Van Sertima's research has been criticized by some of his peers, I encourage you to make an independent judgment of his work.

Sea of the South, the Mar del Sur, reports finding two black men among Native Americans and asking them where did these men come from and they did not know, save that they were in a large settlement off Quarequa in the Isthmus of Panama. Lopez de Gomara sighted blacks. So it is not only Columbus." . . . .

"Since 1964, the Congress of Americanists ruled that there cannot—I quote them—'There cannot now be any doubt that there were visits from the old world to the new long before Columbus'."

The following is just a very small sampling of some of the great ancient civilizations that existed on the African continent:

1. The ancient Nile Valley Civilization of Egypt, the first great civilization of the ancient world, was not a society of olive-skinned, Mediterranean looking people. It was a black, African civilization, as clearly seen in the faces on the Sphinx and the skin color of the people on the walls of the pyramids.
   Bernal, Martin. *Black Athena: The Afroasiatic Roots of African Civilization.* New Brunswick, New Jersey: Rutgers University, 1987 Print On Egypt's impact on Greece:

   "The Greeks had unanimously proclaimed Egypt's African origins and the stony evidence of the sphinx—whose features were clearly etched in the African mold—confirmed it. Was it not one of the crueler ironies of history that the very people who had given the world civilization were now a race of slaves and outcasts?"
   Finch, III, Charles S. "The Black Roots of Egypt's Glory", Washington Post, October 11, 1987

   Slide Show of Egyptian Art and Artifacts
   https://www.youtube.com/watch?v=4V5ntTludYE

2. For a thousand years, the Nubian civilization **also** thrived on the banks of the Nile. By 1700, B.C., the Nubians had built

great walled cities. They invented their own alphabet. [226] They made delicate, superb pottery, were proficient farmers and traders of ivory, ebony and cattle. About Nubia, Paul Richards, in, "Ancient Nubia: A Cultural Crossroads", a May 29, 1995 Washington Post article on an exhibit of Nubian art at the National Museum of African Art, reported, "Like Egypt . . . . Nubia had prospered for 1,000 years on the green banks of the Nile between Aswan and Khartoum." . . . . The old and clearly racist notion that black people of ancient Africa were incapable of building a complex civilization is undone by this exhibit."

3. The Dogon People of Mali are known for their inexplicable knowledge of astronomy. They have been aware, for hundreds of years, of the existence of Saturn and its rings, (which can only be seen from Earth with a telescope), as well as Jupiter and its four largest moons. Additionally, they have correctly placed the Earth within our solar system, and our solar system within our Milky Way galaxy. Most mysterious of all, the Dogon have been aware for centuries, of a distant "dark star" that exists deep within space and thus, not visible from Earth. The existence of the star was confirmed by Western astronomers in 1950.

4. A series of medieval cities existed in medieval West Africa. Cities such as Jenne, Dia, Gao and Timbuktu[227] flourished for hundreds of years and were centers of advanced culture and trade.

5. The ruins of hundreds of sophisticated, well-designed stone towns which date from the 11th to the 17th centuries pepper Africa's east coast, from southern Somalia to Mozambique. Reporting on the towns in her June 6, 1992 Washington Post

---

[226] Deciphered texts of the Nubian people exist today.

[227] The Lost Libraries of Timbuktu: https://www.youtube.com/watch?v=nzqhymaPDNs

article, "Answer to Kenyan Mystery Lies Amid Ancient Ruins: Stone Towns Credited to Arabs May Be of African Origin", Suzie Okie stated that most archaeologists studying the ruins of the town thought that they were too advanced to have been produced by Africans. She reported, "Puzzled by the towns' origin and impressed by such features as elaborate plasterwork and indoor toilets, these researchers viewed them as cultural transplants from another continent, constructed by Arab traders who visited the African coast and decided to stay." Okie continued, however, writing that the head of coastal archaeology at the National Museums of Kenya, after researching the ruins, said that the culture as well as the structure and layout of the cities are all African.

6. A few other great ancient African civilizations among many others:

* The Malao Empire—East Africa
* The Opone Empire—East Africa
* The Mosylon Empire—East Africa
* The Benin Empire—West Africa
* The Kingdom of Ghana—West Africa
* The Lunda Kingdom (a pre-Columbus federation of African states)—Sub-Saharan Africa
* The Nok Empire—Sub-Saharan Africa
* The Mali Empire—Sub-Saharan Africa
* The Songhai Empire—Sub-Saharan Africa
* The Oyo Empire—Sub-Saharan Africa
* The Kingdom on NRI—Sub Saharan Africa
* The Kingdom of Mutapa—Southern Africa

The brochure describing the Time-Life Books series, "Time Frame", summarized the development of the ancient world as follows:

> 3,000 years before the Europeans ever raised a single cathedral . . . Egypt gloried in its god-kings and pyramids. Sumerians were writing epic sagas, and China was fast becoming the exalted Middle Kingdom . . . . It is the

> 25th Century B.C. Along the Nile, thousands of laborers lay stone upon stone to build yet another pyramid for yet another god-king. At Europe's edge, Stonehenge is already under construction. In India, the Harappans boast planned cities and split-level houses—complete with indoor plumbing. While in China, skilled artisans turn out silk robes and even pottery.
>
> Almost incredibly, all of these cultures were flourishing during the same period of history. But just as incredibly, many books today focus on just one culture or development, neglecting the others—and leaving you with an incomplete understanding of the ancient world."

Fortunately, today, works such as*, Africana: The Encyclopedia of the African and African American Experience,* referenced in this note below, provide a history of the people of the African continent which is both much more accurate and more comprehensive than that taught in years past.

African American History

* Benjamin Banneker, born in 1731, (during slavery), was a free African American scientist. In 1791, Mr. Banneker was hired by Major Andrew Ellicott to assist with the preliminary survey of the boundaries of Washington, D.C., the new Federal district that was planned. Specifically, Mr. Banneker was hired chiefly to make astronomical observations that were to be used in determining the location of the survey's start point. Mr. Banneker made astronomical calculations that predicted solar and lunar eclipses and authored a series of successful almanacs. He corresponded with Thomas Jefferson concerning the institution of slavery and on issues of racial equality.

* Phyllis Wheatley was born in West Africa in 1753 and sold into slavery at the age of seven. She was transported to the

U.S. and sold to John and Susanna Wheatley who named her after the slave ship, "The Phyllis" on which she was brought from West Africa. Ms. Wheatley's intelligence was noticed by the Wheatleys, prompting their daughter, Mary, to tutor and educate her. By her twelfth birthday, Ms. Wheatley was reading Greek and Latin classics and had her first poem published. As an adult, her poetry was published in several books by European American supporters. On one occasion, she appeared before and read poetry for George Washington. Many European American readers of Ms. Wheatley's poetry found it difficult to believe that a young African woman could be such a brilliant poet. For that reason, she was required, in 1772, to substantiate the authorship of her work in court. She prevailed in the proceeding, successfully proving that she was indeed the author of her poetry. Ms. Wheatley became so popular as a poet in both the U. S. and England, that she was ultimately freed from slavery in 1773 at the age of twenty.

* Dr. Daniel Hale Williams, born free, in Pennsylvania, in 1858, (during slavery), was the first physician to perform open-heart surgery in 1893, successfully removing a knife from the heart of a stab victim. Dr. Williams founded Chicago's Provident Hospital, the first African American-owned and operated Hospital and the first integrated hospital in the nation.

* Matthew Henson, born in 1866, (the year after slavery was abolished), noted in his day as perhaps the greatest non-Eskimo sled driver of all time, accompanied Admiral Peary to the North Pole and significantly contributed to the success of the mission, and without whose assistance, Perry may never have reached the North Pole. http://www.amazon.com/exec/obidos/ASIN/0780622693/thematthewhenson/002-8215328-4296222

* Elizabeth "Bessie" Coleman, born in 1892, Ms. Coleman was an American civil aviator. She was the first African American pilot to hold an international pilot license and the

first African American female pilot. http://www.youtube.com/watch?v=HPmMHuO5XSY

* "Back in 1899, in Washington, D. C., there were four academic public high schools—one black and three white. In standardized tests given that year, students in the black high school averaged higher test scores than students in two of the three white high schools. This was not a fluke. It so happens that I have followed 85 years of the history of this black high school—from 1870 to 1955—and found it repeatedly equaling or exceeding national norms on standardized tests. In the 1890s, it was called The M Street School and after 1916 it was renamed Dunbar High School but its academic performances on standardized tests remained good on into the mid-1950s.", Sowell, Thomas, "The Education of Minority Children" http://www.tsowell.com/speducat.html

* Bessie Blount Griffin, born in 1914, Ms. Griffin invented a feeding device in 1951 designed to enable World War II amputees, (with whom she worked as a physical therapist), to feed themselves. Her invention was rejected by the American Veterans Administration. She subsequently sold it to France and Belgium.

* African American classical composers Florence Price, William Grant Still and Ulysses Kay made significant contributions to the enhancement of classical music in the United States. In 1941, as a result of the classical music world's barring of African Americans from performing in opera companies, the National Negro Opera Company was formed by Madame Lillian Evanti and Mary Cardwell Dawson.

* In 1992, composer George Theophilus Walker won the Pulitzer Prize for music for his *Lilacs* symphony, which debuted in Boston's Symphony Hall.

* **A Small Sample of Hundreds of African American Inventions (with Patent Dates)**

    * Multiplex telegraph which allowed communication by voice transmitted over wires.—Granville T. Woods, known as "The Black Edison", 1885[228]

    * Heating Furnace—Alice H. Parker—Dec 19, 1919

    * Gas Mask—Garrett Morgan, Oct 13, 1914

    * Automatic Elevator Door—Alexander Miles, Oct 11, 1867

    * Pencil Sharpener—John L. Love—Nov 23, 1897

    * Fireplace Damper—Virgie M. Ammons—Sept 30, 1975

    * Player Piano—Joseph H. Dickinson, June 11, 1912

    * Improved Refrigerator—John Standard—July 14, 1891

    * Ironing Board—Sarah Boone—April 26, 1892

    * Lawn Mower—John Albert Burr—May 9, 1899

    * Golf Tee—George F. Grant—Dec 12, 1899

    * Automatic Gear Shift—Richard B. Spikes—December 6, 1932

    * Shoe-lasting machine—Jan Matzeliger, 1883. The shoe—lasting machine attached the upper part of a shoe to the sole, drastically reducing the price of shoes and launching the mass production of shoes. In 1991, Mr. Matzeliger was

228 Mr. Woods, who held more than 50 patents, was the first African American who was both a mechanical and electrical engineer after the Civil War.

honored for his achievement with the issuance of a U.S. postage stamp in his honor.

* Gamma Electric Cell—Henry T. Sampson, July 6, 1971

  For additional information on African American inventors, see:

  http://inventors.about.com/od/blackinventors/a/black_inventors.htm

* **A Small Sample of African American Contributions to the U.S. Military:**

  * Crispus Attucks—believed to be the first person killed by the British during the Boston Massacre.

  * The 54th Massachusetts "Colored" Infantry's service in the Civil War.
    http://www.masshist.org/online/54thregiment/essay.php?entry_id=528
    https://www.youtube.com/watch?v=3ww5ljU3lx4

    http://www.history.com/videos/gilder-lehrman-massachussetts-54th#gilder-lehrman-massachussetts-54th

  * Approximately 200,000 African American soldiers of the Civil War played a crucial role in the Union's Civil War victory which saved the country.

  * During World War II, The Tuskegee Airmen flew 1,578 combat missions in the Mediterranean and were the only fighter group, black or white, that never lost a single bomber under an escort. Prior to the missions of the Tuskegee Airmen, African Americans were widely believed to lack the intelligence to fly airplanes.
    http://www.history.com/videos/tuskegee-airman-luther-smith
    http://www.youtube.com/watch?v=fMZb7ia_ly4

"What the Tuskegee Airmen were to the skies, the 761st was to land."[229] The 761st tank battalion was the first battalion of African American soldiers to operate armored vehicles. General George S. Patton himself requested the assistance of the 761st in the heavy combat of World War II's Battle of the Bulge. The 761st heroically led the drive across Europe of General Patton's Third Army and guided U.S. forces in liberating Nazi concentration camps at Buchenwald and Dachau.

Most tank battalions fought for a maximum of 15 days at a time. The 761st fought for 183 consecutive days.

On September 30, 1996, the U.S. House of Representatives gave a tribute to the 761st Tank Battalion. Congressional Record Volume 142, Number 138, Monday, September 30, 1996, Page E1876

Prior to the missions of the 761st, African Americans were widely believed to lack the intelligence to operate armored vehicles.
http://www.youtube.com/watch?v=Esh-w6qIyaU

* The U.S.S. Mason's exclusively African American crew and white officers successfully escorted six convoys across the U-boat infested North Atlantic during World War II. Nearly fifty years would pass until in 1994, the crew of Mason would be awarded a letter of commendation for meritorious service.
http://www.youtube.com/watch?v=K5RlEGyxnzY
http://ihffilm.com/dvd272.html

The purpose of this very short sampling of African and African American history was to simply provide a mere **taste** of both the

[229] Quote taken from the synopsis of the movie, "The Story of the Black Panther Tank Battalion, 761th: WWII Had More Heroes Than You Know"

kind and level of historical achievement of Africans and African Americans of which most Americans were never taught in school.

For the most complete compendium of African and African American history currently available, see *Africana: The Encyclopedia of the African and African American Experience,* Kwame Anthony Appiah and Henry Louis Gates at:
http://books.google.com/books/about/Africana.html?id=DfEzhGlnzlkC

Indigenous People (Native Americans)

Charles Curtis, 1860-1936
Member, Kaw Nation

* 31st Vice President of the United States (1929-33)
* U.S. Representative, Kansas, 1892-1906
* U.S. Senator, Kansas, 1906-1929
* U.S. Senate Minority Whip, 1915-1925
* U.S. Senate Majority Leader, 1925-1929

Benjamin Reifel, 1906-1990
Member, Lakota Sioux Nation

* Indian Name: Lone Feather
* Five—Term U.S. House of Representative Member from South Dakota
* Four and a half years of active duty as a Second Lieutenant during World War II
* Doctorate in Public Administration, Harvard University

Maria Tallchief, 1925-2013
Member, Osage Nation

* American ballerina
* Trained both as a pianist and as a dancer.
* Prima ballerina of the New York City Ballet for 18 years
* Numerous tours and television appearances with the American Ballet Theatre

Ben Nighthorse Campbell, 1933
Member, Northern Cheyenne Nation

* Northern Cheyenne Chief and member of the Council of Chiefs of the Northern Cheyenne Indian Tribe
* Former three-term United States Representative from Colorado
* Former two-term United States Senator from Colorado
* Leader in public lands and natural resources policy matters
* Originator of legislation to found the Smithsonian Institution's National Museum of the American Indian
* Captain of the 1976 U.S. Olympic judo team

Navarre Scott Momaday, 1934
Member, Kiowa Nation

* Scholar, Author, Poet and Painter
* Ph.D., English Literature, Stanford University
* Winner Pulitzer Prize for fiction, 1969
* Recipient, National Medal of Arts, 2007, awarded by President George W. Bush
* Recipient, Honorary Doctorate of Humane Letters, University of Illinois

Frank Howell Seay, 1938
Member, most likely Cherokee Nation

* First Native American Federal Judge
* Chief Judge, United States District Court, Eastern District of Oklahoma
* President, Seminole County Bar Association
* Member, Oklahoma Uniform Criminal Jury Instruction Commission
* Member, United States Judicial Council

Michael Anthony Dorris, 1945-1997
Member, Modoc Nation

* Scholar, Novelist
* Recipient, national Book Critics Circle Award for General Nonfiction for *The Broken Cord*.
* BA cum laude, English and Classics, Georgetown University
* MA, Anthropology, Yale University
* Co-founder and first Chair, Native American Studies Department, Dartmouth College

Leslie Marmon Silko, 1948
Member, Laguna Pueblo Nation

* Poet
* Novelist
* Recipient of a MacArthur Foundation Fellowship

Charlene Teters, 1952
Member, Spokane Nation

* Artist, educator and lecturer
* Ms. Teter's paintings have been featured in over 21 major exhibitions

* Ms. Teter is famously quoted as follows:

  "Often, people think about Native Americans as we were envisioned at the turn of the century. If we're not walking around in buckskin and fringe, mimicking the stereotype in dress and art form, we're not seen as real. Native Americans are here, and we are contemporary people, yet we are very much informed and connected to our history."

* Ms. Teters' act of waging a silent protest of the portrayal of the mascot, "Chief Illiniwek" at a 1988 University of Illinois basketball game, resulted in a significant increase in attempts to eradicate Native American mascots in educational institutions and athletics throughout the United States.

* The documentary, "In Whose Honor", highlights Ms. Teter's work in the area.

  http://www.youtube.com/watch?v=lEUl2keJK-w
  http://www.youtube.com/watch?v=8lUF95Thl7s
  http://www.pbs.org/pov/inwhosehonor/film_description.php#.UcSWPlbn99w

John Herrington, 1958
Member, Chickasaw Nation

* First Indigenous American astronaut in space. Mr. Herrington served as Mission Specialist for the Space Shuttle, Endeavor's, sixteenth mission to the International Space Station.
* Commander of the NEEMO 6 mission of the Aquarius Underwater Laboratory. During the mission, Commander Herrington lived and worked underwater for ten days.
* Commander Herrington is a retired commissioned officer and Aviator of the U.S. Navy. As a Naval Aviator,

Commander Herrington trained in the operation of marine surveillance aircraft.

* Master of Science Degree, Aeronautical Engineering, U.S. Naval Postgraduate School, 1995
http://www.youtube.com/watch?v=HKvHsjwAtZQ

Latin Americans

Rita Moreno, 1931
Puerto Rican American

* Internationally recognized singer, dancer and actress
* One of very few entertainers to be awarded an Oscar, Emmy, Tony, and Grammy award.

Mario José Molina-Pasquel Henríquez, 1943
Mexican Contributor to the United States

* Chemist
* Co-recipient of 1995 Nobel Prize in Chemistry for illuminating the threat posed by chlorofluorocarbon gases to the Earth's ozone layer.
* Recipient, 1987 Esselen Award of the Northeast Section of the American Chemical Society
* Recipient, Newcomb-Cleveland Award awarded by the American Association for the Advancement of Science
* Recipient, 1989 NASA Medal for Exceptional Scientific Advancement
* Recipient, 1989 United Nations Environmental Programme Global 500 Award
* Recipient, 1998 Willard Gibbs Medal awarded by the Chicago Section of the American Chemical Society
* Recipient, 1998 Prize for Creative Advances in Environment Technology and Science awarded by the Chicago Section of the American Chemical Society

Antonia Coello Novello, 1944
Puerto Rican American

- Physician and public health administrator
- Surgeon General under President George H. W. Bush from 1990 to 1993. Foci: Public educational campaign on the dangers of smoking and teenage drinking, increase of AIDS education, and improving health care for women, minorities, and children.
- Vice Admiral of the Public Health Service Commissioned Corps

Carlos Augusto Alves Santana, 1947
Mexican American

- World famous musician
- Recipient, ten Grammy Awards
- Recipient, three Latin Grammy Awards
- Listed by Rolling Stone magazine in 2003 as number 20 on their list of the 100 Greatest Guitarists of All Time

Bill Richardson, III, 1947
Mexican American

- Former Governor of New Mexico, 2003-2011; Chair of the Democratic Governors Association
- United States Ambassador to the United Nations, 1997-1998
- Secretary, Department of Energy, Clinton Administration
- U.S. Congressman; sponsored a number of pro-Indigenous American legislation; Chair of the Congressional Hispanic Caucus, 98th Congress, 1983-1985
- United States Ambassador to the United Nations
- Adjunct Professor, Kennedy School of Government, Harvard University
- Candidate for the Democratic nomination for U.S. President, 2008

Franklin Chang-Dìaz, 1950
Costa Rican American

* Physicist, former astronaut and mechanical engineer
* Veteran of seven space shuttle missions
* Member, NASA Astronaut Hall of Fame
* Ph.D., Plasma Physics, Massachusetts Institute of Technology
* Former Director, Advanced Space Propulsion Laboratory, Johnson Space Center, 1993-2005
  http://www.youtube.com/watch?v=JqaHh-R9UUc

Hilda Solis, 1957
Mexican and Nicaraguan American

* U.S. Secretary of Labor, 2009-2013, Obama administration
* Member, U. S. House of Representatives, 2001-1009, 31st, 32nd district, California
* M.A., Public Administration, University of Southern California

Ellen Ochoa, 1958
Mexican and Nicaraguan American

- Former NASA Astronaut—Mission Specialist and Flight Engineer; flew on four space flights
- PH.D., Electrical Engineering, Stanford University
- Recipient, National Aeronautic and Space Administration's Distinguished Service Medal
- Recipient, Hispanic Heritage Leadership Award
- Deputy Director, Lyndon B. Johnson Space Center
  http://www.youtube.com/watch?v=G40G1q1I7u8

Nilo Cruz, 1960
Cuban American

- Renowned playwright
- Recipient, Pulitzer Prize for Drama, 2003 for *Anna in the Tropics*

Maria Hinojosa, 1961
Mexican American

- Internationally renowned journalist
- Reporter for National Public Radio, (NPR), Cable News Network, (CNN), and the Columbia Broadcasting System, (CBS)
- Recipient, four Emmy Awards
- Recipient, John Chancellor Award for Excellence in Journalism
- Recipient, Robert F. Kennedy Journalism Award for Reporting on the Disadvantaged
- Recipient, National Association of Hispanic Journalists' Radio Award
- Recipient, American Women in Radio and Television Gracie Award for Individual Achievement
- Honorary Doctorate of Humane Letters, DePaul University

Asian Americans

Katherine Sui Fun Cheung, 1904-2003
Chinese American

- Overcoming what was then Chinese culture's expectations of women to be meek and quiet, in 1932, Ms. Cheung became the first Chinese American woman to become a licensed pilot. Ms. Cheung also earned an international pilot's license. Her stunt flying skills included barrel rolls and flying loops.

- Member, Women's International Association of Aeronautics.
- Member, the prestigious Ninety Nines Club, an international club of women pilots established by Amelia Earhart four years prior.
- Flew with Amelia Earhart
- Inducted into the American Aviation Hall of Fame
- The Beijing Air Force Aviation Museum declared Ms. Cheung, "China's Amelia Earhart" and opened an exhibit to commemorate her.
- Enshrined by the Smithsonian's National Air and Space Museum as America's first Asian American aviatrix.
- One of only 30 individuals to have a bronze plaque embedded in Los Angeles' Flight Path Walk of Fame which acknowledges and honors historic events in aviation.
- Degree in music from the Los Angeles Conservatory of Music
  http://video.us.msn.com/watch/video/katherine-sui-fun-cheung/12vcplli?cpkey=6fd459be-eed8-4670-967f-72861c66458e%257c%257c%257c%257c

Herbert Choy, 1916-2004
Korean American

- 1971, appointed to the U.S. Court of Appeals for the Ninth Circuit Court
- Doctor of Law Degree, Harvard University, 1941
- U.S. Army, Judge Advocate General Corp, 1942-1946
- Attorney General, Territory of Hawaii, 1957-1958

Young Oak Kim, 1919-2005
Korean American

- Untied States Colonel and decorated War War II combat veteran
- Awarded 19 medals, including three Purple Hearts, two Silver Stars and two Bronze Stars.

Epifanio San Juan, Jr., Ph.D., 1938
Filipino American

- Academic, writer, poet, editor and film maker
- Recipient, Centennial Award for Achievement in Literature from the Cultural Center of the Philippines, 1999
- Graduate, magna cum laude, University of the Philippines, 1958
- Ph.D., Harvard University, 1965
- Fellow, W.E.B. Du Bois Institute, Harvard University
- Taught at various American universities

Ellison Onizuka, 1946
Japanese American

- U.S. astronaut
- Flight test engineer, United State Air Force
- Flew on the Space Shuttle Discovery
- Recipient, National Defense Service Medal, Air Force Meritorious Service Medal, Air Force Commendation Medal, and the Congressional Space Medal of Honor
- Served as Mission Specialist on Space Shuttle Challenger, on which he lost his life on January 28, 1986

Connie Chung, 1946
Chinese American

- Journalist, anchor and reporter for ABC, CBS, NBC, CNN and MSNBC
- Second American woman to co-anchor a national news broadcast on a major network, the CBS Evening News
- Hosted CBS' *Eye to Eye with Connie Chung*
- Hosted CNN's *Connie Chung Tonight*
- Co-hosted ABC's *20/20*
- Teaching Fellow, Kennedy School of Government, Harvard University

Sichan Siv, 1948
Cambodian American

- International bestselling author
- United States Ambassador
- White House Deputy Assistant to President George Herbert Walker Bush
- Deputy Assistant Secretary of State
- Recipient, George H.W. Bush Award for Outstanding Public Service
- Volunteer in the United States Air Force 433rd Auxiliary Civil Air Patrol
- Auxiliary Civil Air Patrol
- Honorary Commander, USAF 433rd Airlift Wing
- Honorary Commander of USAF 12th and 902nd Mission Support Groups
- Recipient, U.S. Army Commander's Award
- Recipient, Brazilian Academy of Art, Culture and History Honors
- Former U.S. Ambassador to the United Nations Economic and Social Council

Venkatraman Ramakrishnan, 1952
Indian Contributor to the United States

- Structural biologist
- Ph.D. in Physics, Ohio University, 1976
- Postdoctoral Fellow, Yale University
- Co-Recipient, Nobel Prize in Chemistry, 2009 for studies of the structure and function of ribosomes.
- Recipient, Louis-Jeantet Prize for Medicine, 2007
- Recipient, Heatley Medal of the British Biochemical Society, 2008
- Recipient, India's second highest civilian honor, the Padma Vibhushan, 2010
- Knighted for services to molecular biology
- Member, National Academy of Sciences

http://www.youtube.com/watch?v=sjSnfhrTnbo

Tammy Duckworth, 1968
Thai American

- U. S. Representative for the 8th Congressional District of Illinois
- Assistant Secretary for Public and Intergovernmental Affairs, U.S. Department of Veterans Affairs, 2009-2011
- Director, Illinois Department of Veterans Affairs, 2006-2009
- Helicopter Pilot, Iraq War—wounded in combat, losing both her legs and suffering severe damage to her right arm.
- Ms. Duckworth still continues to serve as a Lieutenant Colonel in the Illinois Army National Guard
- Recipient, Purple Heart
- Recipient, Air Medal and Army Commendation Medal

Lisa Ling, 1973
Chinese American

- International Journalist
- Host, *Our America with Lisa Ling*, and Investigative Reporter, The Oprah Winfrey Network
- Recipient, numerous awards for groundbreaking investigative documentaries
- Former Host, ABC's *The View,* 1999-2002
- Former reporter and anchor, Channel One News

Salman Khan, 1976
Bangladeshi American

- Educator and entrepreneur
- Founder, YouTube Channel, Khan Academy http://www.youtube.com/user/khanacademy

- Named among the 100 most influential people in the world, Time Magazine, 2012
- Bachelor of Science, Mathematics, Massachusetts Institute of Technology
- Bachelor of Science, Computer Science and Engineering, Massachusetts Institute of Technology
- Master of Science, Computer Science, Massachusetts Institute of Technology
- Master of Business Administration, Harvard Business School
- Author, *The One World Schoolhouse: Education Reimagined*[230]

[230] Khan, Salman. *The One World Schoolhouse: Education Reimagined.* London: Hodder Stoughton. 2012. Print.

Note Three

Unearned Privilege

I have often conducted what is referred to as, "The Privilege Walk" in my diversity workshops. In the exercise, I ask participants to stand in a straight line, shoulder-to-shoulder, in the middle of the room. I then instruct them to listen to my words and based upon their perception of their experience, move in one of two directions, either forward or back. A sample of the kind of questions I ask in the exercise follows:

1. If you believe that when you were a child in school, your intelligence was either doubted or not acknowledged **because of your race**, please take one step back. If you believe that when you were a student, your intelligence was **never** doubted or not acknowledged **on the basis of your race**, please take one step forward. [231]

2. If you believe that you have ever been stopped by the police **on the basis of your race**, please take one step back. If you believe that you have **never** been stopped by the police **on the basis on your race**, please take one step forward.

3. If you believe that you have ever been either followed or watched carefully by sales or security people in a retail establishment **on the basis of your race**, take one step back. If you believe that you have **never** been . . . . take one step forward.

[231] I acknowledge at this early point in the exercise that one may very well have been subjected to any of the experiences described in it for a reason or reasons **other** than race and that those experiences are painful **regardless** of why one underwent them. I then go on to explain why we are focusing **specifically** on the issue of **race** in this particular exercise.

4. If you believe that **based on your race**, you have on at least one occasion, been asked for an unusual amount of ID in writing a check . . . . back. If you believe that you have **never** . . . . forward

5. If you believe that **because of your race**, you have ever been denied a job, a promotion, or a training opportunity . . . . back If you believe that you have **never** . . . . forward.

6. If you feel that you often evoke a fear response in people, **simply because of your race** . . . . back. If you believe that you have **never** . . . . forward.

Nine other similar requests then follow.

It has consistently, i.e., **literally, without fail**, been the case that the one line that was in the room at the beginning of the exercise, has become two at the end, with the European American participants in a line at the front of the room and the Americans of Color, in a line at the back. After the last question, I ask the European American participants to turn around and face their colleagues in the back. Then, in silence, for about thirty seconds, I allow the participants to experience both their and their colleagues' respective places in the room. While still standing in the two lines, we then process the **feeling**s that came up for them during the experience. After a short break, we go back to our seats and process our **thoughts**. The resulting dialogue is **always** profound.[232]

---

232 When I mix race and gender questions in the exercise, there are often three lines at the end. The one in the very front is comprised of European American men because they enjoy both race **and** gender privilege. The second line is a mixture of European American women and Men of Color because European American women **do** have race, but do **not** have gender privilege, and Men of Color have gender but **not** race privilege, The third line in the back is always comprised of the Women of Color in the room who enjoy neither race nor gender privilege. I also conduct the Privilege Walk Exercise focused on the issues of disability, sexual orientation, class, age

Unearned Privilege Learning Points

1. Those who have unearned privilege are almost always unaware of it. Their unawareness of it is as natural for them as water is to fish.

2. Those who do **not** have unearned privilege, are often keenly aware both **that** they don't have it and **when** others receive it in the same moment that they do not.[233]

3. Anger is often the result because it hurts.

4. Thus:

   A. Most of those who **have** unearned privilege are "stuck" in their lack of awareness of:

   i. The privilege in **their** lives;

   ii. The opposite of unearned privilege, i.e., the daily indignities, in the lives of **others**; and,

   iii. Their own actions that result in indignities to others.

---

and religious unearned privilege. The exercise is the same. Only the questions are different. Those exercises and the discussions which follow, are also hugely impactful.

[233] One example: While shopping in a sporting goods store some time ago, I asked a salesperson to unlock the fitting room for me. I was able to see under the three quarter length fitting room door and noticed that the salesperson stood right outside the room the entire time I was using it until I came out with the outfit that I'd tried on. As I continued shopping, I watched as the same salesperson unlocked the door for one European American shopper after another and then promptly walked away, never waiting to see what they existed with. I spoke to the manager about it In the same breadth, he offered both an apology **for** and a denial **of** the event.

B. Most of those who do **not** have unearned privilege are stuck in their hurt, frustration and anger about it.

5. In order for us all to get "unstuck" regarding unearned privilege, the following two things must happen:

A. The unprivileged must begin to speak up in the face of the daily indignities, (e.g., To the store manager: "I noticed that a salesperson monitored me the entire time I was in the fitting room and that she did **not** do that to European American customers. I'd like you to know that I am a paying customer, not a thief, that you have just lost my business and that I'm going to tell my family and friends about my experience here."), and,

B. The privileged must refuse the privilege whenever possible, (e.g., "That gentleman was here before me. You really should wait on him first.")

Doing an internet search of the term, "Unearned Privilege" will bring up a host of information on the subject with respect to privilege in a variety of areas. The following are two of the older, classic articles on specifically unearned **racial** privilege that I have found particularly helpful:

1. **McIntosh, Peggy. "White Privilege: Unpacking the Invisible Knapsack." Wellesley College Center for Research on Women. 1988**
http://www.nymbp.org/reference/WhitePrivilege.pdf

2. **Jensen, Robert. "White Privilege Shapes the U.S." Baltimore Sun 1998**
http://uts.cc.utexas.edu/~rjensen/freelance/whiteprivilege.htm

Note Four

Common Responses to Conversations about Racially-Based Daily Indignities[234]

I have found, over the course of many years of my life, that denial is the most common response to discussions of race and racism with persons who are not regularly their targets. The, "It had absolutely nothing to do with race" response is most assuredly, the most common of all. While that response can and often does stop meaningful communication and learning in their tracks, I have no personal animus against my fellow human beings who respond with such denial. Indeed, I experience genuine compassion for them for I am fully aware that most people who reply with denial were very heavily socialized to not see their own privilege and thus are incapable of responding in any other way **but** with denial. They truly don't know that they don't know.[235] They're totally unaware that there is an entire universe of information and understanding about race, others' experience of it and our nation's racial history, about which they are utterly unaware.

I am fully aware that I don't have a clue about what it is like to grow up in a poor, crime-ridden, drug-infested, gang-overrun neighborhood in an inner city. That reality is so foreign to my

---

[234] The common responses listed in this note are also commonly given in conversations about indignities based on other characteristics, religion, gender, disability, gender identity and expression and sexual orientation, among others.

[235] It has been my experience in many, many diversity workshops, however, that those who don't know, often adamantly **believe** that they know. What they "know", however, is often misinformation, e.g., "The reason they passed all those Affirmative Action laws is so they could lower the standards for our jobs so they could let in minorities and women.

own lived experienced, that I simply cannot imagine it. Having absolutely no mental frame of reference for it, I'm sure that my wildest nightmares would not come close to the actual experience. There is nothing within either my memory banks or my body of acquired knowledge which would allow me to imagine in any real way, what it would be like to live day in and day out in such circumstances. I get that . . . . totally. For that reason, I hope that I would **never** be so arrogant as to dispute the account of what it is like to live there, of any resident of such a community. Statements such as, "Wait a minute. Gunshots **every** night? I can believe once a week or so, but **every** night? C'mon."; or "Ok, so maybe the drug dealers hang out **outside** the school, but drug dealing **inside** the school? I don't think so. The school district would never allow it"; or, "You have **no** regular grocery stores in your **entire** community? Not one? Maybe there's one you don't like, or you think is too expensive, but I'm sure there's at least **one** supermarket **somewhere** in your neighborhood." Such communities are as foreign to me as Mars, and I know it. For that reason, I would **never** purport to tell a resident, i.e., a person who has actual **lived experience** in such a community, **anything** about it, and I would **certainly** avoid expressing doubt about and denying the veracity of accounts of their experiences.

I **know** that I don't have a clue what it's like to live with a disability. I know that I'm **absolutely ignorant** about what it's like to live in a country, the dominant language of which is not my first language. I know that I'm **totally** unaware of what it feels like to be a young Jewish or Muslim, Hindu, Buddhist or atheist child in school during the Christmas holidays. It would be more than grossly insensitive, it would be highly disrespectful of me to deny the reported experience of individuals who live those realities.

I want European Americans to "get" that in like manner, without the lived experience of an American of Color, it is **impossible** for them to know that experience. I want the denial of our experience to stop. I just want it to stop.

When the African American man in my workshop some years ago who was a high-level Human Resources professional in his organization, shared his experience of being stopped and held by police right outside of his home in his upscale suburban neighborhood, I want people to believe him and not ask, "Well, what were you **doing** at the time? Were you doing anything that might've looked maybe a little strange to your neighbors?"

While driving on a training trip in Minnesota some years ago, I was stopped by a police officer on a motorcycle. I was in a line of cars on a two lane highway with only one lane for northbound and one for southbound traffic and I wasn't passing the cars in front of me. At one point, I passed by a police officer who was sitting on a motorcycle observing the traffic. As I passed by the officer, I noticed him doing a "double take" on me. Within a few seconds, he was following me with his lights flashing. I stopped on the side of the road. He got off of his motorcycle and walked up to my car. After looking at me very suspiciously, the following dialogue then occurred:

Officer: So what's your business all the way up here? (I was in northern Minnesota over a weekend).

Me: I'm doing some training in St. Paul and was just taking a ride to see the scenery.

Officer: How long you're going to be here?

Me: Just until Tuesday when I fly back to Washington where I live.

Officer: Where you staying?

Me: A Sheraton in St. Paul.

Officer: Stay in your vehicle.

After taking my driver's license and registration back to his bike and staying on it for what felt like a **very** long time, even though

I wasn't speeding, he gave me a speeding ticket. I chose not to contest it both because doing so would've required me to fly back to Minnesota from the Washington, D.C. area where I lived, and because my argument that I was stopped and ticketed because of my race, while I believed that it was true, would, I thought, have gone absolutely **nowhere** in court.

When I describe the incident to my European American colleague at work the following week, I don't want her to say, "Well you know cops. They have their monthly quotas and if it's getting close to the end of the month, they start giving tickets to **everybody**, no matter who you are." After hearing my story, I want my colleague to understand why I had reason to believe that I was indeed stopped and ticketed because I am African American. I don't want her to speculate about police officers' end of month quotas.[236]

I don't want my account of being closely monitored in a sporting goods store fitting room to be followed by the response, "Well, they probably did it to other people too. You probably just didn't see it."

In a conversation between a European American father and an African American father of teenage sons who are friends in which the African American father explains to the European American father that even though all the kids in their sons' circle of friends are wearing their pants loose and their caps backward, he cannot allow **his** son to do so because the police will view his son differently from the white kids who are dressed the same way, I want the European American father to understand. I don't want him to say to the African American father, "That's just not true. The police see all those kids the same. They just see teenagers. It makes no difference."

---

236 World-renowned jazz musician Miles Davis is reputed to have taken his new Ferrari to the police station near his home in Los Angeles and shown it to the officers in an effort to avoid being stopped as he had allegedly been in the past, under suspicion of having stolen the car.

A couple of months ago, a young male relative of mine, (whom I'll call Lance), and his wife, spent the weekend with Barbara and I. Over the course of the weekend, the four of us visited a tiny local market and restaurant in a nearby town. The very pleasant, very warm, very welcoming restaurant employee engaged the four of us in an interesting conversation about the history of the establishment. I don't remember the context within which she made it, but at some point during the conversation, the employee gestured toward Lance and said, "Now this guy, I don't know about him. He looks kind of suspicious." I immediately responded with, "Hey, hey, hey, that "guy" is my nephew." I don't know whether or not she was serious, but in that moment, Lance left and went outside. He talked on his cell phone out there and never did come back inside. I didn't mention the incident after it was over because I didn't want to put a damper on what was otherwise a very pleasant weekend. I don't know whether or not Lance had just gotten a phone call, but in that moment, I was appalled. It was just the latest example of how, as a Person of Color, race is a monster that's **always** there that can jump out and bite you any time, at any moment. You're not looking for it. You're not even **thinking** about it, and then all of a sudden, there it is. It's **always** there—potentially. When I describe that reality to a European American friend, or colleague I don't want them to tell me that I'm imagining it, that I'm playing the race card, or that I'm just overly sensitive. I'd really **love** to never be met with that reaction again.

I want European Americans to understand that since they do not know what it is like to "drive while black", to "shop while black", or to parent a black child, since their life experience in the United States as a European American is in **many** ways the **total** opposite of that of Americans of Color, it is utterly both hurtful and insulting for them to deny our experiences with race. I understand that it is difficult to acknowledge the extent to which racism is still prevalent in contemporary American society. I understand that it seems easier to deny and not think about it. But I want European Americans to know that being in constant denial about how racism affects the lives of Americans of Color exacerbates the problem itself—tremendously.

Whenever **any** of us stand in judgment of others of us regarding an identity which we do not share with them, we are at risk of responding in ways that are less than empathetic. My hope is that this book will help those of us who engage in the common responses, to understand them and as a result, attempt, in the future, to respond to another's shared experience with increased open-mindedness and compassion.

The following are in my view, the twenty most common and thus most **predictable** responses to stories about people's experiences of the daily indignities:

1. You're overly-sensitive.

2. C'mon, that stuff doesn't happen anymore You must've misinterpreted it. I'm sure it didn't happen like that.

3. Well you know they didn't **mean** it like that. You know they didn't **intend** that, so why do you get upset about stuff like that?

4. Maybe they, (the person who committed the insult), were just having a bad day.

5. Maybe it's just the person's personality.

6. Maybe it's their policy.

7. That happens to everybody.

8. That happens to me too, you know, so it couldn't have happened to you because of your race.

9. What were you wearing? When I dress in a T shirt and shorts I get treated like that too, so it's not about race.

10. Well, if I went across to the ________(Latino, African American or Asian) side of town, (or to the reservation), the same thing would happen to me in reverse.

11. Well, that's not such a big deal. It's not like they kept you from getting a job or something. You're doing pretty well for yourself.

12. Well what did you do? Maybe you did something that made them react like that.

13. What did you do about it? If you didn't say anything, you're just as guilty as they are.

14. I can't be racist because some of my best friends are . . . .

15. You're just looking for it.

16. You're just playing the _____card.

17. I didn't get any unearned privilege. I worked hard for everything I have.

18. Why should I feel guilty? I'm not responsible. I never discriminated against anybody.

19. I've had pain in my life too. Why can't you just deal with it? Why do we have to spend all this time talking about it?

20. I've had pain in my life too. Why can't you just deal with racism the way I deal with my pain. I just handle it the best I can and move on with my life.

If we are to mature beyond racism, we must attempt to answer the following five questions:

1. Why do people so often respond with those common responses? Why do we want to avoid "it" being about race?

2. How do those responses affect the person who is attempting to share their experience of a daily indignity?

3. How do the common responses impact the listener's ability to learn about the experiences of others who are subjected to the daily indignities?

4. How do the common responses affect the possibility of deep, meaningful friendship between people of different races?

5. How do the common responses affect our society's ability to mature beyond racism or any of the other isms?

The Empathetic Response

Upon hearing of another's experience of a daily indignity, rather than responding with one of the common responses, responding empathetically is much more helpful. We listen with empathy when we:

1. Listen attentively, for both facts and feelings;

2. Ask the person about the details of what happened;

3. Ask them how they felt in the moment of the incident;

4. Express our feelings about the event, (e.g., that we're sorry the person experienced the indignity, that they didn't deserve it, etc.); and,

5. Ask if there is anything we can do to help.

In my experience, the common responses are usually not answered very effectively, as a result of which, countless learning opportunities are wasted, time and time again. I offer below, possible replies to the common responses that I believe are more effective than those usually given. In so doing, I am entirely aware that responding in the ways that I suggest, requires quite highly developed self-control and emotional intelligence in general. In that respect, (i.e., having many opportunities over the course of one's life to respond to both the daily indignities **and** the common responses), being an American of Color, provides enormous opportunity for personal growth, for we are challenged to not only **work** for change, but indeed, to **be** the change we seek.

I suggest the following replies to the common responses:

1. **You're overly sensitive**.

   I believe that I perceived <u>exactly</u> what was going on. But if I <u>am</u> sensitive, I hope you can understand that it's because I've had that experience and its accompanying pain many times in the past.

2. **C'mon, that stuff doesn't happen anymore You must've misinterpreted it. I'm sure it didn't happen like that.**

   The way I described my experience is my perception of it. You may not <u>agree</u> with that perception, but I just ask you to understand and accept without judgment, that my perception is based on my many years of life experience with this, an experience with which you may be totally unfamiliar.

3. **Well you know they didn't mean it like that. You know that wasn't their intent, so why do you get upset about stuff like that?**

   There's a big difference between intent and impact. Intent is one thing and impact is totally different. For a number of reasons, an experience can be hurtful without an **intention** that it be. It may be hurtful to the person because they've experienced it many times in the past, and the sheer **familiarity** of it is taxing to them. In other words, maybe what just happened is just the latest add-on to what is an accumulated hurt. It could be hurtful to the person experiencing it because s/he just saw the person in front of them be responded to very differently. It could be any number of things, **regardless** of the other person's intent. Intent and impact can be **related**, but they **are** different. Think about it.

You'd look at me pretty strangely if I stepped on your toe and you yelled, "Ouch! That hurt! And I responded with, "Well I didn't **mean** to step on your toe, so why is it hurting?"

4. **Maybe they, (the person who committed the insult), were just having a bad day.**

   Maybe the person was having a bad day, but it's also possible that they could also have responded to me in that way because they're uncomfortable helping a Latino or Asian, etc. person. Indeed, it is often hard for me to know if I received the indignity because of prejudice and that can make it terribly difficult to know how to respond, which is also uncomfortable.[237]

5. **Maybe it's just the person's personality**.

   It very well may just **be** their personality, but it's also possible that they're uncomfortable helping . . . . (Same response as number three)

6. **Maybe it's their policy.**

   It very well may **be** their policy, but it's also possible that the person responded to me in the way s/he did because of my race. Indeed, ... (Same response as number three)

7. **That happens to everybody.**

   Absolutely. Everyone **does** get a rude waiter every now and then. That's just life. **Of course** it happens to everybody. It's random, like the roll of the dice. Some days, it's just going to happen. I believe that what's different for me, though, is the

[237] I have on numerous occasions, found myself wondering, "Now did that just happen to me because I'm black, or a woman, both or neither?" Not knowing deprives me of a clear response choice, which can be wearisome.

frequency with which it happens to me. My strong suspicion is that it happens to me a lot more often than it happens to you and it's that **frequency**, it's how **often** it happens to me, that's so difficult. It's the **frequency** of my experience of the indignity that affects the quality of my life so significantly in a way that it probably doesn't affect yours.

8. **That happens to me too, you know, so it couldn't have happened to you because of your race.**

   I don't at all doubt that you've had the same experience. I'd be surprised if you haven't. I just ask you to be open to the possibility though, that just because it has happened to you **doesn't** mean that it **didn't** happen to me because of my race. Maybe it happened to you because of your size, or maybe because of your beard. The point is that the person **could** have been prejudiced against or maybe even afraid of **you** because of your size or maybe your tattoos, and they could **also** have been prejudiced against or afraid of **me** because of my **race.** So it could very well have happened to you for a **non**-racial reason and to me **fo**r a racial reason, in other words, because of my race. **Both** could be true.

9. **What were you wearing? When I dress in a T-shirt and shorts I get treated like that too, so it's not about race.**

   I'm sure it's true that sometimes you're treated not as well as others who are more well-dressed. What's different for me, though, is that I've experienced the same thing when I'm wearing shorts and a T-shirt **and** when I'm in a business suit. That's what's different for me. You can change your clothes. I can too, but a lot of times it doesn't' matter for me because what the other person is responding to **isn't** what I'm wearing. It's the color of my skin, and unlike my **clothes**, I can't change my color.

10. Well, if I went across to the ________(Latino or African American or Asian) side of town, (or to the reservation), the same thing would happen to me in reverse.

Sure. That could very well be true, depending upon with whom you'd be interacting. I don't deny that, and whenever it **does** happen to you, it's wrong. **You** also don't deserve to be treated badly because of **your** race. Nobody does. The point, which I hope you can see, is that it's just as wrong when it happens to **me** because of **my** race. The fact that you experience prejudice too, doesn't in any way negate my experience of it.

Also, there's one big difference between my experience and yours,—how easy it is for you to avoid that kind of treatment, compared to how difficult it is for me. If you don't want to be treated that way on a regular basis, all you have to do is not shop on that side of town. In fact, I'd guess that you probably **don't** shop on that side of town. But for **me** to avoid that kind of treatment on a regular basis, I'd have to avoid the entire larger society. It's absolutely wrong for **anyone** to receive that kind of treatment based on their race. The difference is that it's fairly easy for you and nearly impossible for me to avoid.

11. Well, that's not such a big deal. It's not like they kept you from getting a job or something. You're doing pretty well for yourself.

I can understand why you'd think that. From all appearances, I **am** doing pretty well. But just because I have a good job and live in a nice home doesn't mean that I don't experience the daily indignities. In fact, one of the things that's **so** upsetting to me is that I **have** done all the right things; I've **played** by all the rules—gotten the degrees, landed the good job, bought the nice home, have a nice family—and I'm **still** treated like a suspect by the police, by store clerks, and so many others. I just ask you to think about how **you'd** feel if you were me, having worked so hard for so long and accomplished all the things that I've accomplished as a result, and **still** experience these things on a regular basis.

12. **What did you do? Maybe you did something that made them react like that.**

Why do you ask that? I didn't do anything. I was just browsing in the sporting goods section. Your question implies that I'm the guilty one. That's really hurtful.

13. **Well what did you do about it? If you didn't say anything, you're just as guilty as they are.**

Wow. I'm really shocked by that response. I just fundamentally disagree. Sometimes I **do** speak up because it's a matter of standing up for my dignity. But there are other times when I **don't** speak up either because I just don't have the emotional energy to fight that battle again in that moment, or because I'm unable to tell whether it's prejudice that's at play or I'm just dealing with a rude person. But whether I speak up or not doesn't make the other person any **less** responsible for their action and it **certainly** doesn't make **me** guilty. Blaming the victim is really not helpful.

14. **I can't be racist because some of my best friends are . . . .**

I'm glad you have friends who are________. It's possible, though, to have friends who are________ and **still** have unresolved, unconscious bias against or fear of___________. The two are not mutually exclusive.

15. **You're just looking for it.**

Why do you say that? Why would I go around looking for that kind of experience? My life would be **infinitely** better if I didn't have to deal with any of these kinds of experiences, and certainly as often as I do. Rather than looking for it, I expend energy trying to **avoid** it whenever possible.

16. You're just playing the _____card.

That's a very common response when people share their experiences of the daily indignities. The message is that I'm intentionally harping on something that didn't actually happen. Now let's just assume for a minute that the experience I just told you about did **indeed** happen to me. How do you think I'm feeling right now, having been told that I'm just playing the ____ card? (That question will lead to a discussion, hopefully.)

17. I didn't get any unearned privilege. I worked hard for everything I have.

Yes, I'm sure that you've worked very hard for what you have. I don't doubt that in the least. Most people don't get anything **without** working hard, no matter what their race. An important point to understand, however, is that there are people who've worked every bit as hard as you have and didn't get nearly as far as you did. You see, you were able to **yield** all of the benefits of your hard work into what you rightfully earned as a result of it. Many **other** people, however, spent years working **just** as hard as you did, but still weren't given the training opportunities, the promotions and the raises you received. It's not that you didn't work hard. It's that others **also** worked hard but were denied the **benefits** of their work. You shouldn't feel **guilty** about what you have. You didn't make the decisions about who advanced, but it is helpful for you to understand that others were equally as, or perhaps based upon the quality of their work, even **more** deserving, but didn't get the results you did.

18. Why should I feel guilty? I'm not responsible. I never discriminated against anyone.

You're right. You **aren't** responsible for the oppression of whole groups of people**. No one** alive today is. This whole system was set up before **any** of us were born. So no, you **shouldn't** feel guilty. But as the recipient of a lot of unearned privilege, you **do** have a responsibility to **understand** your privilege, to do what you can in your life to work **against** unearned privilege and to educate others about it. Guilt won't allow you to be that empowered ally which others who don't share the privilege need so badly, so yes, move beyond the guilt so that you can be an effective change agent.

19. I've had pain in my life too. Why do we have to spend all this time talking about it?

The discussion about these issues is necessary because it is the majority of people's lack of awareness of them that continues to cause pain, bias and discrimination that have a real impact on people's lives. Imagine, for example, that you grew up in poverty. Imagine also, that in society-at-large, a myriad of stereotypes exist about all people who grew up in poverty, stereotypes that such people are lazy, stupid, criminally inclined and sexually promiscuous. Unless you shared with me that you are a member of that group, though, i.e., unless you were to **tell** me that you grew up poor, I wouldn't know that about you. I'd have absolutely no idea that you are a member of the group for which society holds such dreadful stereotypes. Neither I nor anyone else would be able to simply **look** at you and determine that. You could, indeed, choose to just "be in the closet" about it, living your life with that piece of information as your very own personal, private secret.

As an American of Color, and an African American, (or other racial group), specifically, I'm a member of a group about whom **those very stereotypes** exist on a broad scale in the society in which I live, in the place that I call home, indeed, in the place which **is** my home. Just turn on your television and radio and you'll hear conservative pundits either explicitly say or clearly imply that we're all **four** of those things—lazy, dumb, criminally inclined **and** sexually promiscuous. The huge, indeed **titanic** difference between **your** situation as someone who grew up in poverty and me as a Person of Color, is that you can keep your background a secret but I can't keep my race a secret. You can see it when you look at me. When people **look** at me, they **see** that I'm a member of the stereotyped group. Essentially, I wear the scarlet letter "A" smack dab on my forehead. So I'm being responded to negatively, over and over again, in situation after situation in my life, **because** of that "A". It causes the police to stop and frisk me, for me to be profiled in stores, for people to show a kind of general lack of comfort in dealing with me. I could go on and on. My point, is that I **wear** my membership in the stereotyped group. I wear it **on my face**. **That's** the difference, and it's a huge one and having that difference denied and minimized when it impacts my life so dramatically, is just tiring. It's exhausting to have to **keep** saying, "But race really **does** make a difference in how people regard and treat you. I'm not making it up. It does make a difference!" You know it does. Would you trade places with me right now and live the rest of your life as an American of Color? I just ask you to think about it.

20. I've had pain in my life too. Why can't you just deal with racism the way I deal with my pain. I just handle it the best I can and move on with my life.

[This is the response which, more than all others, requires genuine **compassion**.]

Over many years in numerous workshops, I have observed that it is can be difficult for some European Americans to non-defensively acknowledge race-based daily indignities because they feel that there is an unspoken assumption that racial indignities are taken more seriously and thus given more legitimacy than the non race-based painful experiences which they have had in their personal lives. The statement, "Well, you don't have to be black, or Hispanic or something to understand those things. Everybody experiences negative things in life" speaks to that feeling. Whenever I hear that or a similar statement which conveys the same message, I can, of course, never know exactly to what negative experiences the speaker is referring. I imagine, however, that if the speaker shared their actual sentiment more **specifically**, it may be similar to the following for example: "But about **my** pain? Yeah, I'm white, but I grew up poor!" "But what about **my** pain? I was abused as a child!" or, "But what about **my** pain? I was raped!", or "But what about **my** pain? I've experienced anti-Semitism!" or, "But what about **my** pain? I've experienced sexism!" or, "But what about **my** pain? I've experienced prejudice because of my disability!"

I have never experienced such pain being shared so explicitly, but when I hear the comment, "You don't have to be_____. Everybody has negative experiences in life" or something similar, I respond with compassion, meeting the person where they are, totally agreeing that all human beings experience pain in life. I may then ask the person to share more of their thoughts and feelings about that fact. If at that point, s/he expresses emotion from the heart, I most often feel a deep heart connection to the person, human being to human being, and respond with the deep empathy that I am feeling toward the person in that moment. If they have shared the specific source of their pain, I tell them, in the utmost sincerity, that I am **so** sorry that they went through their painful experience. I tell them that they did not deserve that. I tell them, genuinely meaning every word, that I am **very** happy that they made it through and survived their experience. I tell them that while I **empathize** with their pain, I know that never having had the experience myself, I cannot truly **understand** their pain. It is **that** conversation, **that** sharing of human emotion, which is often the game changer. It is after **that** exchange, after a sincere sharing of personal pain, (even if the speaker doesn't reveal the **specific** source of his/her pain), and being responded to with genuine empathy and deep compassion, human being to human being, that the speaker is then able to empathize with the pain that People of Color suffer as a result of experiencing the daily indignities. The person's pain has been legitimized, making it possible for them to empathize with the pain of others.

After giving **any** one of the above replies, dependent upon the circumstance and the person being spoken to, one may also wish to share with the other person how it feels to be responded to with a common response.

Admittedly, responding to the common responses in the ways I suggest, requires a level of maturity and strength of character that may, unfortunately, be quite exceptional. One thing is sure however . . . . living with daily indignities of **any** kind, whether they are based on race or any **other** ism, affords one **tremendous** opportunity for genuine self-awareness and personal growth. It is a choice. I want all of us who live with daily indignities to **see** that choice.

Final Common Responses Learning Point

The final and a crucial learning point regarding the common responses, is that being a target of the daily indignities is very painful because it deprives one of her/his individuality. The targeted person is not treated as an individual human being; rather, s/he is treated as a member of a group. The experience of not being seen as a person:

(* "Didn't she see how I was behaving? I was very professional."

* "I had on running shorts and a T shirt and I wasn't carrying anything. My wallet was in my pocket. How could I have shoplifted anything?"
* "I was following my colleague in my car. We were **both** doing 75. I was **behind** him and yet, **I** was stopped.")

but being seen, instead, as an entity, a racial entity, is an extremely painful emotional experience which one never gets used to. It is the experience of being constantly objectified. It is, indeed, continuing emotional distress.

Having members of the majority understand how the daily indignities impact the lives of target group people is an absolutely essential piece of the process of becoming more aware. It is an essential part of our collective healing from our tragic history of racism.

Note Five

Societal Attempts to Address the Present Day Effects of Past Discrimination

The American government's attempt to address our long history of discrimination may be summarized by my "Four R" Model:[238]

The First R:

❑ **Rights** **1960's** **Equal Opportunity**

After President Truman integrated the U.S. Armed Forces in1948, we continued our work as a nation, of granting equal opportunity to all to live up to their highest human potential and accomplish their dreams by granting basic civil **rights**, i.e., fundamental **human** justice to the millions who had been discriminated against since the founding of our nation. Much of that work began in the 1960's, a decade of monumental, societal-shifting legislation.

> [We actually began with the Civil Rights Act of 1957, followed by its successor, the Civil Rights Act of 1960, both of which were essentially voting rights acts. Those Acts, however, contained significant loopholes which allowed Southern states to discriminate against African Americans and other People of Color in the voting and voter registration processes, which is why they were followed by the historic Voting Rights Act of 1965.]

The following are by far, the most historically significant pieces of Civil Rights legislation passed during the decade:

- Equal Pay Act of 1963

[238] © Lauren N. Nile 2013

- Civil Rights Act of 1964
- Voting Rights Act of 1965[239]
- Executive Order 11246
- Age Discrimination in Employment Act of 1967

The Equal Pay Act, (EPA), of 1963 made it illegal to pay people differently based upon sex. With the passage of the EPA, the United States Congress declared that the historical practice of paying men more than women for doing the same or comparable work **had** to stop. The practice was keeping millions of women and children, (tens of thousands of whom had lost their husband/ father in World War II), in poverty. Under the EPA, whether one was a woman or a man, did not matter for the purpose of determining compensation for work. Employees performing the same work were entitled to the same salary. Remuneration that was based upon gender was declared to be discriminatory. Period.

The next year, the Civil Rights Act of 1964 was passed and signed by President Johnson. The law made it illegal to treat people differently, i.e., to discriminate against them, on five bases—race, color, religion, gender and national origin, in all public accommodations by entities engaged in interstate commerce, (hotels, restaurants, amusement parks, theaters, etc.), by governmental agencies that receive Federal funds, by most employers, in certain aspects of the judicial system, and in other

---

[239] The Voting Rights Act of 1965 closed loopholes in the first voting rights acts, (the Civil Rights Acts of 1957 and 1960), and represented the strongest legislation in history which prohibited racial discrimination in voting.

The very important Immigration and Nationality Act also became law in 1965. It abolished the U.S.' immigration quota policy which had been the law of the land since the early 20th century, which severely disadvantaged Asian, Latin American and African immigrants. The quotas did not apply to immigrants from independent nations of the Western Hemisphere, providing a significant advantage to European immigrants. In a symbolic move, President Johnson signed the legislation at the foot of the Statue of Liberty

arenas. The Act put an end to segregation and was intended to address discrimination in most areas of society.

The following year, Congress passed and President Johnson signed the Voting Rights Act of 1965. It was one of the few laws which at the time of its passage, was enacted virtually for the benefit of specifically one group. The unambiguous intent of the Act was to make illegal, the unreservedly discriminatory voter registration and intimidation practices that had been widely used for decades throughout much of the South, to prevent African Americans from registering to vote.

Two years later in 1967, the Age Discrimination in Employment Act, (ADEA) was passed and signed into law. The ADEA made it illegal for employers to discriminate against employees who are forty years old and above. With the passage of the law, employers could, among many other things, no longer engage in the then common practice of laying off employees who the employer feared would, due to their age, begin to use more health benefits, and/or who were being paid a higher salary than younger workers. The law established that laying off and otherwise discriminating against workers for those reasons was patently discriminatory. [240]

> [Although Section 504 or the Rehabilitation Act of 1973 prohibited recipients of federal financial assistance from discriminating against qualified individuals with disabilities in employment, in their programs and activities, it wasn't until 1990 that we saw legislation requiring that our society-at-large be more physically accessible to Americans with disabilities and outlawing discrimination against them, as well as those with a history of disability and those **perceived** to have a disability. It happened with the passage of the Americans with Disabilities Act, (ADA)

[240] Although Congress has never enacted legislation protecting **younger** employees from age discrimination, many states, counties and municipalities have.

> of 1990. I have often wondered why this **enormously** significant piece of legislation, affecting the lives of tens of millions of our fellow Americans, came so late in our history and why our awareness of the **need** for the law was so late in coming. I wonder how as a group, Americans with disabilities would be faring today, had the ADA been passed in the 1960's with all of our nation's other anti-discrimination legislation. A much broader and more in-depth discussion of the ADA will be contained in the third installment of *We Are One*, "Sometimes the Same is a Little Different"]

All of the Civil Rights laws passed in the 1960's, were designed to fling wide open, the doors of opportunity which for centuries, had been so tightly closed, which had indeed been cemented **shut,** for Americans of Color, for women, for religious minorities and for immigrants. President Johnson's National Advisory Commission on Civil Disorders, (widely known as the Kerner Commission), described quite aptly in its 1967 report, what was then the nation's racial condition:

> "Our nation is moving toward two societies, one black, one white, separate and unequal." [241]

The Kerner Commission report made clear that if we did nothing to address what were then the present day residual effects of past discrimination, the result, in the future, would be a larger and larger percentage of the American population that was under-educated, under-employed and thus **stuck** in abject poverty and political disenfranchisement. The possibility of such a nation thirty-to-fifty years hence, (i.e., in present day America), was frightening at the time. Thus, the need to give people, **all** people a fair chance to become educated and to join the ranks of the middle class, became crystal clear. It was patently obvious that requiring equal treatment for all Americans was not only the **right**

[241] If it were written today, the report would, of course, be inclusive of many more ethnic groups.

thing to do. It was clear that as a nation, it was undeniably in our **self-interest** to do.

Had we **not**, in the 1960's begun to work in earnest on discrimination, I shudder to think where as a nation, we would be today with respect to equality and understanding of our racial, sex, religious, age and nationality differences. **That** is an alternate reality that I rejoice in saying is unknown to us.

I am thankful that after having lost very nearly a full century after the Civil War during which we did **nothing** to undue our racial mistakes of the past, (while ostensibly engaging in every conceivable thing to do just the **opposite**), I am overjoyed that we **did** start down that road of recovery during the 1960's, the era of my childhood.

The Second R:

- **Representation 1970's Affirmative Action**

  * A remedy for the present day effects of past discrimination . . . .
  * Focuses on underrepresentation
  * Requires a good faith effort by employers to make their workforce generally reflect their local metropolitan area
  * Consequences for non-compliance

The legal mandates for Affirmative Action, including Executive Order 11246, came in the 1960's, but it was in the 1970's that attempts to **implement** Affirmative Action began to capture our attention as a nation.[242] With the implementation of Executive Orders mandating Affirmative Action, we began to work earnestly on the extreme **under-representation** of primarily Americans of Color and women, in the American workforce. Attention was on the extreme under-representation and indeed often the complete **absence** of women and Americans of Color among the ranks of police officers, fire fighters, manufacturing industry assembly line workers, city bus drivers, college presidents, corporate CEOs and in hundreds of other job categories. In the 1960's, even **after** passage of the Civil Rights Act of 1964, with the exception of those employed primarily in either the U.S. Post Office or in segregated school systems, Americans of Color were still, overwhelmingly employed in low wage jobs as elevator operators, janitors, maids, and bell hops. Additionally, a glass ceiling for women was still alive and well in the American workforce.

It was clear that the economic and social results of our long history of racism and sexism were going to remain with us for a **very** long time into the future if all we did as a nation, was to **outlaw** discrimination. In 1964, after 345 years of enslavement,

---

[242] Executive Order 11246 required most employers that received Federal funding to make a good faith effort to diversify their workforce at all levels.

discrimination, harassment and violence, if we had done nothing other than simply **outlaw** discrimination, the expectation that Americans of Color would then be able to compete equally in society, would have been akin to expecting a ten year old who had been prohibited from going to school all her life, to enter fifth grade, sit in her classroom and learn like all the other kids. The "catch up" time required to learn the alphabet and then to read, and to also learn numbers and then to do simple arithmetic, would have been enormous. That expectation, when applied to African Americans and other Americans of Color may be summarized as follows:

> "Ok, we've made discrimination illegal. Now go out there and compete equally with everybody else".

It would have been both utterly unfair and ridiculously unrealistic. If as a nation, we had decided to simply make discrimination illegal and do nothing more to address the **present day** effects of historical racism, we would today, be paying dearly for that grave mistake. We **had** to have another tool to "**jump start**" our way out of the lingering effects of our tragic racial past. Affirmative Action was that tool. Affirmative Action was developed as a means of **accelerating** us toward a more just society, of helping us to march **more quickly** toward the goal of racial equality. It was a way of trying to make up valuable and precious time which we had squandered for so long, time which was critical to our American future. Had we not wasted the ninety-nine years after the Civil War, there would probably have never been a **need** for Affirmative Action as late as the 1960's and 70's. Consider:

The Facts About the Need for Affirmative Action:

* It was never intended to change the past. The past is gone and cannot be changed.

* It was an attempt to dismantle the **present day** lingering **effects** of past discrimination.

* It was intended to be a **temporary** measure, used only until economic parity for the disenfranchised had been reached.

* The American history of racial discrimination has affected those who were the targets of discrimination in all aspects of their lives, and specifically in the areas of employment, housing and education. Employment, housing and education are totally and fully inter-related as follows:

* Education, i.e. public schools, are supported by the real estate values/taxes of their communities. Thus, the quality of the public schools in communities in which the real estate tax base is very low, is also very low;

* When the quality of a community's schools is poor, its children are poorly educated. As adults, those children can therefore not secure employment which pays well enough for them to be able to afford to buy a home; and finally,

* If the majority of the residents of a community cannot afford to be home owners, that community's real estate tax base will not be able to support quality public schools.

* In essence, no good housing, no good schools. No good schools, no good jobs. No good jobs, no good housing.

* Start at any one of the three points and the outcome is the same. It is a **vicious** cycle.

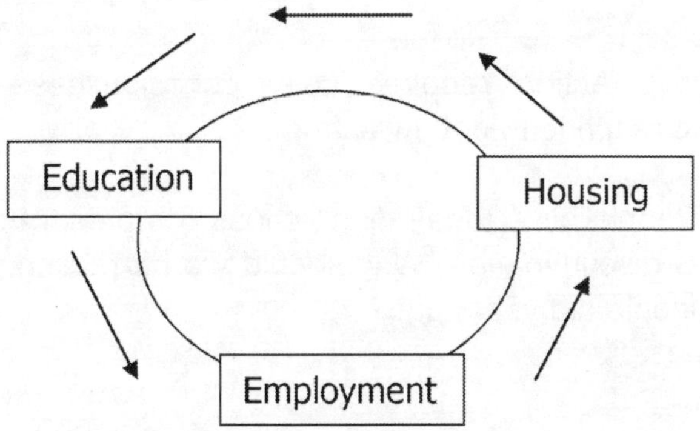

The Inter-Relationship of Education, Employment and Housing

* The objective of Affirmative Action was to break that cycle, to deal it a definitive and final death blow. The stark recognition was that if we **didn't** do what we **could** do to end that three-pronged cycle of oppression, the racial inequities in which our history had resulted and with which we were very clearly still living, would continue well into the future, perhaps becoming **frighteningly** worse over time. It would be a future in which **our** children and our **children's** children would suffer the consequences of our foolish inaction.

* While the original objective of Affirmative Action was to address the present day, lingering effects of past discrimination, Affirmative Action also has the significant advantage of bringing a valuable diversity of thought, outlook and life experience that significantly benefits both institutions and the people within them. Attorney and Harvard Law Professor Lani Guinier has stated that with our present and future contributions, women and Americans of Color arrive at institutions bearing gifts versus grievances.

Common responses to Affirmative Action:

1. Affirmative Action is bad for employers, and in some settings, may even lead to dangerous work conditions because it requires the lowering of standards.

2. Affirmative Action requires color consciousness—the very thing we're trying to get away from.

3. White People alive today didn't cause the present day effects of racial discrimination. Why should we be punished for what white people did years ago?

Responses to the Common Responses to Affirmative Action:

1. **Affirmative Action is bad for employers, and in some settings, may even lead to dangerous work conditions because it requires the lowering of standards.**

   Affirmative Action does **not** require the lowering of standards—any standards. Employers are not required to hire **anyone** who does not meet the minimum standards of the job for which s/he has applied. **Within** the pool of qualified applicants, however, employers **are** allowed to choose the applicant whom they believe best fits their employment needs. Employers were **never** required, even **before** Affirmative Action, to choose the applicant with the very **highest** test score, or **the** most years of experience. **Of those who are qualified**, employers have **always** been able to choose, and **have** always chosen whomever they wished. If, for a sales job, for example, it is highly advantageous for the successful applicant to have a pleasant personality, and if there were two qualified European American male applicants for the position, as long as both men **passed** the qualifying exam, the employer has always been allowed to choose the man who was judged in the interview process to have the nicer personality even if he did not score **as** highly on the exam as the other man.

   Furthermore, employers have always had discretion to determine the narrowly-tailored qualifications that are important to meet the business necessities of their field of employment. **Affirmative Action did not change that**. In the context of race, therefore, if, for example, the employer has made the business decision to try to improve the quality of the services that it provides to senior citizens by hiring employees who have more **experience** working with seniors, as between two applicants, (both of whom have been judged to meet the minimum qualifications for the job), if the applicant who has the more extensive experience working with seniors is an Asian American woman, and the other applicant is European American, the employer has the right to hire the Asian American applicant even if she did not score as highly on the qualifying exam and has fewer overall years of work experience than the other applicant.

Finally, Affirmative Action required not the **lowering** of employment standards, but rather the **review** of them. The goal of such reviews was to ensure that those standards were truly business related and not a pretext for discrimination**.** **Employers are allowed to have any standard they choose for all of their positions** as long as those standards are narrowly tailored to meet a legitimate business necessity.

If, for example, an employer can successfully demonstrate that it's requirement that fire fighters weigh at least one hundred seventy-five pounds, is necessary in order for fire fighters to be able to safely lift, carry and hold industry standard water hoses for a specified minimum period of time, the weight requirement would likely be determined to not discriminate against women, (who on average, weigh less than men within all height ranges), because: 1. It is designed to meet a legitimate business necessity, (the safe handling of heavy water hoses); and, 2. The requirement is narrowly tailored to meet that necessity, i.e., it is not so broad, (requiring, for example, that applicants be "of an appropriate weight"), as to disqualify individuals who may indeed be able to perform the job.

What employers can**not** do, is have a standard that disproportionately disqualifies applicants based upon a protected category, (race, gender, color, national origin, religion and a few others), which either does **not** meet a legitimate business necessity, and/or which is so broad that it disproportionately disqualifies many applicants who are indeed capable of performing in the job successfully.[243] Thus, when standards were thrown out following an Affirmative Action review, it was not done so to allow People of Color and women to qualify for jobs. It was done, rather, for one of two reasons: 1. The standard or requirement was found to **not** be necessary to meet a legitimate business necessity, a requirement, for example, that a successful applicant for a job as a child care provider in a day care center be able to teach the children basic calculus, since teaching basic calculus to children in a day care center is not a legitimate business necessity for the running of a day care center; or, 2. The standard or requirement was so broad as to disqualify applicants who are indeed able to do the job, the requirement, for example, that the successful applicant for a job as a driver for an overnight package delivery company have a minimum score on a test which is not related to the essential functions of the driver job. In this instance, if the test disproportionately impacts applicants of color, for example, who are perfectly able to do the job but who do not on average, get the required score on the test, the test will likely be determined to be discriminatory on its face since it both is not related to the essential functions of the driver job **and** disproportionately disqualifies people based on a protected category. In order for the test to stand, the employer would have to show both that it is directly relevant to the duties of a package delivery truck driver and that passage of it is necessary in order to carry out the duties of a driver.

> [It was quite often the case that when job requirements were changed after an Affirmative Action review, many

---

243 A police department, for example, could not have a requirement that successful applicants must be able to run at a certain speed if the requirement disproportionately disqualifies women, and older male members of the force are **also** not able to meet the same requirement.

European American male applicants were also helped in the process, since the discriminatory standards often disqualified many of them as well.]

As long as an employer is able to establish that the standard or requirement under review is necessary to meet a legitimate business standard and is narrowly-tailored to do so, the standard**, even if it disproportionately impacts people based upon a protected category**, will be allowed to stand. If the employer is unable to demonstrate either, the requirement will be determined to be a pretext for discrimination.[244]

2. Affirmative Action requires color consciousness—the very thing we're trying to get away from.

Justice Harry Blackmun made the observation in the landmark 1978 Regents of the University of California v. Bakke case, that, "In order to move beyond racism, we must first take race into account."

I believe that what Justice Blackmun was saying in that comment can be described by the following story of FTR:[245]

244 There are no protected **people**. There are only protected **categories** such as disability, gender, religion, race and others. Thus, the legal prohibition against, for example, race discrimination, protects **all** people from such treatment, People of Color **and** European Americans. Likewise, the prohibition against gender discrimination protects all people, both women **and** men from being treated differently based upon gender. With the exception of the ADA, which was passed for a specific group of people, the same is true for the other prohibitions against discrimination. It is for that reason that there is no such thing as "reverse discrimination." There is only discrimination, irrespective of who is being discriminated against.

245 To illustrate the need for Affirmative Action, President Johnson referred to the unfairness of bringing to the starting line of a race to

Consider a society in which a minority of the population, when outside of their homes, was required to walk with their legs tied together, and that **in** this society, there was an annual five mile race for all residents. The runners' performance in the race determined the number of the community's children who would be allowed to attend college the following year—its only hope of being prosperous in the future. The "tied minority" was allowed to run one representative in the race every year, but that contestant, because his legs were tied, could, of course, only hop. He did so, as fast as he could, but nonetheless, every year, the quite predictable result was always the same. He'd come in dead last.

Then suddenly one year, to everyone's surprise, an hour before the race was to begin, the judges decided that it really wasn't at all fair for that runner to be required to "run" the race with his legs tied and thus, decided to everyone's utter surprise, to untie them.

Upon untying his legs, however, the judges expected the formerly tied runner, FTR, to immediately compete on a level playing field with all of the other runners whose legs had **never** been tied. Because FTR's legs had been tied together for so long, however, he was unable to compete successfully with the other runners. The circulation in his legs had been compromised, his knees were weak from his having jumped on them for so long, and because he had never run before, his balance was off.

Consequently, in a sincere effort to be fair and to try to compensate FTR for his disadvantages, (which they realized he had acquired through no fault of his own), the judges decided to allow FTR to start the race that year, ten yards ahead of the other runners who had always had use of both their legs and thus had been practicing running for a very

---

compete with all others, a man who for years had been hobbled by chains. That illustration provided the inspiration for the story of FTR.

long time. **At** that ten yard line, just before the race, FTR received five minutes of warm compresses to help improve the circulation in his legs, and support bandages for his knees. The judges knew that there was nothing they could do for FTR's balance problem. That was one result of his legs having been tied for so long that they knew they would **never** be able to make right for him. **If** his balance could improve at all, it would just have to do so on its own, over time.

The judges decided that FTR wouldn't have the ten yard advantage, the compresses and the bandages **forever**, just until he was able to run normally on his legs. At that time, he'd have to go back ten yards and start the race at the same start line as all the other runners. He'd have to compete on his own.

Now, upon hearing that FTR was going to be allowed the advanced ten yard starting point, all of the other runners were outraged. "It's not fair!" they shouted. "We weren't the ones who tied his legs together, so why should **we** be disadvantaged?" they asked with strident indignation. "His legs being tied in the past has absolutely nothing to do with the present and in fact, everybody should just forget about the past", they very passionately insisted. They insisted that FTR should start at the established starting line just like all the other runners, not get the compresses and support bandages, stop wallowing in the past and playing the "tied up card".

The judges explained over and over to the other runners that it wasn't at all unfair of them to give FTR the assistance because he was only being given the chance to **catch up** to them. They explained that he was at that point, not as physically able as they were not due to anything **he** had done wrong, but because of a wrong that had been committed **against** him by their ancestors, through absolutely no fault of his own. They explained that as **soon** as FTR was as physically able as they were, he'd have to compete on his own individual merit, from the same starting point, and without the compresses and bandages, just like all the other runners.

The never-tied runners then very angrily told the judges that it was totally unfair for them to have to pay for the sins of their ancestors. The judges responded that they were absolutely **not** being made to pay for their ancestors' actions because what they were doing for FTR had nothing whatsoever to do with paying for the **past**, but rather that it was about doing the right thing by FTR in the **present**.

The judges attempted to explain that trying to level the playing field for FTR is the moral, the just and the fair thing to do and that doing so required that his **societally-imposed** disadvantage first be taken into account. In other words, that in order to get beyond their society's history of having tied FTR's legs for so long, they must, at least for a while, attempt to address the **present day effect** of that history. They tried to make the never-tied runners understand that although it was true that even **without** the head start, compresses and bandages, FTR would **eventually** heal and catch up to them, it would take him a significantly longer time to do so. Further, the judges wanted the never—tied runners to see that the longer FTR was disadvantaged, the longer their entire society remained fundamentally unfair and thus socially unstable. They tried to make them see that for that reason, getting FTR on an equal footing with all of the rest of the runners as quickly as possible, wasn't **only** the moral, just and **fair** thing to do, it was also the **wise** thing to do for the sake of their entire society. The judges wanted the never-tied runners to see that the more they worked on the issue now, the more stable and healthy a society they would pass on to their children.

The more personally secure, emotionally mature and psychologically sophisticated never-tied runners heard and understood. The majority, however, did not, and remained angry about FTR's "special treatment" and the "reverse discrimination" against them that it represented.

That story illustrates why I believe that Justice Blackmun got it right: "In order to move **beyond** racism, we must first take race into account." Affirmative Action does **indeed** require us to be color conscious for a period. but in order to move beyond color consciousness, **in view of our history**, we must first take color into account.

3. **White People alive today didn't cause the present day effects of racial discrimination. Why should we be punished for what White People did years ago?**

   It is **of course** true that European Americans alive today had absolutely nothing to do with setting up the system of unearned racial privilege in which we all now live. Contemporary European Americans are historically innocent. That historical innocence, however, negates neither our collective moral responsibility nor the practical necessity to end in contemporary American society, the **vestige** of that history—racial privilege.

   Understanding how that privilege affects all of our lives today, is a critical first step in that venture. We must increase our understanding **specifically**, of what is the same and what is different about racial privilege for contemporary European Americans and contemporary Americans of Color.

   What is the **same**, is that **both** groups are historically innocent. **Neither** did anything to set up today's system of racially based unearned privilege. That system was established long before **any** of us alive today, were born. We are all **equally** innocent in this regard.

   What is very **different** about race-based unearned privilege for the two groups, however, are the following:

   A. The ancestors of European Americans are **responsible** for our present system of unearned racial privilege. The ancestors of Americans of Color, are not. Further, the ancestors of Americans of Color were the innocent **victims** of that system.

B. Contemporary European Americans are the **benefactors** of historical and present-day unearned racial privilege. Contemporary Americans of Color are **not**. Indeed, contemporary Americans of Color are the recipients of the **opposite** of racial privilege—daily indignities.

In light of those two historical and present-day facts, not only is Affirmative Action, **not** unfair, not only is it **not** "reverse discrimination" it is indeed the fair thing, it is the right thing, it is the moral thing to do.

A different analogy uses a playground toy. Consider a see saw in which Americans of Color are on one seat and European Americans are on the other. European Americans **from before the United States even became a nation**, have artificially kept themselves in the "up" position by giving themselves every advantage at the expense of Americans of Color, (i.e., by "stacking the deck" **for** themselves and **against** Americans of Color) in every single aspect of life. People of Color, conversely, have been artificially kept in the "**down**" position by being **deprived** of every advantage by European Americans, (through slavery, discrimination, harassment and violence) in every single aspect of life.

In order to bring everyone to the **same** level, the seat of European Americans must go down and the seat of Americans of Color must come up. That "going up" and "coming down" process, the process of making equitable, our system in which millions of us have been historically **under**-privileged and millions of **others** of us have been historically **over**-privileged, will undoubtedly be uncomfortable to those who have been in the over-privileged position for so long. It will be particularly uncomfortable for the historically over-privileged who were not consciously aware that they **were** over-privileged.

If as a result of that discomfort, we decide as a society that taking such affirmative actions is wrong, if we believe that it constitutes discrimination against European Americans, the only other alternative is to allow Americans of Color to continue to suffer the present-day social and economic ravaging vestiges of historical racism for a far longer time than we otherwise would. That alternative, that choice, is utterly morally indefensible. It is also totally unwise for our country.

As previously stated, FTR, without his ten yard advantage, compresses and support bandages would **eventually** have caught up with the other runners. But . . . . it would have taken him a **much**, much longer time, during which he would have continued to suffer. Perhaps even more devastating is that all of the other tied-up people **watching** the race, would have become increasingly more disillusioned, with no hope of perhaps **ever** competing fairly in the race. That hopelessness would in turn have resulted in the well-known negative social consequences to a society of large scale despair in entire communities of "tied up" people, consequences which in time, spill out of those communities into society-at-large.

So, using FTR's example, our question concerning **American** society is whether, in view of all of our laws prohibiting racial discrimination in contemporary American society, Americans of Color will eventually "catch up", socially and economically with European Americans **without** affirmative actions to undo the present day vestiges of past discrimination? Yes, in all likelihood. But it will take a **significantly** longer time if those present day vestiges of past discrimination are **not** addressed affirmatively. We have lost so much time, indeed, a full century after the abolition of slavery. We have to move more quickly now toward the goals of racial equity and understanding. For those who are suffering the horrible present day effects of that past, it is moral, the right thing to do. For our **nation**, it is the prudent, the wise thing to do.

In view of current demographic projections that Americans of Color will comprise the majority of Americans within the next 35 years, a "natural", i.e., unaided progression of Americans of Color would result in so large an under-class of poorly educated, under employed, politically disenfranchised Americans, that the very social fabric of our nation may then be at risk. In such a scenario, the wealthy and upper middle class would likely find themselves more and more isolated from society's majority, living in gated communities, going to gated clubs and even shopping and worshipping in gated structures. Clearly, the work that we do on racial justice and understanding **today**, is squarely in the interest of our children's **tomorrows**—all of our children.

It is for that reason that it is good that Affirmative Action attempts to **speed up** the leveling of the social and economic playing fields—playing fields which have historically been tipped **severely** in favor of European Americans.

One of the most **powerful** responses to this question, however is that not only is Affirmative Action **not** a punishment for contemporary European Americans, the ironic truth is that for the following three reasons, it has actually **benefitted** European Americans, and specifically European American **women** more than any other single American group:

First, an unknown number of European American men who were small business owners, **on paper**, transferred ownership of their businesses to their wives, daughters and other female relatives. Since Affirmative Action is designed to benefit People of Color **and women**, by identifying their wives **on paper**, as the owner of their businesses, European American man were able to acquire for their businesses, all of the benefits of Affirmative Action.

Second, significantly more European Americans, in terms of both their actual numbers in society **and** as a percentage within the European American population, had the educational background and/or business experience or corporate "savvy" required to become a "minority contractor" and to take advantage of Affirmative Action in other available ways.

Third, European American men, when given the choice between hiring and/or doing business with an American of Color and a European American **woman**, would most **often** choose the person with whom he was most **comfortable**—the white woman.

In the final analysis, in helping white **women** as much as it did, (either legitimately, as in the many cases in which Affirmative Action helped white women to get jobs, or as just a name on a piece of paper as the owner of a male relative's business), Affirmative Action actually helped more white **families**, than it did families of color.[246]

The most **compelling** response to the question, however, is that in addition to the **morality** of Affirmative Action as it relates to Americans of **Color**, **and** in addition to the **benefits** that Affirmative Action has in the **past** bestowed on **European** Americans, Affirmative Action is essential to the **future**, to **all** our futures, **including** European Americans because as I learned in a college sociology course many years ago, whatever dysfunction is plaguing the "**ghetto**" in the present, left unabated, will, in roughly fifteen to thirty years, be just as severely plaguing the **suburbs** in the future.

The following two facts are extremely interesting within this context:

First, the life expectancy of both women and men in all age groups in low income communities of color in inner cities, is

246 It isn't only Affirmative Action, however, that has overwhelmingly benefitted far more European Americans than Americans of Color. Because European Americans have been our nation's majority population, a number of **other** civil rights laws, (among them, the Equal Pay Act, the Age Discrimination in Employment Act, Section 503 of the Rehabilitation Act and the Americans with Disabilities Act,) have also helped many more European Americans, by their sheer numbers alone, than they have Americans of Color.

and for many years has **been**, on average, significantly lower than that of European Americans in the same economic strata. It is fascinating, therefore, that (as reported in the article,"*What's Killing Poor White Women*" published in the September 3, 2013 edition of *The American Prospect*, (http://prospect.org/article/whats-killing-poor-white-women) the life expectancy of European American women who did not graduate from high school has declined over the past 18 years such that now, they can expect to die five years **earlier** than the generation before them![247] The team of researchers at the University of Illinois at Chicago who made the discovery, also found that white men who did not complete high school had also lost life expectancy, three years, specifically. The results of prior studies indicated that poor white Americans with the least education actually began to die young in the 2000's.

Second, the kind of epidemic gun violence that has characterized inner city American neighborhoods of color for approximately the past forty years, is now present in American society-at-large. Mass shootings have sadly, tragically, dreadfully, disastrously, **heartbreakingly**, become our "new normal." The ease with which it has been possible to secure all manner of guns in "the hood", (including semi-automatic pistols and rifles), is the same ease which allowed the shooters in all of the mass killings that have occurred in predominantly white communities since the beginning of this very young century, to shoot and kill innocents in a rampage—Columbine, Colorado, Blacksburg, Virginia, Newtown Connecticut, Aurora Colorado and others. Gun violence was **endemic** in inner cities for decades. Still, we did nothing about it. Now, European Americans and indeed, **our entire society** is living in the shadow of the possibility of an outbreak of gun violence at any time, in any place. **None** of our institutions

---

247 American Prospect, "What's Killing Poor White Women?" http://prospect.org/article/whats-killing-poor-white-women
The five-year drop in the life expectancy of white women was first reported in August, 2012 Journal, *Health Affairs*.

are exempt, not our colleges and universities, not our high schools, not our elementary schools, not our places of worship, not our movie theaters, not our shopping malls, not a single one of our institutions is exempt.

Additionally, for several years, all of the **shooters** of whom I was aware, were **also** European American, Eric Harris and Dylan Klebold in the 1999 Columbine High School shootings, Michael McDermott in the 2000 Wakefield Massachusetts shootings, Doug Williams in the 2003 Lockheed plant in Meridian Mississippi, among them. Over time, however, we saw an Asian American shooter, Cho Seung-Hui, in the Virginia Tech murders, African American shooters John Allen Muhammad and Lee Boyd Malvo in the Washington, DC. sniper murders, and Palestinian American shooter Nidal Malik Hasan in the Fort Hood murders. We have also seen one or two Latin American and one Indigenous mass murderer. What began as the crime of white mass murderers, in just a few years, has become the crime of a multicultural cast of men.

We can, of course, add the proliferation of illegal drugs to this discussion for neither drugs nor drug **use** knows any boundaries.

If as a society, we choose to **not** act affirmatively to level the **totally** imbalanced American economic and social "playing fields", we do so at the peril of our entire society and all of us, Americans of Color **and** European Americans, will suffer the grave consequences.

The Earth is indeed round and what goes around, does indeed **eventually** come around.

It was Dr. King, who, in his typically exceptionally eloquent manner, said it best,

> "We are caught in an inexcapable network of mutuality, tied in a single garment of destiny. Whatever affects one directly affects all indirectly."

I long to see us as a nation, reach the point at which a critical mass of European Americans develop a deep understanding of the reality that affirmative efforts to address present-day vestiges of past harms committed against Americans of Color are **not** meant to be and in reality **are** not punishment for the sins of their ancestors. I hope that that critical mass indeed begins to understand that such actions are intended to address the **present day, lingering effects** of our dreadful national historical nightmare of slavery, racial discrimination, harassment and violence. I hope that they begin to understand that as human beings, as members of the same species, we **all** benefit from our giving a "hand up" to each other, whether we be an American of Color, or a European American who is living in poverty. I long for the day on which all Americans understand that doing so is both our moral imperative and is critically important to our future. The point at which that happens will mark a **significant** turning point in race relations in the United States.

The Third R:

- ❑ **Relationships 1980's Diversity Training**

- ❖ **Awareness**
  - ✓ **Personal Awareness**
  - ✓ **Awareness of Societal Dynamics**
  - ✓ **Awareness of Workplace Patterns**

- ❖ **Skills**
  - ✓ **Personal Behavior**
  - ✓ **Intervention Abilities**

It was in the 1980's that in diversity training sessions, we largely began, as a society, to work on cross-cultural relationships in work environments. The quality of the sessions ranged from excellent, leading to increased insight and understanding and thus improved relationships, to poor, leading to resentment and animosity.

In the best training, people learn about how as children, we are exposed to bias. They learn about unearned privilege, about the daily indignities, about the difference between individual, institutional and societal/structural bias. They have the opportunity to reflect on their personal behavior, to learn about the difference between one's **intent** and the **impact** of one's actions and about what as individuals, they can all do, in terms of specific behaviors, (in both relating to others, and intervening as an ally in the presence of a racial indignity), to create a more inclusive and respectful work environment for all. They discuss their particular workplace dynamics, brainstorm ways in which those dynamics can be improved and commit to making those improvements.

Some of the most gratifying training that I have done has been as a co-facilitator with one of my two dear friends, Tom Finn and Jack Straton, both of whom are European American. On more than one occasion, a participant has told me after a session that I co-facilitated with either Tom or Jack, that s/he learned as much from **watching** Tom and I or Jack and I work together, as s/he did from the presentation itself. I believe that what the attendees may find so powerful, is the **modeling** that Jack and I and that Tom and I provide in our sessions, modeling that they may never have seen before—a model of our great trust **of** and total respect **for** each other, a model of obvious deep and genuine friendship across both racial and gender lines.

In sessions that I have facilitated on my own, I have described for the participants, the nature of my friendships with Jack and Tom, friendships, each of which, spans more than twenty years. I tell them about all the things that Jack and I have in common, so many, in fact, that his partner, Theresa, has told us over many years, that Jack, (6' tall with blonde, but now gray, hair and blue eyes, and I, (5'3" tall with black hair and eyes), are twins. I share with them that Tom and I have shared deeply with each other, stories about our families and their histories without either feelings or responses such, as, “Well your people weren’t the only ones that were discriminated against you know. Everybody had it hard. When my ancestors came over from Ireland, they were discriminated against too” and, “Well at least your people weren’t slaves”. I share with the participants that we **do** not, nor have we **ever** done that with each other. I share with them that we have listened to each other with interest, curiosity and profound respect, learning tremendously each time. I share with participants how we engage with each other in that and in other ways that are respectful of who we are both as individuals and as members or our cultural groups.

Finally, I share with participants that that is the manner in which I have had **past** friendships and maintained all of my **current** friendships with all of my European American friends, LJ, and Sandra, Theresa and Jack, Tom and Kathy, Jennell and David, Susan and Nathan, Laura and Matt, Mark and Celie, and many others. I wish that I could bottle the sincere affection that I have shared with all of my European American friends, duplicate it and make it available to all who wish to experience it. Our friendships would be deeper and more genuine for it and our world would truly be a more emotionally intelligent, more compassionate place for it.

The Fourth R:

❑ **Results**	**1990s to Present**	**Inclusivity, Respect & Professionalism**

In work environments in which the lessons learned in excellent diversity training sessions are truly understood **and practiced**, employers have seen significant improvement in employee relationships and thus in productivity and therefore ultimately, in efficiency and/or profits. It is the proverbial “chickens coming home to roost”.

Note Six

How As Children, We Acquire Racial Stereotypes and Their Accompanying Feelings[248]

One of the lecturettes which I most enjoy sharing with participants in my diversity workshops explains the process of how we develop stereotypes and their accompanying feelings. It has the following seven main points:

1. No human being is born with any of the "isms", racism, colorism, sexism, anti-Semitism, heterosexism, classism, ableism or any other form of xenophobia. We are all born innocent human beings.[249]

2. As we began to grow up, however, we, (the vast majority, if not all of us), were exposed to a lot of misinformation about those who the adults in our lives considered to be different from ourselves and our families.

3. That misinformation was combined with a lack of exposure to and experience with those "different others".

4. The misinformation that we received came to us from a variety of sources. For some of us, it was our parents and other adult relatives. For some of us it was from what we were and were

---

248 While this note is focused specifically upon how we acquire **racial stereotypes**, we actually acquire **other** stereotypes in similar fashion.

249 The Rochester Baby Lab has uncovered information that seems to indicate that we **may** be born with an inclination toward things that are more like us than those that are less so, however, it is unknown whether that possible inclination later results in prejudice based upon race, gender, age and other such differences.

not taught in school about the histories of Americans of Color. For some of us, the misinformation about different groups of human beings came from our religious training. For many of us, it came from the images of particular groups of people to which we were exposed in the media.

5. All of that misinformation didn't just go in one ear and out the other. Instead, it went into our subconscious minds and became "mental tapes".

6. Those mental tapes didn't just stay locked up deeply within the recesses of our subconscious minds. Instead, they began to affect us on three levels. They began to affect our thoughts, our feelings and our behaviors. In other words, we went on "automatic pilot" with regard to those whom we consider to be different. Many of us were fully on automatic pilot with regard to racial and other differences very early in life.

7. Fortunately, however, it is possible that over time, and with concerted effort, we can learn to respond to people whom we consider to be different from ourselves and our families as individuals. We **can** become significantly more psychologically healthy and emotionally clear.

I share that lecturette with participants because I want them to know that **none** of us are at fault for having acquired our mental tapes and that as adults, we have the ability, to a large extent, to greatly "turn down the volume" of the messages that are on our tapes. I want them to know that deep and significant personal growth in this area is indeed possible for all of us. I want them to know that they may not be seeing others clearly but that the great potential exists for them to do so, if they choose. I want them to know that as human beings, we truly **can** choose. We can choose to grow.

Study Group Questions

In dialogue groups in which the subjects of race and racism are the topics of discussion, the guidance of a trained facilitator can be extremely helpful if the participants are relatively inexperienced in either conducting and/or participating in such conversations. In the absence of a facilitator, utilization of the principles of compassionate conversation in the group's dialogues can be quite valuable. [250]

Consideration of the following questions provides a starting point for dialogue groups wishing to explore more deeply, the content of *RACE: My Story & Humanity's Bottom Line:*

1. With regard to my early racial messages:

- With what racial messages was I raised?
- How much exposure did I have to Americans of other races in my formative years?
- Are the information that I received and the amount of exposure that I had to Americans of other races in my formative years still impacting me today? If so how? If not, why not?

2. As a result of reading *RACE: My Story & Humanity's Bottom Line*, what do I now fundamentally understand about the following subjects:

- The science/biology of race
- The history of racism in the United States

---

[250] For more information on the principles of compassionate conversation, see the websites of The Compassionate Listening Project and the Public Conversations Project.
http://www.compassionatelistening.org/trainings/about
http://www.publicconversations.org/docs/resources/Jams_website.pdf

- How that history has impacted Americans of Color
- How that history has impacted European Americans
- How that history continues to impact Americans of Color
- How that history continues to impact European Americans
- Unearned racial privilege
- The daily indignities
- The impact of the common responses in conversations about the daily indignities
- Racial justice and equality
- Race relations

3. Is Affirmative Action reverse discrimination? If so why? If not, why not?

4. Is there a legal case for reparations to Indigenous People by the American government? A moral case? If so, what is it? If not, why not?

5. Is there a legal case for reparations to African Americans by the American government? A moral case? If so what is it? If not, why not?

6. Is there a legal case for reparations to Latin Americans by the American government? A moral case? If so what is it? If not, why not?

7. Is there a case for reparations to any other Americans by the American Government? If so, to which group(s) and what is that case? If not, why not?

8. How might the United States be different today if from the beginning of the country, all people, People Indigenous to North America, African People, European People and Asian People, had been free to make contributions in all areas of human endeavor?[251]

---

[251] In such an alternate history, of course, Indigenous People would had to have welcomed people from the other continents to settle in their

9. Where is the United States today with respect to racial understanding, i.e., the awareness of most Americans of the fundamental facts about:

- The science/biology of race
- The history of racism in the United States
- How that history has impacted Americans of Color
- How that history has impacted European Americans
- How that history continues to impact Americans of Color
- How that history continues to impact European Americans
- Unearned racial privilege
- The daily indignities
- Affirmative Action
- The impact of the common responses in conversations about the daily indignities
- Racial justice and equality
- Race relations

10. Would it make a difference in race relations in the United States if more European Americans had an increased awareness of the unearned racial privilege with which they live in American society? If so, what difference would it make? If the increased understanding of racial privilege by European Americans would **not** make a difference in race relations in the United States, why not?

11. Would it make a difference in race relation in the United States if more European Americans had a heightened awareness of the daily indignities experienced by Americans of Color? If so, specifically what difference would it make? If increased understanding by more European Americans of the daily indignities experienced by Americans of Color would **not** make a difference in race relations in the United States, why not?

12. Would it make a difference if more Americans of Color had an increased awareness of:

---

land, a prospect which I believe is quite unlikely.

* The great ancient civilizations of their original cultures
* The great achievements that Americans of Color have made in the United States
* If so, what difference would it make? If not, why would it not make a difference?

13. Would it make a difference if more European Americans had a heightened awareness of:

* The great ancient civilizations of the original cultures of Americans of Color
* The great achievements that Americans of Color have made in the United States
* If so, what specific difference would it make?

14. What are the fundamentals of true racial allyship?

15. What is the most powerful potential for good that racial allyship holds for:

- Individuals
- The United States
- The entire world

16. What can European Americans do to help:

- Heal the painful rifts within European American communities that result from the forms of oppression in which European Americans engage against each other in their own communities?

- Raise awareness among European Americans of many of the issues discussed in *RACE: My Story & Humanity's Bottom Line* in:

    o European American Communities; and,
    o American Communities of Color

17. What can Americans of Color do to help:

- Heal the painful rifts within our communities that result from colorism and other forms of oppression in which we engage against each other in our own communities?

- Raise awareness among Americans of Color of many of the issues discussed in *RACE: My Story & Humanity's Bottom Line* within:

    - American Communities of Color; and,
    - European American Communities

18. As a result of reading *RACE: My Story & Humanity's Bottom Line*, what did I learn, realize, or acknowledge that is most impactful, most profound for me?

- Why was that information, realization or acknowledgement so profound for me?
- How has it impacted my understanding of race?
- How has it impacted my understanding of racism?
- How will it impact my life?

19. If our dialogue group decided to take one action to help raise racial awareness, understanding and compassion either in our local community or elsewhere, what would it be?

20. What one action can our dialogue group take to increase racial justice in our community? In the world?

Short Video Clips

[Please note that the following lists of short video clips, documentaries, movies, television mini-series, training videos and websites do not contain the urls in the six Notes above.]

History

1. **Self-Portrayals of Ancient Egyptians on Pyramids and Other Egyptian Art (Be sure to scroll down the page.)**
   http://www.tuttartpitturasculturapoesiamusica.com/2011/03/ancient-egypt.html]

2. **St. George's Slave Castle**
   http://www.youtube.com/watch?v=Ow2rltUTQtY

3. **Afro Puerto Rico: the Island's Ties to Slavery**
   https://www.youtube.com/watch?v=dh-2E1KReBY

4. **Images of Segregation**
   https://www.youtube.com/watch?v=c-7eNRB2_0Q

5. **Oskar Schindler on the Holocaust**
   http://yearslaterwewouldremember.com/the-memoir-an-excerpt/media/

6. **Human Zoos**
   https://www.youtube.com/watch?v=xedc7pLWyRI]

7. **"Travelin' Man, Ricky Nelson**
   http://www.youtube.com/watch?v=0janfcZ8LUw

8. **The Chinese Exclusion Act**
   https://www.youtube.com/watch?v=hMXrdCNvL04
   https://www.youtube.com/watch?v=GwAhYUgg_uU

9. **Japanese/American Internment during World War II**
https://www.youtube.com/watch?v=6mr97qyKA2s

10. **The 442nd WWII Japanese American Regimental Combat Team**
http://www.youtube.com/watch?v=pu390kDDbi8
https://www.youtube.com/watch?v=lIZC9ihafVs
https://www.youtube.com/watch?v=NOcnz9gvWal

http://www.youtube.com/watch?v=pu390kDDbi8

https://www.youtube.com/watch?v=NOcnz9gvWal

11. **Expulsion of (Mexican) American Citizens**
https://www.youtube.com/watch?v=RZ5pvg5-4Nk

12. **Marion Anderson Sings at the Lincoln Memorial**
http://www.youtube.com/watch?v=mAONYTMf2pk

13. **Dramatization of Dr. Kenneth Clark's Doll Experiment**
https://www.youtube.com/watch?v=85-EC_nDlpY

14. **Brown v. Board of Education**
https://www.youtube.com/watch?v=TTGHLdr-iak

15. **Dr. King Speaking about Mahatma Gandhi's Influence on Him**
https://www.youtube.com/watch?v=-JsbbFHpfSc

16. **Early 1955 Bus Boycotts, Montgomery, Alabama**
http://www.history.com/topics/rosa-parks/videos#bet-you-didnt-know-rosa-parks

17. **"Rosa Parks: Taking a Stand"**
http://www.youtube.com/watch?v=49ALwDsUzrk

18. **Desegregation of Little Rock Central High School**
http://www.youtube.com/watch?v=RGjNqrQBUno
http://www.youtube.com/watch?v=75dhe5Zsy8k

19. The Story of Ruby Bridges
http://www.youtube.com/watch?v=dYM-72AftEo

20. The Sit-Ins of the Civil Rights Movement
http://www.youtube.com/watch?v=iw_Jn-uqWaA

21. The Freedom Riders of the Civil Rights Movement
http://www.youtube.com/watch?v=DcvsWXrS2PI
http://www.youtube.com/watch?v=6T50Ym94k8Y

22. Murder of Civil Rights Activist Medgar Evers
http://www.biography.com/people/medgar-evers-9542324

23. Birmingham Children's Crusade Mighty Times: The Children's March
https://www.youtube.com/watch?v=5c113fq3vhQ

24. March on Washington, August 28, 1963
http://www.youtube.com/watch?v=ZA9TJCV-tks

25. Dr. King's "I Have a Dream" Speech—March on Washington
http://www.youtube.com/watch?v=smEqnnklfYs

26. Ku Klux Klan Bombing of the 16th Street Baptist Church
http://www.youtube.com/watch?v=q-MuWDsv5pg

27. Fannie Lou Hamer—Part 1
https://www.youtube.com/watch?v=TC4CPv1yXaQ

28. Fannie Lou Hamer Part 2
https://www.youtube.com/watch?v=I5RGOhOS_Go

29. Fannie Lou Hamer Part 3
https://www.youtube.com/watch?v=WgaylCQQoRk

30. Assassination of Malcolm X
https://www.youtube.com/watch?v=imV4kqJNP_0

31. **Bloody Sunday**
http://facedl.com/fvideo.php?f=aqauqaoeqoaonokui&selma-alabama-1965-edmund-pettus-bridge-o

http://www.history.com/shows/mankind-the-story-of-all-of-us/videos/bloody-sunday-1965#

32. **Freedom Now: The Civil Rights Movement in Mississippi**
https://www.youtube.com/watch?v=9Kvk8BcUcc4

33. **President Kennedy Announces The Civil Rights Act**
http://www.youtube.com/watch?v=-srOvwG81lw

34. **President Lyndon B. Johnson Signs The Civil Rights Act**
http://www.youtube.com/watch?v=Bygv9u1G6Xo

35. **President Lyndon B. Johnson Signs The Voting Rights Act**
http://www.youtube.com/watch?v=Bygv9u1G6Xo

36. **Affirmative Action and White Privilege—Session One**
http://www.youtube.com/watch?v=vw7ZUAQsHXg

37. **Fair Housing Act: Looking Back, Looking Forward (History of the Fair Housing Act)**
http://www.youtube.com/watch?v=wdKzxSC7DTU

38. **President Johnson Signs the Fair Housing Act**
http://www.youtube.com/watch?v=IDo9mb6-su4

39. **Dr. King's Sermon—"The Drum Major Instinct"**
https://www.youtube.com/watch?v=BcuifZJdyaY

40. **Dr. King Speech on Black Self-Worth**
https://www.youtube.com/watch?v=HlvEiBRgp2M

41. **Dr. King's Last Speech**
http://www.youtube.com/watch?v=Oehry1JC9Rk

42. **Report of Dr. King's Assassination**
https://www.youtube.com/watch?v=cmOBbxgxKvo

43. **"On the Shoulders of Giants"—Movie about the Harlem Rens—Official Trailer**
http://kareemabduljabbar.com/osg/

44. **The Negro Leagues**
http://www.youtube.com/watch?v=9sa7y4lvl1E

45. **Jackie Robinson:**
https://www.youtube.com/watch?v=Ph2cKXA2Mjs

46. **Althea Gibson**
http://www.youtube.com/watch?v=-O2G3pUNdxU

47. **Arthur Ashe**
http://www.biography.com/people/arthur-ashe-9190544

More Recent History

1. **"Vincent Who"**
http://www.youtube.com/watch?v=I_rwnyM1vtE

2. **The Little Rock 9 on Oprah**
https://www.youtube.com/watch?v=aSp4Xdbd8Gk
https://www.youtube.com/watch?v=SAsh_PDr1cc

3. **New York Times' November 14, 2012 Article on the Release of the Audio of Atwater's Interview with Lamis, with the Audio Recording Embedded**
http://takingnote.blogs.nytimes.com/2012/11/14/lee-atwaters-southern-strategy-interview/

4. **Willie Horton Commercial of the 1988 George H. W. Bush Presidential Campaign**
https://www.youtube.com/watch?v=EC9j6Wfdq3o

5. **Jesse Helms' 1992 "Hands Commercial"**
   http://www.youtube.com/watch?v=KIyewCdXMzk

6. **Alleged Gunman in Wisconsin Sikh Temple Attack ID'd as Army Veteran: FBI Explores Links to White Supremacist Groups**
   http://usnews.nbcnews.com/_news/2012/08/06/13141505-alleged-gunman-in-wisconsin-sikh-temple-attack-idd-as-army-veteran-fbi-explores-links-to-white-supremacist-groups?lite

7. **Supreme Court Takes Huge Blow to Minority Voter Rights**
   http://www.youtube.com/watch?v=2Vt9-bXP3Uo

Current

1. **Work of Ms. Charlene Teter on Indigenous Mascots**
   http://www.youtube.com/watch?v=lEUl2keJK-w
   http://www.youtube.com/watch?v=8lUF95Thl7s
   http://www.pbs.org/pov/inwhosehonor/film_description.php#.UcSWPlbn99w

2. **White Privilege: Unpacking the Invisible Knapsack**
   https://www.youtube.com/watch?v=DRnoddGTMTY

3. **ABC's 20/20 What Would You Do: Racism in America-Part 1**
   http://www.youtube.com/watch?v=_cCQU0jt4cs

4. **ABC's 20/20 What Would You Do: Racism in America-Part 2**
   http://www.youtubpe.com/watch?v=VQHdbW36XjE

Other Short Videos Referenced

1. **"I Love My Hair", A Muppet Performance**
   http://www.youtube.com/watch?v=enpFde5rgmw

2. **"A Girl Like Me"**
   http://www.understandingrace.org/lived/video/

3. **The Dance Theater of Harlem**
   http://www.dancetheatreofharlem.org/

4. **Kids React to Cereal Commercial Featuring Inter-racial Couple**
   http://www.youtube.com/watch?v=VifdBFp5pnw

5. **Imagine a World Without Hate**
   http://www.youtube.com/watch?v=3KyvlMJefR4

6. **Charter for Compassion**
   http://www.youtube.com/watch?v=wktlwCPDd94]

7. **It's in Every One of Us**
   http://www.youtube.com/watch?v=op9sUiANKiE

8. **Reflections from Space**
   http://www.youtube.com/watch?v=OGdHmaFGVQk

Documentaries

Science

1. **The Journey of Man: A Genetic Odyssey**
   http://www.youtube.com/watch?v=NPycvh-mYbE

2. **The Real Eve**
   http://www.youtube.com/watch?v=yzAsXRq0XcQ

3. **Scientific Racism: The Eugenics of Social Darwinism**
   https://www.youtube.com/watch?v=-eX5T68TQIo

History

1. **The Canary Effect**
   http://topdocumentaryfilms.com/canary-effect/

2. **In Whose Honor**
   http://www.newday.com/films/InWhoseHonor.html

3. **Who Killed Vincent Chin**
   http://www.youtube.com/watch?v=oX-L6yOtOaM

4. **The Zoot Suit Riots**
   http://www.pbs.org/wgbh/amex/zoot/eng_peopleevents/e_riots.html

5. **Negro Leagues NHD Documentary**
   http://www.youtube.com/watch?v=9sa7y4lvl1E

6. **The Murder of Emmitt Till**
   https://www.youtube.com/watch?v=r9E7aWLq30Y

7. **Eyes On The Prize: America's Civil Rights Years**

http://www.youtube.com/watch?v=9Yd78uDXskQ
http://www.pbs.org/wgbh/amex/eyesontheprize/about/fd.html

8. **Freedom Riders**
   http://video.pbs.org/video/1925571160/

9. **Dr. King on NBC's Meet the Press, March 28, 1965**
   https://www.youtube.com/watch?v=weksRVbNZH4

10. **"442: Live with Honor, Die with Dignity"—Movie Trailer**
    http://www.imdb.com/video/withoutabox/vi1903888153?ref_=tt_pv_vi_1

11. **After Over Four Decades, Justice Still Eludes Family of 3 Civil Rights Workers in Mississippi Burning Killings**
    http://www.democracynow.org/2010/8/13/after_over_four_decades_justice_still

12. **Guns, Germs and Steel: The Fates of Human Societies**
    http://www.youtube.com/watch?v=cLJfZOyFpZo

Other Documentaries Referenced

1. **True Colors—1991, ABC Primetime Live**
   http://www.youtube.com/watch?v=YyL5EcAwB9c]

2. **The Color of Fear**
   http://vimeo.com/40602451

3. **Good Hair**
   http://www.youtube.com/watch?v=1m-4qxz08So

4. **Not in Our Town: A Community Responds to Hate Crimes**
   http://www.niot.org/niot-video/not-our-town-billings-montana-0

5. **Not in Our Town: A Community Responds to Anti-Immigrant Violence**
   http://video.pbs.org/video/2137348207/

Dr. King's Sermons:

The following three sermons of Dr. King were not referenced in this book, but in addition to those which were referenced, they are among my favorite of his sermons.

1. **"A Knock at Midnight"**
   https://www.youtube.com/watch?v=DV7RqizoqJA

2. **"But if Not"**
   https://www.youtube.com/watch?v=pOjpalO2seY

3. **"How Long/ Not Long"**
   https://www.youtube.com/watch?v=TAYITODNvlM

Movies & Television Miniseries

History

1. **Gandhi**
   http://www.imdb.com/title/tt0083987/

2. **Shindi's List**
   http://www.imdb.com/title/tt0108052/

3. **The Diary of Anne Frank—The Movie**
   http://www.imdb.com/title/tt0052738/?ref_=tt_rec_tti

4. **The Diary of Anne Frank—The Television Miniseries**
   http://www.imdb.com/title/tt0246430/]

5. **Into the West 2005 Television Miniseries**
   http://www.imdb.com/title/tt0409572/

6. **Stand and Deliver**
   http://www.imdb.com/title/tt0094027/

7. **Roots—The Television Miniseries**
   http://www.tv.com/shows/roots-the-complete-miniseries/watch/

8. **Something the Lord Made (The 1st Heart Surgeon) HBO Film about Dr. Vivien Thomas**
   http://www.youtube.com/watch?v=dh2TB1M0mY0

9. **Partners of the Heart—PBS Miniseries about Dr. Vivien Thomas**
   http://vimeo.com/26271088

10. **Gifted Hands—The Ben Carson Story**
    http://www.youtube.com/channel/HCz-EqMiPIBjU

11. **Glory Movie Trailer—The 54th Massachusetts Volunteer Infantry—Movie Clip**
    http://www.youtube.com/watch?v=j66i6Ey_IAQ

12. **Glory and Honor Movie at Amazon**
    http://www.amazon.com/exec/obidos/ASIN/0780622693/thematthewhenson/002-8215328-4296222

    https://www.youtube.com/watch?v=lIZC9ihafVs

13. **The Tuskegee Airmen**
    http://www.youtube.com/watch?v=fMZb7ia_ly4

14. **The Story of the Black Panther Tank Battalion—The 761st History, Movie Synopsis and Trailer**
    http://www.761st-movie.com/

15. **Proud—Movie Trailer**
    http://www.youtube.com/watch?v=K5RlEGyxnzY

16. **Proudly We Served—The Men of the U.S.S. Mason—DVD**
    http://ihffilm.com/dvd272.html

17. **Rosewood—Movie Trailer**
    https://www.youtube.com/watch?v=ZoroUDTSY70

18. **The Untold Story of Emmett Till—Movie Trailer**
    http://www.biography.com/people/emmett-till-507515

19. **Neshoba: The Price of Freedom—Movie Trailer (The Story of the Murder of Chaney, Goodman and Schwerner)**
    https://www.youtube.com/movie/neshoba-the-price-of-freedom

20. **Soul of the Game—A Home Box Office Movie about the Negro Leagues**
    http://www.youtube.com/watch?v=LiDULxPh0hU

21. **42—Movie Trailer of Film About Jackie Robinson's Integration of Major League Baseball**
    http://www.youtube.com/watch?v=tkI3RDL5__Y

22. **Cleopatra—Images from 1963 Movie**
    http://www.youtube.com/watch?v=fkRZTiI4ges

Fiction

White Man's Burden (Depiction of an Alternate Reality)
http://www.imdb.com/title/tt0114928/
http://www.youtube.com/watch?v=23DeZKfXN_A

Training Videos

1. **PBS' videos of Jane Elliott's experiments with hair and eye color discrimination**
   http://www.pbs.org/wgbh/pages/frontline/shows/divided/etc/view.html

2. **ABC News discrimination training videos on race, sex, age and attractiveness**
   http://www.videos4training.com/discrimination-videos.html
   http://www.employeeuniversity.com/videos/ABC_News_Discrimination_Series.htm

Websites

Pontchartrain Park

1. **History of Pontchartrain Park**
   http://www.nola.com/175years/index.ssf/2011/11/1955_pontchartrain_park_opens.html

   http://thegrio.com/2010/08/27/the-park-a-history-in-pictures/

2. **Dedication of Pontchartrain Park, January 31, 1955**
   http://nutrias.org/~nopl/photos/ragas/015/015_01.jpg

3. **African American Couples Tour Newly Built Homes in the Pontchartrain Park Neighborhood of New Orleans in the Mid-1950's**
   http://photos.nola.com/tpphotos/2011/11/175pontchartrain_6.html

4. **Golfers Pose at the Opening of the Pontchartrain Park Golf Course**
   http://photos.nola.com/tpphotos/2011/11/175pontchartrain_4.html

5. **Pontchartrain Park Improvement Association Directors' Meeting, November 3, 1957**
   http://photos.nola.com/tpphotos/2011/11/175pontchartrain.html

6. **Pontchartrain Park after Hurricane Katrina**
   http://photos.nola.com/tpphotos/2011/11/175pontchartrain_2.html

Science

1. **"*The Search for Adam and Eve*", Newsweek Magazine 1991**

http://www.virginia.edu/woodson/courses/aas102%20(spring%2001)/articles/tierney.html

2. "***Forget the Old Labels: Here's a New Way to Look at Race***", **Washington Post, November, 1994**
http://www.docstoc.com/docs/17682525/%E2%80%9CForget-the-Old-Labels-Heres-a-New-Way-to-Look-at-Race%E2%80%9D

3. ***The Journey of Man: A Genetic Odyssey,*** **Spencer Wells**
http://press.princeton.edu/chapters/i7442.html

4. ***"Evidence of Very Recent Human Adaptation: Up to 10% of Human Genome May Have Changed",*** **Science Daily, July, 2007**
http://www.sciencedaily.com/releases/2007/07/070711134400.htm

5. "***Who Killed the Men of England*?" Harvard Magazine. July—August, 2009.**
http://harvardmagazine.com/2009/07/who-killed-the-men-england

6. **Cover of Jan/Feb Science Digest Magazine**
http://www.amazon.com/gp/product/images/B005STP9H2/ref=dp_image_text_z_0/192-2064822-5965255?ie=UTF8&n=283155&s=books

History

1. **Tiwanaku: Spirutual and Political Centre of the Tiwanaku Culture**
http://whc.unesco.org/en/list/567

2. **Self-Portrayals of the Ancient Egyptians on Pyramids and Other Egyptian Art (Be sure to scroll down the page.)**
http://www.tuttartpitturasculturapoesiamusica.com/2011/03/ancient-egypt.html

3. "***Great Achievements in Science and Technology in Ancient Africa***", **Sydella Blatch**
https://www.asbmb.org/asbmbtoday/asbmbtoday_article.aspx?id=32437

4. ***They Came Before Columbus*****, Ivan Van Sertima**
http://books.google.com/books/about/They_Came_Before_Columbus.ht ml?id=sPR1AAAAMAAJ

5. **African Stone Heads in Mexico—Photos**
http://www.google.com/search?q=african+stone+heads+in+mexico&rlz=1T4GGLS_enUS494US494&tbm=isch&tbo=u&source=univ&sa=X&ei=eu2qUYqXC6r8igLktlHwDw&ved=0CDwQsAQ&biw=1280&bih=571

6. **Story of Ota Benge**
http://www.npr.org/templates/story/story.php?storyId=5787947

7. **Images of slavery in Puerto Rico**
http://www.google.com/imgres?imgurl=http://www.loc.gov/rr/hispanic/1898/img/slaves.jpg&imgrefurl=http://www.loc.gov/rr/hispanic/1898/slaves.html&h=317&w=500&sz=33&tbnid=58i6cFzg9ZH1yM:&tbnh=90&tbnw=142&zoom=1&usg=__TD7zi42B-l7nCOJ-H6sheaVLcsM=&docid=nNYQ078N7jHcOM&hl=en&sa=X&ei=MIAPUqyvDqrhygGFwoDgDg&ved=0CFAQ9QEwAw&dur=191#imgdii=58i6cFzg9ZH1yM%3A%3BhmY0VgTzGmKtoM%3B58i6cFzg9ZH1yM%3A

8. **Black Inventors A to Z**
http://inventors.about.com/od/blackinventors/a/black_inventors.htm

9. **Lynching in America: The American Experience—People and Events**
http://www.pbs.org/wgbh/amex/till/peopleevents/e_lynch.html

10. **Without Sanctuary: Photographs and Postcards of Lynching in America**

http://withoutsanctuary.org/main.html

11. **The New York Academy of Medicine Report on Mustard Gas Experiments**
http://www.nyam.org/news/press-releases/2008/3096.html]

12. **Digital History of the Internment of Japanese People and Japanese Americans during World War II**
http://www.digitalhistory.uh.edu/learning_history/japanese_internment/internment_menu.cfm

13. **The Zoot Suit Riots**
http://www.laalmanac.com/history/hi07t.htm

14. **1948 Platform of the States Rights Democratic Party**
http://www.presidency.ucsb.edu/ws/?pid=25851

15. **Description of Dr. and Mrs. King's Trip to India**
http://mlk-kpp01.stanford.edu/primarydocuments/Vol5/July1959_MyTriptotheLandofGandhi.pdf

16. **Dr. King's Paper, "My Trip to the Land of Gandhi", July, 1959**
http://mlk-kpp01.stanford.edu/index.php/encyclopedia/encyclopedia/enc_kings_trip_to_india/

17. **Negro Traveler's Green Book**
http://www.autolife.umd.umich.edu/Race/R_Casestudy/Negro_motorist_green_bk.htm

18. **"*Like Something the Lord Made*", Katie McCabe, The Washingtonian, 1989**
http://pdf.washingtonian.com/pdf/mccabe.pdf

19. ***Through My Eyes*, Ruby Bridges**
http://www.barnesandnoble.com/w/through-my-eyes-ruby-bridges/1100752370?ean=9780590189231

20. ***Lies My Teacher Taught Me*, James W. Loewen**
http://www.residential-life.unh.edu/diversity/aw_article14.pdf.

21. **African American Expats**
http://www.biography.com/people/groups/african-american-expats/photos

22. **Africana: The Encyclopedia of the African and African American Experience**
http://books.google.com/books/about/Africana.html?id=DfEzhGlnzlkC

Freedom Songs

1. **Freedom Song: "Ain't Gonna Let Nobody Turn Me 'Roun"**
http://www.gospelsonglyrics.org/songs/aint_gonna_let_nobody_turn_me_around.html

2. **Freedom Song: "We Shall Not Be Moved"**
http://www.youtube.com/watch?v=4WXSI6PcjkE

3. **Freedom Song: "Oh Freedom"**
http://www.youtube.com/watch?v=yHmUPqI6w9g

4. **Freedom song: "We Shall Overcome"**
http://www.youtube.com/watch?v=qRWR6lZ3pF8
http://www.youtube.com/watch?v=130J-FdZDtY
http://www.youtube.com/watch?v=bKDVNSpsBZE

Other Websites Referenced

1. **"Racism in the English Language: A Short Play on 'Black' and 'White' Words",** Robert B. Moore
http://www.femi.pwp.blueyonder.co.uk/race.htm

2. **"White Privilege", Robert Jensen**
http://uts.cc.utexas.edu/~rjensen/freelance/whiteprivilege.htm

3. **"Beyond Guilt", Jack Straton and Lauren N. Nile**
http://rise.pdx.edu/GuiltMultEdNileStraton2.pdf

4. **"Parable of the Ups and Downs"**
http://resources.css.edu/DiversityServices/docs/parableupsanddowns.pdf

5. **Developmental Model of Intercultural Sensitivity, Milton J. Bennett, M.D.**
http://www.library.wisc.edu/EDVRC/docs/public/pdfs/SEEDReadings/intCulSens.pdf

6. **Finn, Tom. *Are You Clueless.* Reston: Kells Castle, 2007. Print.**
www.areyouclueless.com

7. **"Travelin' Man", Ricky Nelson, 1961**
http://www.youtube.com/watch?v=0janfcZ8LUw

8. **"Some Children See Him" Christmas Carol**
http://www.youtube.com/watch?v=s49gEmTlOTk
http://www.youtube.com/watch?v=_1gZuabWfb8

9. **"Some Day at Christmas Time Christmas Carol"**
http://www.dailymotion.com/video/xw6dpt_stevie-wonder-someday-at-christmas-w-lyrics_music

10. **Inside Higher Ed**
http://www.insidehighered.com/quicktakes/2013/11/25/fourth-student-suspended-san-jose-state
http://www.insidehighered.com/quicktakes/2013/11/25/3-colleges-party-themes-or-costumes-offend-many
http://www.insidehighered.com/news/2013/11/25/ucla-grad-students-stage-sit-during-class-protest-what-they-see-racially-hostile

Current

1. **The Southern Poverty Law Center's March 5, 2013 report on hate crime in the U.S.**
   http://www.splcenter.org/home/splc-report-antigovernment-patriot-movement-continues-explosive-growth-poses-rising-threat-of-v

2. **A Southern Poverty Law Center report on hate incidents in general**
   http://www.splcenter.org/get-informed/hate-incidents?page=11&year=&state=TX

3. ***The New Jim Crow, Mass Incarceration in the Age of Colorblindness,*** Michelle Alexander
   http://newjimcrow.com/

4. **Hope in the Cities Program**
   http://www.us.iofc.org/hope-in-cities-iofc

5. **Portland Oregon's Office of Equity and Human Rights**
   http://www.portlandoregon.gov/oehr/

6. **The Public Conversations Project**
   http://www.publicconversations.org/docs/resources/Jams_website.pdf

7. **The Compassionate Listening Project**
   http://www.compassionatelistening.org/trainings/about

8. **Charter for Compassion**
   http://charterforcompassion.org/

The Grand Trilogy
to
Save and Mature Humanity

Book I
We Are One
(A Five Part Series)

W— Who Are the Parents of Humanity? Africans
We All Began as African
The Fundamental Truth About Race
(This is RACE: My Story & Humanity's Bottom Line)

I — In the Beginning, In Utero, We All Develop as Female
The Fundamental Truth About Our Sexes

S — Sometimes the Same is a Little Different
The Fundamental Truth About People with Disabilities

E — Either Be Straight or Be Wrong: Why That's Just Not Right
The Fundamental Truth About Gender Identity, Gender Expression and Sexual Orientation

R — Religion: Different Paths—Same Journey
The Fundamental Truth About Faith and Spirituality

Coming Next in Book I The *We Are One* Series:

Great Fact Five on Religion

A. My Spiritual Memoir:
A Lifelong Journey . . . . A Pilgrim's Path

B. Our Conventional View of Religion and Spirituality: Our Very Simple Story

C. Our History with Our Religious Differences

D. The Fundamental Truth about Religion and Spirituality

E. Our Compassionate Evolved View of Religion and Spirituality

I have chosen to release next, the fifth segment of the *We Are One* series because it is matters of the spirit that more than the subjects of any of the remaining four segments, are dearest to my heart. In truth, spirituality is of far deeper interest to me than is the subject of race as well. I chose to release this segment on race as the first in the series, however, because I wanted to introduce myself to you, dear friend, through the lens of that issue which has so profoundly impacted my life and will, by necessity, be interwoven into my descriptions of many of my experiences with the other issues in *We Are One*.

Book II
Truth II—We Are Brilliant

This We Must Know: Our Trilogy of Profound Truth about . . . .

1. The Limitations of Our Senses;
2. The Workings of Our Brains; and,
3. The Potential of Our Minds

This We Must Do: Our Trilogy of Transformative Action to . . . .

1. Think Critically;
2. Behave Rationally; and,
3. Balance Our Brains with Our Hearts

This We Must Be: Our Trilogy of Ultimate Being as . . . .

1. Transformers of Our Present;
2. Guardians of Our Progress; and,
3. Visionaries of Our Future

Book III
Truth III—We Are Divine

This We Must Know: Our Trilogy of Profound Truth that . . . .

1. We Can Be Happy, Healthy and Wise;
2. We Can Be Compassionate Keepers of Both Ourselves and Our Planet; and,
3. We Are Limitless and Eternal

This We Must Do: Our Trilogy of Transformative Action to:

1. Individually Heal:
   Meditate/Pray and Practice;
2. Spiritually Evolve:
   Experience the Divine in Ourselves; and,
3. Socially Mature:
   Witness the Divine in Every Person & in Many Religions

This We Must Be: Our Trilogy of Our Ultimate Existence as . . . .

1. Human Beings;
2. Spiritual Beings; and,
3. Divine Beings

Postscript

Several months ago, a jury acquitted George Zimmerman of the murder of seventeen year old Trayvon Martin. Millions of African Americans as well as Americans of all races were horrified by the verdict.

To the millions of Americans who do not understand that reaction, I ask you to try to understand only this . . . . **The outrage is about being judged by how we look**. It is about being judged by how we look. It is about being perceived, **at first glance**, to be dangerous, to be threatening, to be a thief, to be a drug dealer, **based upon how we look**. It is about the total loss, in the **moment** of that judgment, of our individuality and thus, of **our very humanity**. It is about living our lives every day, seeing those judgments and the fear in which they result, on people's faces. It is about knowing that the judgments are all **about** our race, a God-given characteristic, and then hearing from those who **make** them, that they had nothing to **do** with race.

In young Trayvon's case, it is about our knowing that while no law, no legislation, no civil rights regulations can legislate **away** those judgments and their resulting fear, we now have laws that allow our lives to be taken, **laws that allow us to be killed**, based **upon** those fears. It is about the fact that now, if the killer says, "I was afraid", and the jurors believe that the fear was legitimate, (jurors who are likely to emotionally connect with and thus **understand** that fear, i.e., jurors who **themselves** would likely have been afraid of the victim based upon his race), the killer will literally get away with murdering us.

It is for **that** reason, that the acquittal of Geroge Zimmerman of the murder of young Trayvon Martin stings so much. **That** is why it is so painful.

To all young African American men like Mr. Martin, please know that regardless of how **others** view you, millions of us see you. We see you. We see you.

My heart goes out ***sincerely*** to Trayvon's mother, Mrs. Sabrina Fulton, to Trayvon's father, Mr. Tracy Martin and to Trayvon's brother, Mr. Jahvaris Fulton.

Lauren Joichin Nile is an author, keynote speaker, trainer and licensed attorney.

Since 1990, Lauren has specialized in assisting nonprofit organizations, educational institutions, governmental agencies, and Fortune 500 corporations increase their emotional intelligence in a variety of areas, facilitating workshops including the following: "Inspiring Leadership", "Fun and Effective Team Building", "Empathetic and Successful Organizational Communication", "Positive and Efficient Conflict Resolution", "Sexual and Other Harassment Prevention and Intervention", "Training-of-Trainers", Conducting Workshops Using Mindfulness Principles", "Facilitating Compassionate Dialogue", and "The ABC's of Diversity Awareness and Diversity Competence." The goal of Lauren's work with organizations is to help create environments in which understanding and kindness are valued and as a result, every person is equally welcomed and uniformly appreciated irrespective of all demographic differences.

The goal of Lauren's speaking and training in the greater society, is to help the human species grow in both wisdom and compassion. Her fervent desire is to help all people see The divine in themselves and themselves in each other.